THE STORMRIDER GUIDE
NORTH AMERICA

LOW PRESSURE

THE STORMRIDER GUIDE NORTH AMERICA

LOW PRESSURE LTD
Unit 11 Efford Farm
Bude Cornwall EX23 8LP
Tel/Fax +44 (0)1288 359867
E-mail guides@lowpressure.co.uk
Web www.lowpressure.co.uk

LOW PRESSURE – Europe
Tel/Fax +33 (0)5 58 77 76 85

First published in 2002 by **LOW PRESSURE LTD**

A catalogue reference for this book can be obtained from the
British Library. ISBN Softback: 0 9539840 1 X

Printed in the UK by Bath Press Ltd
Lower Bristol Road Bath BA2 3BL

THE STORMRIDER GUIDE
NORTH AMERICA

Foreword

Publishing Directors
Ollie Fitzjones Dan Haylock Bruce Sutherland

Researched and Written by
Bruce Sutherland Drew Kampion Michael Kew

Editor
Drew Kampion

Project Co-ordination
Bruce Sutherland Dan Haylock

Design and Production
Dan Haylock

Photo Editors
Dan Haylock Bruce Sutherland

Copy Editor
Vik Sell

Production Assistance
Graham Waldron Tim Nunn

Finance and Distribution
Ollie and Andrea Fitzjones

Editorial Contributors
Sid Abruzzi Greg Arnold (Makah Nation) Jim Austin Burgess Autrey
Gene Bagley Billy Barwick Richard Bell Dickens 'Dickey' Bishop
Allene Blaker Karsten Boysen (Quileute Nation) Will Brady
Carter Brereton Brian Broom Rob Brown Kent Brummitt Charlie Bunger
Tony Butt Chuck Carter Dick Catri Chuck Michael Crews Joe Doggett
Mike Doyle Jack Endicott Clay Feeter Harry Fentress Stu Foley
Henry Fry Paul George Scott Goodwin Kevin Grondin Joe Grottola
Dave Hadden Dave Hamby Drew Hazzlerigg Scott Heffernan
Bruce Henderson Glenn Henning Brian Heritage Leo Hetzel Ed Hewitt
Steve Hoiles Bob Holland Bill Hoopes Gail Hull Julie Hume
Aaron Jackson Mike Jipp Robbie Johnson Phillip Johnson Paul Jones
Hunter Joslin Rick Kahn George Kaminsky Mitch Kaufman Paul Kennedy
Peter Kennedy Paul Klarin Kenny Kooyenga Greg Lapin Cecil Lear
Tom LeCompte Bob Ledbetter Mike Lorusso Joe Luce (Elwha Nation)
Phil Luther Gary Lynch Dave Macri Tim Malins John Marra Mickey Marsh
Ed. Mazzarella Kyle McCarthy Mickey McCarthy Bob McClay
Geoff McCormack Joe McGovern Tim McKevlin Bill McKinnon
Elaine McLemore Missy McMillan Markus Mead Jamie Meiselman
Dick 'Mez' Meseroll Lance Moore Jeff Mosely Nathan Myers
David Newell Steve O'Hara Sean Ollice Peter Pan Dorian Paskowitz
Kathy Phillips Ellis Pickett Kevin Ranker Jim Ready Jamie Risser
Dick Rosborough Lisa Roselli John Sapienza Art Schultz
Scooter Simmons Luis Skeen Gary Smith Richard Spies Tom Sterne
Ken Stevens (Quinault Nation) Mark Straka Peter Strazzabosco
Paul Taylor Bob Tema Charlie Tuna Peter de Turk Kevin Upton
Wyman Wade Matt Walker Tom Warnke Chip Weinert Cory Wells
Dana Williams Bryson Williamson Randy Young Ricky Young Dan Zindler

Photographic Contributors
Don Balch Doc Ball Bob Barbour Mike Baytoff Mike Boyd
David Burhardt Sylvain Cazenave Michael Chaplinsky Bruce Chrisner
Gina Dempster Jeff Devine Glenn Dubock Tom Dugan Vern Fisher
Gibber Rob Gilley Doug Gotthold Leroy Grannis Kevin Hall
Ray Hallgreen Dan Haylock Mark Hill Bill Hoopes Robbie Johnson
Bob Kemp Paul Kennedy Michael Kew Jeremy Koreski Bob Ledbetter
Aaron Loyd Paul Mann Mickey McCarthy Boots McGhee Joe McGovern
Markus Mead Dick 'Mez' Meseroll Mike Meseroll Jamie Meisinger
James Metyko Tim Neil Brian Nevins Christopher Polk David Pu'u
Richard Quinn Geoff Ragatz Jim Ready John Ruebartsch Jim Russi
Mo Daddy Sanford Richard Spies Stumpphoto Ron Stoner/Surfer Magazine
Bruce Sutherland Bob Tema Patrick Trefz Kevin Upton Doug Waters

Special Thanks
El Monte RV for providing fantastic vehicles to enable the lengthy
research. All the surf shops who gave assistance. The Eastern Surfing
Association and all the Surfrider Foundation chapters that helped. Eastern
Surf Magazine The Surfer's Journal Surfer Magazine and The Surfer's Path
Alex Dick Read Jim Peskett and all at Permanent Publishing
Tiki Yates Camilo Gallardo Tim Rainger Antony Colas Simon Mahomo

Extra Special Thanks
Andrea Dillon Sheila Jake Shani and Marla Fitzjones
Louise Aedan Anna Ella and Jamie Millias Jim and Nancy Sutherland
Vik Sell Sue John Mathew and Adam Haylock
Susan Kampion

W hen these blokes from Europe contacted me about helping out on their upcoming *Stormrider Guide North America*, I wasn't sure what to think. I didn't know quite how I felt about surf guides. There seemed to be something politically incorrect about them, and yet one of my favorite books from long ago was David Stern's and Bill Cleary's *Surfing Guide to Southern California* – a genuine classic that was my intimate companion on my own California explorations.

Apart from aggravating hostile locals, I wondered what the point of the whole guide thing was. And seeing as how 90% of North American surfing took place in Southern California and Santa Cruz, it seemed a little pointless to do a NorAm guide, since everything else would be kind of boring. And then I found myself looking through the books they'd already published: *The Stormrider Guide Europe* and snowboard guides to both North America and Europe. I liked them the same way I liked the Stern-Cleary books. They had great photos, good maps, amusing and informed text, and they were beautifully printed, but sturdy. These guys were obviously experienced surfers and travelers themselves. So I agreed – first to help edit, then to write some of it.

Since then it's been a journey – directly, through Oregon and Washington, and indirectly, down the East Coast through Florida, along the Gulf of Mexico, across the Great Lakes, up to Alaska and British Columbia, on down to Baja, and finally across to Nova Scotia. What a trip! This Foreword might better be called "Forward!" That's what all of this is about anyway – getting out of town and getting wet. Forward, march! Forward, paddle! Forward, charge!

North America is a huge place, a continent of sublimely variegated wave-riding resources. This particular volume doesn't cover it all, but it opens a lot of doors. It catches us up on the environmental status of our coasts and beaches. It tells a good bit of the history of surfing in North America. It paints a picture of the way things are at a thousand places we'll never surf or maybe even see, but somebody does.

Each of us has our favorite waves, along with a résumé of spots we've surfed – here or there, my break or your break. It's my hope that this book will help to erode the walls being built up on our wild shores – be they walls of rock or ignorance – and that it will help to spread the message of free access to free beaches and free waves, where we can all ride and have a good time. That would be a major step Forward.

I imagine that most every surfer would love to have the experience of surfing the world's greatest waves. With luck, we'll sample a few, but most of the time we'll ride something else. This book isn't a guide to the world's greatest waves (the Low Pressure team has already performed the ultimate cherry-pick – *The World Stormrider Guide* – and is now on a second compendium of elite destinations), this book is a guide to the real world, at least the real world of riding waves in North America.

There's a reason our eyes and feet point the same direction. Informed by a good heart and an open mind, great strides can be made. The idea here is to travel light, smart and stoked. Practice the way of the surfer – pack your shit, be a good citizen of the world, try not to leave a trace except friendship.

Drew Kampion

This page – **Huntington Beach.**

Cover – **Ventura vortex.** PHOTO: DAVID PU'U

ROB GILLEY

Contents

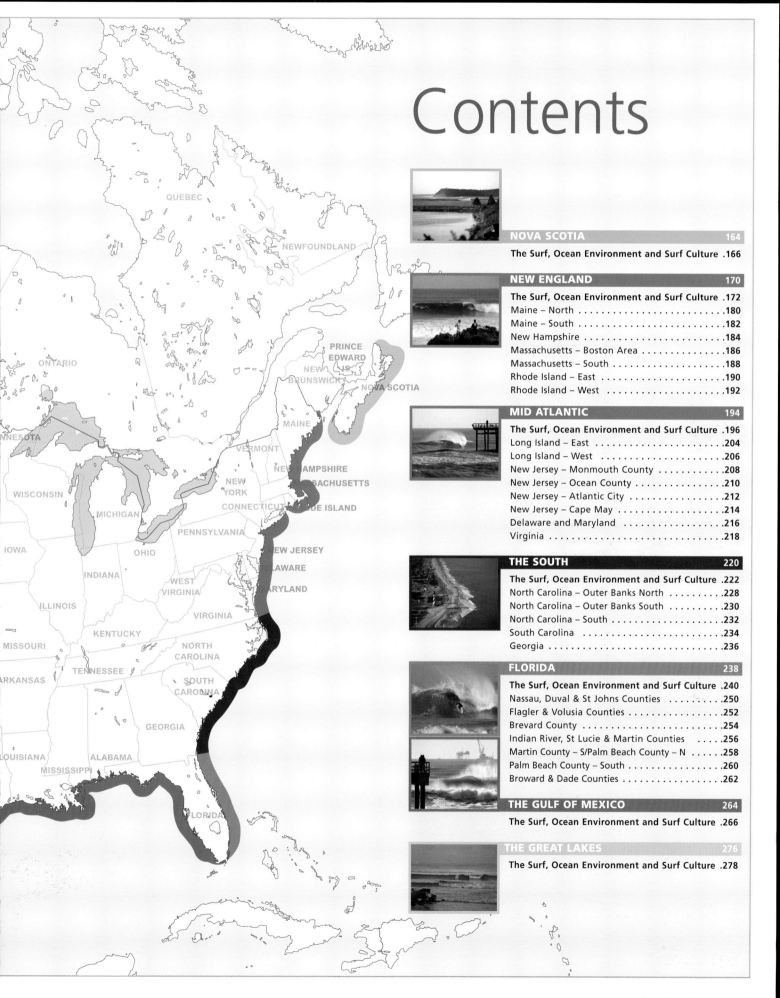

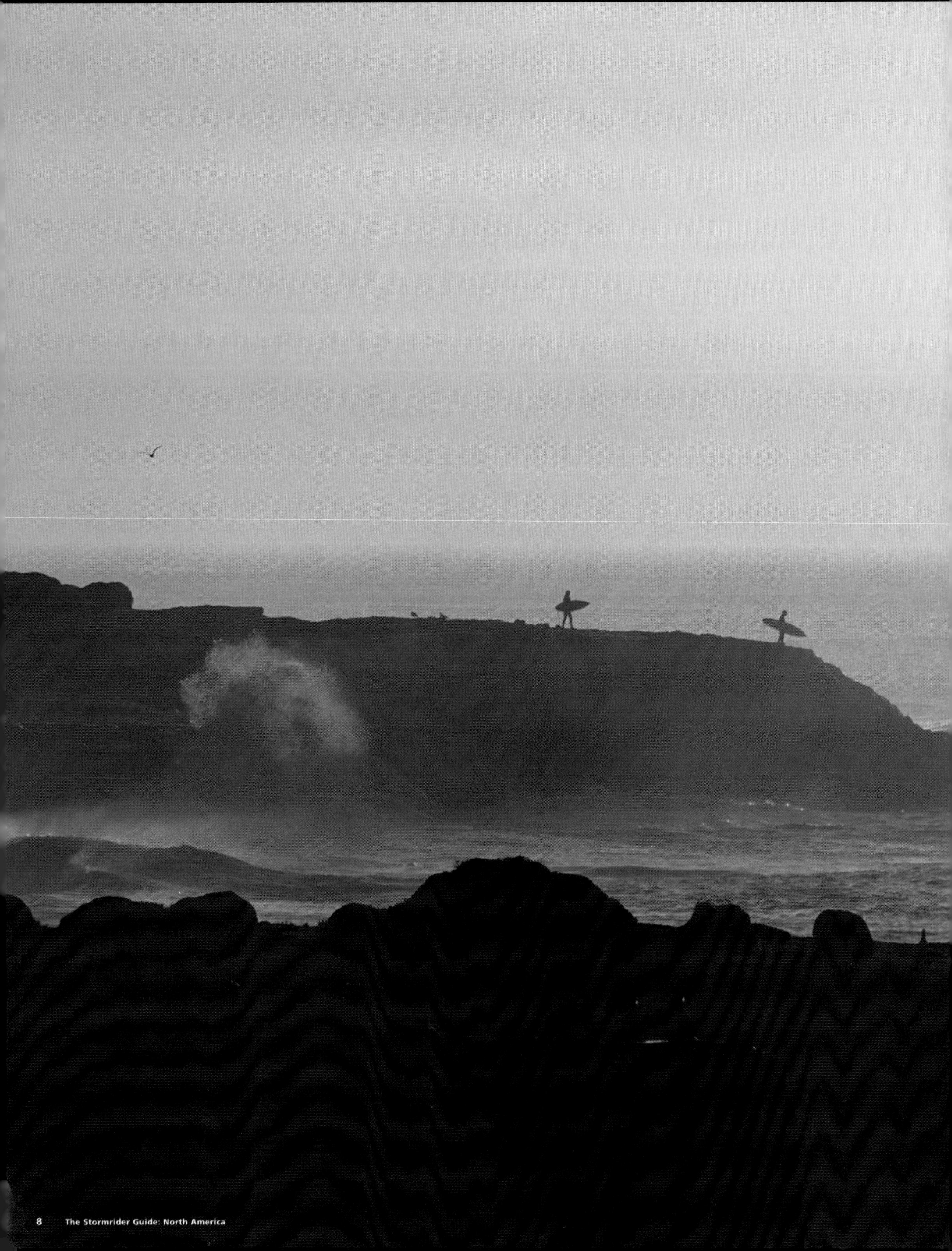

PATRICK TREFZ

Steamer Lane, Santa Cruz.

Introduction

Continental Stormrider Guides are designed as useful tools for surfers to increase their knowledge and understanding of the coastal fringes of Earth's largest land masses. The subtleties of this dynamic zone, where land meets sea, shape the waves which create the places where surfing is practiced and defined. More than just directories of surf spots, Stormrider Guides include illuminating appraisals of the ocean and beach environment along with authoritative discussions of the surf culture that feeds off this interaction.

North America is perhaps the most fertile surf continent on this watery planet. Its immense littoral range is washed by the mightiest oceans, gulfs, and lakes. Here, a surfer will discover an endless supply of wave-riding possibilities. But all of this wealth is jeopardized both by natural cycles and by man's continuing poor stewardship of the vulnerable ocean environment.

With its far-reaching exploration of the pioneering American surfers and innovators, this book is a celebration of the rich mosaic of modern surf culture in North America. This diverse tribe of surfers cherish equally the warm beachbreaks of Florida, the icy reef waves of Lake Superior, the chill wilderness peaks of Alaska or the crowded pointbreaks of Southern California. Each is chasing a taste of perfection, each one wants the free ride. Remember this wherever you go – get wet, give thanks, and share a smile. That is surfing's reward.

North America's Oceans

North America is a tale of two oceans, dividing the mighty North Pacific to the west and the stormy North Atlantic on the east. Further exposure occurs on the south shore where the continent meets the Gulf of Mexico.

The Pacific Ocean   63,838,000mi² (165,384,000km²)

Accounting for 45% of the global ocean coverage, the Pacific Ocean is the largest body of water and single biggest feature on the planet Earth. It is also the deepest ocean with an average depth of 13,800ft (4,200m), plunging to the unequaled depth of 35,826ft (10,920m) at the Mariana Trench.

In the winter, the northern half of the North Pacific is raked by high winds of over 35mph (55kmh), usually blowing from the west. These winds can generate sustained seas of over 15ft (5m) which pound the western shores of North America. Generally light winds are experienced in the eastern Equatorial Pacific throughout the year and wave height is maintained by swell propagation from both the North and South Pacific westerlies.

The Atlantic Ocean   31,736,000mi² (82,000,000km²)

The Atlantic is the world's second largest ocean with 22% of the global sea area, but it's only half the size of the Pacific. The greatest distance from east to west in the

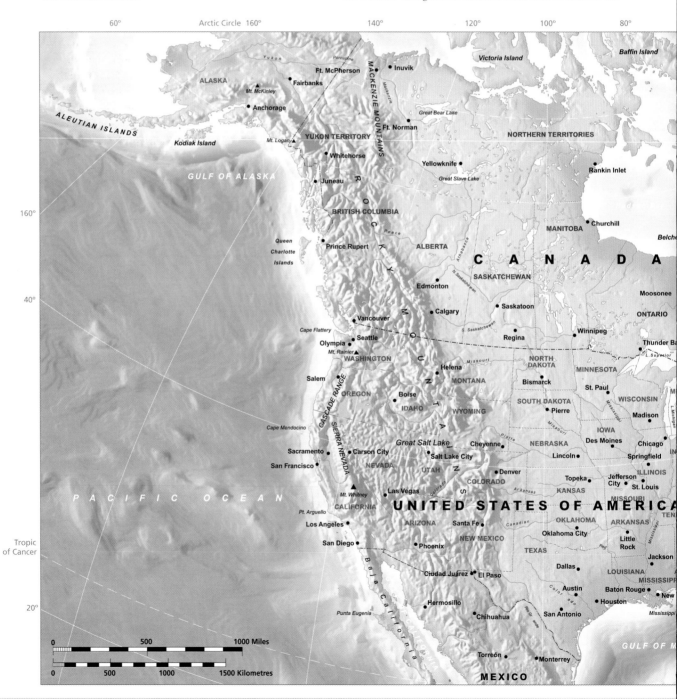

North Atlantic is Morocco to Florida – 4475mi (7,200km). The average depth is 12,000ft (3,660m).

The North Atlantic is the windiest and roughest ocean, with strong winter westerlies of over 35mph (55kmh), generating a band of seas greater than 15ft (5m) between Nova Scotia and the UK. There is significant seasonal variation with much milder conditions occuring in summer. The NE trade winds blowing from the sub-tropical highs around 30°N towards the Equator are sustained throughout the year but weaker than those in the North Pacific.

Overall, the Atlantic trades are the weakest of all oceans. The strongest swells occur in winter and spring, produced by the westerlies in the 30° to 60° zone, sending the biggest waves to the eastern shore of the basin.

MICHAEL KEW

The Gulf of Mexico   596,000mi² (1,554,000km²)

The Gulf of Mexico measures 1060 miles (1700km) at it's widest point and extends 720 miles (1200km) from north to south, with a maximum depth of 13,570ft (4377m). This large gulf is almost completely enclosed by Florida, Cuba and the Yukatan Peninsula, excluding the possibility of swells from either the Atlantic or Caribbean. Trade winds are from the NW in winter, generating seas around 5ft(1.5m). This wind direction is maintained through summer but at much lower speeds, resulting in 3ft (1m) seas. Late summer and early fall can see Atlantic hurricanes enter the Gulf of Mexico, causing average wave heights and wind speeds to be greatly exceeded.

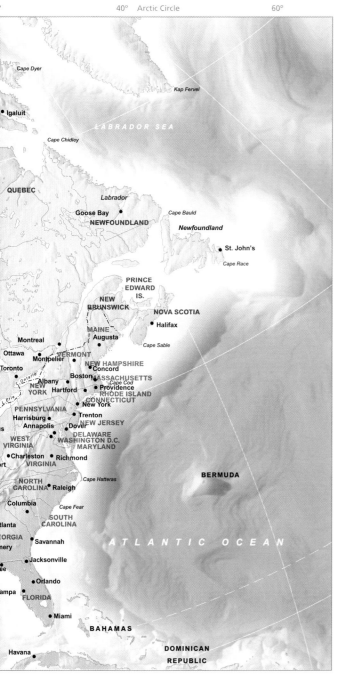

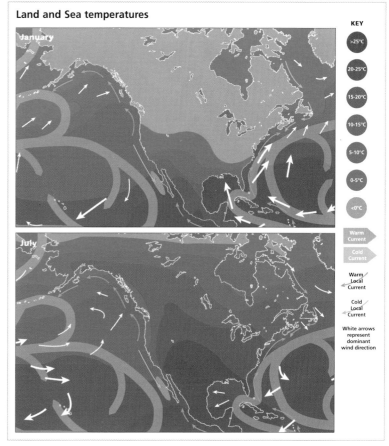

Land and Sea temperatures

KEY

>25°C	
20-25°C	
15-20°C	
10-15°C	
5-10°C	
0-5°C	
<0°C	

Warm Current

Cold Current

Warm Local Current

Cold Local Current

White arrows represent dominant wind direction

The Creation of Wind

The Earth's weather is a complex system designed to redistribute the heat energy that the Sun delivers. The Sun's rays strike the equatorial regions with more concentration, causing the surrounding air to be heated. This lighter, hot air rises in updrafts, then travels towards the poles, high in the atmosphere. When it cools, the air becomes denser, sinks down to sea level and returns towards the Equator, replacing the warm air and completing the heat exchange process. These parcels of air are measured by barometric pressure, whereby the warmer, lighter packages of air are known as high pressures and the colder, denser air is called an area of low pressure. The air in a high pressure is attracted to areas of low pressure and rushes towards it, creating winds. The rotation of the Earth deflects the wind from taking a direct route to the poles, a phenomenon known as the coriolis force. In the northern hemisphere, this causes the air to spin clockwise around a high pressure and counterclockwise around a low pressure. The winds spin in the opposite direction in the southern hemisphere and these rotations are mirrored by the ocean currents. The Coriolis effect is also responsible for bending any wind (or pressure system) in the northern hemisphere to the right of its direction of travel. This right turn will be regardless of which way it is flowing between the Equator and the poles and will be a left arc for winds south of the Equator. This produces the NE and SE trade winds that blow towards the Equator from each hemisphere and also angles the mid-latitude westerlies from the SW and NW respectively. Besides these two dominant bands of circulating winds, there are polar cells at the extremities of the planet and doldrums directly over the Equator.

A low pressure or depression will strengthen when a warm air mass collides with it and slides over the top, lowering the barometric pressure and creating instability

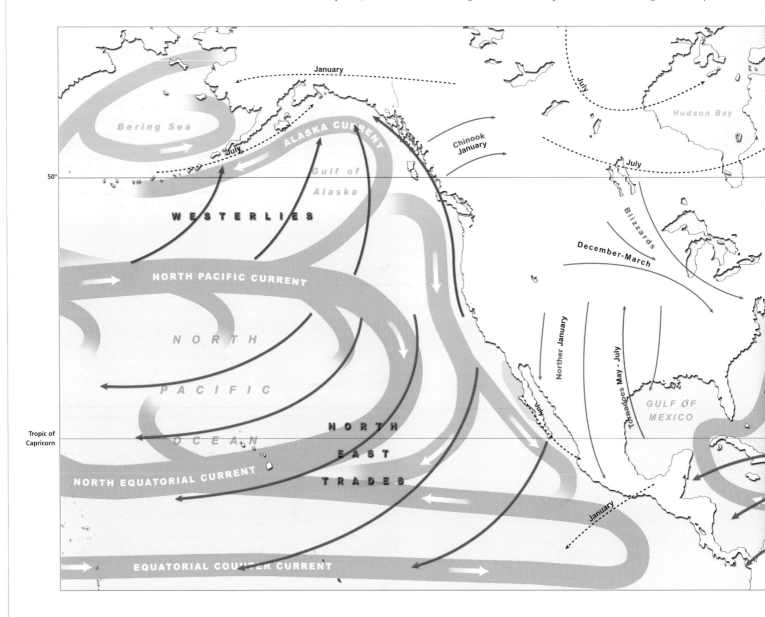

High level jet stream

Meandering waves called Rossby waves

Meanders produce rotating frontal weather system

The polar jet stream meanders gently from north to south. Beneath it large frontal systems form along the boundary between polar and tropical air masses.

which makes the air spin faster. These mid latitude systems become more energetic in the winter when the temperature difference between the Equator and the poles increases. A primary influence on the west to east movements of these weather systems is the flow of air in the upper atmosphere called the jet stream. The jet stream moves at much higher speeds than the surface air and dictates the speed, intensity and trajectory of surface weather systems. A jet which takes a polar heading will create surface low pressures that deepen, while a jet leading towards the Equator will cause the low to fill and fizzle out.

The most violent of all low pressures are formed over warm, tropical oceans when huge differences in temperature get a storm spinning extremely fast. Massive amounts of water vapor are drawn up into the vortex of destructive tropical storms that are known as hurricanes when refering to the Atlantic and north-eastern Pacific.

Land and sea breezes are a small scale version of the global convection currents governed by heat. During the day, the land quickly heats up and hot air starts rising. This brings in cool air from the sea in the form of the afternoon onshore sea breeze. At night when the land cools, the flow is reversed and the offshores blow.

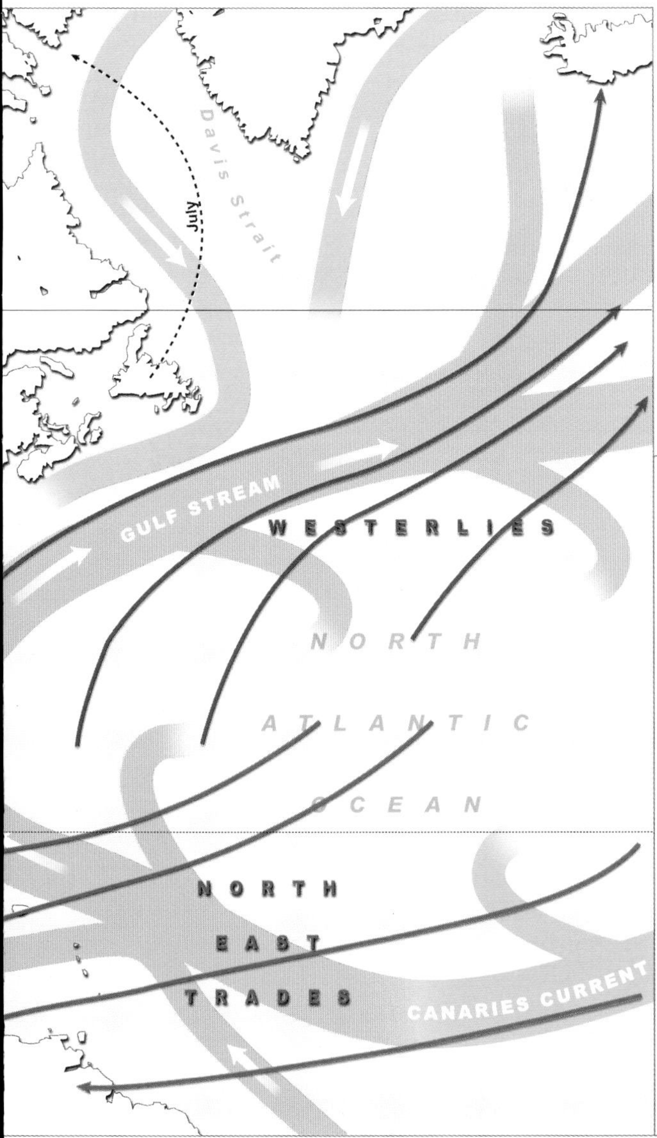

Wind strength measured with the Beaufort Scale

Force	Strength	km/h	Speedmph	Land Actions
F0	calm	0-1.5	0-1	Smoke rises vertically
F1	light air	1.6-6.3	1-3	Smoke drifts slowly
F2	light breeze	6.4-11	4-7	Wind felt on face; leaves rustle
F3	gentle breeze	12-19	8-12	Twigs move; light flags unfurl
F4	moderate breeze	20-29	13-18	Wind moves dust and paper; twigs move
F5	fresh breeze	30-39	19-24	Small trees sway; wavelets on inland waters
F6	strong breeze	40-50	25-31	Large branches move; whistling in telegraph lines
F7	near gale	51-61	32-38	Whole trees sway; difficult to walk against wind
F8	gale	62-74	39-46	Twigs break off trees; very difficult to walk
F9	strong gale	75-87	47-54	Roof tiles blown down
F10	storm	88-101	55-63	Trees uprooted; considerable damage to buildings
F11	violent storm	102-117	64-73	Widespread damage to buildings
F12	hurricane	118+	74+	Devastating damage

Wind Types

Prevailing winds:

Westerlies ➝

Blow in the mid-latitudes (30° to 60°) and produce the groundswells. The rotation of the Earth causes them to blow more SW in the northern hemisphere and more NW in the southern hemisphere.

East Trades ➝

Blow in the sub-tropical latitudes (5° to 30°) and produce constant small windswells. They tend to blow more NE in the northern hemisphere and more SE in the southern hemisphere.

Local winds:
Warm ➝
Cold ➝

Seasonal ---------➝
(can be either warm or cold)

Wind direction is a reference to the wind's compass point of origin: i.e. the direction it is blowing from and not blowing to.

Currents and Upwelling

These vast moving belts of water, convey warm water from the Equator and return cold water from the poles. Like a big heat exchanger, currents (and winds) keep the Earth evenly distributed with warmth. Surface currents are mainly wind driven and can move extremely quickly (from 10km/6mi up to 220km/136mi per day) while deep ocean currents barely move (3ft/1m per day) and work on differences in ocean density and salinity. Open ocean, wind driven, surface currents form large round circulation patterns known as gyres. As with the wind, they circulate in a clockwise direction in the northern hemisphere and counterclockwise in the south. While the wind is the major motivating force, the currents do not follow the exact same path, because the Coriolis effect steps in to alter the current's course. Northern hemisphere currents will swing to the right (clockwise) of the dominant wind direction, while it's left and counterclockwise south of the Equator. Wherever there is a cold current heading back to the Equator combined with trade winds blowing away from the land, the phenomenon of upwelling occurs. Warmer surface water is driven offshore and colder water rises up from depth to replace it. This colder water is usually rich in biological species, which is fortunate because these areas of upwelling are almost exclusively situated next to deserts.

Warm ➝
Cold ➝

Area of upwelling

(Map labels: Davis Strait, July, GULF STREAM, WESTERLIES, NORTH, ATLANTIC, OCEAN, NORTH EAST TRADES, CANARIES CURRENT)

The Creation of Swell and Surf

The main creator of rideable waves is wind blowing over the surface of the water. The wind comes in different strengths and goes by different names but essentially, it always has the same affect on wave creation. Wind blows across the surface of the globe from the four points of the compass and everything in between, but it also changes direction in the vertical plane, exerting a downward pressure on the surface of the sea. At first, this produces ripples on a calm surface, which are then easier for the wind to get a grip on and increase their size. This two part process starts with the ripples or capillary waves, which are still small enough to be pulled back down by surface tension. As the ripples grow, small disturbances of rotating air form between the ripples adding more height to the waves, which in turn creates more uniform pockets of turbulence between the quickly growing waves.

Surface tension is no longer strong enough to restore the rippling disturbance and gravity now attempts to push the waves back down. This self-perpetuating cycle increases wave height exponentially until gravity limits further growth and the wave reaches saturation point. The wave height can also be limited by white-capping, where storm force winds literally blow the tops off the cresting waves. The main factors that determine the size of the waves will be the strength and duration of the wind plus the fetch, meaning distance over which the wind blows.

Propagation, Dispersion and Grouping

Once the wind has done its job and the waves begin to travel or propagate away from the source, they organize themselves into lines of swell. As the swell fans out, the waves lose some height, which happens at a set rate. This is called circumferential dispersion, and the further a swell travels, the more this process will cause it to spread out. The width it spreads out is directly proportional to the distance it has traveled. For every doubling of the propagation distance, the height reduces by about one-third, which doesn't include other height reducing factors like white-capping and opposing winds in the propagation path.

Radial dispersion is the term used to describe how swell cleans itself up into the orderly lines that surfers love to see hitting their local beach. This revolves around wave

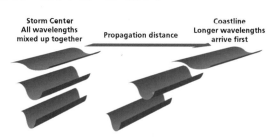

When swell travels away from the storm, swells with a longer wavelength travel faster and overtake shorter wavelength swells.

speed, which is governed by how far apart each wave is, known as wavelength. The longer the distance between two crests, the faster the waves will travel across the open ocean. When the swell is first created, many different wavelengths will be mixed in together, producing messy, disorganized waves. As the swell starts to propagate away, the faster waves with the longer wavelengths will progressively overtake the slower, shorter wavelength swells. Given enough time and distance, the faster swells will hit the coast first, bringing the clean, well-spaced corduroy lines that produce quality surf. The shorter wavelength swells will arrive later with less organisation and power, and some of the weaker, choppy waves won't even make it at all. Differences in wavelength are also responsible for the creation of sets. Technically referred to as wave grouping, sets are the result of two different swells traveling in the same direction and merging together. When the peaks of two different wave-trains coincide, a larger wave will result. However, when the peak of one wave-train coincides with the trough of another, a canceling out effect occurs, resulting in the dreaded lulls at the beach. There are other complicated influencing factors and most non-surfing oceanographers are theoretically dismissive of wave grouping, indicating that further research is necessary to understand why sets occur.

Speed, Shoaling and Refraction

Wavelengths are also a major factor in determining the speed of waves. A straightforward equation is used for the velocity of deep water waves. Speed is equal to the wavelength divided by the time it takes for two waves to pass a fixed point (period). This means that a well spaced, long period, big swell will travel at up to 25mph (40kmh).

As waves approach the coast and come in contact with the sea floor, they slow down, but only lose a little bit of energy to friction. The excess speed or velocity energy is channelled into making the waves higher, which happens when they start to feel the bottom at depths around one half of their wavelength. Unlike open ocean swell, the shallower the water, the slower a wave will travel. As they slow down, they squash together, forcing the period to shorten, as it must remain constant throughout the swell. Similar to traffic approaching a bottleneck, this slowing and bunching is termed shoaling, it increases wave height

---

The stages of development of open ocean swells.
(left to right)

1. Turbulent fluctuations in the wind cause the surface of the sea to become bumpy and agitated while surface tension tries to restore it.

2. The agitated sea modifies the flow of air causing more turbulent fluctuations which further agitates the sea's surface.

3. The following wind adds more energy to the waves and makes them grow.

GRAVITY

GRAVITY

SURFACE TENSION

and the effect is more pronounced the steeper the shelf. If a section of one swell starts to feel the bottom while an adjacent section does not, then it will start to refract (bend) the swell. Depending on the swell direction, refraction will bend the swell one of two ways. If an obstacle (reef) is situated next to deep water, and a swell hits it straight on, then the part of the swell that hits the reef will slow down while the rest of the swell line will maintain speed. This faster traveling section will start to bend in towards the reef, resulting in concave refraction. The energy gets concentrated towards the peak, making the wave bigger, more sucky and bowly, but it often makes the wave shorter or far smaller on the inside. Convex refraction describes what happens at many classic pointbreaks, especially if they are at right angles to the prevailing swell direction. As a swell line hits the tip of the point, the bulk of the swell will continue on its way while only the part right on the point will be slowed and start to break. The breaking part of the wave then tries to catch up to the faster advancing swell line, which creates a fanned out appearance. Convex refraction spreads the wave energy over a wider area, so power and size will be less than in a concave set-up but the wave will be a long, walled-up type ride and sometimes even get bigger down the line.

Breaking Waves and Bathymetry

Waves will break when the bottom part of the wave is slowed down so much that the top of the wave overtakes it and spills forward. A simple equation is used, stating that a wave will break in water at a depth of 1.3 times the wave height. This equation can be affected by other factors such as wind, swell type and beach slope. An offshore wind will hold up and delay the top of the wave from overtaking the bottom, resulting in the wave breaking in shallower water. Onshore winds have the opposite effect and can push the waves over before they reach the critical depth. Different types of swell may break in different depths of water. Fast lined-up groundswell will get to shallower water before breaking while short wavelength, choppy windswell is more likely to crumble in deeper water. A gently sloping beach will cause waves to break prematurely while a steep slope makes them overshoot their normal breaking depth. Combining all these factors, a small, onshore, windswell wave, on a flat beach would break in very deep water, while a large, groundswell in an offshore wind, on a steep reef would break in very shallow water.

Concave refraction – Hazard Canyon, San Luis Obispo

ROB GILLEY

Convex refraction – Rincon Point, Ventura

ROB GILLEY

Bathymetry refers to sea floor features like reefs and points (that are part of the refraction process). Two other important bathymetric features from a surfer's point of view are beaches and rivermouths. Beachbreaks need a certain shape of sandbar to provide a good forum for rideable waves. If the sand under the waves was totally flat and featureless, then when swell arrived it would almost certainly close-out. An ideal sandbar formation will be vaguely triangular with slightly deeper water on either side of the bar. This is formed when a wave breaks on a bar and starts pushing water towards the beach, picking up sand along the way. The water starts to get pushed sideways until it loses forward momentum and looks for a way back out to sea. This is where rips and currents form, aiding the circulation of water and sand. The rip gouges out a handy paddling channel and deposits more sand out towards the peak for more swell to focus upon. Rivermouths work on the same principle whereby sand is constantly deposited at the sandbar, and are far more reliable for well shaped bathymetry.

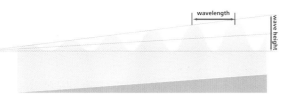
As waves propogate into shallow water they slow down, the wavelength is shortened and the wave height rises

Swell Forecasting

Swell forecasting has changed radically in recent years. Gone are the days of checking the newspaper for the surface pressure map and trying to decipher the twisting mass of isobars. Connecting to the World Wide Web serves up an abundance of surf-related forecasting sites, which offer a range of wave and wind models with funny names like WAM, FNMOC, and Wavewatch III from national weather institutions like NOAA, NCEP, and NWS. Constantly updated maps show wave size, direction, and period along with wind speed and direction, even predicting these most crucial surfing elements up to six days ahead. If that's not enough, there are hundreds of surf cameras pointing at hundreds of line-ups, beaming up images to thousands of web-surfers looking for the best waves. If all this seems just too complicated, there's the option of real-time eyewitness reports from somebody on the beach, relayed to your cell phone via text or email – just to make sure you don't miss a wave.

Despite all this technology, the fundamental skill of reading a weather map is not obsolete. All forecasting services relate directly back to these basic charts for much of their formative information.

The spiral of lines on a weather map (surface pressure chart) are called isobars and join together areas that have the same barometric pressure. This air pressure is a measurement of the weight of air being exerted on the surface of the planet. Measured by a barometer and expressed in millibars (or kilopascals), the average sea level pressure is 1013mb, roughly equal to the weight of an elephant spread over a small coffee table. The lower the air pressure and the closer the isobars are together, the stronger the winds generated by a weather system will be. This results in larger swells radiating out in the direction in which the isobars are running. Straighter isobars will increase the fetch or time the swell has to build from one direction, while tighter curves are more likely to create changes in swell direction.

Once a swell has propagated away from the influence of a low pressure system, it will remain on a fairly straight course. The duration of a swell is dependant on how long a particular swell window is exposed to a low pressure system. Low pressure systems tend to move far quicker than high pressure systems and the swells they generate travel up to 25mph (40kph).

The Pacific Ocean

A constant procession of low pressure systems march across the northern Pacific from October to April. Their exact paths are determined by the meandering trajectory of the upper atmosphere jet stream, but they usually make landfall between British Columbia and Northern California. These lows are responsible for sending swells as far as Peru and establishing the NW swell pattern for California; further north, pulses from due W and SW can combine to create chaotic mixes of swell.

January

July

The jet stream controls the path of North Pacific low pressure systems. The summer pattern brings onshore winds and the occasional hurricane (chubasco) from the south.

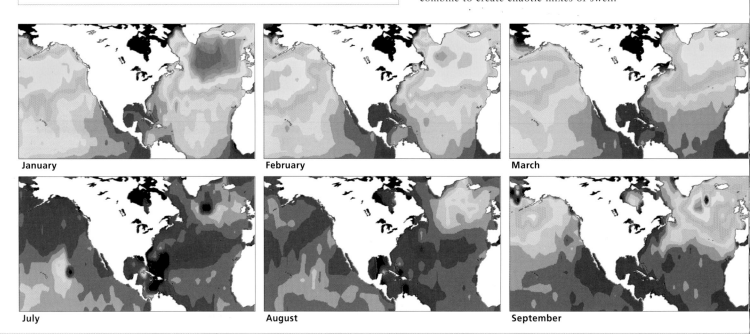

January

February

March

July

August

September

Outside of these months, deep low pressure systems are rare, allowing large high pressure systems to establish themselves offshore. These highs generate the summer afternoon onshores as well as weak windswell from the W or NW, depending on latitude. From a surfer's perspective, this seasonal slump is most extreme during July and August, when the Southern Hemisphere storms are the most likely source of a salvation swell from the S or SW. Smaller storms or frontal activity can sometimes contribute SW lines from equatorial latitudes; the occasional chubasco (tropical storm heading W from Mexico or Central America) is another source of summer swell.

The North Atlantic Ocean

As with the Pacific, the jet stream drags an incessant stream of winter storms across the northern latitudes of the Atlantic. However, unlike the West Coast, these storms are almost always moving away from North America. Consequently, the East Coast has to survive on the swells that propagate off the backs of low pressure systems. Many of these storms are spawned in Baffin Bay between Newfoundland and Greenland and will pump NE swell down the Atlantic seaboard, especially if they remain stationary. Usually, however, these lows are quick to spin off towards Europe, taking the swell with them.

Cold fronts sweeping across the North American continent also bring predominantly NE swell to the East Coast. In winter, energized by the warmer waters of the Gulf of Mexico, these frontal systems can take a more southerly path, usually reaching the ocean between the Carolinas and Northern Florida. Alternatively, cold air descending from the Canadian interior will arc down through the Mid Atlantic states, before swinging north again to join with the established low pressure systems off Newfoundland. These fronts are dubbed Alberta (or Canadian) Clippers and, once again, are most likely to send out NE pulses in their wakes.

Nova Scotia and New England score extra size from proximity to these weather systems, while the Outer

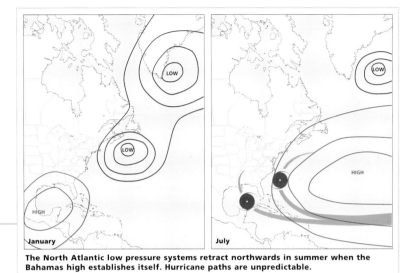

The North Atlantic low pressure systems retract northwards in summer when the Bahamas high establishes itself. Hurricane paths are unpredictable.

Banks and Southern Florida protrude into the deeper waters of the Gulf Stream current, which acts as a conveyor belt for the NE swell to head down the coast.

Summer is a feast or famine scenario on the Atlantic shore, with sizable surf completely reliant on hurricane swells. These most powerful of tropical storms are the only low pressure cells that travel towards the East Coast, bringing large swells along with the threat of widespread damage if they make landfall. Swell direction is dictated by the storm's track, which can range from westerly (aiming into either the Caribbean Sea or the Gulf of Mexico) to an arcing trajectory up the coast to the north, where cooler ocean temperatures signal its demise.

Hurricanes can materialize anytime between June and November, with September and October being the statistically most likely time for scoring these swells, which usually have an element of S to them. 'Canes aside, summer can be diabolically flat, relying on weak E to SE windchop from the stationary Bermuda High, which dominates the western North Atlantic.

Wave Models such as the WAM predict wave size and direction for up to six days. Both the North Pacific and North Atlantic show a strong pattern of seasonal variation.

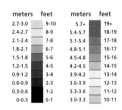

meters	feet		meters	feet	
2.7-3.0	9-10		5.7+	19+	
2.4-2.7	8-9		5.4-5.7	18-19	
2.1-2.4	7-8		5.1-5.4	17-18	
1.8-2.1	6-7		4.8-5.1	16-17	
1.5-1.8	5-6		4.5-4.8	15-16	
1.2-1.5	4-5		4.2-4.5	14-15	
0.9-1.2	3-4		3.9-4.2	13-14	
0.6-0.9	2-3		3.6-3.9	12-13	
0.3-0.6	1-2		3.3-3.6	11-12	
0-0.3	0-1		3.0-3.3	10-11	

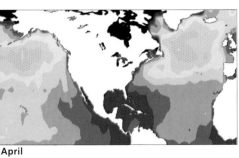

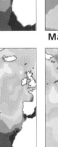

April

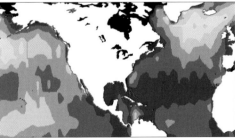

May

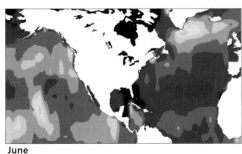

June

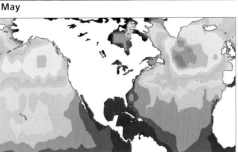

October

November

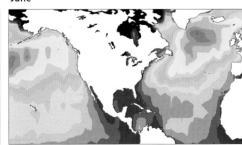

December

Tides

Tides are the result of the Moon's gravitational force producing a bulge in the sea, directly in line with the Moon's position. An equal bulge forms on the opposite side of the Earth to balance the planet out during orbit. The two bulges are the high tides and the areas in between are the low tides. The Earth spins on its axis and every point on the ocean's surface will experience at least one of these bulges every day. Throughout the time it takes for the Earth and Moon to go round each other (a lunar month), the Moon has four phases: opposition, quadrature, conjunction and quadrature (again). The Sun has a smaller gravitational pull on the oceans, which also produces bulges. So when the Sun and the Moon are lined up (in opposition or conjunction), their bulges are added together, making the tides bigger, known as spring tides. When the Sun is at an angle of 90° to the Moon (quadrature), they create bulges at right angles to each other. The water is evened out over the Earth's oceans, producing neap tides.

Tidal Range

Depending on latitude and underwater topography, tidal ranges (heights) vary massively from one region to another. The Gulf of Mexico has minimal tides whereas places like Nova Scotia's Bay of Fundy can experience a depth difference of 50ft (16m) between low and high water. Micro-tidal range means that spring tides never exceed 6ft (2m). Even this small amplitude will affect most spots, especially shallow reefs, but the tide won't be the key factor. Under 3ft (1m) will be insignificant and between 3ft-6ft (1-2m), some sensitive spots won't work on all tides. For meso-tidal range, including much of the west and east coasts, spring tides oscillate between 7ft (2.3m) and 13ft (4.3m) – a tide table is essential. Many tide sensitive spots will only work for about one third of the tide (low, mid or high). The Pacific Northwest and Eastern Canada experience macro-tidal ranges of over 14ft (4.6m) on spring tides. This results in extremely unstable surf conditions, where tide will be the main priority, rather than the swell and wind.

On the Pacific coast tides grow in range as you travel north and are uniformly semi-diurnal. Atlantic tides are small and predictable in the south,

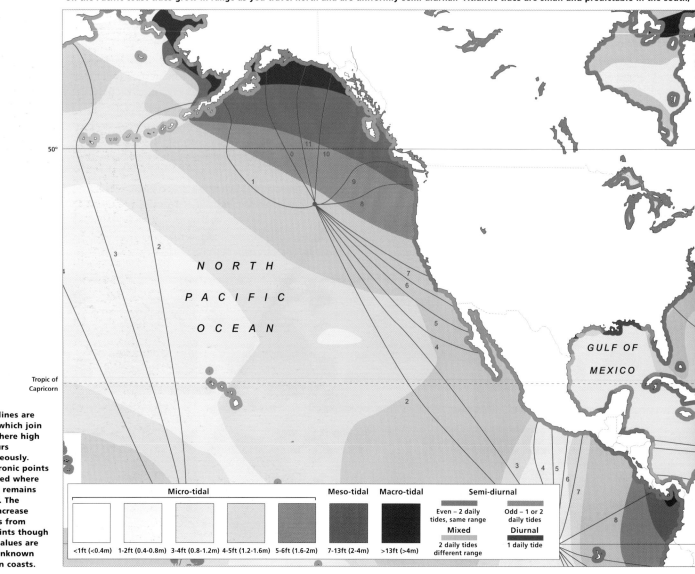

— Co-tidal lines are isolines which join places where high tide occurs simultaneously.

• Amphodronic points are located where sea level remains constant. The ranges increase outwards from these points though precise values are largely unknown except on coasts.

Micro-tidal					Meso-tidal	Macro-tidal	Semi-diurnal	
							Even – 2 daily tides, same range	Odd – 1 or 2 daily tides
							Mixed	**Diurnal**
<1ft (<0.4m)	1-2ft (0.4-0.8m)	3-4ft (0.8-1.2m)	4-5ft (1.2-1.6m)	5-6ft (1.6-2m)	7-13ft (2-4m)	>13ft (>4m)	2 daily tides different range	1 daily tide

Tide Cycle

A tide cycle is made of outgoing (ebb) and incoming (flow). Because the moon phase is 24hr 50min, the average length of a tide is 12hr 25min. High and low tide times move forward every day and the tide increases and decreases in increments of twelfths. 50% of the tide occurs during the 3rd and 4th hours. The graph below represents a semi-diurnal type, from low tide to high tide and back down over twelve hours.

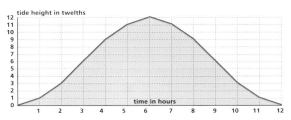

Tidal Types

Because of the Earth's rotation, different latitudes and uneven underwater topography, there are four types of tides. Semi-diurnal 'even' is the most commonly occurring, with two high tides and two low tides every day that are of the same range. Semi-diurnal 'odd' also has two tides but the daily range is different. Diurnal refers to areas that only have one tide per day. Mixed tide describes those tropical latitudes where some days have two tides and some days only one.

Tides make a difference, Murph Bar, Santa Cruz.

PATRICK TREFZ

but the further north you go, the greater the range.

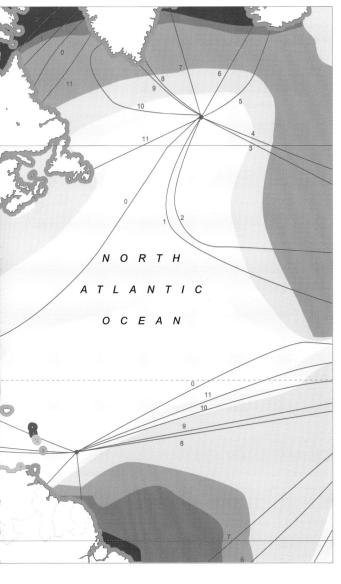

Springs Conjunction

Springs Opposition

Neaps Quadrature

Larger tides (spring tides) occur when the gravitational pull of the Moon and the Sun are combined in line. Smaller tides (neap tides) happen when the Sun and the Moon are at right angles to the Earth evening out the bulge.

The Surfrider Foundation

"I love to think of nature as an unlimited broadcasting station, through which God speaks to us every hour, if we would only tune in." George Washington Carver

I am continuously amazed at how much information we, as a global community, are provided in this modern era. We are seemingly turned on, tuned in, and hard-wired to the events unfolding around us at all times. Through the internet and 24-hour cable news channels, we are continuously fed everything from last weekend's box office grosses to the weather in Southeast China. Yet, as technologically advanced as we've become in dispensing media and information, our mother ocean's cries for help continue to go unheard.

Between 1999 and 2000, the number of beach closures across the United States doubled. In California, beaches were closed or had warnings almost 6,000 times during 2000, nearly twice as many as in 1999. Extended closures/advisories (those lasting 6 to 12 weeks) more than quadrupled from the previous year. Although some of this increase can be attributed to increased monitoring, it indicates a growing problem with chronically polluted beaches. Also disturbing, comes the news that more than 10% of California's, Florida's, Maine's, and South Carolina's shoreline is covered with beach-destroying shoreline armoring.

Sadly, commercial and private development continues to threaten dozens of North American surf spots, including a number of world-class breaks such as Tres Palmas in Puerto Rico, Ma'alaea in Hawaii, Scorpion Bay in Baja, and Trestles in California.

Perhaps it is because we spend so much time reading the clouds, studying the horizon, looking for swells that we can actually feel the struggle of our mother ocean. Perhaps it is because we are surfers that we hear her cries for help.

It was this awareness, this intuitive empathy that we share with our oceans, that was the impetus behind the formation of the Surfrider Foundation. Our grassroots organization is dedicated to the protection and enjoyment of the world's oceans, waves, and beaches for all people, through conservation, activism, research, and education. Our chapters across the United States and Puerto Rico, as well as our affiliates in Australia, France, Brazil, and Japan, continue to work each and every day in an effort to make the public aware of the precarious state of our oceans, coastlines, and beaches.

The ocean is the cradle of all life here on earth. As surfers and ocean-sport enthusiasts, we are her ambassadors. Through your travels, please take the time to share her message with those who would listen.

Aloha, Chris Evans
Executive Director, Surfrider Foundation

Surfrider Foundation.
www.surfrider.org

1% of all sales of *The Stormrider Guide North America* will be donated to Surfrider Foundation.

BOB BARBOUR

Man's interference with the coastline will either create or destroy waves. Dredging at the harbor, Santa Cruz.

The Surfrider Foundation

Founded in 1984, the Surfrider Foundation is an international non-profit environmental organization dedicated to the protection and preservation of oceans, waves, and beaches for all people to enjoy, through conservation, activism, research, and education. With a growing membership (over 31,000 nationwide), Surfrider attracts people through a grassroots network of 60 volunteer chapters and a specific menu of effective environmental programs such as water-quality monitoring and beach preservation.

The vocal presence of Surfrider chapter activists in coastal communities has resulted in 18 years of environmental victories for our beaches and oceans. From stopping the construction of sand-swallowing seawalls to implementing water-testing programs and using the resultant data to support community-based pollution prevention strategies, Surfrider has proven the efficacy of its grassroots chapter network, solid environmental programs, and issue-based advocacy campaigns.

The Surfrider Foundation believes that the decline of coastal habitat and concomitant reductions in marine animal and fish populations cannot be reversed by addressing any single aspect of the ecosystem or any one species above another. Nor can the situation be ameliorated through regulatory means alone. Viable solutions require long-term, multi-year commitments to education and raising public awareness to effect changes in public attitudes and values. These changes require scientific assessments, inventories, and monitoring of habitats critical to the entire life cycles of our marine resources. This means involving a broad segment of the public in restoration and reclamation of critical habitat already lost. And it means bringing the full force of existing law to bear on protecting what remains while cleaning up what has already been degraded.

Surfrider's well-distributed network of local chapters, its menu of environmental programs aimed at ocean education and stewardship, and its 18 years of activist experience reflect these beliefs. The Surfrider Foundation is uniquely positioned to address coastal issues like pollution, erosion, and access. It does this through its community-based chapter structure, which provides an integrated link to 60 coastal locales dotting America's coastlines. We are already providing an undeniable voice in the preservation and stewardship of coastal resources. As issues develop nationally or regionally, we are poised to develop additional chapters in communities not currently represented. Surfrider's co-ordinating national structure and local chapters provide an excellent base from which to deploy our grassroots environmental programs.

These programs include:

Respect the Beach – RtB embodies an attitude and spirit of coastal resource awareness and stewardship. RtB engages local participants to better understand and assume "ownership" of the coastal and marine ecosystems in specific regions through hands-on educational curricula, through schools or via informational outreach in the community. RtB is a key component in Surfrider's strategy to combat nearshore water pollution by teaching students and citizens about preventing pollution before it begins.

Respect the Beach is a coastal educational program that includes field trips, classroom lectures, handouts, video, interactive computer applications, and hands-on projects designed to teach ocean safety, marine ecology, and coastal-area stewardship to students and community groups. Most surfers are natural students of weather, coastal physical processes, and water-quality. Teaching oceanography and environmental protection from a surfer's perspective captivates students of all ages and makes learning about the ocean exciting, fun, and very cool. The RtB program is brought into classrooms by Surfrider Foundation members, who represent ocean environmentalism from personal experience and who are role models that students can relate to.

In the short term, RtB participants improve coastal conditions by performing activities such as beach clean-ups, stormdrain stenciling, and repairing damage caused by uncontrolled access, as well as by reducing activities that contribute to coastal degradation. In the longer term, RtB will give participants the tools to become stewards of their own coastal landscapes and to engage their communities and decision-making agencies as leaders in coastal resource preservation and management.

Respect the Beach was launched in California schools in 1991 and in junior lifeguard programs in 1992. Since that time, it has been successfully implemented by chapters across the US. The Surfrider Foundation now plans to revise and re-package this program to reflect up-to-date scientific information and a holistic approach to understanding coastal and ocean environments.

Beachscape – As a Geographic Information System (GIS)-based program, Beachscape utilizes our network of dedicated activists to create a database of coastal conditions and characteristics. Beachscape is providing gap analysis and "ground truthing" of larger scale, mostly aerial datasets collected by other NGOs. The ultimate goal of Beachscape is to support sustainable coastal management through dynamic resource inventory at the local level with the aim of protecting and preserving our critical shoreline ecosystems.

Who knows a beach better than a local does? This is the philosophy that is driving the Surfrider Foundation's newest program – Beachscape. Many of our members visit their local beaches on a daily or weekly basis and observe trends in swell direction, local weather and its effects on the beach, shifting sands, other notable shoreline impacts, and, perhaps most importantly to them, how all of these factors affect their favorite surf breaks. They might not realize it, but these Surfrider members are in fact 'surfer scientists.' Their diligent study of the coastal surroundings makes them experts on their beaches. Beachscape wants to tap into this precious local knowledge and put it to use to defend our beaches.

Above – **Untreated waste...**
Left – **Coastal erosion is an uncontrolable natural process. Attempts to prevent it usually exacerbate the problem.**

DAVID PU'U

Above –
Diminishing access is a major issue around the entire continent.
Right – **Polluted run-off in urban areas is a major cause of beach closure.**

Beachscape is being developed to empower our chapters with information about their coastlines. This is a community-based coastal mapping program that employs chapter volunteers to map our beaches for features such as coastal armoring, stormdrain outfalls, beach access ways, erosion hotspots, and beach characteristics. Once mapped, this information will be entered into a Geographic Information System (GIS) to be used by the chapters and coastal management agencies. The maps will also be used as reference material to 'fill in the blanks' in Surfrider's *State of the Beach Report*, especially where states have incomplete data.

To accommodate the broad range of capabilities and time commitments of our chapters and volunteers, Beachscape has several levels, from 'entry level' mapping activities to 'advanced level' collection of long-term data about the coasts.

The Blue Water Task Force is a water-quality monitoring, education, and advocacy program aimed at alerting citizens and officials in their communities about water-quality problems and working toward solutions. The BWTF is providing a grassroots voice advocating the implementation of the Beaches Environmental Assessment, Clean-up and Health Act (BEACH bill), the first federal legislation requiring national beach water-quality testing standards and public notification.

Blue Water Task Force is the Surfrider Foundation's most visible and successful program to date. It was established with the following objectives: to provide concerned citizens with the opportunity for hands-on involvement with an environmental problem-solving effort; to gather coastal water samples on a regular basis to determine pollution patterns in the near shore environment; to raise public awareness regarding the extent and severity of coastal water pollution; to use the data collected to bring polluters into compliance, and to develop a model program that could influence national legislation and enforcement.

BWTF has been successful in raising public awareness of coastal water pollution levels and precipitating the establishment of state and local government water-quality monitoring programs in many communities where the program has been implemented. We are still working to raise awareness about the need for a comprehensive national beach water-quality monitoring program. Ongoing changes in the scientific methods of monitoring and reporting water-quality mean the Blue Water Task Force and Surfrider chapters must constantly evolve, since all monitoring programs are updated to reflect the most advanced and easily administered testing protocols.

A new application of the program will be dedicated to developing and deploying techniques and information that will empower our chapters to collect, analyze, and distribute agency water quality data in their communities. Another part of the new program will address a range of water-quality improvement strategies. Surfrider will conduct annual surveys of chapters using the program; survey results will be published in annual reports and used to refine and further develop program and training materials.

The Surfrider Foundation anticipates that by maintaining, expanding, and updating the Blue Water Task Force program, we will be better able to educate citizens about coastal water-quality problems and build support for establishing national coastal water-quality testing with adequate provisions for high monitoring standards.

FURTHER INFORMATION	
Surfrider Foundation	www.surfrider.org
The Programs	www.surfrider.org/programs

DON BALCH

Localism   **by Drew Kampion**

Each and every day now, the instant global news network channels the world's disasters, wars, murders, and an apparently infinite list of other horrors straight into our mutual consciousness. Young or old, urban, suburban, or rural, few of us (like those in comas) are exempt from something that approaches immediate worldwide awareness of all things negative. As if by a divine alchemy, 9/11 crystallized this paradigm into full-frontal reality. What you see is what you get, or got. Now we're all watching country vs. country or whatever vs. whatever in real time, all together.

Man's inhumanity to man has dogged and characterized the species from the very earliest good-old days, and some say nothing has changed, that our inconsequential strife over waves and associated 'turf' is just another fruit of our territorial family tree, our natural animal essence.

But time is running out. All human systems are on overload, red-lining, growing greedily, heading straight off the charts. The bottom line must be sustainability on all levels, and this includes relationships. The hostile local who dominates his surf spot like the tribes of the Great Plains once dominated particular hunting grounds will always lose the battle – he'll move away or grow old and die – and others will ride the waves he once rode. The problem is in what happens to the area he's trying to hoard or 'protect.' His influence, the aura of negativity he projects at others – newcomers or invaders – conditions the environment, creates a paradigm, a way of thinking that others are forced to adopt unless they are stronger, more intelligent, or more agile. This paradigm is self-perpetuating and helps to explain the global fix we all share in.

These people are nuts; they live in hallucinations – they need to be ignored, marginalized, and unrespected. There's a reason local or regional bullies are seen as "little Hitlers or Napoleons," and that's because they are. We look at the evolutionary pattern in any dictatorship or oppressive autocracy, and we see the same thing — weak-minded individuals buy in for approval or keep silent in the hopes it will go away, and it doesn't. It just gets bigger, until some courageous souls make a stand and reveal the nakedness of the 'emperor.'

"Surfers are the blessed sons and daughters of Kahuna gliding through Neptune's kingdom," writes Surfrider Foundation founder Glenn Hening, "until they start acting like troops of baboons defending territory against outsiders while engaged in internecine conflicts typical of lower order primate communities. Or maybe a better comparison would be to the behavior of the sea's most instinctually violent species, predatory sharks."

In his essay on *The Toxic Spill of Localism*, Hening continues: "I don't know if there is another sport/art/ lifestyle on the planet that offers as phenomenal an

experience as riding a wave and yet is cursed with human behavior in a classification with sharks and gangbangers. Surfing is an amazing thing to do, but seen through the prism of localism, it comes off looking pretty lame."

We require a different paradigm, a new way of thinking more reflective of how far we've come in so many other ways. This kind of territorial logic only makes sense on a certain scale; it is only logical on a certain level on consciousness. Fighting over a carcass, while ignoring an onrushing wildfire is patently stupid, and so is fighting over waves while our beaches erode or our access is being revoked or the world goes to hell in a handbasket.

"Your attitude is your surfboard," I believe, and you could just as well add Owl Chapman's famous saying, "Give a smile, get a smile," to it. But remember what Bob Dylan said too: "He not busy being born is busy dying." At every stage, attitudes of responsibility and respect are challenged by new waves of creation, which effectively

wipe away the past and its paradigms of context. A new set comes, and everyone wants the best wave. Who cares about the last set, it's history. Well...haven't we traveled far enough down that road already?

Surfing is the ultimate metaphor. Life is all sets and lulls, hard paddling and sweet rides. Surfing ocean waves teaches the fundamental principles of the real world, so we should know that bringing issues of ownership out into the ocean is nothing more than illusion. We're all renters on this planet, and surfers are coastal nomads. It's unnatural for them to stay and surf in one place. Which hardened local doesn't ride other waves in other places? Which of them can honestly claim ownership of anything, let alone the ephemeral resource of ocean waves? Fighting over waves at the expense of the quality of the surfing experience is an utterly bankrupt activity. Give it up. Please. We get so much from our experiences in the ocean, it's our responsibility to give something back, even if it's just a smile.

Crowds are a given in any urban area, but there's always enough beauty to go around. Newport, Orange County, LA.

ROB GILLEY

Surfin' USA – A brief history by Drew Kampion

If Polynesian Hawaii is the essence of surfing, California is its personality. It may have been the Beach Boys' "*Surfin' USA*" that crystalized contemporary surf culture as catalyzed by the book and film *Gidget* in the late '50s, but surf culture was seeded on the Mainland many years before.

In 1885, three young Hawaiian princes rode waves off the mouth of the San Lorenzo River in Santa Cruz using surfboards milled from local redwood. Jonah Kuhio Kalaniana`ole and his brothers David Kawananakoa and Edward Keli`iahonui were nephews of Queen Kapi'olani, wife to Hawaii's last king, David Kalakaua. They were attending St. Matthew's Military School over the coastal mountains in San Mateo when they became the first to surf California's waves.

Twenty-two years later, in the spring of 1907, 23-year-old Irish-Hawaiian beachboy George Freeth was brought to California by developer Henry E. Huntington to demonstrate the sport of Hawaiian kings to the astonished throngs at Redondo Beach as a promotion for Huntington's new train line. Freeth must have enjoyed the warm welcome he received, because he stayed on in California to become the first official lifeguard on the Pacific Coast, distinguishing himself in the winter of 1908, when, after a violent storm capsized a fishing boat in the South Bay, he single-handedly rescued six Japanese fishermen, earning the US Life Saving Corps Gold Medal. Freeth died in the line of duty in 1919, after performing strenuous lifesaving work in storm conditions off Oceanside, then succumbing to a bout of influenza. He was just 35.

Surfing had received quite a bit of press in the years following the US annexation of Hawaii in 1898. *Woman's Home Companion* published Jack London's paean to wave-riding, "A Royal Sport: Surfing at Waikiki," in '07. *Collier's* countered two years later with Alexander Ford Hume's "Riding the Surf in Hawaii," which covered the Waikiki Beach scene as well as the physics of wave-riding. And London's travel book, *Cruise of the Snark*, published in 1911, included a version of "Surfing: A Royal Sport," in which the author described Freeth, Francis Ford Hume, and the surfing life at Waikiki. During this period, the first surf clubs – the Outrigger Canoe and Hui Nalu – were founded at Waikiki.

Public interest in surfing was further fanned by Duke Kahanamoku's gold medal performance at the 1912 Olympics in Stockholm, where he set a world record in the 100m swim (63.4 seconds); he also collected a silver in the 4x200m freestyle relay. On his return from Stockholm, he surfed for the crowds and cameras near the steel pier at Atlantic City, New Jersey, thus introducing surfing on the East Coast. Four years later, Duke was the first to ride the waves of Ocean Beach in San Diego. And then in 1920, after he Gold Medaled again in the 100m with a new record time of 60.8 seconds, the 30-year-old beachboy was on a cross-country victory lap with his teammates when he met a young man from the north woods of Wisconsin, Tom Blake.

Blake was inspired by Duke and his aloha spirit to devote his life to the Polynesian sports of swimming, paddling, and surfing. When he arrived in Waikiki in 1924, he was immediately drawn to Hawaiian culture and lore. The course of surfing history was forever altered when he discovered a few ancient surfboards at Honolulu's Bishop Museum and set about creating replicas, notably the fabled

LINDLEY

Peter Cole and Kit Horn, Malibu

1946

Kit Horn

Bob Simmons' Model B

Old Man's, San Onofre

1939

DOC BALL

Peter Cole and Kit Horn

San Onofre

Long Beach flood control

1941

1981 **Tom Blake**

Blake hollow paddleboards, which became popular around the world as lifesaving tools. Blake's many innovations (the first waterproof camera housing, the first surfboard fin, the first sailing surfboard) set the tone for the continued innovation and technological development of the surfboard which followed.

The 1920s saw the growth of surfing in Southern California, as both Kahanamoku and Blake tried their hands at the movie business, and Duke gave an exhibition of surfing at Santa Monica's Hotel Virginia before a crowd of 5,000. He then demonstrated the surfboard's utility as a lifesaving device by rescuing eight survivors of a boat capsize in big surf off Corona Del Mar. About that time (1925) Sam Reid and Tom Blake hiked into the Rindge Ranch and discovered the beautiful peeling waves of Malibu.

During the 1930s, surf clubs sprang up around California's major surfing areas (San Diego, San Onofre, Corona Del Mar, Palos Verdes, Hermosa Beach, Santa Cruz, etc.) and the first Pacific Coast Surfriding Championships were held. Tom Blake's patented

Finally, however, the war fanned the flames of surfing's growth as material developments were soon put to use in the evolution of the modern surfboard. The brilliant Bob Simmons (4-F during the war because of an earlier arm injury) created the first balsa-foam-fiberglass "sandwich" surfboards in the late 1940s. Then, Joe Quigg built a surfboard for his girlfriend, Darrylin Zanuck, a 10'6" made of lightweight balsa with rounded rails and a fiberglass fin. Les Williams took it for a spin and discovered a whole new world of maneuverability. The era of the Malibu surfboard was born. Beach luaus drew big crowds to the grass shacks at Windansea and San Onofre.

At the dawn of the 1950s, Dale Velzy opened the world's first real surfboard shop in Manhattan Beach, California, and others soon followed suit – Hap Jacobs, Jack O'Neill, Hobie Alter, Dave Sweet, Dewey Weber and so on. Bud Browne's surf movies (inspired by the early surf photos of Tom Blake and Dr. John Ball) stoked surfers up and down the West Coast in the mid '50s, and he was soon joined by the likes of John Severson, Bruce Brown, Greg Noll, and finally Hollywood with the milestone release of *Gidget* in 1959.

1965

Dewey Weber, Malibu

STONER

1964

Sequit Pt (aka Secos), LA County

LEROY GRANNIS

1966

Steamer Lane, Santa Cruz

LEROY GRANNIS

1962

Miki Dora, Malibu

BOB JOHNSON

LEROY GRANNIS

Hawaiian Hollow Surfboard (#1872230) went into production, California surfers stowed away on steamships to 'mythical' Hawaii, and Meyers Butte created the first production surfboards at his family's Pacific Ready Cut Homes factory in LA, choosing the Tibetan symbol of eternal recurrence for his logo, a year before Adolf Hitler seized upon the same image to symbolize his Nazi Party.

World War II effectively put a stop to surfing in America, with only a rag-tag group of kids and physically unfit adults left at home to ply the waves. Some of these kids – like the Malibu crew of Kit Horn, Goodwin M. 'Buzzy' Trent, and Peter, Lucky and Corny Cole – later remembered these as golden years of crowdless wave-riding.

Perhaps signaling the end of an era, Simmons drowned at Windansea (San Diego) in 1955, the same year Tom Blake hung up surfing and left Hawaii for good. Soon Hobie and Sweet were making surfboards out of polyurethane foam and fiberglass, and Jack O'Neill (O'Neill) and Bev Morgan and Bobby Meistrell (Dive 'n Surf) started designing wetsuits for surfers, thus effectively expanding the seasonal and territorial scope of the sport. Waimea Bay was ridden for the first time by a crew of mainland surfers in November of '57, and Grubby Clark started blowing foam for Hobie in 1958 near Laguna Beach. This process greatly facilitated the mass production of surfboards.

Back in the 1950s, surfing's big adventure was a winter trek to Hawaii for the big surf, and surfers in the know got their trunks custom-made from M. Nii, a Waianae tailor. In 1959, Nancy and Walter Katin, Newport Beach makers of canvas boat covers, started making similar surf trunks. These, along with the Hawaiian (or Aloha) shirt, were the foundation of the modern surfwear industry. That same year, the first West Coast Surfing Championships were held at the pier in Huntington Beach.

The 1960s dawned with the creation of *The Surfer* magazine by filmmaker John Severson, and the boom was on. Fueled by its own films and magazines, plus sensational articles about the 'cult' of surfing in the mainstream press, surf culture grew into a significant fashion force in the '60s, backed by the rhythms of California rock 'n' rollers Dick Dale and His Del-Tones, who emerged from the inland smog to play the coastal ballrooms with the "big and wet" sound of surf music.

In 1961, surf/skier Joey Cabell and UDT frogman Buzzy Bent launched the Chart House restaurants, the United States Surfing Association was founded by Hoppy Swarts, and a song titled *Surfin'* (written by a Hawthorne kid named Brian Wilson and his cousin Mike Love) became a SoCal hit. Meanwhile, Hang Ten founder Duke Boyd signed Phil Edwards as the first surfer to have a signature clothing line designed and marketed around his image and prototypical hot-dogger Matt Kivlin, overwhelmed by the crowds, rode his last wave at Malibu.

The flames of surfing's popularity were fanned by the arrival of Bruce Brown's milestone film, *The Endless Summer*, which hit the surf-film circuit in 1964, then went mainstream in 1966, acclaimed at theaters coast to coast. On the flip side, Hollywood was spinning out surfploitation films like *Beach Blanket Bingo*, any surfer with a name was celebrated with a signature surfboard model, and the first man-made wave pool opened in Tempe, Arizona.

This era – sometimes seen as a 'golden age' of sorts – was endo'd with the social upheavals precipitated by the cluster bomb of the civil rights movement, psychedelic drugs, rock 'n' roll, and opposition to US involvement in the war in Vietnam. This nexus of forces disrupted established relationships at all levels and ushered in an era of impetuous change. Surfing was as much a medium for transformation as any other subculture on the planet.

Catalyzed by the short, neutral-buoyancy wave-riding vehicle of Santa Barbara knee-rider George Greenough, surfers cut two feet from the fronts of their surfboards in 1967-68, kicking off the pivotal shortboard revolution, first in Australia, soon after in America. Amidst a cultural imperative to 'do your own thing,' surfers turned on, tuned in, and dropped out.

1969

Gerry Lopez, Huntington Pier

1969 Trestles, San Diego County

Swamis, San Diego

1971 David Nuuhiwa and the Brotherhood's John Gale, Laguna

Although surfing's popularity was exploding in California, the fastest-growing market was on the East Coast, where hordes of young people found their identity in beach culture. During the mid '60s the major manufacturers sold more surfboards in New Jersey, Virginia, and Florida than they did in California, Oregon, and Washington. Business was booming, contests started paying prize money, and guys who had cut school to surf were suddenly making money at the beach.

Reflecting a growing awareness in the culture at large, increasing numbers of surfers began to migrate towards spirituality and environmentalism in the late '60s. The budding competition scene was essentially displaced by a 'back to the roots' movement in the sport, and things got very mellow indeed. For a short while.

Necessity is the mother of invention, and surfers couldn't surf all day every day unless they were paid for it, so they formed themselves into the International Professional Surfers in 1976, cobbled together a world tour, and have been chasing sponsors with increasing success ever since. Although the first nine world champions were from the Southern Hemisphere, the tide finally turned in 1985 with the ascension of another

Santa Barbara surfer, Tom Curren, son of legendary big-surf pioneer Pat Curren. Curiously, the situation was almost exactly the opposite for American women, who captured the first 12 world titles, yet got virtually no respect in a male-dominated sport and media.

By the 1980s, the surfboard had gone through yet another transformation. A multitude of experiments in the '60s and '70s resolved themselves into a short, lightweight, wide-tailed board with a pointed nose that lifted like an Arabian slipper. The design was dubbed the "thruster" by its innovator, Australian Simon Anderson, and it had three fins.

Six-time world champ Slater parlayed his good looks and unnatural abilities into a starring role on the heavily overwatched television show, Baywatch and a well-publicized relationship with the actress Pamela Anderson. An übermensch with no known detractors, Slater was widely accepted as the greatest surfer who had ever lived. Except for maybe the ultimate übermensch, Laird Hamilton, adopted son of Laguna Beach stylist Bill Hamilton, who boldly and almost single-handedly led surfing's extreme wing into the world of strap- and tow-in surfing. Pioneered on the outer reefs of Maui, tow-in surfing eventually found its mainland arena at a spot called Mavericks near Half Moon Bay, California, and its most suggestive potential at the Cortes Banks, a seamount some 100 miles (160km) off the coast of San Diego.

Note: Miki Dora died on the 3rd of January 2002 at his father's home in Montecito, California. On that same day, after a month of calm seas, a rising swell hit Dora's adopted home break at Guéthary in the south of France. It was 6ft by Friday, 8-10ft by Saturday, and bigger on Sunday. Winds were offshore and perfect.

1987

Kelly Slater, OP Pro, Huntington

1997

Computer aided shaping

JEFF DIVINE

1994

Proto-aerialist, Christian Fletcher

1988

1988

Tom Curren, Stubbies

JEFF DIVINE

Peter Mel, Mavericks

ROB GILLEY

This three-fin business changed everything. A tradition of spin-outs and side-slips gave way to turn-on-a-dime handling that allowed riders a complexity of trajectory never dreamed of before.

While many older surfers (and some younger ones too) staged a parallel 'longboard renaissance,' most young, fit American surfers embraced the thrusters and, in the spirit of one-upmanship, took their "new school" surfing into the aerial dimension, led by pioneers Kevin Reed and Christian Fletcher (California) and Kelly Slater and Lisa Andersen (Florida). Andersen won four consecutive women's championships in the 1990s while galvanizing the spirit of women's surfing into a commercial and competitive force to be reckoned with. The growth of surfing's popularity with women was one of the defining evolutionary streams of the 1990s and continues unabated.

There in January of 2001, a group of California surfers, including Mike Parsons, Brad Gerlach, Peter Mel, and Kenny 'Skindog' Collins, teamed up to ride 50-foot plus waves in the middle of the ocean, far out of sight of any land and a long, long way from those three Hawaiian princes testing the waters off Santa Cruz 116 years earlier. A long way too from Mickey Dora's mythic days of dominance at small-wave Malibu, but, overall, just another step in the evolution of surfin' in the USA.

JEFF DIVINE

1998

Taylor Knox

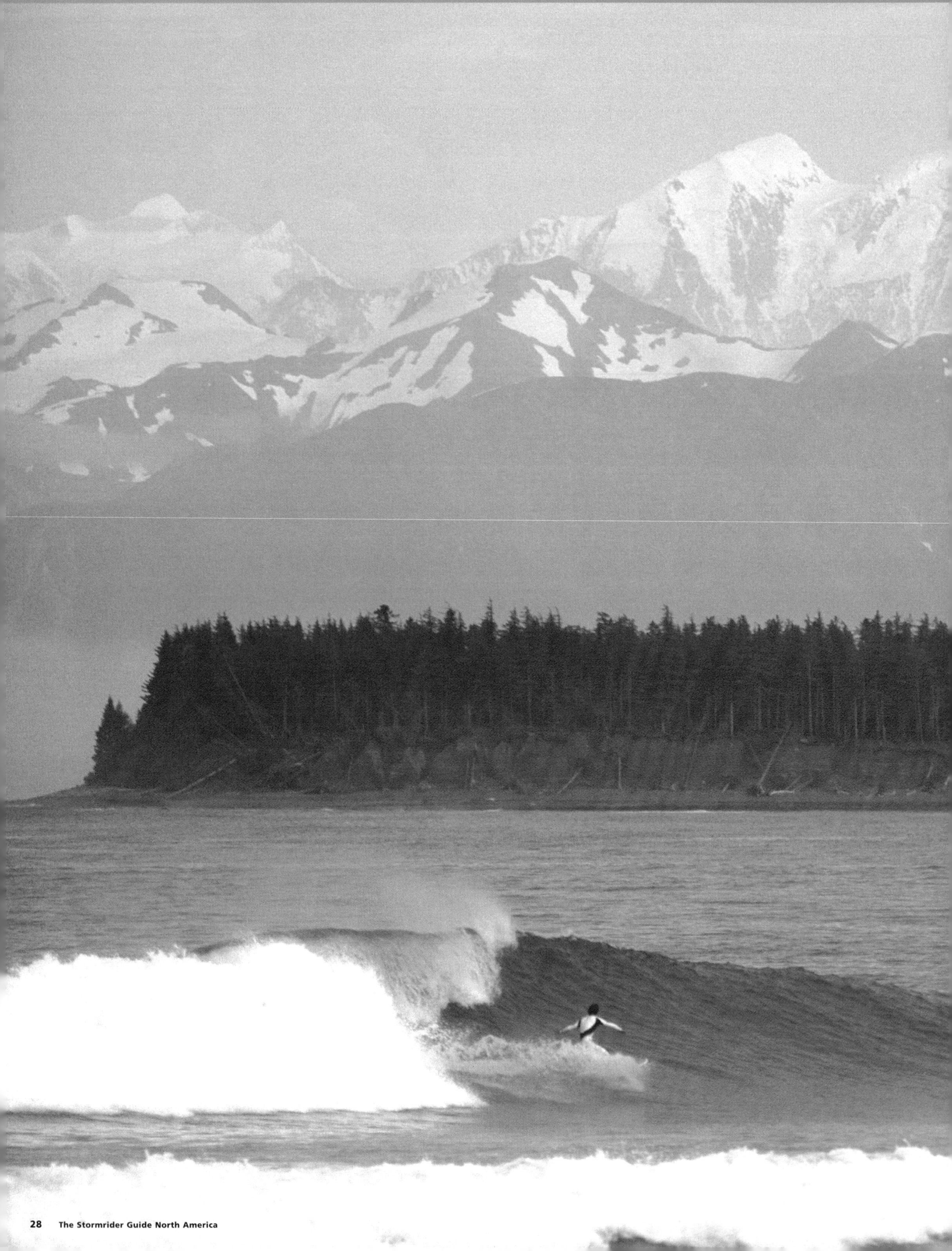

Alaska and British Columbia

'The Wild North' perfectly describes the arc of wilderness seashore that ranges from the far-western Aleutian Islands through the Gulf of Alaska and down to the islands and peninsulas of Canada's Pacific coast. A true surfing frontier containing untold surfing secrets in some of North America's most spectacular wilderness, the exploration potential is huge, but access is limited, and this raw corner of the Pacific is not for the faint-hearted.

From barren islands with sheer cliffs plunging into the sea, to vast glaciers grinding and calving off into frigid waters, to primordial old-growth temperate forests wreathed in mist, this northern landscape is home to a kaleidoscope of wildlife – from whales and bears to eagles and king-sized mosquitoes. There are problems to overcome in exploring these remote shores, not least the cold, rain, fog, and fiercely unpredictable weather. Escaping the full brunt of mutant Aleutian depressions, blasting swell and gale force winds into the Gulf, is the greatest challenge. Fortunately, the contorted coastline provides the shelter as bays, channels, estuaries, and fjord-like coves pock the islands and mainland, bending, refracting, and grooming unruly swells into more organized and manageable shapes. Understandably, most surfers will congregate at a handful of easy-access spots. Meanwhile, the intrepid searcher should be rewarded with quality waves in solitude.

BOB BARBOUR

Graveyards, Yakutat, SE Alaska.

WEATHER AND WATER STATISTICS	J/F	M/A	M/J	J/A	S/O	N/D
Anchorage, AK						
rainfall (inch/mm)	0.7/18	0.5/13	0.6/15	2.1/54	2.4/61	1/26
consistency (d/mth)	6	5	5	12	13	7
average sun (hrs/day)	2	7	9	7	4	2
min temp (°F/°C)	7/-14	20/-7	41/5	46/8	34/1	9/-13
max temp (°F/°C)	23/-5	39/4	59/15	64/18	50/10	25/-4
water temp (°F/°C)	36/2	38/3	49/9	52/11	47/8	39/4
wetsuit						
Vancouver, BC						
rainfall (inch/mm)	7.2/183	4.2/107	2.6/66	15/38	4.7/119	8.5/216
consistency (d/mth)	18	15	12	7	13	20
average sun (hrs/day)	3	5	7	8	5	3
min temp (°F/°C)	32/0	37/3	50/10	54/12	46/8	37/3
max temp (°F/°C)	43/6	54/12	68/20	74/23	61/16	46/8
water temp (°F/°C)	45/7	48/9	52/11	53/12	52/11	48/9
wetsuit						

TRAVEL INFORMATION	
Alaska	www.travelalaska.com
British Columbia	www.bc.worldweb.com
Vancouver Island	www.islands.bc.ca

The Surf, Ocean Environment and Surf Culture

*Below – **Aleutian line-up.***
*Opposite – **Boat trips are the only way of accessing much of the Wild North's coastline while some mountain ranges hem the coast, making access virtually impossible and surfable waves unlikely.***

Alaska is the USA's largest state and its sprawling, convoluted coastline has scarcely been explored by surfers. Beyond the distance and the cold, access is the main obstacle to surfing the 2,800-odd miles (4500km) of Pacific shore, where airplanes and ferries are virtually the only available modes of transportation, and only a few areas (like Kodiak Island and Yakutat) have some coastal access, usually via weather-beaten roads and tracks, barely navigable by the pricey, well-used rental cars. This leaves thousands of watery miles to be mapped by surfers with a sturdy boat and total faith in their survivability in this humbling environment.

British Columbia's western shores, from the Queen Charlotte Islands to Vancouver Island, are somewhat milder but scarcely closer to civilization; they are difficult to explore without concerted, well-outfitted expeditions. Most of the coast north of Vancouver Island is similar to Alaska's – remote, unpopulated, and littered with hundreds of islands and bays, vast areas where it's boat exploration only. Portions of the Queen Charlotte Islands are a World Heritage Site, so admittance to large areas is by special permit only. The southern part of Vancouver Island is the only coastal zone of BC with a sizable year-round population and easy road access. These roads convey thousands of summer tourists to pristine beaches and what remains of the island's much-marauded forests and substantially denuded mountains.

Current theory has it that Asians were first to colonize Alaska, crossing the land-bridge from Siberia during

BOB KEMP

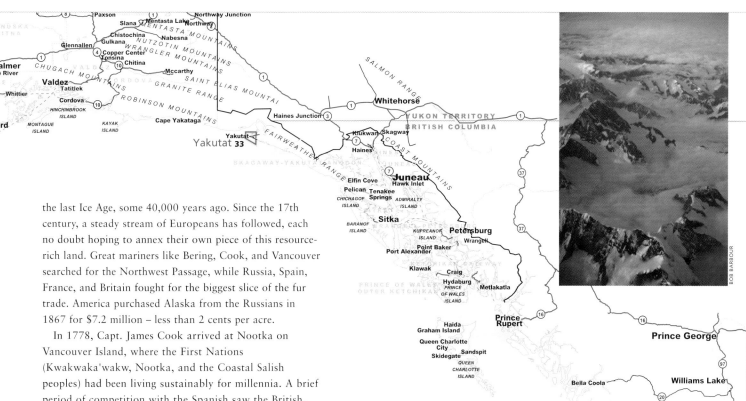

BOB BARBOUR

the last Ice Age, some 40,000 years ago. Since the 17th century, a steady stream of Europeans has followed, each no doubt hoping to annex their own piece of this resource-rich land. Great mariners like Bering, Cook, and Vancouver searched for the Northwest Passage, while Russia, Spain, France, and Britain fought for the biggest slice of the fur trade. America purchased Alaska from the Russians in 1867 for $7.2 million – less than 2 cents per acre.

In 1778, Capt. James Cook arrived at Nootka on Vancouver Island, where the First Nations (Kwakwaka'wakw, Nootka, and the Coastal Salish peoples) had been living sustainably for millennia. A brief period of competition with the Spanish saw the British, with the help of the fur-trading companies, take control of the area by 1795. Lumber barons and gold prospectors followed until Victoria was declared the provincial capital of British Columbia in 1868.

PATRICK TREFZ

Although most of this region is still considered wilderness, man has managed to upset the equilibrium. Most notably, in 1989, the *Exxon Valdez* ran aground, spilling 11 million gallons of crude oil into Prince William Sound; the resultant slick contaminated over 1,500 miles (2400km) of pristine shoreline, bringing a tide of black death to thousands of birds and sea creatures. Meanwhile, large-scale logging operations in both Alaska and BC have disrupted the habitat of numerous species, bringing changes to surfing line-ups in the process.

While the surf culture of Alaska is currently evolving, there have been a few notable pioneers, but Vancouver Island surfers have been at it since the 1960s, braving the cold waters even in pre-fullsuit days.

Swell Forecasting

In winter, storms track across the North Pacific from Japan into the Gulf of Alaska, usually close to the 50°N line of latitude. These are the same intense low pressure systems that spawn the giant waves that batter the North Shore of the Hawaii Islands. Powered by potent jet stream currents, these systems are known as semi-permanent Aleutian Lows, generally sandwiched between high pressures in Siberia and in the Pacific. Often, an almost continuous procession of tight-gradient tempests assaults the Gulf of Alaska with hurricane-strength winds and enormous seas. Winter gales can persist for days and usually blow from the S or SE. Where exactly these chaotic systems decide to cross the coast determines the center-of-gravity of the wind motion, and the best chance of an offshore is directly before or after a low has passed overhead.

During a rather brief summer season, the North Pacific undergoes a marked transformation, and big lows and large swells are unlikely. Southeastern Alaska is better equipped for smaller localized windswells than the east-facing coast of Kodiak Island. As with many places in the Northern Hemisphere, late spring and early fall are generally the best seasons for clean conditions.

Vancouver Island is directly in the path of the same Aleutian lows that pinwheel down from the Gulf of Alaska. Close proximity to these low pressure systems can result in messy, blown-out conditions as the winds can veer from storm S to NW onshores while the storm passes over. Other swells of less intensity can originate from western Pacific storms at lower latitudes, or arrive courtesy of localized weather systems. Distant Southern Hemisphere swells can show at Long Beach on Vancouver Island, but Washington's Olympic Peninsula blocks S swells from reaching the Island's fertile southern shore.

Alaska

The coast of Alaska is an enormous arc of swell-trapping shoreline that can be roughly divided into several distinct surfable areas.

The Aleutian Islands get hit by (and can hold) serious monster swells. Although a recent *Surfer* magazine expedition ended up getting no swell (always a possibility in the milder summer months), the incredible potential did not go unnoticed; subsequent exploration will undoubtedly unearth some classic waves. There are no roads and very little else on these treeless, wind-ravaged islands. There is no true lee side of the islands either, because the north sides are fully open to Bering Sea swells. Once a month (from May to August and twice in September), the Alaska Marine Highway ferry service runs from Seward to Unalaska, briefly dropping in at tiny settlements along the Alaska Peninsula and the island chain throughout the 6-day voyage. While it stops in the large fishing port of Dutch Harbor for 5-6 hours, it is not enough time to get wet. The town has a large summer population and (expensive) flight connections to Anchorage, making it the obvious base for any Aleutian surf exploration. Chartering a fishing boat or similarly seaworthy vessel to take you exploring is an expensive plan but the only one likely to net some quality

waves. Quad bikes make it possible to search some of the Unalaska coastline, but camping permits must be obtained from the Ounalashka landowners. One thing you don't have to worry about out here: the bald Aleutian landscape doesn't support any bears.

Kodiak Island is shielded by the Aleutians from W swells and relies on S and E pulses for its surf. A single, short road provides some access to the island's east coast as it skirts the 2,500 sq mi National Wildlife Refuge, which occupies two thirds of the 120-mile long (192km) island. With surfaces ranging from paved and gravel to deeply rutted 4WD track, driving on Kodiak's coast-hugging Chiniak Road is a scenic delight. Much of Kodiak City is in the swell shadow of Woody and Long Island, which definitely have some spots on the north- and east-facing coasts. North of town, near Fort Abercrombie, Mill Bay provides sheltered waves in big NE-E swells. At the end of the road on the north side of Monashka Bay, a rare but perfect wave, peels down a protected sandy cove in NE storm conditions. Another mile-and-a-half (2.5km) hike to the north is Termination Point, where abundant reefbreaks are open to NE-E swells but are plagued by the strong currents of Narrow Strait.

Driving south from Kodiak City, there are three deep NE-facing bays that need serious E swell to get going, and their protruding points are a long hike from the road. Chiniak Road winds past Cape Chiniak and terminates on the due east-facing coast at Cape Greville, where you'll find cliffs plunging into deep water and very few surfing options. Pasagshak Bay Road leads to a State Recreation Site of the same name where free riverside camping and, of course, awesome salmon fishing can be had in a wilderness area that has great surf potential. The wide, sandy beaches of Narrow Cape have good southerly exposure.

Flights to Kodiak Island arrive at the local airport near Kodiak from Anchorage. There is also a ferry service from Homer, located a 100-plus miles (160km) southwest of Anchorage on the Kenai Peninsula.

BOB KEMP

Above – **Kodiak Island beachbreak.**
Right – **Aleutian juice. Finding protection from battering winds and swells is the trick.**
Opposite top – **Turnagain Arm.**

BOB KEMP

The area from the Kenai Peninsula (Cook Inlet) through Prince William Sound to Kayak Island is not suitable for surfing due to tidal flats (combined with enormous tidal movements) and giant mountains bordering the ocean. The only surf-related attraction in this area is the tidal bore in Turnagain Arm, southeast of Anchorage. Huge 40ft (13m) tides flow into the Cook Inlet at up to 12 knots, causing a wall of whitewater at Bird Point, where a bend in the Arm refines the surge into rideable 1-6ft waves that can run for 2 miles (3km) up the channel. However, sucking mud and vicious currents make this a dangerous thrill. Careless people have been trapped in the fine alluvial silt (which displays all the properties of quicksand) and drowned by the rapid advance of the tide. Story goes, one unfortunate woman was pulled in half when a helicopter tried to lift her out of the deep muck as the tide was rushing in. Accessible directly off Seward Highway (Alaska's busiest tarmac), Turnagain Arm is popular with windsurfers and not far from the Alyeska ski resort.

Southeast Alaska holds the best potential for surf. Take one look at a map of the fjord-pocked coastline with its hundreds of islands, rivermouths, and headlands, and the potential is obvious. However, roads are virtually non-existent, and huge mountains barricade the coastal fringe in the north and east. Except in the scattered small towns, travel to the SE is via plane and boat, and it's expensive. Alaska Airlines flies from Anchorage to Seattle, stopping (much like a bus) at Cordova, Yakutat, Sitka, Petersburg, Wrangell, and Ketchikan along the way. From each of these locations small planes (usually amphibious De Havilland Beavers) can be hired to cruise the surrounding coastline. Further south, inter-island ferries ply the 'Inside Passage' from Juneau to Bellingham, Washington.

Yakutat is the best-known surf destination in SE Alaska, but this former Tlingit village is only serviced once a month in summer by the Alaska Marine Highway, so it's well off the usual tourist trail. Accommodation is limited and expensive, with all mod-cons lodges catering to sport fishermen or Malaspina and Hubbard Glacier sightseers. The other option (most favored by surfers) is to hire a van (expensive) from either of the two rental locations, drive to the forest bordering the beach, and pitch camp, taking all necessary bear precautions. There is only one paved road in Yakutat, and it leads from the airport to the harbor. The harbor is the center point of the 'town', which consists of a fish-processing factory, a couple of (large) hardware stores, a couple of bars, a marina, enough housing to shelter the small community of fishermen who live there, and a rubbish dump where bears scavenge for food.

It's a 7-mile (11km) drive from the harbor out to the main beaches; head west from the town crossroads. The unpaved, ever-deteriorating, potholed road leads to an impossibly rickety bridge deep in bear country. Taking the left after the bridge takes you out to the most westerly point, Ocean Cape, a rocky headland that provides views across 20-mile (32km) wide Yakutat Bay to Mount St Elias and the giant Malaspina Glacier, sideways rain and soupy fog permitting. At Ocean Cape there are some pockets of beachbreak held together with rocks marking the northern end of Canon Beach, a long, black sand expanse, so named after the WWII tank relics rusting in the woods. Canon Beach faces SW, is fully exposed to the swell, and is regularly onshore and enormous. Between Ocean Cape and Point Carrew there are more open beachbreaks and a left off the Cape that suffers from horrendous currents. These spots are only worth a check on small summer swells.

A right turn at the bridge winds past a graveyard in the forest, which gives way to sand dunes leading to the predictably-named surf spot, Graveyards. This is the furthest east of a series of three points located inside the estuary itself. Bigger swells wrap around Point Carrew, cleaning themselves up on the way, and by the time they reach Graveyards, they've swung almost 180° from their original SW direction, and howling onshores have become dead offshores. Naturally, it's always bigger further west towards Point Carrew. On small days, the left offers an

Top – **Rare small, clean conditions at Cannon Beach.**
Above – **The route to the surf in Yakutat.**

BOB BARBOUR

Above – **As Graveyards increases in size the right becomes more surfable.** Below – **Many a perfect set-up awaits the intrepid surf traveler in SE Alaska.**

Kuroshio extension, it moderates the whole Gulf of Alaska. Yakutat bottoms out at around 39°F (4°C) and can climb to 62°F (16°C) in an El Niño August, with Kodiak a bit colder throughout the annual cycle.

You'd expect all hazards in this remote area to be natural ones, but it seems past military operations managed to pollute this otherwise pristine environment. In fact, the huge *Exxon Valdez* oil spill was smaller than several of WWII catastrophes in the Gulf. Fortunately, this huge landscape seems capable of recovery. Unfortunately, an Agent Orange dump has been found (out near the Yakutat breaks), which is leaching into the aquifer, poisoning clams (for starters). Other isolated incidents of illegal toxic dumping are probably a result of a "Who's gonna find it way out here?" mentality.

uncomplicated take-off, projecting into an open wall which suddenly warps and actually bends through almost 90°. There are barrels and power on the inside. The whole set-up favors lefts, although there's a small swell right that's shorter but steeper. Since several local surfers own boats, exploring the great potential of the islands inside the estuary has likely progressed to advanced stages.

South of Yakutat, the Southeast Alaska coastline continues to provide an inexhaustible number of possible surf spots throughout the islands above the Canadian border. Russian-named islands like Chichagof, Kruzof, and Baranof, as well as the Prince of Wales and the outer islands west of Ketchikan, present fertile opportunities for exploration. The historical city of Sitka (on Baranof), the only population center open to the Pacific, is a jumping-off point for outer island forays and some road-accessible surf south of town.

Considering the latitude, water temps should be extremely cold, but as the Alaska Current splits off the

The US Congress has (so far) narrowly defeated bills that would open up the nation's greatest coastal wilderness (Arctic National Wildlife Refuge) to oil exploration and drilling. Exploitation of the state's abundant natural resources (oil, timber, salmon, etc.) is the main issue on the environmental agenda. Spruce bark beetle infestations have decimated forests in South Central Alaska and while salmon stocks have recovered in some managed areas, salmon farms have flooded the market with product. Mixing farm-raised fish with wild stocks has huge implications for the survival of already threatened species.

Kodiak is, of course, most famous for its eponymous species of brown bear, the largest terrestrial carnivore in the world; some tip the scales at over 1,500lbs (680kg). The 3,000 Kodiak bears resident on the island gorge themselves on salmon during the late summer runs and can be seen foraging on beaches. These and the small brown

BOB KEMP

and black bears should be kept foremost in your mind, especially if you're camping. Food-storage precautions include wrapping everything edible in three layers of plastic and hanging it high from tree branches at least half a mile from camp (no kidding). Before walking any distance, tie bells to clothing and/or baggage to warn bears of your approach as you don't want to surprise a bear, especially one with cubs. Low-impact camping etiquette involves packing out whatever you take in, so plan on it. Use bio-degradable soaps and wash away from water sources. Use small sticks and split pieces of deadwood for fires; never leave one burning, and cover fire pits with natural materials after use.

Seals, sea lions, and orcas are three consecutive members of the food chain patrolling the Alaskan waters. Take care during the spring season when pupping is taking place. Both seals and sea lions have been known to chase surfers from the water. Seasonal salmon sharks (fisheaters – no reported attacks) bear an uncanny resemblance to white pointers, which can't be discounted in these waters, either, particularly in summer. Beluga whales follow salmon runs up Cook Inlet and can be spotted cruising Turnagain Arm from the viewpoints on the Seward Highway.

Talented Washington surfer Greg Wheaton pioneered Alaskan line-ups in the late '70s and '80s, but is sadly no longer around to tell us of his early experiences. Sitka-based writer Richard K. Nelson wrote about surfing his neighborhood in the obscure but excellent spiritual/naturalist book, *The Island Within*, published in 1989. Alaska burst onto the mainstream scene in 1995 when a shot of Josh Mulcoy appeared on the cover of *Surfer*. Modern high-profile pioneers like Doc Renneker and Dave Parmenter surfed Yakutat and beyond in the early 1990s, but there's still a huge amount of potentially surfable coast to explore. Meanwhile, more than a few feral hellmen are out there, guys who fled to the land of cold waves long before the *Surfer* article. Only they know who they are.

Yakutat has become the best-known Alaskan surf town, where Icy Waves Surf Shop sprung up in 1999 to service a growing number of locals. With little infrastructure available for practicing more mainstream sports, surfing provides an ideal focus for the local kids right on the doorstep.

There is surf along the entire exposed British Columbia coast, to be sure, but access is challenging, as are the conditions. The Queen Charlotte Islands are nicely positioned to receive all sorts of swell energy, but there are almost no roads and little coastal access. One of the exceptions is on the north island – Graham – near the town of Masset at the mouth of the Sangan River. From there up to Rose Spit, there is potential, although you'll need a reliable 4x4 or dune buggy to check it out. Although water temps are moderated somewhat by the Kuroshio Current, you'll need a fullsuit, boots, and gloves to enjoy the best months for surf – October through April – and if you like fishing for salmon and steelhead, it's bonus time. Despite all this, the Queen Charlottes are seldom surfed.

British Columbia

The only part of British Columbia where people surf in any number is the semi-accessible southern half of Vancouver Island. There are only two roads that lead to the coast, the main one being the Pacific Rim Highway (Highway 4) to the 19-mile (30km) long, SW-facing beaches bounded by Tofino in the north and Ucluelet in the south. This area includes a large slice of the Pacific Rim National Park, which features many rocky outcrops and coves, but the waves are predominantly beachbreaks. Cox Bay is the favored contest beach; it's close to Tofino, which is the nearest thing to a surf town in western Canada. With an extensive southern headland, Cox Bay is sheltered from S winds. Other spots close to town include Chesterman Beach and MacKenzie Beach, which offer less wind protection than Cox Bay.

JEREMY KORESKI

Smoothed by kelp beds, this north Vancouver Island spot is only accessible by boat or seaplane.

The Pacific Rim Highway connects Tofino with Ucluelet, passing through the Long Beach area on the way. Long Beach is the first coastal access point and many people stop there after a long drive from Victoria or the mainland. With almost 6 miles (10km) of gently curving sand, it handles the summer crowds, who choose this beach for its easy access. The central expanse of the bay is named Combers Beach; the southern corner is Wickaninnish Beach, where an interpretive center displays natural and cultural information on the Long Beach unit of the Pacific Rim National Park. An open, SW-facing beach, Long Beach enjoys little protection from the wind, except in the northern reaches, where the more westerly Schooner Cove also holds waves.

South of Long Beach is Florencia Bay, another SW-facing strand with good N wind protection. The length of the walk in and back out deters the lazy, leaving plenty of peaks, which are sprinkled with the odd rock. South to Ucluelet, surfing opportunities decrease as the coast becomes rocky, except for a couple of tucked-away pocket beaches called Big Beach and Little Beach. The Wild Pacific Trail is a circuitous cliff walk past the lighthouse that the tourist office touts as a place for "winter tourists to witness enormous breakers pounding the rugged coast."

Across Barkley Sound lies the West Coast Trail, which started life in 1906 as the Dominion Lifesaving Trail to provide access through the impenetrable forests for rescuers searching for survivors of the frequent shipwrecks. This stunning coast is walled with sandstone cliffs, pocked with caves and graced with waterfalls, sea stacks, deserted beaches, and undoubtedly some lonely waves. But this is a heavy-duty hiking trail that requires permits and orientation sessions from the Pacific Rim National Park staff before members of the public are admitted, and only then between May and September. Unfortunately, surfing is not permitted along the West Coast Trail, perhaps because there are 25 ladders of over 100 vertical feet that need to be negotiated along the 48-mile (77km) trail. Pachena Point used to be ridden, but it is now off-limits, the dominion of boaters who must remain at a depth of 10 fathoms (20m) along the park's boundary.

BOB KEMP

Above – **BC presents many possibilities for finding and riding an un-named peak.**
Below – **South Vancouver Island lineup.**

Once inside the Juan de Fuca Strait, the accessible surf spots begin again. From the logging town of Port Renfrew, Highway 14 shadows the coast down to Sooke near the southern tip of Vancouver Island. The underwater topography is well-suited to reefs and pointbreaks, which mirror the lefts across the Strait in Washington. Port Renfrew has waves where the Gordon River flows into Port San Juan. Sombrio is a cobblestone beach at the mouth of the Sombrio River with a choice of waves that includes a fast, steep reef peak, which attracts a crowd, sometimes with attitude. The most notorious wave on the Strait is Jordan River (River Jordan on the maps), where

long righthanders wind down a rocky point, occasionally in ruler-edged fashion. The outside wave is The Point, a wave the pioneers with their heavy longboards at first considered too fast to ride. Further inside is Sewers, named for a defunct sewage-outlet pipe. This break has recently acquired a reputation for incidents of intimidating localism, which can include violence and vandalism to non-local vehicles. The wave is suited to experienced riders, so only paddle out if you're very sure of your ability and are able to withstand some stink-eye. SE winds will chop up most Juan de Fuca breaks but the area can clean up quickly after strong westerlies abate. These spots inside the Strait usually rely on big winter storms to push swell in and are very tide reliant. Secret spots exist, but it takes local knowledge to catch them firing. The Long Beach area is far more consistent and reliable for visiting surfers looking to score a decent session.

The remainder of Vancouver Island and the BC coastline is remote and hard to explore. Logging trails, boat access, or a guided tour are the only way to reach the wild and spectacular spots that undoubtedly pound the coastline on a daily basis. The coming years will see more spots revealed but it's going be a long time before the whole area has been fully explored. At present little information exists and what does is closely guarded by those who have had the will and stamina to find out.

The maritime climate delivers cool, foggy summers and mild, wet winters, resulting in an average of 300cm (120in) of rain annually. Near-shore ocean temperatures drop down to a chilling 8°C (46°F) in winter and reach a maximum of 15C (59°F) in summer. The Kuroshio (or Japan) Current brings warmer water from the Eastern Pacific before splitting north to feed the Alaskan Current or heading south to rejoin the North Equatorial Current, which completes this huge Pacific gyre. The offshore currents run strong and the continental shelf drops off to almost 2 miles (3km) directly off Queen Charlotte Islands, 150 miles (240km) to the north of Vancouver Island.

Coastal Vancouver Island is predominantly National Park and First Nations reservations, maintaining much of its pristine character, where logging hasn't ravaged the

GEOFF RAGATZ

landscape. Wildlife diversity is staggering; the waters teem with whales, seals, sea lions, otters, and schooling fish. Shark danger is relatively low from the few great whites that might have strayed too far north; the local species, like the six-gill and salmon shark, are mainly piscivorous. The British Columbia inter-tidal zone is one of the richest on the planet, where invertebrates and bivalves make their homes among the rocks and tide pools. The backdrop is a blanket of temperate rainforest, dominated by conifers, where the world's largest black bear, cougar, and wolves roam the remnants of dense old-growth forests.

Indeed, logging is the biggest threat to the island's (and all of British Columbia's) fragile ecosystems. Rampant clear-cutting has gutted the island's forests in the past, but environmental consciousness has been raised by an army of dedicated 'tree-huggers,' who have put their lives on the line to slow the damage at Clayoquot Sound (just north of Tofino) and the other remaining stands of old growth. There has been a recent increase in broad-based committees that include water and logging company representatives working with concerned residents (including surfers) and environmentalists.

At Jordan River, surfers often ride the waves in 'woody' conditions, a result of bark and tannic acid flowing to the rivermouths from the timber booms upstream. Silt deposited downstream from clear-cuts within the island's watershed is actually crucial in the formation of good sandbars at breaks like Port Renfrew.

Exactly when the first surfers paddled out at Long Beach and Pachena is as obscured as an approaching swell in a fog bank, but it most likely occurred back in the early 1960s. Certainly Tofino surfer Jim Sadler was one of the pioneers; he was often seen with plywood paddles lashed to his wrists to improve horsepower.

Vancouver Island had become a haven for alternative lifestyle proponents in the late '60s. They were joined by draft dodgers from as far away as Hawaii and California; inevitably, there were surfers in their numbers. Timber shacks were constructed on the sandstone cliffs above Wreck Bay (Florencia Bay), and a subsistence commune enjoyed the summer waves until the National Parks Service cleared them out in 1973.

Jordan River was pioneered in the mid '60s by a core crew, some of whom can still be found riding there on occasion. By 1973, the West Coast Surfing Associates were well established in their clubhouse – with sauna and commanding views of the point. China Beach, Sombrio, and Port Renfrew had all been ridden by then, and Sombrio had become another communal refuge for open-minded individuals, keen to avoid mainstream existence.

Early island shaping facilities were crude and rudimentary; Jim Van Dame, who lived at Jordan River, had a small lean-to on his barn, which housed a country-style

shaping bay. Wayne Vliet, Chuck Dillon, Dave Maxwell, and probably Van Dame all tried their hand at shaping, crafting some interesting mid '70s experiments. In the late '70s, a small influx of South African surfers (the second wave of draft dodgers) joined the tightly-knit dozen or so in the JR line-up. The following decade was fairly static, until recent growth spurts, which have spawned the intolerant attitude that pervades the modern JR line-up as BC catches up to the global surfing reality and those who remember the good ol' days try to hold on to them and each other.

Moving north in 1976, LA surfer Don Leschuk was amazed to find such good waves and a laid-back crew of friends to share them with. He opened Redbeard's surf shop in Sooke in the late 1980s, hoping to serve as a much-needed source of equipment; but lack of business combined with local resentment doomed the shop to permanent closure.

The surfing population remained small for years, but has grown rapidly in recent years, and it's now common to see 80 surfers in the water at Long Beach. Wetsuit technology has helped make Canadian surfing more accessible, as the numbers of year-round locals almost double on an annual basis. Tofino's local population of 1,300 swells to 22,000 in summer and a number of surf schools have sprung up to satisfy the demands of visiting novices. Check www.coastalbc.com. for surf schools, camps and environmentally friendly surf tours like Tatchu.

While certain easy access spots are suffering from crowding and localism, waves beyond the roads are seldom sessioned.

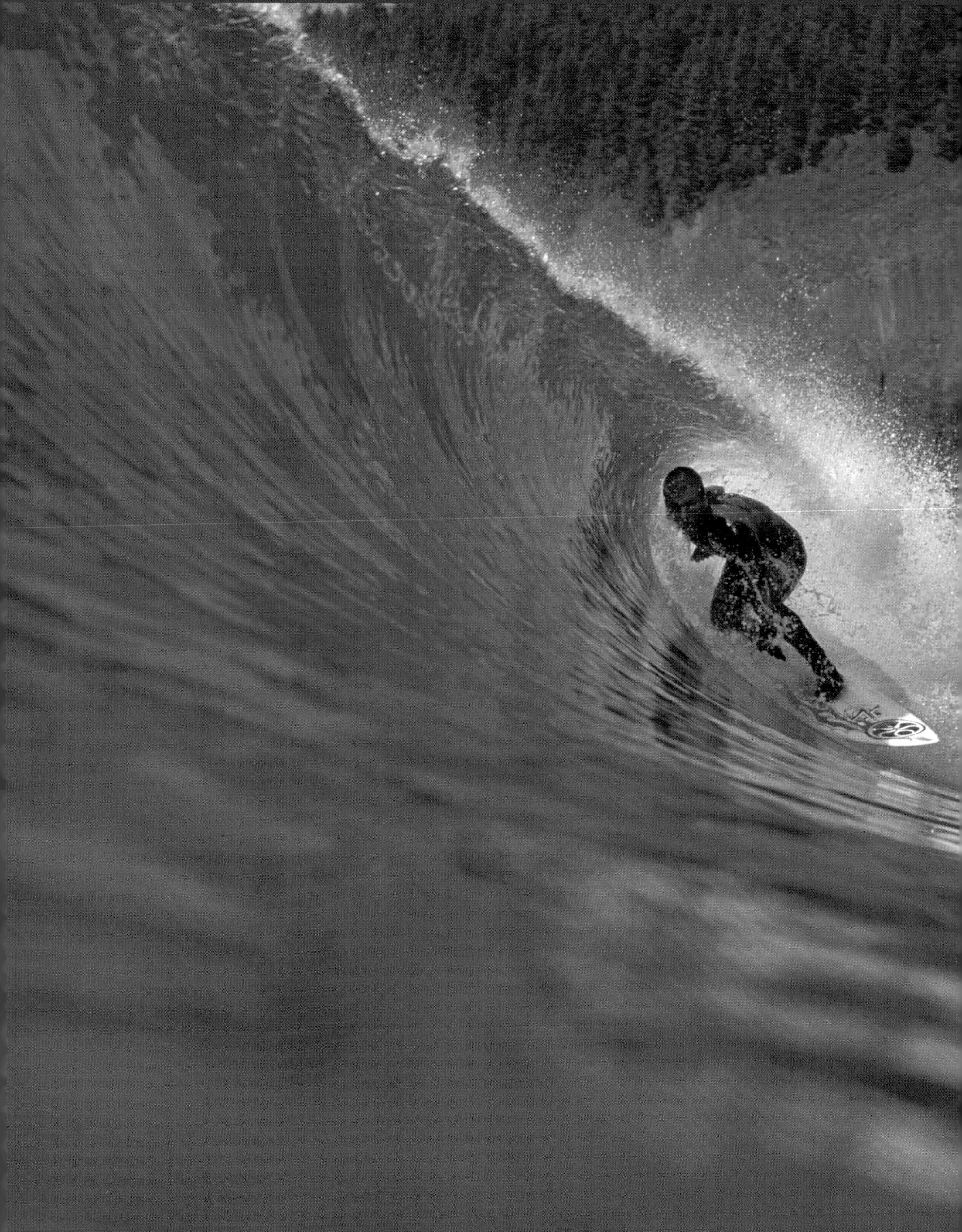

Washington and Oregon

In the early days of surfing, Santa Cruz and San Francisco were popularly considered the remote northern outposts of West Coast surfing. However, surfers have been riding waves north of San Francisco (and even north of the California-Oregon border) for many years. How many exactly is a subject of some debate. What is not subject to debate is the clear fact that there are, indeed, good, surfable waves in Washington and Oregon, an area of the United States commonly known as the Pacific Northwest...but to locals more often experienced as the Pacific Northwet.

This northern coast is, indeed, the wild edge of the continent. Unbuffered by offshore islands or the broad, shallow continental shelf found on the US East Coast, swells arrive near shore with most of their raw energy intact. Further, the virtually north-south orientation of the coast from Washington's Cape Flattery to Northern California's Cape Mendocino ensures maximum exposure to NW and W swells and to both frontal and thermally-generated winds.

In a word, this is a rugged and ruthless coast, virtually bereft of the more sensually forgiving aspects of the south. There are pockets of perfection, to be sure, but the rule of thumb is, the more north you go, the rougher it gets. Expect frigid water, lots of rain (except August, and maybe even then), harsh terrain, and long drives between spots. But when you score, you can score high. There are some great spots, many of the local surf tribes have a wonderful camaraderie, and there's always a sense of anticipation and adventure in the air.

Oregon tree-lined point.

BOB BARBOUR

WEATHER AND WATER STATISTICS

	J/F	M/A	M/J	J/A	S/O	N/D
Seattle, WA						
rainfall (inch/mm)	4.2//106	2.7/68	1.6/41	0.7/18	2.3/58	5.2/132
consistency (d/mth)	17	14	10	5	10	18
average sun (hrs/day)	3	6	8	9	6	3
min temp (°F/°C)	36/2	41/5	50/10	55/13	50/10	39/4
max temp (°F/°C)	47/8	54/12	68/20	72/22	62/17	48/9
water temp (°F/°C)	45/7	48/9	52/11	53/12	52/11	48/9
wetsuit						
Seaside, OR						
rainfall (inch/mm)	5.5/140	3.7/94	1.8/46	0.5/13	2.5/63	6.6/168
consistency (d/mth)	18	15	11	3	10	18
average sun (hrs/day)	3	5	7	9	6	3
min temp (°F/°C)	34/1	41/5	50/10	56/13	48/9	39/4
max temp (°F/°C)	47/8	58/14	68/20	77/25	66/19	50/10
water temp (°F/°C)	49/9	50/10	53/12	55/13	54/12	52/11
wetsuit						
Brookings, OR						
rainfall (inch/mm)	5.4/137	4/103	1/26	0.3/7	2/52	6.2/158
consistency (d/mth)	13	12	5	2	6	15
average sun (hrs/day)	5	7	9	10	7	4
min temp (°F/°C)	42/5	44/6	49/9	53/12	50/10	43/6
max temp (°F/°C)	55/12	56/13	59/15	63/17	62/16	56/13
water temp (°F/°C)	51/10	52/11	54/12	58/14	56/13	52/11
wetsuit						

TRAVEL INFORMATION

Washington	www.tourism.wa.gov
Oregon	www.traveloregon.com

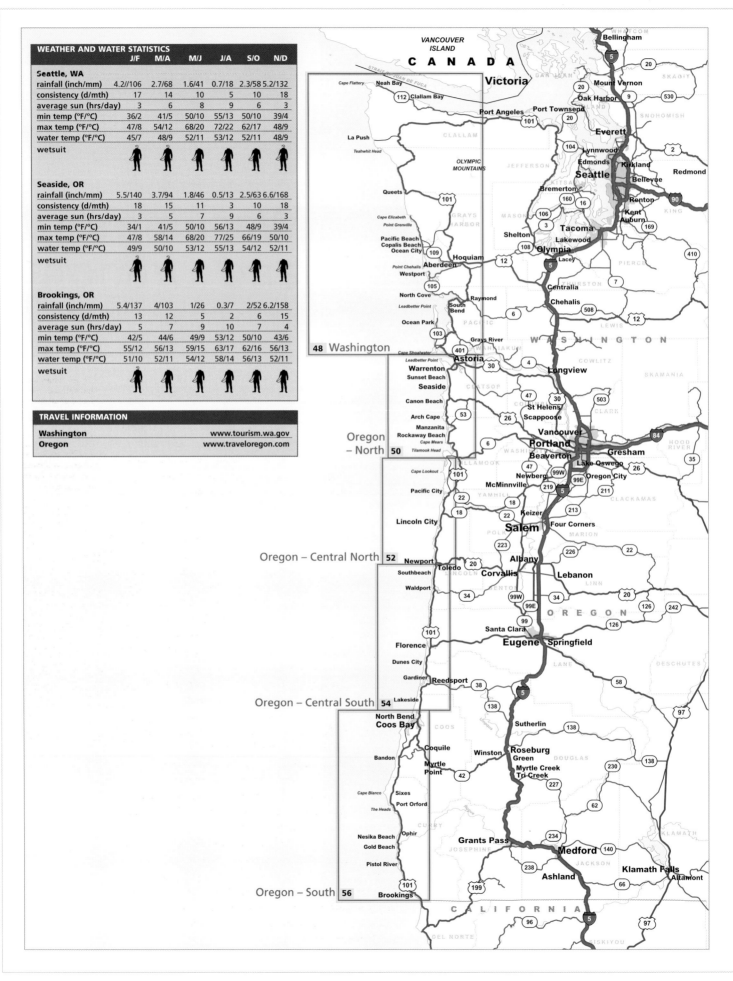

GEOFF RAGATZ

The Surf, Ocean Environment and Surf Culture

Nested in the southern lee of Vancouver Island in the northwest corner of the Lower 48 states, Washington State appears strategically located to intercept the bountiful North Pacific storm pulses and transform them into great surf. The 200-odd-mile (320km) west-facing coast angles nicely away from the witches' cauldron of great Northern Hemi storms, the Gulf of Alaska, evoking expectations of countless righthand point waves and huge, gnarly outer reef spots. Unfortunately, nothing could be further from the truth.

While the Washington coast is indeed bombarded by an extravagance of winter swell, this rainy, bleak, and economically-challenged shoreline offers just about the toughest and least rewarding wave grounds on the entire continent. A chill stretch of coast, ravaged over the years by clear-cut logging and commercial fishing, the shoreline ranges from the inhospitably rocky tip of Cape Flattery in the far north down to a giant expanse of a generally broad and featureless sand beach in the south.

Fringed with sentinel sea stacks and broken by the occasional timber-strewn rivermouth, the northern Washington coast is predominately a fantastic desolation of National Seashore, tribal reservations (Makah, Elwha, Quileute, and Quinault) and the Olympic National Park. The state's southern coast is composed largely of sandbar peninsulas enclosing two large bodies of saltwater (Grays Harbor and Willapa Bay) terminating at the mouth of the mighty Columbia River separating Washington from Oregon.

As a result of rapacious forest practices, the region's rivers are silted and choked with slash, and the formerly prodigious salmon runs have been depleted, putting some species on the endangered list.

While some Washington surfers live on the coast, the great majority are commuters from nearby towns or as far away as Puget Sound, Seattle, Bellevue, and the inland empire east of the Cascade range. Choices being few, they all tend to gather and get to know each other at a handful of decent surf spots.

Oregon is a state of mind. A cold, wild coast that can regularly chalk up numbers like 24-foot swells at 8-second intervals with 100mph wind gusts and a sea temperature of 46°F (8°C), Oregon is neither for the faint of heart nor the physically frail. Pronounced 'organ' by true locals, this 360-mile-long (576km) stretch of uniquely pristine Pacific shoreline enjoys more regulatory and environmental oversight than any other US state. The coast is defined by a series of prominent headlands, punctuated with a large number of rivermouths shedding the abundant waterfall from the coastal mountain ranges and transporting huge volumes of sand, which has accumulated into vast coastal dunes, mighty spits, and expansive beaches. This alternation of ragged rock and the finest sand – the hard and soft – defines the splendid Oregon shore.

Surfwise, Oregon's got it all. If the state was relocated to a warmer part of the world, it would rival Southern California in its variety of beaches and surf. Alas (and thankfully), it's no California; although its waves and beaches are the most accessible of any state in the country, the fact is, it's Oregon. The water's cold, there are lots of snappy white sharks, the wind and rain are intense (especially during surf seasons), and swells are often generated by storms so near to shore that it's hard to make it out through the short-period waves. Still, on a good day, surfing in Oregon can be as fun and rewarding as surfing anywhere in the world.

The Oregon surf culture is dispersed into tight regional pockets that reflect the topography of the coastal zone, from the surf-rich north to the remote, low-key south. While each beach town has its local population, a series of east-west roadways over the coastal mountains drains inland enthusiasts to the coast whenever the buoy reports herald the arrival of a new pulse.

Above – **Long walk-ins, full wetsuits and a peak to yourself – the reward of Pacific NW exploration.** Below – **There's a lot of wild, untouched coast in the Pacific NW, but also a lot of clear-cuts.**

CHRISTOPHER SPEAKMAN

Washington

Access to much of Washington's coast is attained by side roads, primitive lanes, or trails. The situation is complicated by the state's relatively arcane property laws, which have privatized huge tracts of shoreline to as much as a quarter mile below the mean high tide line, and the

fact that the lion's share of tribal reservation land has been set aside in the more remote regions of the state, and that includes the rugged, storm-wracked coasts. The ocean is cold here, although the Japan (or Kuroshio) Current moderates conditions somewhat.

Too far north to feel much in the way of Southern Hemi energy in the summer months (when the action is mostly windswell or weak area lows), during a typical winter, relentless storms bombard the Washington coast with huge swells, torrential rains, and wave-mangling S winds. There aren't too many places to hide, which is why many a Washington surfer seeks solace in the Strait of Juan de Fuca, in the windshadow of the Olympics and shoreline bluffs. The problem here is access. While there are a few highly regarded surf spots, entry is through tribal or private lands, and past indiscretions have generally made surfers personae non gratae.

Out on the coast, there are really only a couple of accessible, sheltered winter spots, and one of them (Westport) is the closest thing in the state to Surf City. Here, in the shelter of the jetty at the entrance to Grays Harbor, it's possible to enjoy clean swells, manicured by S winds that can whip the place into offshore perfection due to the E-W angle of the beach in this rare surf sanctuary.

On the north side of the Grays Harbor inlet is Ocean Shores, a seaside town with even less to offer surfers than Westport. However, the jetty at the north entrance to Grays Harbor creates a rare S wind block while leaving

Above – **Quileute natives in canoe, La Push.**
Below – **Seastacks are commonplace off the northern Washington coast.**

the way open to W and N swells. North of Ocean Shores, it's over 20 miles (32km) of sand and beachbreak until you get to Washington's lost treasure, Point Grenville. An anomaly on an otherwise almost pointless coast, Grenville is a big headland that hooks out into the Pacific, sheltering a large scoop of bay under its southern flank. Located within the lands of Quinault Indian Nation, Grenville was once Washington's version of Malibu, back in the first boom era of the early 1960s. Not that Grenville shows any similarity to Malibu in wave quality – this is not a classic, peeling point wave. But the rocky promontory interrupts the relentless NW winds and creates an eddy of atmospheric tranquility on this heavily thrashed coast. Depending on tide, there might be a half dozen spots working over a 2-mile (3.2km) stretch of glorious natural terrain. But the free-and-easy access of those days was lost. "Kids painting graffiti, trash, parties...it all added up to the demise of a great family beach," says Tom LeCompte, a veteran of those years, now a teacher up in Ketchikan, Alaska.

From Westport, it's mostly beachbreak south almost to the Columbia River. Not a lot of character – big beaches and nondescript sandbars open to the alternating surges of N and S winds, with only the occasional glassy or E wind day to set up some surfable peaks.

US Highway 101, which loops around the entire Olympic Peninsula, runs along only a short stretch of the coast before cutting inland and crossing the Columbia (and the border) into Astoria. Out of the heart of this large 90mi by 90mi (144km by 144km) peninsula erupt the majestic and aptly named Olympic Mountains. Once girded in dense rainforest, the slopes of these many peaks are now an ugly patchwork of the worst kind of environmental 'stewardship,' much of it ironically known as 'National Forest' land. It's quite clear from a good look around the Olympic Peninsula (and the Pacific Northwest in general) that the US Department of the Interior considers its forests little more than timber mines or cropland for wood pulp.

In many ways, Washington is a scarred and awful place, scarcely the pristine natural wonder portrayed on postcards and in guidebooks. Still, most of the beaches are remote enough and superficially appear untouched by man.

The Surfrider Foundation's presence in Washington State has been growing rapidly in the past five years. Surfrider's first annual Winter Clean Water Classic surf contest was held in Westport in February 2002. The event pulls the tribe together in midwinter for a rousing good time in the state's surf capital. A Surfrider membership comes with the entry fee.

Since most ocean beaches are relatively remote from large concentrations of human population, water quality is not generally a huge issue. However, according to Surfrider, Washington State fails to conduct regular monitoring, with the exception of one local agency. Much of the state's Pacific shoreline is Marine Sanctuary, National Wildlife Refuge, or National Park, so reasonable protections are, for the most part, in place. The moratorium on drilling in the Outer Continental Shelf (OCS), in place since the first Bush administration, was extended in 1998 by President Clinton (until June 2012). It affects the coastal waters off Washington, Oregon, and California.

In the spring of 2002, the Bush administration weakened endangered-species protection for salmon and steelhead throughout the West, while underfunding Clean Water Act projects (proposing only $1.21 billion of the $20 billion needed for improving sewage treatment systems and reducing polluted runoff).

Especially important to surfers is the ongoing struggle over the armoring of the shoreline at Westport and Ocean Shores. Local Surfrider members have made diligent efforts to work with the Army Corps of Engineers to reverse damage done by earlier ACE projects in the area. A dialogue has commenced, and Surfrider has brought valuable input (science and usage) to the discussion, and the courts have already ruled in SF's favor, ordering mitigation of negative armoring impacts and restoration of the surf break at Westport's cove. However, there are differences of opinion on how this can be accomplished.

In general, the state's coastal management practices are behind the times in dealing with erosion problems; it's mostly reactionary measures rather than long-term planning. Bottom line: we're heading towards sand starvation of the beaches in SW Washington.

"The day after Ernest Hemingway committed suicide, there was a cold NW wind hitting the coast at La Push on an Indian reservation up near the border of Canada. However, the surf looked beautiful at about 5-6ft, as a strong side wind feathered the tops of these waves – quite beautiful, but bone-bruising cold. No wetsuit! I was able to stay out close to an hour. Some Indians sat on the beach, and they invited me to their beach fire, which probably saved my life. They also passed around a bottle of red wine, and I thanked them profusely."

A lot has changed in the 40-some years since Hemingway shot himself one Sunday morning in July of 1961. As Fred Van Dyke sat among the Quillayute (or Quileute, as tribal members spell it), he may not have seen another surfer, but, in fact, the pioneer big-wave surfer of California and Hawaii wasn't the first to surf the Washington coast.

With few spots to choose from, Washington surfers are a relatively close-knit tribe, and their tribal history is a closely-held body of knowledge. Its obscurity reflects the general isolation and secrecy of surfing in the far US Northwest. Ray Walters is the generally acknowledged 'father of Washington surfing.' An engineer for Boeing

(the state's largest employer) in the '50s and '60s, Walters built up his cold water tolerance as a marathon swimmer in Puget Sound. Walters was a pal of Dick Wald, who surfed big Seaside in the early '60s on some bizarre longboard shapes.

The gathering place in the 1960s was Point Grenville, where surfing started in Washington State. "The magic of Grenville was in being there," says a veteran of the early days. "It was more a 'happening' than it was ever a good surf spot." He describes the "powerful Native American spirit" of the place and rues the day the Quinault Tribe

Rare beachbreak beauty on the Olympic Peninsula.

DON BALCH

closed it to surfing in the spring of 1966 for a short while. George South, a protégé of Ray Walters from Seattle, was especially distraught at the loss of the spot and lobbied strongly for the surfers. Largely through his efforts, the spot was reopened and Washington's first surf contest was held there on the 4th of July in 1968.

The core Washington regulars of that era included Hank Simmons, Tom LeCompte (who started surfing at the Westport jetty in '66), Mike Friegang, Tom Burns, Darryl Wood (the man at La Push), Lee Evans, Brian Jett, Kent Wienker, Steve Lewis, Dan Norton, and the late Greg Wheaton (a terrific surfer who pioneered Alaska surfing in the late '70s and '80s). Arriving on the scene in '66, Peter de Turk (like several of these guys) was from Southern Cal, a surfer who joined the Naval Air Corps, got posted on Whidbey Island, was a great competitor (the first Oregon champ), and an even better explorer. Times were different, de Turk recalls: "As a California surfer with seven years in the water, I was embraced by the fold, given high status and total access to their world."

South lived in a beach shack, had a milk truck, rented boards, and gave lessons (to tribal kids too) until he headed off to Vietnam in the fall of '69. Unfortunately, no one else really took care of the place. Lack of sanitation and refuse management hurt the surfers. Painting "Renton High Class of 67" on sacred rocks didn't help, nor did the tribe appreciate the surfers driving on the clam beds, living on the beach in driftwood huts, and smoking weed. There was drunken debauchery, out-of-control campfires, and when psychedelics hit, the tribe closed it for good – on Labor Day 1969.

"We were all sent packing," recalls Kent Brummitt. "The Washington diaspora began. That's when we started really exploring. We went north and south. I went to Westport with some of my mates. Ray Walters (now deceased) was our leader, mentor, and guide during those years."

Prominent surfers of the 1970s included hot California transplants Mark and P.J. Wahl, Randy Harrison, Kenny 'Cheetah' Sunde, Lonnie Smart, John Messmer from Aberdeen, and Abner Agee (the state's informal goodwill surfing ambassador). Then Tom Decker and Bruce Prater came storming onto the scene. Mike Galbraith was the first real shaper in the state; now a famous Seattle architect, he did some innovative stuff back in the '70s. P.J. shaped too, but the state's first real surf shop didn't open until Big Al Perlee opened The Surf Shop in Westport in 1985. A couple of years later, Ricky Young Surfboards opened in posh Bellevue (since sold and renamed Off The Beach), over a hundred miles from the beach. Since then more and more surfers and shops have appeared, including Rob Brown's Boarding Factory and Jetty Java. Ricky Young's contests at Westport have been the events of the summer in recent years; he's gifted a lot of boards and gear to the Quinault kids. A spokesman for the Quinault recreation department said the tribe is considering allowing a semi-annual surf contest at Grenville over the Labor Day weekend in early September.

Today, Westport is Washington's Surf City. It's where you'll find most of the surf shops, most (or all) of the contests, and most of the state's big surf-related environmental meetings taking place. As far as the fluky, finicky, frustratingly fickle remainder of the state, there's still magic to be found for the intrepid explorer – mysto reefs and creek mouths that almost never get seen, let alone seen breaking. You have to be there. Chances are slim, but as surfer and fisheries biologist Tom Burns says, "Seek and you shall find."

The Surf Shop in Westport – the capital of the Washington surf scene.

BOB BARBOUR

Oregon

Near the mouth of the Columbia River, Highway 101 connects the historic town of Astoria with the broad, sandy beaches of northern Oregon. Nondescript and windblown, the only place you're likely to find another surfer up here is during the summertime in the southern lee of rivermouth's south jetty. However, 15 miles (24km) down south is the bustling tourist burg of Seaside, tucked into the northern hook of Tillamook Head. The lefts that wrap around the north side of that promontory on a W or SW swell can be some of the best on the West Coast. From here to the California border, Highway 101 stays close to the coast, alternately maintaining a polite distance to avoid the shifting sands of the broad dunes then swinging close in to the undulating curves of projecting headlands (or sometimes sweeping discretely behind them). The scale of the place is immense, and the number of surfable peaks (the lion's share of it beachbreak) uncountable. But, as is the reality on this planet, the truly good spots are few and far between.

The northern coast of the state is punctuated with large headlands, beginning with Tillamook and then Capes Falcon, Meares, Kiwanda and Lookout, then Neskowin and Cascade Head. Things smooth out a little after that, through the surf hub of Lincoln City, with its surrounding reefs and beachbreaks down through some lovely coastal geography past Boiler Bay, Otter Rock and the big beach at Agate at Yaquina Head (both great learning spots), then slim-pickin's through the central coast from Waldport to the great dunes from Florence to Reedsport and on down to Coos Bay (the North Pole of the southern Oregon surf scene) and the big headland at Cape Arago. South of there – from Bandon out to Cape Blanco and Port Orford on down to Gold Beach is a little more varied and esoteric. From Gold Beach past Cape Sebastian to Brookings (the South Pole) and the border is hit or miss, but you can get lucky.

Conditions vary widely along this long and winding road, but for every rare, crowded spot you come upon, there are miles and miles and more miles of deserted surf – usually funky, but not always. Many swells that will hit California from the NW come straight out of the W to ramp up off Oregon's beaches, which means excellent swell exposure even at spots that are shielded from N or S winds. Like Washington State, a fair number of Oregon's most reliable waves are the result of man-made structures, mostly the series of rivermouth jetties that begins at the Columbia and ends with the Chetco in Brookings. With most of these situations you can expect wind protection during favored storm cycles. For instance, on winter NW swells accompanied (usually) by S winds, the north side of a jetty will be optimum; on summer S or SW swells accompanied by prevailing NW winds, the south side of a jetty will be the spot. The numerous headlands along this coast comport themselves in a similar fashion.

The nutrient-rich waters off the Oregon coast play host to the full food chain, and any Oregon surf shop worth its salt displays a local board that has been allegedly chomped

Left – **Oregon barrel.**
Below – **Jetties
provide shelter from
the wind, paddle-
out channels and
organized sandbars.
Unforunately, they
are also a hang-out
for sharks.**

by a great white shark. In fact, only 16 unprovoked shark attacks have been recorded in Oregon since 1620, so it's not all that big a deal. However, compared to Florida and California, there are few surfers here, so when there is an attack, it seems a bit closer to home. At least two surfers have been the subject of shark attacks in the last 25 years, but nobody's been seriously tormented. In August of 1976, a white attacked a guy who was surfing the South Jetty at Winchester Bay (Umpqua Rivermouth), then in September of 1994, another surfer was attacked at Short Sand Beach in Oswald West State Park, near Seaside. Both attacks occurred in small, clean swell conditions and involved big fish – 12-15ft (4-5m) – but neither was a proper attack on a surfer, since both bites were inflicted on their boards. Perhaps word will get around among these predators that foam and fiberglass make a nasty nibble.

On the surface of things, Oregon has a relatively aggressive and progressive coastal environmental bureaucracy. On the other hand, the state's shoreline communities are relatively small and seasonally-challenged, and (despite its relatively remote, rural character) Oregon has earned Surfrider's 'Beach Bum' designation. In its *Testing the Waters 2000: A Guide to Water Quality at Vacation Beaches*, the Natural Resources Defense Council cited inadequate coastal-water monitoring programs in four states, noting: "Two states, Louisiana and Oregon, still lack any regular monitoring of beachwater for swimmer safety."

Fortunately, the situation is changing. According to Oregon surfer Paul Klarin, who directs the Oregon Ocean Coastal Management Program (OCMP), the state is now receiving funds from the EPA to initiate an ocean recreation water-quality testing program. "Our Dept. of Environmental Quality has been working with the state Surfrider chapter, taking their samples to the lab for

analysis," he says. "The bum rap is off." Klarin received a special grant from NOAA a few years back to do a statewide coastal access inventory under the aegis of the OOCMP. The project includes an extremely detailed GIS inventory of over 1,200 access sites, complete with a broad database of exact locations, geology, landscape, facilities, aesthetics, ownership, digital photos, and maybe some videography. All available via a handsome website set up through Ecotrust.

His group is also attempting to locate, map, characterize, and photograph every ocean shore protective structure for a GIS project. "We are doing the same with all the outfalls on the beach," he adds, all of which will be combined into an *Oregon Coastal Atlas*, "a cutting-edge web-based interactive mapping and data download site, which will include sections on sandy shores, rocky shores, estuaries, and the ocean." This online *Oregon Coastal Atlas* is scheduled to launch in 2004. "We partnered with OSU and Ecotrust to build it and got an National Science Foundation grant to make it happen, along with a special grant from NOAA," concludes Klarin. You can view the early stages of this work at: www.inforain.org/interactivemapping/coastalaccess.htm

And then there's CoastWatch, the 6-year-old brainchild of the Oregon Shores Conservation Coalition, which has 1,000 individual volunteers watching over Oregon's 362-mile (579km) coastline. Based on the idea that a dedicated volunteer can get to know a one-mile stretch of shore very well, this army of 'CoastWatchers' provides collective vigilance and constructive action along the entire coast. Coordinated by Phillip Johnson (who founded the program as an OSCC board member), volunteers make a minimum commitment of four visits per year (once per season) to 'their' mile. The aim is to have volunteers track land-use changes and erosion-control efforts, test for water-quality, measure beach growth or loss, survey bird and animal populations, and watch for such abuses as dumping, illegal harvesting, and wetland filling. Volunteers also 'advocate'

Uncrowded, large waves are easy to find, but glassy conditions are not.

for their mile, educate others about its value, and gather information that becomes part of the state's monitoring overview. At this time, CoastWatch is working with the Oregon chapter of Surfrider to create the state's new joint water-quality testing program.

Although there is some speculation that Duke Kahanamoku, Tom Blake, and other early 20th century watermen may have surfed some of Oregon's vast wave grounds long ago, the verifiable history of surfing in the state begins much more recently. In fact, the lion's share of this coast was pioneered by refugees from California, fleeing the Gidget-fueled surf boom of the early 1960s. The best known and most revered of them is a well-traveled San Diegan by the name of Dana Williams. A surfer throughout his youth, Williams joined the Navy in 1958, went to Guam, where he enjoyed excellent warm water reef barrels, then wound up in godforsaken Astoria, assigned to a crew decommissioning old ships on the Columbia River. It was 1962, and he couldn't find another soul surfing in Oregon, and then he discovered Seaside. A member of the Windansea Surf Club and best friends with Butch Van Artsdalen, it was Williams who got the local

kids into the waves. "The water was so cold...and no rubber suit," recalls Williams. "Guys learned in the first couple of days, to get away from the water!"

Williams was the first surfer to move into Seaside, where he promptly became the subject of considerable local suspicion. "Because of me, Seaside banned surfing and skateboarding," he laughs. "So I put on a tie and got the Cove and Point opened up." But that was it – the sandy beach remained off-limits. As a lifeguard he surfed those same sandy beaches despite the ban and wound up in the clink. The mayor once referred to him as "Communist California riff-raff." To this day, Seaside holds the dubious honor of having the only no-surfing stretch of beach in Oregon (from Avenue U north to the city limits).

Dick Wald, a Portland diver and waterman, started surfing with a bunch of friends in the summer of '63 and met Williams at Indian Beach in August, where he was teaching a pack of kids the fundamentals. Williams invited Wald up to Seaside, where they surfed Avenue U that October. It wasn't till the two were caught in a rip and carried south that they discovered the peaks and channel of the Cove, and it was from the line-up on a big day at the Cove that the two surfers really got a good look at the waves at the Point. The two started working on going left, and one day soon paddled out to ride this mysto lefthander, which Williams had described as "just like the Pipeline" – except it broke directly onto Volkswagen-sized boulders. But Wald, totally at home in the ocean, loved it and was soon famed for riding HUGE Seaside Point on a Jim Sagawa pintail.

Early Oregon locals included Dan and Dave Matthews of Portland, the Scribers (Marty, Steve, and Jackie), who started in the early '60s down in at Newport, and Jack Brown in Cannon Beach. Bobby Jensen was shaping boards in Astoria as early as 1964-5; Jim Sagawa made boards in Portland during the same period. Peter de Turk started coming down from Whidbey in '66 and used to seek out Bill Fackerell as good big-wave company when the Point was macking. "Pre-leash Seaside was a serious commitment," says de Turk, who spent all of October there in the late '60s and early '70s.

SoCal competitive machine Corky Carroll surfed Seaside alone in 1964, then returned yearly thereafter, winning the Oregon State Championship at Agate Beach in 1967. "I used to stay in the Lanai Motel right there on the point in Seaside," he recalls. "I remember when a bunch of longhairs from Santa Cruz showed up and started making boards in an old garage at the turnoff to Cannon Beach. Art Spence was one of the dudes."

Art Spence was the Santa Cruz kid, who got everyone on ultralight shortboards in the late '60s; he lived at Seaside Point and taught Bill Barnfield how to shape. Along with

Dan Matthews and Jerry Herrington, Spence started Tillamook Head Surfboards; their scene attracted a group of core guys (including Kent Weinker), who surfed the Head spots for Spence's movie camera. His *Free Ride* (predating Bill Delaney's famous flick of the same name by almost eight years) is a classic visual saga of the late '60s surfing and skating lifestyle in the Tillamook Head subculture. By 1972, Spence had started up Evergreen Surfboards, and the core group included the Holbrooks from Newport, Dave Copra, Tim Spence, Perry Shoemake, Bruce Prader, Josh Gazdavich (founder of Cleanline Surf Shop), de Turk, and 20 more guys who shared the log fires in the cold and wet after feasting on lonely outpost lefts that could make you or break you. De Turk: "Jack Mullins went from kook to big tube-rider in a matter of two years."

PATRICK TREFZ

Meanwhile, John Kelsey was making boards in the Newport/Agate Beach area, where Sagawa's Sag Surfboards were also popular. Scott Blackman was there, along with intrepid explorers, like Neahahkanie/Insanities pioneer Mad John Fink. Down in Coos Bay, near Cape Arago, another community jelled. The pioneers there were Dave Sheldon, Dan Matthews, Ron Coleman (The Reverend: "Thou shalt not drop in"), Dave Bond (Bastendorff regular), Al Kreiger (president of the Kahuna Surf Club in the mid-'60s), Pete Cochran (made boards, now in Seaside), Arden Keylock, Ellis and Willie Lark, Don 'Ducko' Garrett (a Coquille native and the best guy in the area) and Bert Moffitt.

It was Moffitt who let the genie out of the bottle with his article in the Aug/Sep issue of *Surfer* ("Oregon: As We Like It"). Sniffing something interesting, California waterman Mike Doyle moved up to Port Orford in 1973; he was soon joined by Walt Phillips, who lived up the road a piece, and the two surfed the Creek and entertained curious visitors, like Joey Cabell, who "came up to see what the hell we were up to," says Doyle. "There were no surfers in the south except a few around Coos Bay; the fisherman on the Port Orford pier used you ask me if I was going out on my shingle today." Doyle remains impressed with several life-and-death midwinter sessions on the north side of Cape Blanco, one of the gnarliest venues for marine disaster ever concocted by the Author of all our joys and sorrows – "Thirty feet easy," he marvels.

Today, the Oregon coast remains a harsh place to live, and the decreasing coastal population proves it. But the surf scene thrives in an Oregon sort of way. There are spots of intense localism and areas of extreme mellowness and Aloha of the kind promulgated by Paul George, owner of Rocky Point Surf & Sport in Coos Bay. George spent most of his youth in Hawaii and ran with the likes of Larry Bertlemann, then bailed and came to Oregon, he says, to save his life. Involved in prison ministry and fully involved with his family and the local youth, he is profoundly upset by the hostile localism perpetrated by a few (generally older) surfers. "A strong etiquette is necessary here," he says. "Surfers have to keep the spirit of aloha alive."

Reflecting the Northwest's 'seek and ye shall find' ethic, Salem-based Paul Klarin hints that sometimes you find surf in all the wrong places: "There are a series of mystery waves that form on the inside of most every major bay spit and river jetty during really big swells of 20ft-plus (6m). They usually grind away in the friendly confines of the mixing zone of the estuary at up to shoulder size after the wave propagates up the channel and sometimes around the bend. Don't be surprised if on a really big day you look down as you are driving over the Yaquina bridge in Newport and see some longboarder gliding over the sandy bar at the elbow of the channel."

Meanwhile, Dana Williams continues to articulate the other Pacific Northwest surf ethic: "We shall suffer!"

BOB LEDBETTER

Above – **Mist and sea fog is always a possibility along Oregon's picturesque coast.** Below – **The godfather of Oregon surfing – Dana Williams.**

WASHINGTON

OREGON

Washington

1. The Strait

Fluky and finicky, but when juicy W and NW swells pump out of the North Pacific, Washington surfers looking for quality waves head for the Strait of Juan de Fuca, where it's all lefthanders (okay, there are a few mysto right shoulders) from Neah Bay to Port Angeles and occasionally even further up the strait. If the swell is strong enough and the tides incoming, there can be waves as far east as Whidbey Island, 100 miles (160km) from Cape Flattery and the Pacific. Winter S winds are offshore or side-off at most spots on the Washington side of the strait. Outgoing tide kills all but the biggest swells. If you're a regular foot, take the ferry over to Vancouver Island, where it's all rights inside the strait. Different spots work on different tides, but it's mostly mid tides incoming.

The Strait

The Strait

The main issue in the strait is access. Just about all of the good spots are on either tribal (check in at tribal offices any time you're entering Sovereign Lands) or private land. Inconsiderate behavior has cost the open access of earlier days, and surfing the strait now requires subterfuge, guerilla tactics, and lots of respect. Regrettably, most of the hostile locals are non-native surfers.

2. Hobuck/North Coast

Average beachbreak abounds on the northern Washington Coast, but conditions are unpredictable, and you've gotta hike to get there. Hobuck Beach offers minimal access to inferior beachbreak on Makah reservation land. Follow the trail a couple of miles south past Portage Head for better quality, but nothing world-class.

Cold water, strong currents, sharks, and a long way from help if you need it.

3. La Push

The most popular spot is First Beach, a small, relatively sheltered cove at the end of La Push Road. (Route 110) about 15 miles (24km) from Highway 101. Sand and gravel at the mouth of the Quillayute River (La Push comes from la bouche or 'the mouth') creates several distinct, fat peaks on the outside with reform sections working into the beachbreak. Mid tides, all swells from S to NW. James Island frames the north side, blocking NW swells - try the beachbreak on the north side of the rivermouth for some clean winter barrels.

Summer is best here, but if it's not an El Niño year, it's still plenty cold. This is Quileute [sic.] tribal land, so check in at the La Push Ocean Park Resort for a parking permit. Camp for $15; refurbished cabins $78-180. Big kayak event here in January, called Maytag Surf for obvious reasons. Chronic auto break-ins have subsided in recent years.

4. Point Grenville

A rocky headland creates a sheltered stretch of coast with a variety of reef and beachbreak surf. The state's most popular surfing area back in the early 1960s, mindless acts of vandalism and imperial attitudes soon alienated the Quinault people. Several decent surf spots offer excellent learning conditions at a safe, family-style beach. Good contest venue.

Although you should check in at the tribal office (off Highway 109) for beach access, your permit will say NO SURFING on it. Over the past decade, the Quinault Nation has periodically allowed surfers access to Grenville to stage a summer contest or two. However, recent run-ins with trespassing surfers aggravated relations between the tribe and outsiders, and even this limited access was suspended. The tribal council is considering reviving a semiannual surf contest on Labor Day weekends.

5. Westport

Westport is just about the only reliable, publicly-accessible surf spot on Washington's Pacific shoreline – thanks to the Army Corps of Engineers. Two long rock jetties flank the entrance to Grays Harbor interrupting a long stretch of featureless coast. There are three major spots: **The Jetty** or **The Corner** is the south side of the south jetty, where W and SW swells converge over ample sandbars to create powerful, well-shaped beachbreak waves on N or E winds. When the wind blows out of the S, locals move inside the jetty to **The Cove**, where the wind will be offshore and the waves manicured into clean walls. Lacks shape in recent years, however, due to increased sand erosion. Better shape when the swell is W or on a strong SW can be found at **The Groins**, predominantly left beachbreak peaks, but some hollow rights too. Low to mid tides best. All areas get crowded. Smile and take your turn. Across the channel, there's good beachbreak on the leeward side of the north jetty on S winds.

Conditions at the Cove and Groins change dramatically with tide swings. Perfect waves can yield to raging rips or surfless bumps in the course of an hour. Beware of dangerous rips and currents. Strong timber-industry presence in the Grays Harbor area brings likelihood of pollution. To get to the Cove and the Jetty go to Westhaven State Park. Parking is no problem at either Westport or Ocean Shores, but getting there is, since there are no straight lines to these sandbar peninsulas.

6. Long Beach Peninsula

Miles and miles and miles of average beachbreak fully exposed to the slings and arrows of summertime NW and wintertime SW winds. Still, you can own your own peak!

Dunes and fine white sand beach and a few topographic surprises. Beware rips and currents in bigger surf conditions. Most of the Washington State shoreline is much like this.

La Push

STUMPPHOTO

Westport

BOB BARBOUR

Oregon – North

1. Seaside Cove

Where the crescent of beach fronting Oregon's ultimate beach town turns rocky and bends westward towards the long, bouldered point, Seaside Cove behaves pretty much like a northside jetty wave. There are lefts off the head side at fuller tides, closing out at tides below 2ft (0.6m) with a permanent rip along the Cape transporting surfers relatively dry-haired out into the line-up, with waves breaking over the rip on a 10ft-plus (3m) swell. Sandbar peaks to the north open up into nice rights and lefts, especially on a NW swell.

Hollow and hefty when conditions are right. Mushy, sectiony longboard waves at higher tides. Good beginner/intermediate surf spot. A much friendlier crowd than you'll find out at The Point, and less shark danger too. Although surfable peaks continue north of here, except for the rocky margins of the Cove and Point, Seaside beaches have been closed to surfing since pioneer waverider Dana Williams showed up here in the 1960s with long hair and a surfboard.

2. Seaside Point

When it's firing on a W or SW swell, this is the most well-known wave in the Pacific Northwest (it may actually be the finest lefthand pointbreak in North America). Swells wrap around the north end of Tillamook Head and peel off in perfect, hollow, lefthanded zippers that leave little margin for error. **Second Point** is the shorter, juicier indicator wave. Further inside and the main spot, **First Point** is long, lovely, and frequently glassy on the gnarliest of winter days since the head shelters the break from the predominantly southern winter storm winds. A classic barrel – think Indo or consistent El Capitan (reversed). Works on most any tide, although high tide can generate some backwash from the rocky shoreline. On a perfect SW swell, the take-off area can be as narrow as a Toyota truck bed. As the swell direction moves N, the peak section becomes broader. Although this may spread out the crowd, getting caught by a section here can and will pin you to the shoreline boulders unless you know the place intimately.

This is a challenging wave with a challenging crowd, and they won't want to see your face in the line-up. The Point's reputation as the heaviest local scene on the West Coast is well deserved. Enter the water after a 650 yard (600m) hike over big, slick boulders at the Point. Beware a fierce shorepound on all but the most southerly swells. Roadside parking at the end of Edgewood. The City has just constructed a cement bunker-style restroom and shower facility across the street from the parking lot, however, it's shut off in winter, when the surf's good. Expect flat tires and other damage to out-of-state vehicles. Oh yeah, the break is way out in the ocean, so there are sharks, too.

3. Indian Beach, Ecola State Park

Located on the south side of Tillamook Head, opposite Seaside Cove and Point, you might think the waves here would be a mirror of Seaside. No dice. A lovely rocky cove at the mouths of the Ecola and Canyon creeks – nice sand-and-gravel bar formations make for clean peaks with lefts and rights at mid to high tides (incoming best). Don't expect long rides except on the most epic days. Sheltered from the prevailing NW wind, this is a pleasant summertime spot.

Very popular with summer-only Portland surfers and their families. During the north wind or foggy days of summer, this place can be partly cloudy and glassy. A great place to paddle out and check the sea stacks to the south toward Cannon Beach. Pay $3 to get into the park for a surf check. If it's no good, you have 10 minutes or so to get your butt out and take your refund with you.

4. Cannon Beach/ Tolovana Beach

Portland's favorite vacation playground, Cannon Beach is an increasingly upscale tourist town offering only marginal beachbreak and breathtaking sunsets as backdrop to the overdeveloped shoreline. Can get good mornings and evenings or on small, glassy days.

Majestic sea stacks along this stretch of coast include Haystack Rock, at 235ft (76m) the third tallest monolith in the world. Recent shark attack here. Plenty of free parking everywhere. Lots of slow summer traffic on the main drag.

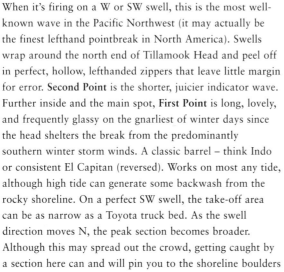

Seaside Point

Cannon Beach

MICHAEL KEW

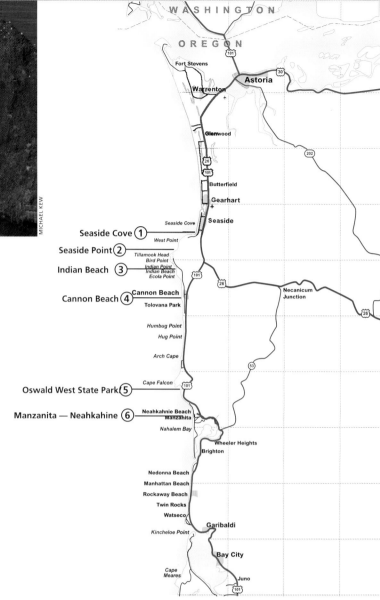

5. Oswald West State Park/ Short Sands/Smugglers Cove

Another beautiful cove fed by twin creeks (in this case Short Sand and Necarney). It's a half-mile walk down through old-growth forest to a beautiful white sand beach. More Oregon surfers probably have their first Oregon surfing experience here than anywhere else. The beautiful paved-trail hike through the forest, along the creeks will definitely give you the Pacific Northwest surf adventure feeling.

Protected from summer N and winter S winds by picturesque rocky headlands, the surf gets hollow and snappy on lower tides, when it usually closes out on any swell over 6ft (2m). More often it's mushy and forgivable, especially on a high. There are peelers off the north (juicier) and south headlands with a rip along the south end used on bigger days to get to the line-up. Sand bottomed peaks make this horseshoe cove a big hit with beginners. Free parking at Oswald State Park (use the second lot near the restrooms and interpretive kiosk). The trail down to the beach begins near the highway overpass. There's a campground just up from the beach. Proximity to Portland, wind protection, scenery, and campground facilities make this spot frequently crowded, especially on summer weekends. Even so, the vibe is generally good, and this is one of the few 'beach scenes' in Oregon. Caution: Thieves work the parking lot, especially summertime; take precautions.

6. Manzanita — Neahkahnie

Average beachbreak at Manzanita is made more attractive by easy access and a cute, upscale beach community. NW wind accelerates around the Cape Falcon-Neahkahnie Mountain headland making this spot one of Oregon's saltwater windsurfing Meccas. The reef just north of Neahkahnie Beach can fire on a clean N to W swell, producing a long grinding righthand point wave. Legends abound, information is scarce.

Large rocks in the impact zone along the cobble point make for limited surfing opportunities anywhere but the beach-headland corner on smaller swells. From the headland south (Rockaway Beach and beyond), miles of

Neahkahnie

DON BALCH

featureless beachbreak, driftwood, and grassy windblown white sand beaches and dunes. Surf potential on small, clean swells with E or no wind, but that's a rarity indeed. Park where any small lane meets the sand.

Oregon – Central North

1. Cape Lookout

Oregon has two 'legendary' spots. Seaside Point is the left, this is the right. A solid cobble and table rock reef near the protruding headland hosts a classic righthander when conditions are perfect. Best on a W swell. Outside kelp beds help smooth things out too. Just about the cleanest and clearest water in Oregon. Otherwise, most of the action is beachbreak, much like anywhere else in Oregon, but conveniently windshadowed by the longest cape on the coast. Sometimes a good left breaks into the channel between the beachbreak and the point. Blows out on S wind. The north side has nice beachbreak too, which is naturally sheltered from winter S winds.

Due to limited swell window, Lookout is unpredictable and rarely does the 3mi (5km) walk pay off. Still, it's beautiful. Surfing the south side may be Oregon's version of the Palos Verdes Cove experience. Some of the local crew are hostile and have been known to steal gear left at the bottom of the trail, slash tires, and intentionally drop in on new faces. Surfing here involves leaving your car in

the lot at the top and hoping it's got wheels when (and if) you make it back up the daunting switchback trail. Call the cops if you have serious hassles. Access the north side through Cape Lookout Campground at the bottom of the cape.

2. Cape Kiwanda – Pacific City

There's a good righthand reef peak on the south side of the cape that works when the sandbars are right on a big clean W or WNW swell. There's a clean beachbreak on the inside that's sheltered from N and NW winds. The number of peaks south of the cape varies – as the tidal change shuts down one peak, another one will usually start to work just next door. Directly in front of the parking lot at PC there's a very user-friendly stretch of beachbreak peaks, great for beginners, longboarders, the whole family. Best in spring and fall. Straight out is **Toilet Bowl**, to the south is a left called **Gas Chambers** – hollow at low tide, mush at high. There's also good beachbreak straight out from the bridge and further south in Robert W. Straub State Park. On S winds, try north of Cape Kiwanda towards Tierra Del Mar for often excellent and powerful beachbreak with some wind protection.

The main Pacific City beachbreak gets more crowded each year. It's a State Park and parking is limited, typically filling by 10am on spring weekends and earlier in peak summer season. The surf contest held here each August is known for being a real gathering of the Northwest tribe and a fun event. Celebrity guest stars of recent years have included John Peck and Gerry Lopez. Possible shark danger, and watch out for renegade jetskis and dory boats, which are both permitted to launch from the beach. Hard to tell how Pacific City got its name, since Bob Ledbetter's South County Surf shop is just about the biggest operation in town, and it's in his home (okay, there are some restaurants and a post office!).

3. Lincoln City

Three resident surf shops give this 6mi (10km) long shoreline town a certain surf consciousness that isn't generally known to be reflected in the local surf quality. Don't be so sure. While it's more or less standard beachbreak towards the north and south ends of town, the beach below the central bluff-lined shore is nicely marbled with reef formations, mostly covered with sandbars. On smaller summer and autumn swells with glassy or E wind conditions, you can find an uncrowded spot on this long stretch of beach if you take the trouble to walk in. About midtown, check out the '**D**' **River** State Wayside on a small, clean swell. The river flow moves the bars around frequently, so you never know. South of 'D' River is the area known as **Canyons**, named after the little county beach park, just over the hill from the factory outlet stores on Highway 101. The main break is left of the parking lot, about an 100-yard (90m) walk down the beach. Mostly good lefts but some rights. Like all Lincoln City spots,

Cape Lookout

BOB LEDBETTER

Cape Lookout

MICHAEL KEW

Parking Lot, Pacific City

hollower at low tide, mushier at high. There's a reef far outside that arches into a perfect A-frame on 15ft (4.5m) plus swells. Locals claim to have ridden the place. South of Canyons is **Nelscott**, a popular sand-covered reef often exposed in spring. Locals say it gets good about every other year for some reason. A 100yd (90m) walk north is **Shark Fin Rock** (it's the shape), which has been known to serve up a sandbar right. At the extreme north end of town at **Roads End** Beach State Roadside, an outside reef holds up to 12ft (3.6m) with good shape, and a series of beachbreak peaks offers a diverse selection of rides. At the turnaround in the park look for hard-breaking tubes with strong rips and sharks lurkin'. Blows out readily. South of Lincoln City, the top spots are the quality beachbreak at Gleneden (recent shark attack) and the challenging rock-reef right at Boiler Bay, just north of Depoe Bay. For advanced surfers only, Boiler will work on a 20ft (6m) swell if the wind is strong S and the swell SW to W. Best at about 10ft (3m), depending on wind. Super hollow at low to minus tide.

No public access in mid-town, otherwise easy parking at the most surfed spots in the Lincoln City area, which are either north or south of town.

4. Otter Rock

Somewhat sheltered from summer NW winds by Cape Foulweather, Otter Rock is popular with beginners and longboarders. Several mushy, soft-rolling beachbreak peaks are open to most swells but best on a small W. Occasional snap on the inside under exceptional conditions. Can get good on a small S summer swell. Experiences a lot of rips along the rocks in the winter and early spring, which can work like a ski lift. Sometimes gets a good peak towards the Cape serving up good lefts and rights.

Nice recreational beach, gets crowded with surfers, spongers, and all kinds of people. Located at Devil's Punch Bowl State Park. One veteran refers to the Otter Rock scene as the Old Man's/Waikiki of Oregon. Has a large parking lot that often fills, plus restrooms, nearby food, and a long stairway down to beach. More surfers probably learned to surf here than anywhere else in Oregon, though some folks down at Agate make the same claim.

Roads End, Lincoln City

Oregon – Central South

1. Newport

Average beachbreak from one end of this busy beach town to the other, but even so a pretty surf-stoked stretch of coast. North of town is **Agate Beach**, the area's most popular spot, a wide expanse of decent beachbreak protected from N wind by the massive promontory of Yaquina Head. Great longboard waves at Agate, which works at most tides, breaking close to shore on high tide, then getting hollower and more lined up as it goes lower and moves out. Good beginner spot when small, can hold a huge swell – easily double overhead. Close to the head, a rip provides genteel transport out to the line-up. However, after the El-Niño of 1998, the sandbar south of the head has lost its former glory and doesn't peel like it did before the storms rearranged the bar. **Avalanche**, an outside sandbar spot off Yaquina Head, works at 12ft (3.6m) plus and surfing it requires a dangerous jump off the Cape – a very treacherous entry not to be attempted without local guidance. This outside sandbar seems to have been less affected by the El Niño storms, and is still good on a big WNW or W swell. On the north side of Yaquina Head, **North Agate** can work on a high tide when the wind is S; flat reef completely exposed and dangerous on low. Further north is **Moolack**, a reef and sandbar set-up with wedgier, punchier peaks, popular with shortboarders. In the opposite direction, over the Yaquina River bridge

south of Newport, **South Beach** offers miles of typical beachbreak with predominant lefts, except at **The Box**, in the lee of the south jetty, where you can find nice, wedging righthanders on a S swell with full N wind protection. Excellent (and popular) summer spot.

Plenty of parking at the Agate Beach wayside. Parking on the dirt turnout overlooking the surf at Moolack. Asphalt parking lots, paths, trails, and signs galore at South Beach State Park, along with a large campground with tent, RV and YURT (Year-round Recreational Tent) facilities. Be careful: The Box can produce some dangerous currents (not to mention powerful pitching waves) when the swell exceeds 8ft (2.5m). Some shark danger. Surf shops to serve all your aquatic needs.

2. Yachats

Tiny town at the mouth of a river of the same name. Beach access through Yachats State Park for good mid tide rights and lefts at the north end reef. Nice looking peaks off the north side of the rivermouth too. To the south, Yachats has some general open beachbreak, subject to all wind and swell directions. If it's clean, you can definitely surf alone here all day.

Rivermouth area could be sharky. Area has potential – worth checking on glassy days or with an E wind.

3. Florence

Just south of the exquisite Heceta Head and lighthouse, Highway 101 sweeps inland to bypass some 50mi (80km) of coastal sand dunes, interrupted in only a few places by major rivermouths. The northernmost of these is the Siuslaw, and the nondescript town of Florence perches on its final bend before emptying into the Pacific between massive rock jetties. The **South Jetty** juts out and angles to the south, creating a sheltered nook to ride S and SW swell waves on small N-wind summer days. On big W swells at lower tides, there's a good left that peels between the jetties (breaking off the south jetty), which can be about a third the size of the outside swell.

On S wind days, head over to **The North Jetty** where there can be excellent beachbreak surf when the swell's small. In Florence, Jetty Road will lead you out to the north jetty. To get to the south jetty, cross the river to Glenada and turn into the Oregon Dunes National Recreation Area. Follow the narrow blacktop for about

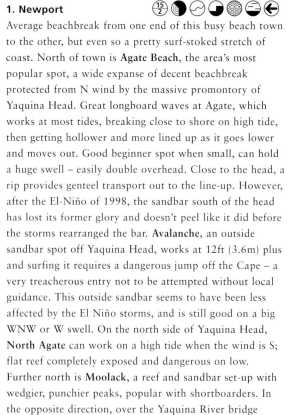

Florence, Outside South Jetty

Florence, Inside South Jetty

Umpqua Jetty

GEOFF RAGATZ

GEOFF RAGATZ

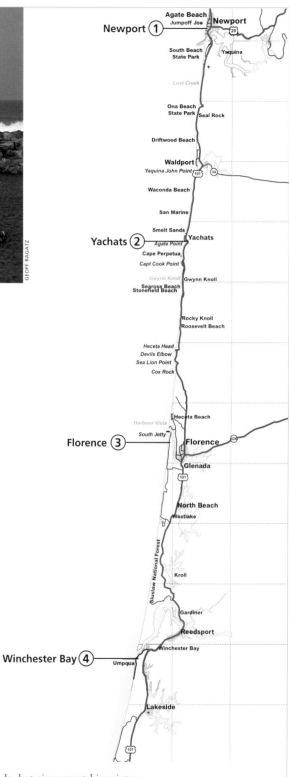

Agate Beach
Newport ① Jumpoff Joe Newport
20
South Beach
State Park Yaquina
Lost Creek
Ona Beach
State Park Seal Rock
Driftwood Beach
Waldport
Yaquina John Point 101 34
Waconda Beach
San Marine
Smelt Sands
Yachats ② Agate Point Yachats
Cape Perpetua
Capt Cook Point
Gwynn Knoll Gwynn Knoll
Searose Beach
Stonefield Beach
Rocky Knoll
Roosevelt Beach
Heceta Head
Devils Elbow
Sea Lion Point
Cox Rock
Heceta Beach
Harbour Vista
South Jetty
Florence ③ Florence 126
Glenada
101
North Beach
Westlake
Siuslaw National Forest
Kroll
Gardiner
Reedsport
Winchester Bay
Winchester Bay ④ Umpqua
Lakeside
101

5mi (8km). When it disintegrates into a moonscape of giant potholes, you're getting close. Walk out on the jetty and check both sides. Moderate shark worries. Die-hard locals confuse this place as a world-class spot and may be unfriendly. If you're surfing between the jetties, use caution. A lot of water drains through here, and an outgoing tide can transport you from the break out past the bar, no matter how fast you can paddle. Check the tide charts. The Coastguard charges a lot of dough to pluck you (and not your board) out of the water.

4. Winchester Bay/ South Umpqua Jetty

One of those man-made wonders, a delta of Army Corps rock projects about a 1000yds (910m) into the Pacific on the south side of the mighty Umpqua River entrance, creating another convenient wind block and a good place for sand to pile up and form bars. In this case a reliable, sometimes dredging, righthander that peels away from the jetty in often classic form. A rip usually sets up right along the jetty, providing a convenient conveyance back to the line-up. This is one of Oregon's good big-wave spots on a NW and W swell. Although the sandbars do shift, the place will handle a significantly larger swell than most (if not all) of the state's outside jetty breaks. However, the

spot is exposed to S winds; but since most big winter swells are accompanied by S winds, good conditions are rare. On most S to NW swells, a nice left peak sets up a 100yds (90m) to the south. If it's glassy, there's a near-infinite stretch of peaks to the south along the majestic dunes of the treeless Siuslaw National Forest. All tides.

Despite the fact that this spot is visible from Highway 101 (check it from the overlook at the top of the hill just south of Winchester Bay), and the beach is public, you might encounter the odd ugly local. Grin and bear it. Relatively major shark hazard here.

Oregon – South

1. Coos Bay-Bastendorff Beach

South of the dunes and moated by a complex system of bays and estuaries, the North Bend/Coos Bay area is the epicenter of surfing in south-central Oregon, thanks to a complex system of rocky headlands and coves leading out to Cape Arago. First stop on the Cape Arago Highway is the popular Bastendorff Beach, a wide, sandy cove flanked by Yoakam Head and the south jetty at the entrance to Coos Bay. Offshore on winter S winds, the various peaks are loosely divided into spots like **South End, Gray Houses, Middles, Crappers (a.k.a. Shitters), and North End**. All tides except extreme high and low. Rips at point or jetty ends, depending on swell direction. There are several regularly-surfed spots further out on the Cape, including **Simpson's Reef**, which one regular describes as "a hard-breaking, rocky-climb-down-the-bluff, time-your-entry, sucking wave right inside the largest concentrated sea-mammal haulout in the Pacific Northwest."

Bastendorff is one of the most polluted spots in the NW; some local regulars report skin problems. Paul George, who owns the Rocky Point Surf Shop in Coos has worked hard to cultivate aloha spirit among the surfers here, so bring a smile. Sharky area with strong rips when the swell is large.

BOB LEDBETTER

2. Port Orford

South of Coos Bay and Cape Arago, the shoreline topography changes – fewer areas of dune, less expansive sand beaches, shoreline bluffs – as the coast flares out to Cape Blanco, the westernmost point of Oregon. South of the Cape, the coast fades eastward to Nellies Point and the town of Port Orford, where the prevailing NW wind is offshore. Most of the significant winter swells capable of entering the Port Orford hook are accompanied by S or W winds. Big NW swells are significantly shadowed, but when tide, wind, and swell all work in coordination this place can work. Here, you'll find occasional S swell beachbreak at Battle Rock, and less than a mile south, the finicky sandbars at the mouth of Hubbard Creek can reel off good, hollow rights and lefts from several distinct peaks.

Beautiful scenic overlook on the south end of Port Orford overlooks Battle Rock and Humbug Mountain in the distance. Easy park beachside at Battle Rock. Roadside parking in the dirt across from Hubbard; trail to beach starts at opposite guardrail. Easy access, so it gets plenty crowded.

3. Frankport-Nesika Beach

About six miles (8.5km) south of Humbug Mountain on the windy, winding, always-sliding 101, watch for a large, partially excavated headland and pull off on the dirt road that leads to the north-facing cove called Frankport. Big W or SW swells wrap around the head, cranking off occasionally good lefts. In the middle of the cove, a decent peak (especially on a NW swell) forms off a small rock (exposed at lower tides), sending a reeling right into achannel near the rocky shore. Can get big. Left can be good too.

Good shelter here from S wind. A few miles further down the road, NesikaBeach offers up better than average beachbreak, notably at the south end of the beach. Blows out quickly with NW wind; best when glassy or light S. Park at the top and walk down to Frankport; there are craters on this so-called road that can swallow anything less than a Hummer whole. For Nesika, park near the rest area (renovated toilets), as the sandbars have been best in that area in recent years.

4. Gold Beach

Long stretch of exposed beachbreak, but the short south jetty of the Rogue River offers shelter from the N wind and some excellent sandbar rights and lefts. Heavy currents. Expect competition in the line-up from a gang of seals that ride the place regularly. A couple miles down the beach, check out the beachbreak at South Park or (further still) the reefs and sandbars around Hunter Creek, which can all work when a clean, long-period swell and offshores coincide. About 7mi (11km) down the coast, the south side of Cape Sebastian is worth a look for some howling offshore winds and occasional good surf at lower tides.

Watch out for interesting and sometimes classic left-breaking spot (called Little Joes or Between the Jetties) inside the jetties on strong W swells at lower tides. With the large seal and fish population here, sharks are definitely in the area (recent encounters). The area from Cape Sebastian to the Pistol River is one of the USA's great windsurfing Meccas.

5. Rainbow Rocks

Sand beach pockets amid nondescript jumble of rocks that some claim produce a shape-shifting rideable wave over near-shore reef on a W or NW swell. A nook of relatively unencumbered beach about 3mi (5km) north of Brookings, right across the cove (S) from the Rainbow Rocks condo complex. Can be decent on any small swell from SSW to NW on a glassy or light E wind day. Good dawn patrol spot before the wind picks up.

Look for the turnout above the break. It's a scramble getting down to the beach.

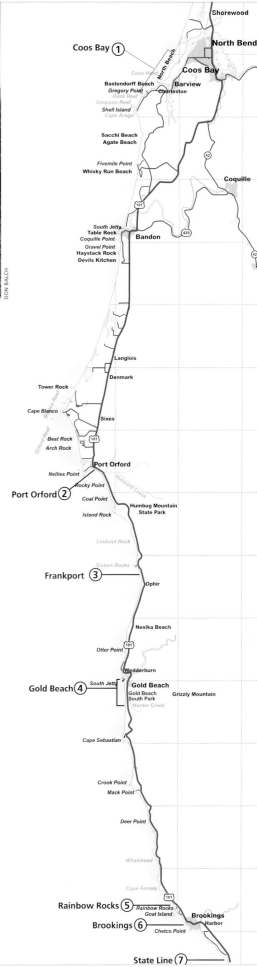

6. Brookings/South Jetty

Protected from prevailing NW summer winds by the Chetco River Jetty, this popular Brookings spot is a rare summertime haven. Takes anything from a NW to a S swell, which produce two-way peaks that break over a sand bottom on most any tide. A nice beachbreak, greatly enhanced by E and NE winds. Good fun at a foot or two, it'll handle surf up to about 8ft (2.5m). Good beginner spot, although, as with other NW rivermouths, sharks are a concern.

Free parking fronts on the beach, big RV park right across the street. The quiver of amenities includes free outside showers, restrooms, and phones. Most luxurious set-up on the southern Oregon coast. Watch out at low tides: it gets super shallow and the waves start to dredge. Gets crowded.

7. State Line

Enter via Pelican State Beach at the California-Oregon state line and drive north a couple hundred yards (220m) to tree-fringed parking area. Sand beach and bars between rocky areas, which produce better than average beachbreak in glassy or offshore conditions on a small swell at mid and higher tides.

Seldom crowded, nice parking area, interesting wave action in both directions. Modest shark worry.

Southern Oregon Beachbreak

MIKE KEW

Northern California

Northern California (including Del Norte, Humboldt, Mendocino, Sonoma, and Marin counties) is one of the most iffy surf destinations on the globe. This wild and wooly landscape will delight, disparage, or horrify even the hardiest of souls. Bottom line: unless you live there, it's most likely one of those places you'd really like to visit someday, but never quite muster the time. For good reason.

If the very real prospect of becoming a great white shark's evening meal fails to deter you, the adverse weather patterns with their horizontal rain storms and raw Jurassic swells might. Throughout the winter months, the National Weather Service's offshore buoys repeatedly report groundswells in excess of 20 feet and occasionally top 40, but they're rarely anywhere as clean and rideable as, say, Mavericks gets on an average day. Come February, the surf usually fails to stoop below double overhead. In fact, it takes a veritable mini-miracle for tide, wind, and swell to coalesce into surfable conditions on this largely 'lost' coast.

Even so, the Northern California seascape is a haven for the big-wave surfer with the mettle to endure its gray chill, its fickleness, its ubiquitous hazards, and its mostly unspoiled grandeur.

With break names like Devil's Gate, Shark Pit, Deadmans, and Obituaries, it's not hard to imagine that many North Coast surf spots are aptly named. But every spot has its day, and Northern California's gems are no exception. To quote one famous surf photographer, "Luck is the intersection of preparation and opportunity."

Inaccessable points.

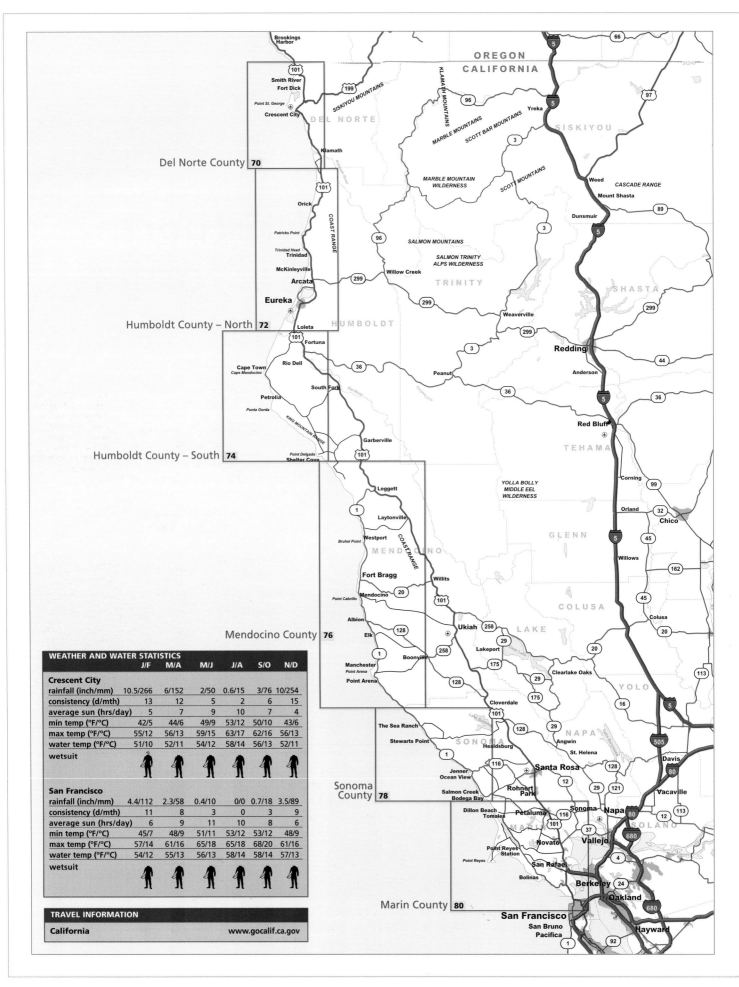

Del Norte County **70**

Humboldt County – North **72**

Humboldt County – South **74**

Mendocino County **76**

Sonoma County **78**

Marin County **80**

WEATHER AND WATER STATISTICS

	J/F	M/A	M/J	J/A	S/O	N/D
Crescent City						
rainfall (inch/mm)	10.5/266	6/152	2/50	0.6/15	3/76	10/254
consistency (d/mth)	13	12	5	2	6	15
average sun (hrs/day)	5	7	9	10	7	4
min temp (°F/°C)	42/5	44/6	49/9	53/12	50/10	43/6
max temp (°F/°C)	55/12	56/13	59/15	63/17	62/16	56/13
water temp (°F/°C)	51/10	52/11	54/12	58/14	56/13	52/11
wetsuit						
San Francisco						
rainfall (inch/mm)	4.4/112	2.3/58	0.4/10	0/0	0.7/18	3.5/89
consistency (d/mth)	11	8	3	0	3	9
average sun (hrs/day)	6	9	11	10	8	6
min temp (°F/°C)	45/7	48/9	51/11	53/12	53/12	48/9
max temp (°F/°C)	57/14	61/16	65/18	65/18	68/20	61/16
water temp (°F/°C)	54/12	55/13	56/13	58/14	58/14	57/13
wetsuit						

TRAVEL INFORMATION

California　　　www.gocalif.ca.gov

MICHAEL KEW

The Surf, Ocean Environment and Surf Culture

Northern California is truly a land of feast or famine, with the big feedings few and far between. The reefs aren't perfect, the sandbars are temperamental, and it's seemingly 20 feet and unrideable all winter. But this isn't to say that NorCal is devoid of classic days. To the devoted residents and the serendipitous visitor, NorCal has proven to be more than capable of serving up a heaping portion of coldwater perfection.

But first, you might be better off if you don't even tell anybody you saw this book. Surfers north of the Golden Gate Bridge can be a trifle xenophobic and paranoid, because the good spots are few and far between and seldom get any good, so most of the folk in this isolated region prefer to keep their surf zones under wraps. NorCal has giant surf, trees and terrain, not to mention unbelievably violent storms, icy water, huge white sharks, and seemingly endless stretches of lonely beach that, if you ran into serious trouble, could possibly become your grave. See all those photos and videos of Mavericks in Central California? It's like that all winter and much of spring and autumn up here, albeit more raw and vastly more unridden. This coast is not for everyone, but the scenery is enchanting, and you might find yourself slipping into some heavy, cold, double overhead caverns with no one watching except some shorebirds and sea lions.

North Pacific storms bare their teeth, torturing the coastline mercilessly and whisking surfers indoors for weeks on end. The elements are harsh, the surf is extremely fickle, and the weather is usually 50 shades of gray. Marijuana is both potent and ubiquitous, it rains a lot, and roads are about 80 times longer than they appear on the map. You'll need wads of gas money, optimism, patience, strength, rain gear, a 5-millimeter fullsuit (with hood, booties, and gloves), big-wave boards, extra leashes, and a low profile.

Although the local surfers can be less than welcoming, a surfer's biggest environmental hazard is what lives in the water (and the waves themselves), not what humans have done to the land and sea. Pesticides and animal waste in the runoff are negative health factors at the rivermouths (not to mention attracting sharks), but rivermouths aren't typically surfed during the winter, when most of the rain falls, due to the volume of turbid water and accompanying flotsam.

Sharks? The land o' plenty. Blood Red Triangle, for sure. Equate the teeming whitey populations of Central California with far fewer people to rescue you, and you have Northern California. If the rivermouths are spooky haunts for sharks, the reefs and pointbreaks can be just as bad. Surf with someone else, if you can. There have been several shark attacks on surfers over the years (all non-fatal). If you dwell on the fact that this place is indeed Shark Heaven, you probably won't enjoy yourself. The perspective that seems most philosophically realistic up here: if it happens, it happens. If it doesn't (and it probably won't), you can soak up NorCal's wooly, majestic splendor and go home happy.

Northern California waves have been surfed since the 1950s, though inconsistently. A lack of wetsuits played a major part in adhering to a 'surfing lifestyle' in those days. The advent of leashes and contemporary wetsuit technology catapulted surfing into vast new dimensions, such that today it's the activity of choice for thousands of NorCal men and women. Like anywhere else, places once rarely surfed and uncrowded are now banner spots, and the days of driving down Highway 1 and not seeing another car with a surfboard on top are long gone. Still, NorCal remains a frontier for the hardy souls who live there.

MICHAEL KEW

Above – **The winding Redwood Highway takes a lot longer to navigate than a look at a map would suggest.** Below – **There's plenty of wild life up north.**

MICHAEL KEW

Del Norte County

With the exception of Wilson Creek, none of the Del Norte (the 'e' in Norte is silent) coast is really accessible until you hit Crescent City, but there are some fine vistas from Highway 101 along the way. Wide open to wind and swell, miles of moody dune-backed beachbreak can be accessed through the towns of Fort Dick and Smith River. The hub of the county's surfing, however, is Crescent City, a true south-facing 'crescent.' As a result, South Beach is always a lot smaller and cleaner than surrounding spots, making it rather popular, especially during the persistent N winds of spring. Del Norte takes all swells, although S and SW are quite rare. Similar to Oregon, Del Norte is never flat, but the issue of access and actual number of legitimate surf spots is a tough one, not to mention frequently unfavorable winds and an often depressing, gray climate. Most of the swell comes from the NW, and since storms are relatively close offshore, conditions are frequently junky with swells accompanied with strong winds. Most of Del Norte's surf is beachbreak.

Del Norte beaches are and always have been pristine. The area's biggest environmental issue has been logging, which doesn't noticeably affect the surf, apart from the increased mud and silt runoff from the rivers. In

*Above – **Big swells battering the gateway to Del Norte County. Gold Bluffs Beach.**
Right – **Del Norte's most famous surf citizen, Greg Noll.***

typical capitalist fashion, Del Norte is economically the poorest county on the California coast, thanks in part to the crash of the logging and fishing industries due to non-sustainable levels of harvesting.

Rugged individuals typify the Del Norte surfer. The county is small and there are relatively few surf spots, so most of the surfers either know one another or have seen each other at one of the area's few breaks. Surfing started at Crescent City's Pebble Beach in 1959 after locals Jim Rooney and Mike Morgan encountered the book, *How to Build a Surfboard*. Today, surfers of every ability level with every sort of surfcraft go to South Beach, the focal point of Del Norte wave riding. While many Del Norte spots are more longboard-friendly, only a few spots are surfed mainly by shortboarders, and these are the places where you can look to encounter the most aggression in the water. Del Norte surfers are generally a friendly breed and learn to live with horrible conditions and weeks of rain.

The place for all your wave riding needs (including talking story) is the Rhyn Noll Surf Shop in Crescent City (Rhyn's the son of Greg Noll, who moved to Del Norte 20 years ago). He puts on the Noll Longboard Classic over the first weekend of October, billing it as "a contest for the good, sorta good, and not so good."

RON STONER/SURFER MAGAZINE

Humboldt County

Almost everything is big in Humboldt County, especially the waves. Never a lack of swell, but also never a lack of adverse conditions and weeks of poor wave quality. Most of the coast is beachbreak only surfable during small, clean swells, so during winter's big-time swells, the only places people really ever surf are the Harbor Entrance, the North Jetty/Bunkers, Patricks Point and Camel Rock. Call it the Winter Congregational Theory. Things spread out when the surf is small, however. Humboldt receives swell from all directions: North Humboldt is more susceptible to the prevailing NW swells, while South Humboldt can pick up S swells during the summer. Generally, South Humboldt (Shelter Cove) is smaller than North Humboldt. Windswells work well at the North Humboldt beachbreaks, while solid groundswells are key for the points and reefs. The surf can get huge any time of the year. Winter rarely sees waves below head high. North Humboldt is mostly offshore with SE storm winds, while South Humboldt blows offshore with N winds. Perfect days are rare, as the junky/stormy/huge/scary days are the rule. Bottom line is, don't visit Humboldt expecting to score. But there's always a possibility.

Humboldt County has loads of environmentally-active citizens, many of them associated with the Surfrider Foundation. Historically, people have made their livings here from resource extraction; logs, gravel and fish have been the basis of the local economies. Now all those natural resources are in jeopardy. These days, largely due to poor forest practises, rivers are silted and once-plentiful salmon are nearly extinct. Fierce battles between loggers and 'tree-huggers' have created a media portrait of an extremely polarized region, but it was a run-in with the Surfrider Foundation that may have had the biggest impact.

Every day for decades, two pulp mills on North Humboldt's Samoa Peninsula spewed some 40 million gallons of coffee-colored effluent and toxic chemicals into the ocean near the North Jetty, Humboldt's most popular

surf spot. The mills were found guilty of more than 40,000 violations of the Clean Water Act in the course of a lawsuit brought by Surfrider and joined by the Environmental Protection Agency. The 1991 settlement resulted in the biggest environmental victory in the history of surfing, as both mills agreed to pay $6 million in fines, conduct $100 million of improvements to one mill, and pay Surfrider a heap of money – $350,000 ($175k each). Within a year, Simpson Paper Co. closed down its mill and built the world's largest pulp mill in Chile, where they didn't have to worry about environmental laws. But Louisiana-Pacific's mill, still at the North Jetty, operates a hundred times cleaner today.

A small but key condition of the settlement, says Mark Massara, Surfrider's lead attorney in the suit and a sometime south county denizen, was a shower for the North Jetty (Massara initially demanded the shower be built in the form of an effigy of Rob 'Birdlegs' Caughlan, Surfrider President at the time). This little island of comfort on an otherwise harsh coast isn't the only thing that's changed in Humboldt in recent years. "Now," says Massara, "just about everyone agrees that what few trees, rocks and salmon remain must be saved."

Above – **Humboldt County has always been synonomous with logging and pulp mills.**
Below – **The Humboldt Bay harbor jetties are a perfect foil for large winter swells, providing stable line-ups and paddling channels.**

BILL HOOPES

Right – **Arnold Sharpes' 58 Chevy station wagon with several NSSA members looking over the surf at South Beach in Crescent City, CA. L to R: Tom Rigden, Steve Coppin, Gary LD Poncia, Craig Fleckenstein, Jim Rooney, Steve Warnow, Andy Westfall and John Phillips in 1965.**
Below – **Arnold Sharpe going left at Crescent City, 1966.**
Bottom – **Shelter Cove.**

BILL HOOPES

Today, thanks to Arcata's Humboldt State University, the Humboldt Bay region is the hub of the county's surfing populace. "HSU is really the basis of the economy here," says Massara, "and the surfing population too!" In fact, there are enough surfers to officially classify the place as 'crowded.' The vast majority are transplants from Southern California or elsewhere. Even so, a dedicated Humboldt surfer is one who can withstand the elements, excels in large waves, and boasts a rugged individuality (and mentality).

All types and levels of surfers live in North Humboldt, sometimes congregating at the heavier spots in clumps of 15-30 people jockeying for position in a take-off zone about the size of a postage stamp, rife with grumpy middle-aged men on 9'6" guns. Other spots are softer, with gobs of room for everybody, including the old lady kooking in the whitewater and the blind kayaker cartwheeling on the outside. South Humboldt (Shelter Cove) hosts a generally unfriendly and tight-knit local crew, most of whom grew up here and are wary of outsiders. This is also Marijuana

In 1953, alarmed by the population explosion in Southern California, pioneer surf photographer Doc Ball moved his family and dental practice to the tiny town of Garberville in southern Humboldt County. Why he chose this nondescript wayside along Highway 101 might be explained by the south-facing cove, a twisting 15-mile (24km) drive to the west. That year Doc and his friend John Kerwin brought surfing to Shelter Cove. Surf culture came to the north county in 1959, when two Hermosa Beach transplants (Howie Skihan and Chuck Ehlers) rode the first waves at Camel Rock and Moonstone Beach. Local boy Ed Cox was the first to ride a mysto spot called Stinky's (inside the harbor) in the early '60s. North Jetty was ridden in 1966 by Kim and Willie Robinson, and South Jetty about the same time by Jim Sylvia. The next big spate of pioneering came in 1972, when Bob Hallmark, Jr. and Steve Grant (Malibu) first rode Patricks Point, and Grant, Trevor Smith, Tom Leshe broke the ice out at the harbor entrance.

MICHAEL KEW

Central: the land of dope-growing surfers with their new cars, big houses, and no visible means of income. (Best not ask these locals what they do for a living.) It is speculated that more high-potency, Grade-A marijuana is cultivated in Humboldt County than anywhere else in the United States, and the herb is undoubtedly the largest contributor to the area's otherwise cash-strapped economy. (Notice how many folks book tickets to Fiji shortly after harvest.) A federal program dubbed Campaign Against Marijuana Planting (CAMP) has government helicopters roaring all over the countryside at tree level, searching for the illegal gardens and this has forced many outdoor growing operations inside. The result is an increasingly bitter war between the pot growers and the government, which many argue should focus on abolishing the area's true scourge – meth-amphetamine manufacturing and abuse – rather then squander boodles of dollars on a relatively harmless, multi-use plant, whose main deleterious effect seems to be inducing a state of euphoria.

Arcata's Humboldt Surf Company is the most well-stocked, legitimate surf shop in the county. It's a good idea to get your goods here if you plan on driving around (which you will). South Humboldt has two small shops that are not well-stocked, and they have spotty hours of operation. But for something completely different, check out Bill Hoopes' Born Again Boards in Eureka. Hoopes is a Humboldt native with a small rustic woodshop specializing in reproductions of '30s redwood boards and balsa-redwood combinations. He also makes balsa blanks and finished boards in modern or retro templates. By appointment only. Info at www.bornagainboards.com.

Mendocino County

Not a stellar surfing destination, but even the Mendocino coast can have its day. Much of this stretch of coast is either inaccessible or unrideable, so don't get your hopes set on finding a coldwater paradise. From Westport all the way south to Gualala, there are no world-class pointbreaks, reefs, or beachbreaks, but the spots Mendocino does have can get quite good on rare occasions, generally during autumn or on the smaller days of winter. Most popular North Mendocino spots are Virgin Creek and Chadbourne Gulch, and although there's a lot of coast beyond those spots, for some reason surfers seem to flock together. North of Westport, the coast intensifies and morphs into the 'Lost Coast,' a harshly forbidding stretch of cliff and rock remaining inaccessible and unridden.

Wide open to swell and wind from all directions, this rugged coastline can play with a surfer's degree of optimism, no matter what season it is. Prevailing swells come out of the NW and are often lumpy due to the proximity of the generating storms. The prevailing winds are also from the NW, so the surf is often blown-out. As with the rest of Northern California, Mendocino gets very windy. South swells generally go unridden except in the Point Arena vicinity, and W swells have basically the same effect on the coastline as NWs do – without high-quality

Above – **Local Rig.**
Below – **Clean up set at a south Humboldt point.**

MICHAEL KEW

Above – **Southern Mendocino Point.** Below – **Just to remind you sharks are a given in Nor Cal.** Right – **Shapers and surf shops are few and far between in parts of Northern California.**

bottom contours, much swell is wasted, and the beachbreaks can't handle size. Large stretches of the Mendocino coast are unfortunately publicly inaccessible, but it doesn't really matter since the private stuff hides no gems. Sheer cliffs and insanely rocky beaches are the norm in South Mendocino.

Mendocino County is a very fickle wave ground, but the surf is seldom flat, so there's almost always somewhere rideable, even during the smallest of summer swells. Much of winter is unsurfable, while spring can feature howling onshore winds for weeks on end. Summer is often junky and foggy; autumn is the best bet for favorable conditions. Don't come to Mendocino expecting good waves, and you won't be disappointed. Still, you might get lucky.

As to the north, much tussling has gone on between loggers, fishermen, and environmentalists over the depleted natural resources that were the lifeblood of this county back around the turn of the 19th century. Once brilliant rivers and creeks are now brown with silt and largely devoid of their former prolific fish populations; old-growth forest is virtually non-existent. Nonetheless, ocean water quality has always been quite good considering the poor river conditions. Bucolic South Mendocino has been known to experience some pesticide and cattle-waste pollution. Curiously, Mendocino is the only California county without a Surfrider Foundation chapter, which may be indicator of its good ocean water quality or, more

likely, small population. This coast has lots of rocks, seaweed and places for seals and sea lions to hang around, so expect an omnipresent shark population. With relatively few options for surfing, it's always a roll of the dice.

Surfing came late to Mendocino County. It wasn't until the winter of 1969-70 that Central Cal explorers Paul Acklin, Mark Ricci, Rick Carroll, Randy and Ron Vetterly, and Terry Thompson slid into the first waves at Arena Cove. San Francisco hellman Mark Renneker surfed a nice big-wave reef off nearby Saunders Landing in 1983.

Mendocinians are rural-minded surfers, who live in a beautiful surf setting unspoiled by crowds or rampant development. Many residents are transplants, evacuees from urban life in the Bay Area, and they try their best to protect their newfound paradise from outside intrusion. Many other surfers are Mendocino natives, well-schooled in the difficulty of maintaining a surfing lifestyle in a harsh environment, so when the surf gets good, they tend to act like they'd all just won the lottery. Crowds congeal in the spots near Fort Bragg and Point Arena, and the pecking order is usually apparent. All spots are easily accessible from Highway 1 and, since tourism is huge business here, locals are accustomed to unfamiliar faces at the beach. Highway 1 can be clogged with tourists in summer, then blessedly deserted in winter. Though the vibe is generally mellow, it's best to lay low and soak up the surroundings – and hopefully get some good waves to yourself. Mendocino has no surf shops.

MICHAEL KEW

PAUL MANN

Sonoma County

The tranquil Sonoma coast is not a prime surfing destination, but it's a special shoreline nonetheless. Bodega Bay is generally affluent, and the Russian River Valley is a western gateway to world-renowned wine country. Unfortunately, the surf in Sonoma doesn't compare to the quality of its vintages. While the numerous rocky coves are beautiful beyond scenic, most of the Sonoma coast is inaccessible or does not break at all due to deep water and sheer cliffs.

There are only four towns on the Sonoma coast, and between them lie miles and miles of inaccessible or unsurfable beaches. There may be a real jewel or two, but these are only scored by the locals. The best spots are few and far between, so most surfers tend to congregate at all the same places. Salmon Creek is the county's best-known

break on small swells. Beware of brutal currents. Beginners will be most at home at Doran Park than anywhere else in the county thanks to its shallow, more graduated bottom and wind protection.

Several encounters with white sharks have occurred at Salmon Creek, and there's been a handful of incidents involving both divers and surfers all the way up to Black Point. Located just north of the Sea Ranch Lodge, Black Point is a fickle beachbreak along the controversial, 10-mile-long (16km) shoreline of the 5,200-acre Sea Ranch subdivision. When the first single family dwellings were erected inconspicuously behind windbreak trees in 1965, Sea Ranch was supposed to remain a quaint clustering of small, unique homes that blended into the landscape, leaving the entire coastline open to the public. Things didn't exactly work out that way, and public access to

MICHAEL KEW

spot, while south-facing Doran Park is favored by beginners and anybody else looking for some relief from the persistent NW winds. For the traveler, a number of spots will be obvious, but finding the sublime will require some very open locals to point you in the right direction, since the forests and abundant steep cliffs lining Highway 1 do hide a few secrets.

Winter swells are relentless and lumpy, colliding violently with Sonoma's ragged coastline, deeming the surfable spots few and far between. NW swell is the predominant direction, as are NW winds. Storms bring SE winds – blowing offshore at a few select spots. South and due west swells are uncommon. The reefs are very tidally sensitive and fickle. The beachbreaks like Salmon Creek are very consistent but often junky, and it's difficult or impossible to make it out when there's a solid swell or even windswell. Many of the beachbreaks come up from deep water to throw treacherous shorepounds and don't

most of the Sea Ranch beaches was denied in the late '60s after a lengthy and tiresome court battle between Sea Ranch advocates and the California Coastal Commission regarding public beach access. Quickly, developers from the city honed in, stamping out 2,300 lots in an all-too-typical flurry of unsightly development. Thus, the original, idyllic concept of Sea Ranch became a network of overgrown vacation homes, private roads, and well-heeled transplanted or seasonal residents. Now, instead of unhindered coastal access to a handful of breaks, there remains only Black Point, and even here you have to shell out $3 to the county for the privilege of parking before you walk a quarter-mile to the beach.

The Sonoma Coast Surfrider Foundation chapter has expanded its water-testing program, thanks to a core group of young volunteers. Two to four weekly tests are conducted throughout the winter and spring, from the Russian River to Doran Park, with spot samples taken at other popular surf

Finding a little tube time in Sonoma can be a tricky business.

Marin County

Marin is the smallest of the NorCal counties, and it's not exactly known for its surf. It is all beachbreak with rare exceptions. This is also one of the sharkiest places on Earth (it's the northern boundary of the so-called 'Red Triangle'), so Marin is hardly worth visiting if you're not feeling lucky. Most of the county's shoreline is within the immense Point Reyes National Seashore, a wonderland of tangled woods, serene estuaries, grassy knolls, and windblown (and wind-sheltered) beachbreak. But, if not for the surf, check this place out just for its unspoiled vastness.

When the rest of the Marin coast is flat, there will be some kind of surf at Point Reyes Beach (north side), albeit often junky. It's a good option during the summer if the winds are calm. The place sticks so far out into the sea, it's susceptible to all kinds of weird currents and wind fronts coming from the open ocean. The waves do get good in Marin, albeit seldom, and since distances are far between surf spots, you'll surely encounter some sluggish tourist traffic, especially on weekends. Bolinas is a hot area, as is Stinson Beach. North, at the mouth of shark-infested Tomales Bay, Dillon Beach sees a fair number of

locations. The chapter continues testing during the summer, especially in Salmon Creek and the Russian River, as these areas have been problematic in the past.

While public access is a problem in Sonoma County, the Surfrider chapter recently implemented the first phase of its Beachscape coastal mapping program, which is documenting coastal armoring, erosion, stormdrain outfalls, and the general condition of the beaches.

Inland urban sprawl filters dozens of surfers to the coast. Most surfers frequenting Salmon Creek Beach drive from cities like Santa Rosa and Sebastopol, much to the dismay of coastline natives. Thus, you get your mix of the clean-shaven, new-Toyota-truck types from the big city versus the hard-edged, rusty-pickup-driving Bodega fishermen types. The number of Sonoma surfers has increased dramatically in recent years with the advent of the Internet boom and influx of people into the Bay Area. Locals tend to be protective of their spots, which usually contain adverse rocks or sandbars riddled with currents adding to the fickleness of the shifty line-ups. Sonoma surfers are resourceful because the surf is rarely good.

Bodega has a couple of surf shops. Nothing exists north of there, so if you need something, better get it in Bodega.

Top – **Sunset lines.**
Above – **Sonoma's rocky inaccessible coast hides a few challenges.**
Bottom – **Marin is deep in the Red Triangle. Not the sort of sign you want to read before paddling out.**

SHARK ADVISORY

A shark attack has occurred here at Stinson Beach. This attack occurred in 5 ft. of water within 50 yds. offshore. Be aware of the potential for sharks close to shore along the entire length of the beach.

Golden Gate Natl. Rec. Area

surfers on any given day, but Bolinas and Cronkhite Beach are by far the most crowded (Cronkhite is most easily accessible from the San Francisco Bay Area). Check out other beaches along the Golden Gate National Recreation Area and Marin Headland for other good spots that come and go as conditions vary.

Point Reyes blocks winter NW swells from making it into Bolinas Bay, but a W will get in nicely – a good place during bouts of huge winter swell and NNW winds, which blow offshore at the south-facing beaches. Bolinas Bay does pull in S swells, although they are rare and when they do arrive, the place is packed with surfers. The south side of Point Reyes is also exposed to S swells, which take the prevailing summer NW winds right in the face. Of course, S winds spell disaster at these spots.

The ocean off Marin is teeming with white sharks. Recent encounters include a bodyboarder, who was bitten at Stinson Beach in August of 1998, and a surfer, who was attacked at Dillon Beach in October 1996. The Marin Surfrider Foundation chapter regularly tests water quality at various beaches; pollution here is usually blamed on animal waste runoff and/or pesticide residues. The Bolinas Lagoon is an ongoing area of concern. Fronting as it does on a few of Marin's most popular and consistent surf spots, the lagoon is beginning to fill with silt at a very rapid pace; it is projected that the lagoon could completely lose contact with the ocean in the near future. This would eliminate crucial sediment flow, which nourishes and forms the sandbars at the breaks around Bolinas and Stinson Beach. Some of this 'silting in' is due to natural causes, but the majority is from the destruction of the forests and the surrounding grasslands (from overgrazing) and the resultant acceleration in runoff. In 1994, citizens formed the Bolinas Lagoon Foundation in an effort to prevent the destruction of the lagoon. They were able to convince Congress to study the situation, and Bolinas Lagoon was subsequently designated a national treasure. The U.S. Army Corps of Engineers continues to monitor the watershed system to determine what steps need to be taken to restore its natural state. There are various options, including several forms of dredging, which could affect surf quality.

Marin County surfing was pioneered back in the early-to-mid 1950s by Stinson Beach lifeguards Bill Wilson and Jim Sylvia (the same guy who snagged the first peak at Humboldt's South Jetty ten years later). These two intrepid lads were the first to ride the expansive Point Reyes Beach, the sheltered peaks of Bolinas Bay, and the fickle beachbreak at Stinson in pre-wetsuit days.

Only slightly more rugged than the more southern badlands of San Francisco and San Mateo counties, Northern California's infancy begins smack-dab in the middle of the Golden Gate Bridge, once you pass the green 'Marin County Line' sign headed north. As such, Marin's coast endures a massive contingent of wealthy Bay Area vacationers, many of whom own vacation homes in the quaint coastal villages. Even so, West Marin is drastically distanced from its inland counterparts of Novato, Sausalito or San Rafael: instead of affluent yuppies, giant homes and strip malls, it's huge fetches of green, rolling hills dotted with barns, cattle, sheep and horses, meandering gently down to the Pacific. Stinson Beach is a super-popular San Francisco-Marin weekend getaway zone overflowing with snooty homes behind gates, puffy poodles and Rolls Royces. You may have a little difficulty finding Bolinas in light of the local paranoid xenophobes: for 20 years, residents have removed every turnoff sign that Caltrans posted. The department finally relented, leaving it up to travelers to find this relatively alternative community on their own. Otherwise, the Marin vibe is rich but mellow. Most Marin surfers live in inland cities like Novato, San

Below – **The long curve of Stinson Beach was first ridden by lifeguards back in the fifties.** Bottom – **Marin County is just about all beachbreaks.**

Rafael and Petaluma, but there are many scattered in the small mountain towns. A few locals actually live in Dillon Beach, Point Reyes Station, and Stinson Beach. Marin is regularly surfed and has been for decades, but there really isn't much of a problem with localism. Most of the surfers here are organically-minded and unusually accepting of outsiders, especially when you consider that the place lies so near to huge population centers.

There's one small surf store in Stinson Beach and another in Bolinas, so you're pretty well-covered if it's only small things (like wax and leashes) you need. The big shops are inland (San Rafael, etc.)

Klamath Rivermouth

Del Norte County

1. Smith River-Kellogg Road area

Miles of sharky dune and marsh-backed beachbreak accessed through the enclave of Fort Dick and off Hwy 101. Rideable only when small and clean; some heavy shorebreak and no one around. Widely exposed to all wind and swell. Check it when the seas are small and clean. Other spots include Gilbert Creek (access is difficult since there's a house right in front of this spot), Toilets, Cow Paddies, Pelican State Beach, and State Line.

Toilets and Cow Paddies are accessed from the Clifford Kamph Memorial Park. Above that, you're in Oregon.

2. Point St George

A lefthand reef and a good right sandbar that come alive during large winter swells, low tide, and SE wind; a semi-pointbreak set-up. Some hollow sections. The outside sea stacks and reefs drain the energy of large swells, so a 15-foot (4.5m) swell could be head high here. The inside beachbreak rights just north get good, especially during SE winds and smaller swells.

Point St George

Check out the St. George Light, 7 miles (11km) offshore on St. George Reef. The break is reached by way of a grassy knoll trail at the end of Radio Road.

3. Garth's Reef

A subdued, gutless beginner's righthand reef off of Pebble Beach Drive, just south of Point St George. Large swells filter around the outer reefs and rocks, which, like Point St. George, shave the beards off large winter swells.

N winds blow offshore here. Low tide. Check it only during big swells.

4. Whaler Island

A semi-hollow, rocky righthand reef outside of the Crescent City Harbor South Jetty. Low tide needed, with a medium/large winter swell.

Small take-off zone and protective locals.

5. South Beach

The main break of Del Norte County. A wide, flat, expansive beachbreak near the Crescent City Harbor right alongside Highway 101. The north end of the beach is the most sheltered and blows offshore during north winds, so it's a good place to go during springtime and between winter storm fronts. Getting out can be a problem. Best during high tide on SW swells.

Rhyn Noll (Greg's son) hosts an annual October longboarding contest here.

6. Enderts Beach

Rocky beachbreak below South Beach, rarely surfed. Needs small, clean swells and a medium tide.

Only medium consistency, so few takers. Rip currents and a rocky line-up. Easy access and parking with restrooms and telephones.

South Beach

MICHAEL KEW

7. Wilson Creek ⑥/②

A fickle summertime beachbreak with several rocks, the south end being the most surfed. Nasty shorepound; only rideable when small. Often hollow and powerful; best during an incoming tide.

Lies in plain view of the highway; watch for the roadside creek marker.

8. Klamath Rivermouth ⑩/②

A wicked, heavy righthand sandbar barrel with its own miniature ecosystem in the water and a huge pinniped rookery on land. Sealife galore, making it the easiest place around to get attacked by a shark, as a few surfers will testify. Usually ridden during clean swells from chest high to a few feet overhead. Incoming tide. Mainly a summer and autumn spot, though autumn is the sharkiest time of year due to salmon runs. The currents and the shorepound are severe.

Deep Native American vibe. The second largest river in California. Essentially, the Klamath is very dangerous but can provide some mind-bending barrels for experienced surfers.

MICHAEL KEW

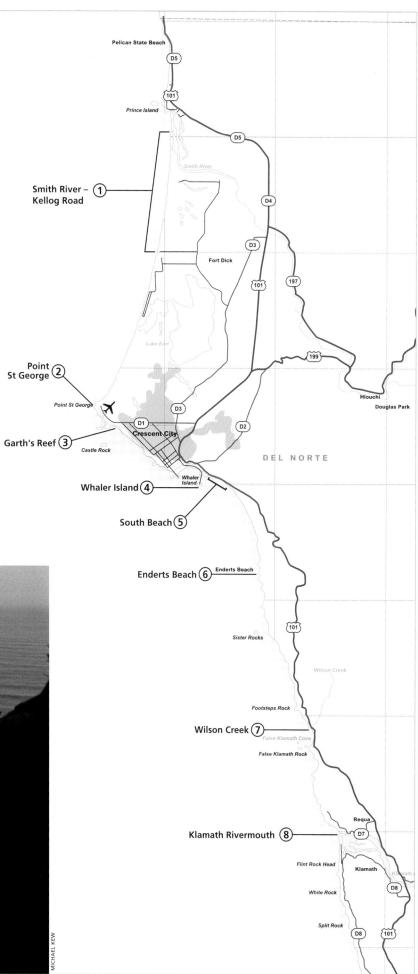

Pelican State Beach

Prince Island

Smith River – Kellog Road ①

Fort Dick

Lake Earl

Point St George ②

Point St George

Garth's Reef ③

Castle Rock

Crescent City

Whaler Island ④

South Beach ⑤

DEL NORTE

Hiouchi

Douglas Park

Enderts Beach ⑥

Sister Rocks

Footsteps Rock

Wilson Creek ⑦

False Klamath Cove

False Klamath Rock

Klamath Rivermouth ⑧

Requa

Flint Rock Head

Klamath

White Rock

Split Rock

Humboldt County – North

1. Gold Bluffs Beach

A long stretch of sharky, variable beachbreak, surfable when small and clean. Far off the beaten track, but a lush environment including wild elk. Do not approach them!

Expect solo surfing in this medium-consistency area. Check out Fern Canyon at the end of the dirt road leading out here from Highway 101. Camping available inside the large Prairie Creek Redwoods State Park.

2. The Lagoons

Four of them (Humboldt Lagoons State Park) occupying nine miles (14km) of coast; each of them (Big Lagoon, Dry Lagoon, Stone Lagoon, Freshwater Lagoon) features the same basic characteristics. Big Lagoon has evil shore-

Moonstone Beach

pound. You'd want a clean, head high swell with lower tide and E wind for all four lagoons. Sharky.

The lagoons above Big all break consistently, but the shape of the waves is very temperamental. Sandbars change constantly due to the strong currents, and the undertow can be severe. Freshwater Lagoon is the most popular since it's right alongside the highway. You can camp there.

3. Patricks Point State Park

This deep-water left is rocky, bumpy, mushy, huge, powerful, long, and mean. It holds swells as big as the biggest Mavericks, which says a lot about Humboldt's most popular big-wave spot. Winter-only, Patricks is sheltered from S winds. Although definitely not a user-friendly place, it's very beautiful. Waves slam into the outer boils and rumble on through more boulders to the inside, where a potent peak exists: Agate Beach, which is a sandbar with a few lethal submerged boulders of its own. Very hollow and steep, Agate snaps boards like toothpicks.

A winter break, it's good during low tides, SE winds, and larger W swells. Nice camping available in the park.

4. Trinidad State Beach

Funky, rocky beachbreak/reef set-up with a few decent peaks. Rideable during peaky swells. Good place to go when the NW wind is howling.

Very scenic surroundings. Accessed through the tiny town of Trinidad.

5. Camel Rock

A crowded beachbreak adjacent to twin-humped Camel Rock in a lush, verdant setting. On the best days, rights

Patrick's Point

Mad River Beach

MICHAEL KEW

will peel pointbreak-style for a hundred yards into a nice channel, but the wave is usually a mushy, sectiony right with hollower lefts on the inside near the rock. Best at low tide with a light E wind.

River-like paddling channel alongside the rock at this highly-consistent spot.

6. Moonstone Beach

Another popular spot just down the beach from Camel Rock. A wide, flat bottomed beachbreak with plenty of room for everyone. High tide, no wind, with a small, clean swell from any direction; can either be saggy mushburgers or snappy tubes with speed to burn.

There have been four documented shark attacks on surfers here (all non-fatal) plus several sightings.

7. Little River State Beach/
Clam Beach County Park

Rarely-surfed fetch of quirky, nondescript sandbars along the highway, only rideable when small and clean at high tide. If it's good here, it's most likely better elsewhere.

A juvenile white shark attack occurred here in August 1997 (non-fatal). Free camping allowed.

8. Mad River Beach

More miles of sharky, seldom-surfed beachbreak. Wicked currents, rip tides, undertow, and massive barrels in winter.

Small and clean conditions only; high tide and E wind.

9. Samoa Peninsula

About four miles of variable beachbreak along the road between Samoa and Fairhaven, best during SE winds, incoming tides, and small swells.

Popular access points are Power Lines (the first place you can see the ocean coming from the north), Pulp Mills (directly across the road from the Louisiana-Pacific Pulp Mill) and Bay Street. Sometimes crowded, always sharky.

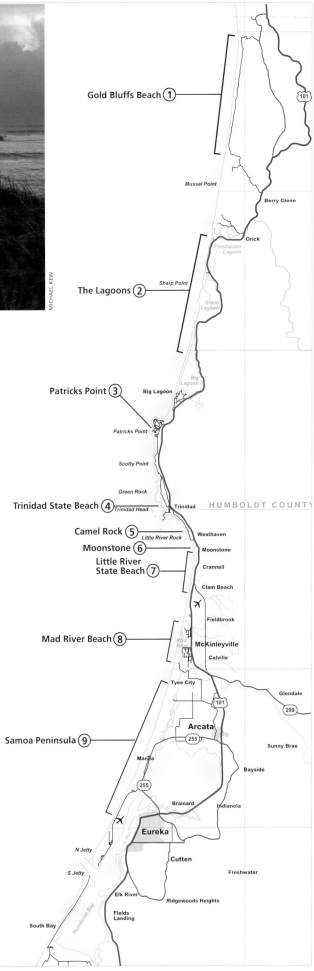

Humboldt County – South

1. Bunkers

A thick peak often resembling a bombora when big. Good when the North Jetty is too small, but it can hold its own when the conditions permit. Getting out can be difficult, but the place can moonlight as a cold water Sunset Beach when it's really good – barrels and all. Higher tide. Requires the same conditions as the rest of the peninsula.

Shark attacks have occurred here.

Bunkers
MICHAEL KEW

North Jetty
MICHAEL KEW

2. North Jetty

The premier surfing arena of Humboldt County, widely known due to its proximity to Humboldt State University and because of its famous Pulp Mill lawsuit initiated by the Surfrider Foundation in the early 1990s. When properly arranged, the sandbar here can provide either freight-train, barreling rights and/or longer, steep, hollow lefts. Holds up to three times overhead and is offshore during SE storm winds. Very powerful and gets crowded. Best during an incoming tide and any clean NW pulse. River-like paddling channel next to the jetty.

A few non-fatal shark attacks here over the years, plus numerous shark sightings.

3. Harbor Entrance

For mariners, it's one of the most dangerous harbor entrances in the world, nicknamed "Jaws." For experienced surfers, it's a crowded albeit intense, thick, and shallow sandbar peak on the north end of the entrance. Pipeline-style lefts and steep, dredging rights à la Backdoor when epic. Surf it an hour before and up to an hour after low tide only or else get sucked out to sea or into the bay, depending on which way the tide's headed. Access is by leaping off or scratching back onto the craggy North Jetty rocks. If you surf it on an incoming tide, you'll continually get sucked toward the bay and into the impact zone of every set.

The heaviest wave around when it's on; don't even think about giving it a go unless you've had solid experience in serious surf. Guys have been trying tow-ins here lately.

4. South Jetty/
Table Bluff County Park

Since South Jetty Road was closed a few years ago, the South Jetty has rarely been surfed. Access is permitted only if you have a key to the gate or if you paddle across the harbor entrance. However, Table Bluff is publicly accessible and is a good choice for small, clean, summer swells. Incoming tide.

Rarely surfed.

5. Centerville Beach

Several summertime, sandbar miles backed by grassy dunes and dairyland. Steep beach drop-off, harsh currents, and gaping barrels...if you can get out.

Needless to say, it's sharky.

6. Cape Mendocino

The westernmost and windiest area in California – very sharky, wild, and desolate. If you don't live here, you probably won't score it. Access is arduous along twisting Mattole Road from Ferndale, but once you reach the coast, the ocean is easily accessed from the road. Clearly visible as you drive is Sandbox, a wide, flat beachbreak with boulders offshore. Can be good on any tide with a small swell and zero wind.

North wind is sideshore. Just before the road heads inland is McNutt Gulch, a punchy beachbreak surfable on small swells and medium-low tide. Must be windless or offshore and clean. Quick, wedgy, shifting peaks; some rocks. Semi-steep beach slope.

7. Deadmans

A small, boulder reef/peak in Shelter Cove. A long, steeply twisting mountain road to get here. The most popular spot in the Cove. Best during an incoming tide. Blows offshore with N wind. S swells do get in, transforming the peak into lined-up walls that shoot all the way to the black sand. Park at the boat ramp and walk down the beach to the knoll.

Gets semi-crowded. Unfriendly, marijuana-growing locals and big white sharks.

Cape Mendocino

Bunkers ①
North Jetty ②
Harbor Entrance ③
South Jetty ④

Centerville ⑤
Beach

Cape Mendocino ⑥

8. Third Reef

Directly between Deadmans and No Pass is this reef peak, which breaks relatively far out from the beach. Fast, lined-up lefts and long, easy rights. Needs a clean, medium-sized swell and a low tide.

Not surfed often as thoughts of shark attacks prevail. A five-minute walk south from Deadmans.

9. No Pass

A very rocky, sharky left over a horseshoe-shaped boulder reef, a long walk down the beach from Deadmans. Steep take-offs followed by a fast wall when it's on. A real lip-smacker with solid cutback sections. Best with an incoming tide. Unfriendly local crew.

Rock hazards too in this shark infested area.

Deadmans

Deadmans ⑦
Third Reef ⑧
No Pass ⑨

Mendocino County

1. DeHaven Creek/ Howard Creek

Two similar, smallish beachbreaks with several rocks, both accessed through barren Westport-Union Landing State Beach and easily seen from the road. Watch for the creek markers along Highway 1. Small, peaky and glassy swells are required with a medium tide and no wind.

Cheap camping available in the park.

Chadbourne Gulch

2. Chadbourne Gulch/ Blues Beach

Punchy, beachbreak popular with the Fort Bragg crew. Needs to be small and glassy with no wind; medium tide works best. A good left at the beach's south end.

Park at the end of the dirt spur west of Highway 1 milepost 75.40.

3. Seaside Creek

An unsigned, rocky, fickle beachbreak only surfable during small swells, preferably from due W.

Very visible at Highway 1 milepost 70.65. Minimal parking.

4. Ward Avenue

Just north of Cleone, this road leads to a peaky, rocky beachbreak, which can get good on low tides with SE wind. A summer/early autumn spot.

High consistency in small swells and rarely crowded.

5. Virgin Creek

The most surfed break in the Fort Bragg vicinity offers quality peaks over a soft, sandy bottom; a small cove with wedgy rights peeling into a channel. Rocks on the inside and quite sharky. The lefts usually section more.

Located just north of Airport Road at the northernmost end of Fort Bragg; park in the wide dirt lot across the street from the Fort Bragg City Limits sign. Often crowded.

6. Caspar Creek

A small cove with a gravely beachbreak that suits beginners. Caspar needs a giant swell to break since it's flanked by large headlands. There are a few rocks at the south end, but the sandy bottom occasionally cooperates to form some fun peaks. Any tide can be workable as long as the surf is clean; a good spot to surf when the rest of the coast is maxing and/or blown out.

Often crowded on the peak, on the beach, and in the parking areas, which are minimal.

7. Big Rivermouth

At the township of Mendocino, the mouth of the Big River's 1,500-acre estuary is a washy, shallow area best at high tide on small, peaky swells. Usually sectiony, Big River can offer up some fun waves, and it's real easy to check from Highway 1. A good beginner's spot with a wide, sandy beach when the tide is out.

The usual rivermouth hazards of rips and sharks.

8. Navarro Rivermouth

A rare sandbar set-up worth checking only after considerable rainfall and a minor miracle of sand movement. There's always a bad shoredump.

Cheap camping on the beach.

9. Manchester State Beach/ Alder Creek

Five miles (8km) of windswept, sharky beachbreak, surfed only during the summer months or during a tiny swell. The beach faces NW, so it receives the brunt of winter storm surf and all other swells throughout the year; a good place to check when Point Arena isn't breaking. Heavy rips, uneven bottom contours, littoral currents, undertows, and a nasty shorepound. The northernmost end of the beach is called Alder Creek and is the exact same as the rest of the place, though a bar sometimes forms at the creek mouth. Best at higher tides.

Located at the bottom of Alder Creek Beach Road. This is where the San Andreas Fault leaves the land and heads north into the ocean.

10. Point Arena (Arena Cove)

Easily one of the best spots north of San Francisco, found off Port Road at the south end of the Point Arena township. When conditions are prime on the north side of the pier, you'll find a steep, hollow, ledging righthander with a thick wall roaring into the deep channel. Beware of the rusted ship's boiler on the inside during low tide.

Virgin Creek

Southern Mendocino

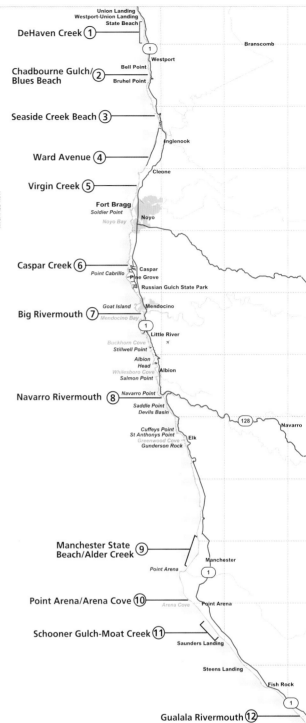

DeHaven Creek ①
Union Landing
Westport-Union Landing
State Beach
Branscomb
① Westport

Chadbourne Gulch/ ②
Blues Beach
Bell Point
Bruhel Point

Seaside Creek Beach ③
Inglenook

Ward Avenue ④
Cleone

Virgin Creek ⑤

Fort Bragg
Soldier Point
Noyo
Noyo Bay

Caspar Creek ⑥
Point Cabrillo
Caspar
Pine Grove
Russian Gulch State Park

Big Rivermouth ⑦
Goat Island
Mendocino
Mendocino Bay
① Little River

Buckhorn Cove
Stillwell Point
Albion
Head
Whilesboro Cove Albion
Salmon Point

Navarro Rivermouth ⑧
Navarro Point
Saddle Point
Devils Basin

Cuffeys Point
St Anthonys Point
Greenwood Cove Elk
Gunderson Rock
128 Navarro

Manchester State ⑨
Beach/Alder Creek
Point Arena Manchester
①

Point Arena/Arena Cove ⑩
Arena Cove Point Arena

Schooner Gulch-Moat Creek ⑪
Saunders Landing

Steens Landing

Fish Rock
①

Gualala Rivermouth ⑫

Needs at least a clean, head high swell (the bigger the
better) to break, with an incoming tide. When it's smaller,
the wave peels dangerously close to the inside ledge. The
paddle-out is through a keyhole in the rock ledges near
shore. There's also a good left breaking to the south of the
pier, best at about head high and offering some punchy
sections in front of the exposed rock shelf. N wind blows
sideshore/offshore at both the point and the left, but
forget about it on a S wind.

The waves and the crowds are consistent. Ditto for
white sharks.

11. Schooner Gulch-
Moat Creek

About three miles south of Point Arena is the public access
to Moat Creek, a joint project of the Surfrider Foundation
and the State Coastal Conservancy. A very short walk from
the dirt parking lot will lead you to a small, subdued reef
that works best during clean SW swells. The place is
sheltered from prevailing NW winds, so Moat is a good bet
during the springtime. It's a mushy peak, good up to about
head high, with lots of seaweed and rock obstacles during
low tide. The beach itself is very small, so don't expect to do
much sunbathing if you're coming here at high tide; some
cool tidepools emerge at low. Schooner Gulch State Beach is
a rocky beachbreak that's only surfable when small and
clean; it's a state owned pocket beach in front of a shallow,
wooded canyon.

Park along Highway 1 at the confluence of Schooner
Gulch Road and walk down by the bridge. Rarely crowded.

12. Gualala Rivermouth
Various sandbars relying on rainfall and river flow. The
mouth does get good on occasion, but, like all other
North Coast rivers, is only surfable during the small
swells of summer and early autumn. Since the mouth is
basically divided in half by the Sonoma-Mendocino county
line, you need to go through Sonoma's Gualala Point
Regional Park to publicly access the dune-backed beach.

In the town of Gualala itself, beach access is only
through adjacent restaurants and inns. This isn't to say you
can't reach the north side of the mouth, but you might have
to briefly explain your quest to a maitre d' or innkeeper
while tromping through with your surfboard underarm.

Near Gualala

Sonoma County

1. Black Point Beach (Sea Ranch)

Spew $3 to the county for parking before you strut the quarter-mile to this spot, a NW-facing beachbreak known for its power and shape during the wintertime S winds. A good place to check if the swell is small and clean, or if you enjoy taking leisurely strolls along wild flower-studded bluff tops.

Somewhat consistent with a low crowd factor.

Black Point Beach

MICHAEL KEW

North Sonoma

MICHAEL KEW

2. Secrets

At the north end of Salt Point State Park, Secrets (a.k.a. Horseshoe Cove) is a lefthand reef/point that works during S winds and winter swells. The name 'Secrets' is a misnomer, because everybody and their brother will be out surfing here when the S wind is howling offshore. It's a low tide spot, achieving prime shape with a larger W swell.

Beware of several submerged rocks and such. The take-off spot is small and the currents can be bad, but Secrets will probably provide you with your best Sonoma waves north of Salmon Creek (that is, if the Russian Rivermouth isn't happening). Camping nearby.

3. Timber Cove

As if you didn't need any more rocky surf spots, the next one down is called Timber Cove and, yep, it's a real paradise for our friend, Mr. Barnacle. Timber Cove is a low tide right at the north end of the cove; it only breaks during big NW swells, so go here during the between winter storms (i.e. sunny days), when the wind is from the N.

Oodles of rock hazards, so it isn't a beginner's spot. Access is via a steep lane through the privately-owned Timber Cove Campground & Boat Landing, so you'll have to dispense a small day-use parking fee to the good man at the booth if you want to surf here.

4. The Fort

Around the corner from Mystos lies a creatively named break called The Fort (named after Fort Ross State Park), a rock-infested, grumpy lefthander, working best during big S swells and high tides.

Gobs of boils, weird double-ups and freaky suck-outs at lower tides. A pretty spot, but we suggest you utilize your 'beater board' here, and don't forget your booties.

5. Mystos

A craggy righthand reef near the Fort Ross Reef Campground. Big S swells and higher tides work best at Mystos, plus it's sheltered from N wind. Not a real consistent spot, but worth a look on those rare days when a S swell is running.

Cannot hold any sort of a crowd, which is unfortunate since it's often crowded.

6. Russian Rivermouth

A classic, righthand barrel when it's on, although good lefts too have been surfed here over the years. As with all other rivermouths, the spot is slave to the river's flow and the shape of the sandbar. Fires on small, clean swells from the SW to W but is sensitive to tidal shifts.

Easily seen from Highway 1. Really only a summer/autumn break, it is shallow with lots of currents and sea life. Shark infested. The sandspit here is a seal pup haul-out, but it's illegal for you to approach them. Questionable water quality from the Russian River.

7. Goat Rock

The south side/cove can boast some decent sandbar peaks, which are semi-sheltered from NW wind. Low tide is better, with a smallish, peaky S swell running. Not a stellar break, but good enough at times to warrant yanking on that cold 'n' clammy 5-mil.

Goat Rock was once an offshore sea stack, but man stepped in with his altering ways in the 1920s and connected the rock to the mainland with a paved causeway.

8. Salmon Creek

The most popular surf spot in the county; meaty beachbreak resembling San Francisco's Ocean Beach in

Black Point Beach ①   *Black Point*

Secrets ②

Timber Cove ③

The Fort ④

Mystos ⑤

Russian Rivermouth ⑥

Goat Rock ⑦

Salmon Creek ⑧

Doran Beach ⑨

terms of size and consistency. Getting out can be difficult, but, if you're lucky, you can find a natural paddling channel. Heavy sandbar peaks are the norm at Salmon, which gets crowded but usually offers room for all. Rarely flat, so you can surf it all summer long.

Most surfers paddle out in front of the signed parking lot, but a stroll down the beach could yield a solo session at a comparable peak. Numerous white shark sightings. Camping nearby.

9. Doran Beach

A crescent of hard-packed beachbreak, basically only ridden during bouts of N wind and either large winter swells or summertime S swells. Hollow and lined-up, but not much length to the wave. Fewer close-outs at high tide.

Usually not much shape, but it'll do if you're itching to get wet during the soggy dregs of winter. A good beginner's break. Camping nearby

Russian Rivermouth

Marin County

1. Dillon Beach-Shark Pit

Shark-infested beachbreak boasting a non-fatal surfer attack in October 1996. Shifty sandbars, sometimes mushy, sometimes hollow, but always sectiony. Usually smaller than northside Point Reyes and Sonoma's Salmon Creek. Best with higher tides and due W swell. Pay $5 to enter the car park here.

At the mouth of Tomales Bay is Shark Pit, an epic lefthand barrel which peels over sand but is a feeding ground for white sharks. The best left in Northern California. Ask the locals about this spot.

2. Point Reyes Beach (North Side)

A wooly, windswept fetch of sandbars and rip tides which can get good during small, peaky swells. Any tide, preferably incoming, and SE winds are offshore. Bigger days can be ridden, but the challenge then becomes simply making it to the outside and avoiding the deadly currents and white sharks.

Easiest access lies at the ends of the signed roads leading to North Beach and South Beach.

3. Drakes Estero

An exceptional albeit seasonal sandbar at the mouth of the Estero's delta, about a mile walk east from Drakes Beach, on the south side of Point Reyes. Generally only good during the summer and late spring, when S swells can focus onto the bar and bend the waves into speedy tubes in either direction. Incoming tide. Offshore during N winds. Score it good and you'll never forget the experience.

Sharks galore.

4. The Patch

Gutless, sheltered beginner's spot facing southeast, at the end of Bolinas' Overlook Drive. Bottom slopes gently, causing some genuine longboard sliders. Works on big winter swells or big southerlies. Low tide. The prevailing NW winds are offshore here, but it's not like the wind makes the wave hold up and pitch.

Weak surf despite the mixed rock and sand bottom. Nice view to the south.

5. Bolinas Jetty

Reputable beachbreak lefts on the west side of the Bolinas Lagoon mouth. Very sheltered from big winter swells, so the jetty area comes alive during clean S pulses. Offshore during NW winds. Medium tide the pick.

Sharky and crowded, compounded by scant parking and protective locals.

Point Reyes Beach

MICHAEL KEW

Stinson Beach Park

DON BALCH

Dillon Beach-Shark Pit ①

Point Reyes Beach ②

③ Drakes Estero

The Patch ④

Bolinas Jetty ⑤ ⑥ Stinson Beach

Fort Cronkhite/Rodeo Beach ⑦

MICHAEL KEW

6. Stinson Beach

A sheltered crescent of fine, white sand popular with sunbathers and tourists. The surf can get good, but the swell must be small and clean. Windswells work wonders here. Higher tides work best.

Summer lifeguards along with a snack bar and a vast car park. There was a non-fatal shark attack on a bodyboarder here in August 1998.

7. Fort Cronkhite/Rodeo Beach

Various sandbar peaks with profuse backwash and funky currents. Not a stellar break. Occasionally a decent right rebounds off the cliff. Regularly surfed, but essentially a summertime spot. Semi-sheltered from N wind.

Often crowded and suffers from currents and the ever-present patrolling white sharks.

MICHAEL KEW

Dillon Beach

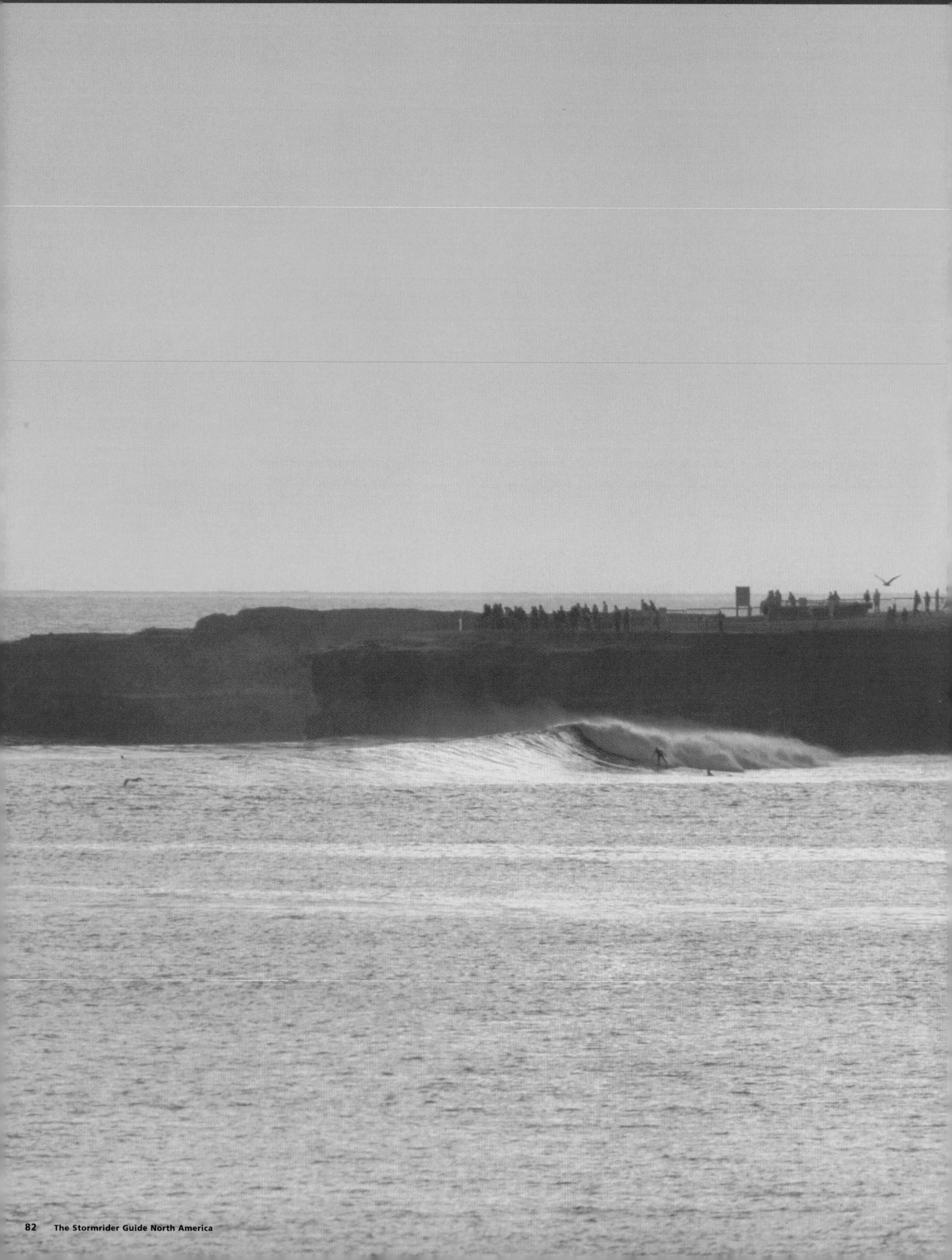

Central California

The Central California coast between San Francisco and Point Arguello is one of the world's most fickle, weather-beaten, rugged, frustrating and beautiful stretches of shoreline. Surf-wise, it's magically diverse, picking up the same swells and winds that buffet NorCal year-round, but here the coast angles a bit more to the SE (not to mention the S-facing haven of Santa Cruz), which offers some respite from the wind. Central California is a veritable paradise for the persistent surf-seeker who doesn't mind icy water, narrow serpentine roads, or the virtually inevitable disappointment of fluctuating wave quality.

Highway 1 is a blessed ribbon of pavement, much of it enabling easy checks on the conditions, and (with the exception of San Francisco and the towns of Santa Cruz, Monterey, Pismo, and a couple others) a coast that is mostly open and rural, still hopefully light years from Southern California saturation.

Central California offers something for the novice and the maniac alike. There's 25ft winter surf heaving onto treacherous reefs at San Mateo County's Mavericks, and there are the beginner-friendly rollers of Cowells in Santa Cruz or Sand Dollar in southern Monterey County. The savvy surf traveler will have a versatile board quiver in tow if the aim is to experience Central California at its finest and most true. In many ways, this is the place for the quintessential California surfing experience.

PATRICK TREFZ

Steamer Lane.

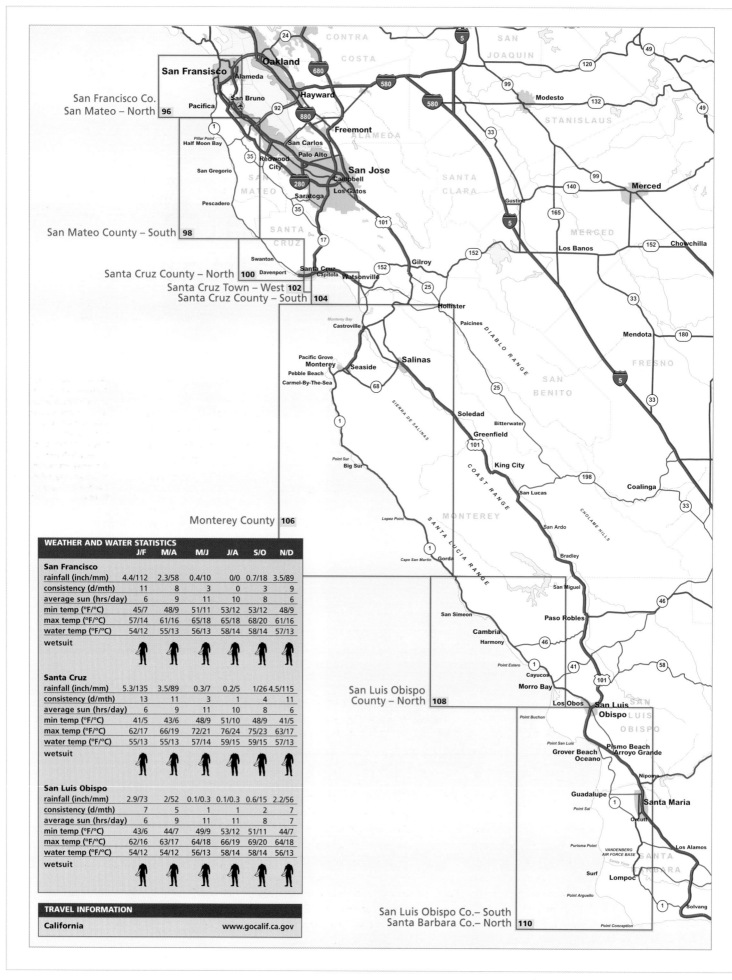

San Francisco Co.
San Mateo – North 96

San Mateo County – South 98

Santa Cruz County – North 100
Santa Cruz Town – West 102
Santa Cruz County – South 104

Monterey County 106

San Luis Obispo
County – North 108

San Luis Obispo Co.– South
Santa Barbara Co.– North 110

WEATHER AND WATER STATISTICS

	J/F	M/A	M/J	J/A	S/O	N/D
San Francisco						
rainfall (inch/mm)	4.4/112	2.3/58	0.4/10	0/0	0.7/18	3.5/89
consistency (d/mth)	11	8	3	0	3	9
average sun (hrs/day)	6	9	11	10	8	6
min temp (°F/°C)	45/7	48/9	51/11	53/12	53/12	48/9
max temp (°F/°C)	57/14	61/16	65/18	65/18	68/20	61/16
water temp (°F/°C)	54/12	55/13	56/13	58/14	58/14	57/13
wetsuit						
Santa Cruz						
rainfall (inch/mm)	5.3/135	3.5/89	0.3/7	0.2/5	1/26	4.5/115
consistency (d/mth)	13	11	3	1	4	11
average sun (hrs/day)	6	9	11	10	8	6
min temp (°F/°C)	41/5	43/6	48/9	51/10	48/9	41/5
max temp (°F/°C)	62/17	66/19	72/21	76/24	75/23	63/17
water temp (°F/°C)	55/13	55/13	57/14	59/15	59/15	57/13
wetsuit						
San Luis Obispo						
rainfall (inch/mm)	2.9/73	2/52	0.1/0.3	0.1/0.3	0.6/15	2.2/56
consistency (d/mth)	7	5	1	1	2	7
average sun (hrs/day)	6	9	11	11	8	7
min temp (°F/°C)	43/6	44/7	49/9	53/12	51/11	44/7
max temp (°F/°C)	62/16	63/17	64/18	66/19	69/20	64/18
water temp (°F/°C)	54/12	54/12	56/13	58/14	58/14	56/13
wetsuit						

TRAVEL INFORMATION

California	www.gocalif.ca.gov

PATRICK TREFZ

The Surf, Ocean Environment and Surf Culture

Central California picks up the same swells and winds that buffet Northern Cal year-round, but here the coast angles a bit more to the SE, and there is the haven of Santa Cruz, which offers respite from the wind and, in turn, huge crowds. The Monterey Peninsula attracts fairly consistent surf and people with big bank accounts in Monterey, while the majestic Big Sur coast to the south is home to maddening fickle waves and self-sufficient forest living. Further down the road, relaxing, university-powered San Luis Obispo County hosts all walks of life and has a few wave gems of its own to offer. Swell conditions can vary dramatically in a hurry – from too big to ride to small and piddly – while the weather will regularly switch from hot and sunny to cold and rainy with plenty of coastal fog sandwiched between.

San Francisco, San Mateo, and Santa Cruz counties lie within the 'Red Triangle' – a notoriously sharky zone, despite the fact that only 26 attacks and 3 fatalities occurred in waters off the three counties between 1926 and 2000.

Central California is generally clean as far as pollution goes, but that isn't to say there isn't any. Several environmental groups are based here, and little or nothing goes unnoticed by them. Land disputes and public access are the two main issues, although pollution continues to be a problem at a handful of populated hotspots.

This coast became the birthplace of North American surfing when three visiting Hawaiians practiced the art of he'e nalu at the San Lorenzo Rivermouth in 1885. The three, students at St. Matthews Military Academy in Burlingame, were the children of David Kahalepouli Piikoi and Esther Kinoiki Kekaulike, sister of Queen Kapiolani, who was married to King Kalakaua. The visiting students were David Laamea Kahalepouli Piikoi Kawananakoa, Edward Keliiahonui, and Jonah Kuhio Kalanianaole. It is unclear why none of them bore their father's name. King Kalakaua, their uncle, named them

as princes in 1886, perhaps because he and Kapiolani had no children.

From this propitious beginning, a notable surf history (with a long line of notable surfers) followed, and Santa Cruz has long vied with Huntington Beach in SoCal for the rightful title of Surf City, USA. After all, Duke Kahanamoku first surfed Santa Cruz in 1924; he didn't paddle out at Huntington until '26.

It is the home of the Lighthouse Surf Museum, one of the finest West Coast repositories of surf culture, sited on Point Santa Cruz (a.k.a. Steamer Lane). San Francisco and Santa Cruz have witnessed a number of pioneering surf developments over the years, including the invention of the modern surfing wetsuit by Jack O'Neill in 1952, the popular introduction and innovation of the surfboard leash by Pat O'Neill and Roger Adams in the early 1970s, and leading-edge production of molded surfboards (from honeycomb in the early 70s to Randy French's Surftech technology today).

World-famous for many reasons, the Central Cal coast has spawned a diverse crew of celebrated surfing personalities over the years – from 1950s shortboarder Jim Foley to the lone Mavericks' pioneers Boyd Scofield and Jeff Clark, from early North Shore chargers Fred Van Dyke, Ricky Grigg and Peter Cole to aerial pioneers like Kevin Reed. Today's talented Central Cal roster includes the well-hung lads who charge Mavericks at its meanest, the dexterous boys and girls who bust airs in waist high Carmel and Cayucos beachbreaks, and the gritty dawn-patrollers who paddle into the icy teeth of monster Ocean Beach shorepound. While modern-day crowds continue to stimulate the grumpy localism that prevails at many breaks, it is nonetheless possible to snatch an occasional good wave at a few of the more consistent nooks.

Above – **The Central California coast is laden with diverse wildlife and waves. Mitchell's Cove, Santa Cruz.**
Below – **Santa Cruz is the birth place of the modern surfing era, courtesy of the Hawaii'an royal family.**

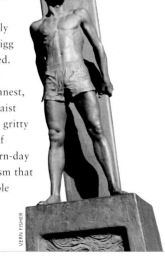

VERN FISHER

San Francisco County

The City & County of San Francisco is a certified surfing metropolis. Surrounded on three sides by saltwater, battered with solid swell on its western and northwestern shores, you're only a few miles from the surf from most anywhere in the city. Standing in the midst of chaotic noise, cars, trucks and exhaust fumes, stoplights, pedestrians, and the general hustle and bustle, it's hard to imagine that a world-class beachbreak lies just over that way. But it's true!

The options for surf in The City are limited, however. Two spots (Fort Point and Deadmans) are lefthand reefs that require large winter swells and S winds. Your other choice is the five-mile (8km) stretch of sandy shore known as Ocean Beach, home to some of the heaviest and most consistent beachbreak this side of Puerto Escondido, its north end (Kelly's Cove) is the focal point and most

Where the city meets the surf – Ocean Beach, San Francisco

PATRICK TREFZ

crowded surf arena in San Francisco. Ocean Beach takes all swells and is never flat, but suffers from a lot of foul wind, ball-numbing water temperatures, impossible paddle-outs, surfboard-snapping power, lethal currents, and sneaker close-out sets. Big-wave boards are essential. Winter brings frequently (almost constant) large swell, S wind, and seemingly endless rain, while N winds prevail most of the year, blowing the shape all to hell. Ocean Beach has no shelter, so any wind besides offshore is a bad wind. Still, the place gets perfect on those glassy mornings or those rare E wind days. The City's two reefbreaks are far more fickle and inconsistent, but equally hostile. Bottom line: surfing in San Francisco for any extended period of time will either harden your nerves and dish up a healthy main course of heavy water, or you'll rarely surf at all.

The San Francisco chapter of the Surfrider Foundation has implemented the National Basic Beachscape program to monitor area beaches. Beachscape is a community-based coastal mapping program that employs chapter volunteers to map beaches for features such as coastal armoring, stormdrain outfalls, beach access, erosion hotspots, and other beach characteristics. Natural erosion and beach-building processes have been effected by continued development along San Francisco's coast. Inappropriate seawalls and rock revetments have been built to protect public or private property. Although the structures may protect the property behind them, these structures usually cause increased erosion and permanent loss to the beach itself. Erosion along Ocean Beach has recently threatened the Great Highway south of Sloat Boulevard. In the past, the city has used emergency tactics to protect the road by adding boulders; creating a rock revetment without any environmental review or public comment. Although effective as a stopgap measure to save the roadway, it may be causing irreversible loss of the beach. Surfrider has been working hard to ensure sand, not rocks, will be used as a short-term fix while an acceptable long-term solution is found. The San Francisco Surfrider chapter was praised for its innovative Beach Information System for coastal water-quality reporting in receiving awards from Senator Barbara Boxer and EPA Region 9 at the Environmental Awards Ceremony held in the city in 2001.

Surfing came rather recently to the City and County of San Francisco. When Tom Blake arrived with his paddleboard to stroke across the Golden Gate in 1948 (in 13 minutes and 45 seconds), there were a number of bodysurfers regularly tackling the beachbreak, but nobody surfing. It was Pedro Point Club surfers Al Peace and Charlie Grimm who opened up the city's major spots in 1949 – Kelly's Cove, Fleischackers, VFW, and Ocean Beach.

Over 50 years later, all kinds of people surf in San Francisco, from the grizzled gray guru to the latest millionaire high-tech yuppie, from the doctors and lawyers to adolescent McDonald's busboys. 'The City' (as it is sometimes called) truly is a melting pot of cultures, counter-cultures, classes, creeds, and personalities. You're likely to see more surfers of ethnic diversity here than, say, some place in Oregon. The city's surf population has increased dramatically over the last decade as surfing has acquired social cachet. But the dedicated waveriders here are tough as nails and on-task. As with Northern Californians, core San Francisco surfers are adept at dealing with thick barrels, relentless monster swells, rain, heroic paddle-outs, gnarly rocks, edgy line-up companions, and minor bouts of hypothermia. Nature lovers will be disappointed with the general lack of pure, quiet nature at the beach. Anywhere you surf is backdropped by concrete and cars, although surfing under the Golden Gate Bridge at Fort Point is definitely unique. The city has anything anybody could ever want/need, including a few well-stocked surf shops in the Ocean Beach vicinity, close to where Jack O'Neill opened his first Surf Shop in the 1950s.

PATRICK TREFZ

San Mateo County

Raw and rocky, home to huge-wave Mavericks and a handful of other big-wave spots, plus several breaks only surfable when small, this shark-infested epicenter of the 'Red Triangle' has only seen two shark related deaths in the past 75 years. Surfwise, there's not much middle ground here, but quality waves are to be had when desirable conditions coalesce. Swell catchment varies from NW to S, with NW being dominant. Winds are unpredictable and often strong, and can wrack and wreck the surf for weeks. Generally no lack of swell at any time of the year, the soothing, rural ambiance of San Mateo (once you get south of Daly City and once-laid-back Pacifica) is a favored escape zone for San Franciscans, Santa Cruzers, and the rest of the super-saturated Bay Area.

Follow Highway 1 past the burly Pacifica beachbreaks and the much revered big-wave left at Pedro Point, snaking around the curves past Devil's Slide, and you come to a beautiful, expansive coast stretching from the popular Montara Beach down to the intimate, cold, and truly sharky cove at Año Nuevo. Not far along that road you'll find now world-famous Pillar Point and the surf spot called Mavericks. A remote, derelict headland just a few years ago, a veritable circus atmosphere now prevails whenever the big swells come barreling in from the N and W. Jetskis, boats, helicopters, the world's best big-wave surfers, tripods, cameras, photographers, galleries of spectators, and so on. It's all here today, gone tomorrow.

Surfers lacking the proper heavy-water experience have attempted Mavericks; they're usually slapped down. The wave is potentially lethal, and the near-shore topography of the spot adds to the mayhem, even for seasoned riders. Like the old Mexican proverb says, "If you ride the bull, be prepared to take the horns." What was once a secret reef ridden by one or two hellmen has exploded – much like the wave itself – into the limelight, becoming a household name by taking well-known waterman Mark Foo's life. Never short of drama or glory, Mavericks always packs a mean punch and, as break pioneer Jeff Clark has said, the spot "will take care of itself."

South of Half Moon Bay is a lot of funky beachbreak, a few occasionally decent stream mouths, and a tasty reef or two. This stretch of coast generally needs a small swell to

Above – **Rear view of Mavericks, inside the Monterey Bay National Marine Sanctuary, which may soon ban the use of jetskis.** Below – **The summer face of San Mateo County.**

ROB GILLEY

be surfable. Exposed to the same giant pulses that rouse Mavericks to horrendous heights, options are slim during winter. But summer is another story, as breaks like Pomponio and Pescadero can get good...but crowded. The beautiful and infamous Año Nuevo corner sandbar is another gathering spot – you might spot dozens of shortboarders strutting across the bluff and down to the beach. Shallow, hollow and as sharky as any place on Earth, Año is not for the unsavvy or easily-frightened. But neither is the whole of San Mateo. If you like a little bite to your wave, give the county a go.

A major issue is the proposed ban on personal watercraft (a.k.a. PWCs or jetskis) from the line-up at Mavericks, since the epic spot breaks within the Monterey Bay National Marine Sanctuary, which stretches from Marin to San Luis Obispo County in the south. The issue involves tow-in surfers vs. paddle-in surfers and the rules and regulations of the Sanctuary (home to 11 endangered

Hop Swarts at Pedro Point during a 1940 springtime excursion with E.J. Oshier and Doc Ball.

and seven threatened species of bird, fish, turtle, and marine mammal) that live in or migrate through the area.

Environmental groups say that PWCs are noisy, polluting, dangerous and a threat to wildlife. Many paddle-in surfers, who count tow-in surfers as friends, simply hate what they're doing, denouncing them as intruders and dangers to themselves and those around them. In October 2001, the National Oceanic and Atmospheric Administration banned PWCs from the Gulf of the Farallones (bordered to the west by the Farallon Islands National Wildlife Refuge), just north of the Monterey Sanctuary, claiming "no other vessel type has demonstrated so many wide and varied detrimental aspects." NOAA's report cited the machines' abundant exhaust and their tendency to disturb marine mammals and birds. The issue in the Monterey Bay Sanctuary is expected to receive a ruling sometime in 2003. If PWCs

are banned from the Sanctuary, we will never again see (legal) tow-in surfing at Mavericks, and rogue winter swells will presumably go unridden.

The San Mateo chapter of the Surfrider Foundation is a fundamental force for retaining the pristine qualities of San Mateo beaches for surfers to enjoy, establishing a Beach Clean-up Program and successfully campaigning for public beach access to areas like Pillar Point. The chapter also launched its own Blue Water Task Force, working with the Department of Health and Safety to continually test the water quality at San Mateo beaches and bring unsafe levels of contamination to the attention of residents. The results are published in local newspapers.

Pedro Point was the early seedbed of San Mateo County surfing as the wave-riding community jelled around the great waterman, Dick Keating, who went to Hawaii, learned to surf, and returned in 1935 to start the Pedro Point Club. His nephew, Dick Keating (the younger), pioneered area breaks into the late '50s, including Ross' Cove and Princeton Breakwater (Pillar Point/Half Moon Bay) before the breakwall. Another Pedro Point Club member was Charles Grimm, who started San Francisco slidin' with Al Peace in the late '40s. The first to surf Año Nuevo, way back in 1951, was Al Wiemers of Santa Cruz. While Pedro Point is still the most surfed spot in the county, the center of gravity has definitely moved south to Half Moon Bay and the wave called Mavericks.

Always a mix of Santa Cruz, San Francisco and the small towns along its own coast, expect a mixed crowd at any given San Mateo spot, except Mavericks, where only the most experienced big-wave riders need apply. Santa Cruz surfers drive up when their spots are flat (or, conversely, when it's booming), and San Francisco surfers drive down when they crave a scenic alternative to the mundane week-after-week reality of moody Ocean Beach. Most of the spots are not longboard-friendly, so you'll see a large contingent of young shortboarders at the beachbreaks. Año Nuevo locals are not the most welcoming people in the world. Localism bouts are rare however, and as long as visitors maintain respect and lay low, there should be no problems. Some locals like to intimidate or frighten newcomers with bogus shark stories to keep outsiders (especially foreign tourists) from surfing their local breaks. San Mateo surfers are a rugged, persevering bunch, enduring a lot of bad weather and junky waves to fill their quotas. They're used to surfing with the spooky presence of white sharks, erratic currents, unfriendly sea lions, and large, shifty waves. Area locals are not without a good supply of surf gear, as Half Moon Bay and Pacifica both sport several quality surf shops.

PATRICK TREFZ

Santa Cruz County

Surf-wise, Santa Cruz is just about the most diverse county in California. It's got the consistent, quirky reefs and beachbreaks of the north, user-friendly, ultra-clean and crowded points and reefs in 'Town' and the powerful, uncrowded, often merciless beachbreaks of south county. Starting at Waddell Creek, just south of the county line, the Santa Cruz County coastline angles SSE before bending around into a south-facing arc, an inverted bowl on the north end of Monterey Bay that catches NW, W, SW and S swells, making 'Cruz' one of the most wave-rich areas on the entire West Coast, as long as you know where to go.

Except when S or SW, the wind is usually blowing offshore somewhere. If the more W-facing spots to the north and south are unruly or blown-out, Town (divided into Westside and Eastside) almost always offers an option – for every surfer in the county, that is, which translates into severely congested line-ups, overflow parking, and lots of frustration. Even the breaks north of town get can super crowded, especially Waddell, Scott Creek, Davenport, and Four Mile. Town (and the eastward bend of the coast) is only a few, flat highway miles south of these spots. South of Town, Manresa is really the only spot that sees a pack.

During the winter, large NW swells bend around the western points and headlands and wrap into Monterey Bay. Groomed and elongated, they are further refined by thick kelp beds into often perfect, glassy (unless the S wind is blowing) reef waves at world-famous spots like Steamer Lane and Pleasure Point. All Town waves can handle a lot of NW wind, which blows sideshore, offshore, or misses the area altogether. S winds are bad news, but summer S

swells, though relatively rare, can bring excellent waves to the S-facing shores of Town. Sometimes, these can be the best swells of the year, although they don't begin to approach a good NW swell in terms of juice. Rainstorms always bring S winds, so most of the coast is a no-go if it's very stormy. All said, the county generally has some sort of rideable wave, even if it is the long but mushy walls at Cowell Beach (a.k.a. Cowells), the hotdog lefts at Davenport, or the often closed-out barrels of Manresa. The biggest problem, again, is avoiding a crowd.

Santa Cruz County is never short on environmental issues, or participation. Ocean water quality is regularly monitored by the Santa Cruz chapter of the Surfrider Foundation, which is also fighting a 'cliff stabilization' project fronting the famous waves of Pleasure Point, proposed by the Santa Cruz County Redevelopment Agency. Based on information provided by the county,

Above – **All types of surfers and surf-boards frequent Steamer Lane, where three's just the beginning of the crowd.**
Below – **Not all waves in Santa Cruz are long performance walls. Thick peak – Blueball Reef.**

PATRICK TREFZ

Above – **Pleasure Point: the proposed site of a new cliff stabilization scheme strongly opposed by locals.** Below – **Santa Cruz surf club in its heyday 1940, before rowdy behaviour closed it down.**

people that all such drains flow to the ocean, and using them to dispose of toxics and other damaging materials is inappropriate. Surfrider conducts stormdrain stenciling on the third Saturday of each month and beach clean-ups on the first Saturday of each month.

Santa Cruz is also home to the Surfer's Environmental Alliance, a grassroots organization with similar aims to the Surfrider Foundation, which has been very active in the region. Additional efforts at environmental education have been launched by Jack O'Neill, who, besides a strong interest in saving the great white shark from extinction, has developed the O'Neill Sea Odyssey program, which provides free educational cruises aboard the Team O'Neill catamaran, acquainting kids with the microbiology of the Monterey Bay Marine Sanctuary, which begins at Jack's East Cliff Drive doorstep. So far, over 16,000 kids have gone through the O'Neill Odyssey program (as many as 5,000 were expected in 2002 alone)

By 1896, just a decade after the visiting Hawaiian princes demonstrated the sport off the mouth of the San Lorenzo River, local Santa Cruz kids were riding the waves on makeshift surfboards at Seabright Beach near the center of Town. In 1938, newly arrived San Onofre and Palos Verdes veteran E.J. Oshier met Harry Mayo and other locals, the Santa Cruz Surfing Club was founded, with a headquarters shack and surfboard storage near Cowell Beach ($1 a month for non-members). By 1952, accusations of drunken, rowdy behavior and destructive antics (like setting fires and pushing cars off the cliff at the Wild Hook) put the club out of business.

Duke Kahanamoku visited Santa Cruz in 1924 and surfed Cowell Beach. The indicator outside of Cowells,

chapter activists are calling this nothing more than a seawall, saying there are undoubtedly better alternatives, which offer more environmentally friendly and long-term solutions. County representatives claim the cliff stabilization is necessary to protect a road and sewer line that spans the area. Chapter activists aren't buying this argument, saying the best long-term solution is to relocate the road and sewer line altogether. They say the road is not critical to vehicle traffic and that it would be better used as a pedestrian parkway. The scientific issues involved range from wave refraction – causing loss of beach to access – to damage of the nearshore ecosystem. The chapter has enhanced its Blue Water Task Force program, stormdrain stenciling program, and educational outreach programs. The stormdrain signage reminds

LEROY GRANNIS

called Cypress Point and now known as Steamer Lane, was first surfed by Lloyd Ragon in 1937. According to Mayo, it was Claude 'Duke' Horan who named Steamer Lane, when he was heard to say, "My God, look outside, they're breaking clean out in the steamer lanes." He was referring to the shipping lanes, which were much more active along the coast in those days. Duke Kahanamoku also visited in 1938 (for the second time); at the time most surfers rode Tom Blake-style hollow paddleboards, which floated 'em high and dry out of the cold water.

Pleasure Point was first surfed by Southern Californian Bill Lidderdale and local Dick Anderson in 1940. The following year, Wild Hook was ridden by locals Ray Miser and Norm Cromwell. Waddell Creek was first surfed in 1951 by Al Wiemers, who pioneered the Santa Cruz Harbor wave the same year. January 10, 1953 was an especially epic day at Steamer Lane for future oceanographer Rick Grigg, who has said that "Steamer Lane was our Mavericks." Grigg's friends Peter Cole and Peter and Fred Van Dyke were there on that day, too, and soon they went on to pioneering the big waves on Oahu's North Shore.

Over the years since then, many professional surfers have risen from the Santa Cruz County ranks. In large measure this is due to the quality and consistency of the area's surf. So, expect the level of surfing in the best line-ups to be high and blatantly competitive. The Westside, home to famous Steamer Lane, is generally bigger and less refined than the relatively soft Eastside arenas. These two sides of Town have some sort of traditional rivalry, with the Westsiders seen as more raucous than Eastsiders (despite the old Pleasure Point Night Fighters organization); the waves are just about good, east or west, but the mentalities differ. Such is the human condition.

In a nutshell, you'll find every imaginable sort of person surfing Town from San Jose yuppies to UCSC students (the bane of many locals; home-grown Westsider Vince Collier once described the university as "a friggin' conveyor belt for surfers."), which is constantly attracting new surfers to the area and its clogged line-ups. Stress levels run high, often on par with gridlock rush-hour traffic heading over Highway 17 to or from Silicon Valley. Bad attitudes abound, particularly with young punk shortboarders who are hell-bent on landing aerials and whacking the lip as many times as possible. Still, the county has a long and colorful surfing history, and you'll find just as many mellow, older longboard types hassling for waves alongside young longboarders,

BOB BARBOUR

bodyboarders, kayakers, bodysurfers, and the aforementioned aggressive contingent. Women now constitute a significant percentage of the surfing population, especially at name-brand spots like Steamer Lane and Pleasure Point; in fact, Santa Cruz has more female surfers than any other area in America.

Highway 17 is a direct artery to the coast for thousands of inland dwellers hungry for their saltwater fixes. Most Santa Cruz locals resent this. The Town has been nicknamed "Silicon Beach" in light of the recent technology boom just 'over the hill' and closer – in Scotts Valley and other nearby communities. Home and rent prices in Santa Cruz have skyrocketed since the nouveau riche looked toward the beach instead of the valley for housing. 'Cruz is now one of America's most expensive places to live. Predictably, the place is not without several slick, well-stocked surf shops catering to a surfer's every need.

Top – **Steamer Lane 1960, pre-surf leash. Preventing boards getting thrashed on the rocky points of Santa Cruz must have been strong incentive for leash inventors Pat O'Neill and Roger Adams.** Above – **Modern day surf vehicle nostalgia at a Santa Cruz woody rally.**

Monterey County

Oodles of swell exposure in Monterey County, but it's tricky knowing where to go and when. To the north, Moss Landing and the surrounding beachbreak is pretty basic in that you need ESE winds and medium-sized swell to see it really working. And when it's working, Moss serves up world-class beachbreak barrels which can be cold water rivals to Hossegor and Puerto Escondido.

Barrels abound in Monterey County, particularly at Moss Landing and Carmel. Above – **Exclusive Seventeen Mile Drive is famous for golf but there are some fair-waves too.**

Down around the Monterey Peninsula itself are a bunch of quirky and fickle reefs, a point or two, some rocky beachbreak, and some booming sandbar spots – all breaking on different swell and wind directions. It's quite possible you could live an entire year in Monterey County and surf nowhere but the Peninsula. You'd get some good days and some bad ones, but it's almost always possible to find some spot blowing offshore with a wave to ride.

Big Sur is another story. Without fail, one glance at a topographic map of this section of the California coast sparks incoherent blather from the unenlightened surf-trekker who's intent on raiding this rocky maze because,

dude, anywhere with that much serrated coastline must offer barrel after sparkling barrel. Not so. This coast's highly-venerated rugged beauty has been celebrated in stacks of 'coffee table' books. A legendary tourist destination and romantic escape, where a twisting, treacherous stretch of Highway 1 runs along the rims of sheer cliffs, it's a lovers' wonderland, but a hoodwinker for surfers the world over. Yeah, it's true. Despite the recurring lure of protected coves, bulbous headlands, white sand beachbreaks, and auspicious point set-ups, the 72 miles (115km) of photogenic shore from Carmel Highlands down to Ragged Point hold, at best, maybe a half-dozen funky surf spots. Big Sur's handful of spots is brutally fickle, rendered almost impossible to score epic unless you reside in the region. This is surf turf where local knowledge really comes into play.

The mouth of the Big Sur River (in Andrew Molera State Park) is the northern focal point of Big Sur surfing. A fairly long walk in tends to keep the crowd down, and the spot blows offshore on a prevailing NW wind, which whips around the headland, shooting directly into the oncoming waves – sometimes so fiercely it won't let you make the drop. Elsewhere, ample big swell, ample bad wind, and sharp, sheer terrain are the reality. Highway 1 through Big Sur is periodically closed during the winter due to natural calamities like floods and slides, the latter sometimes precipitated by earthquakes in this less-than-stable geology (the infamous San Andreas Fault passes through the coastal range). The sights and sounds of a gray, messy ocean are impressive here, but the surfing is not.

The entire Monterey County coast lies within the Monterey Bay National Marine Sanctuary, so, as you can imagine, it's a clean fetch. The sanctuary is a briny kingdom of vast kelp forests, submarine canyons, rocky shores, coastal estuaries, and bone-chilling water. Marine wildlife is everywhere – a dizzying variety of fish, birds, mammals, invertebrates, algae, etc. – so throw yourself into the teeming pot and you're transformed into another link of the food chain. Sharks? Uh, yeah. The Santa Cruz-based Surfer's Environmental Alliance successfully campaigned against chumming for white sharks in the Monterey Bay. Big Sur is also home to the California Sea Otter State Game Reserve, so, as you can see, the place is teeming with a healthy aquatic populace – lots of animals, seaweed, rocks and cold, nutrient-rich saltwater. Monterey's coast is a marine biologist's dreamscape.

Monterey County surfing followed hard on the heels of its more richly-endowed neighbor to the north. The first report of surfing here was at Spanish Bay, when a guy named John Widenmann rode the waves here in the late '40s. Danny Garcia was the major pioneer. Inspired by photos and how-to articles in *National Geographic* and *Popular Mechanics*, he built his own board and was surfing Asilomar and Carmel beaches by 1947.

Today, Moss Landing is renowned for its unfriendly locals. Keep yourself in check, and you should have no problems. Expect cat-calling, hooting, heckling, and hassling at any given time. Locals resent passers-through and often attempt to make the individual(s) feel unwelcome. There's plenty of rocks to throw, but don't count on any of the locals partaking. Just keep your distance and avoid eye-contact with the bad seeds. The same fellow who'll hassle you at Moss Landing will probably try to do the same thing at Asilomar, but ignore him and surf to your heart's contempt.

The Monterey Peninsula is very wealthy as a whole, and most surfers there drive shiny new SUVs and ride the newest boards. They sometimes cop a bad attitude when visiting Big Sur, claiming 'local' status, for some reason. Big Sur localism is a misnomer if you simply smile and stay out of the way of the guys who actually live there, but there's always the possibility of some revved-up grayhair loud-mouthing his way into sets. Besides the generally lackluster surf, one real big bummer for summer around here are the tourists: Flocking to Highway 1 from June through early September, they stuff the road and hog all the roadside surf-check spots, and the parking lots above spots like Willow Creek and Lovers Point can fill early with looky-loos and picnickers, so come early.

The nauseating tourist hype and countless coffee table photo books have certainly done more than their fair

share of exploiting the rest of the county, but, thankfully, Monterey's tourist industry doesn't surf. Big Sur is basically smack-dab between San Francisco and Los Angeles, so poor old Highway 1 bears a constant load of SUV and oversized-RV traffic. Turnouts at frequent precipitous overlooks are jammed in summer.

Out in the water is a whole other ballgame, however. A Big Sur 'crowd' is a relative term when the entire actual resident surfing population hovers at about a dozen guys. If it's a hot, sunny day at Sand Dollar Beach, there'll be girls in bikinis, families tossing the frisbee around, and beer being swilled by all. Up at the Big Sur Rivermouth, you might encounter some Monterey boys claiming local status, but let them know their opinion means nothing to you and go about your business. Chances are, anybody you see surfing Big Sur will be a visitor like yourself, so don't worry about a thing besides the random windshield-waxing. The only surf shops exist in the town of Monterey itself.

Above – **Asilomar Beach on the tip of the Monterey Peninsula, circa 1984.** Below – **One of the very few hidden gems on Big Sur.**

GEOFF RAGATZ

A gorgeous coast, San Simeon attracts people of all types, including surfers, who are generally disappointed with the area's nicely convoluted yet maddeningly volatile surf breaks. Pico Creek is the popular spot here. If you're heavily invested in scoring big in San Simeon, there's a 97 percent chance you'll be severely let down. You'll likely find yourself in search of a rideable peak somewhere else, burning a deep hole in your gasoline fundage as you hunt. Random, medium-quality reefs and spotty beachbreaks line the Highway 1 coast down through Cambria, where tourists are the norm and B&Bs rule the roost.

San Luis Obispo County

Kicked-back San Luis Obispo County (or 'SLO' for short) is better recognized for its esteemed California Polytechnic State University and opulent nearby Hearst Castle than for its surf. Not a pointbreak graces this bucolic, 85-mile (136km) stretch of coastline, though connoisseurs of fickle beachbreaks and quirky reefs might find SLO intriguing. Very consistent in terms of swell and onshore wind, SLO has few sheltered spots and a lot of hit-and-miss reefs and beachbreaks. The prevailing wind direction is NW, and the surf is usually blown-out by noon. Few spots blow offshore with SSE storm winds, but there are a handful that are sideshore/offshore with NW wind. NW swell is the predominant direction, often junky. Springtime is basically one big blow-out with the coldest water temperatures of the year due to upwelling. Summer S swells definitely ignite a few places. Rocky inlets and heaps of seals, sea lions, and elephant seals are hallmarks of the shore abutting pleasant San Simeon, as are excruciatingly slow tourist traffic, bitter onshore wind, and velvety-green marine terraces.

Top – **Morro Bay. If its gentle beachies you want head here.** Below – **Alternatively head north for some seriously localized reef action. Killers.**

Few secrets remain, as far as SLO surf spots go. Santa Rosa Creek/Moonstone is the focal point. Since Morro Bay's beach faces due west, any and every kind of swell hits the sandbars there, occasionally converting an ordinary California beachbreak into a magical mile or two of feathering A-frames and vomiting tubes. Besides Hazard Canyon, Morro Rock is the most famous spot in SLO County, and it's usually crowded. Below Morro Bay is a big knob of earth best known for the lovely Diablo Canyon Nuclear Power Plant and Hazard Canyon. A 24-karat spot and one of the most well-known breaks in California, the Canyon is a serious righthand reef with a legendary local posse. Neither Avila, Shell Beach, Pismo, or Oceano offer much in the way of perfection; rather, it's whole tractor-trailer loads of beachbreak after beachbreak after friggin' beachbreak, but for a few quirky reefs below the bluffs at Shell Beach. One of the more consistent and shapely of all Central Coast beachbreaks, the Pismo Beach Pier is the hub of south-county surfing. North of Pismo, Avila Beach can have something during large swells and bouts of that pesky NW wind, but don't get your hopes up. The area just north of Cayucos can be semi-offshore during N wind, and San Simeon Bay, although not really a surf spot, can prove valuable in times of true desperation.

Beach access is a hot SLO topic, the primary example being

DAVID PUU

the Hearst Corporation land, to which most of the San Simeon coast belongs. There is an underlying threat of development along the San Simeon coast to accommodate tourists and funnel money into the region. Local infrastructure is scarce, however, including water and the carrying capacity of Highway 1, which is already overburdened. The Piedras Blancas land swap between Cal-Trans and the Hearst Corp threatens public access to San Simeon Point and beaches north. A highly controversial golf course has also been proposed for San Simeon Point. The San Luis Bay chapter of the Surfrider Foundation stages monthly beach clean-ups, and its Blue Water Task Force samples and tests ocean water quality along the SLO coast. The chapter hopes to eventually get SLO schools involved in a 'Teach and Test' program to increase public awareness of the chapter and its goals, through displays, school lessons, and newsletters.

PWCs are an ongoing issue, and there's a movement to ban them from the pristine waters of the Monterey Bay National Marine Sanctuary, which begins at Cambria and runs north into Marin County. Surfrider's San Luis Bay chapter supports a total ban on the use of motorized watercraft in the surf zone, except for the purpose of surf rescue by 'lifesaving professionals'.

As far as pollution goes, the chapter is involved in bringing attention to both the Guadalupe Dunes and Avila Beach oil spills, pressing to ensure that industrial petro-development (namely UNOCAL) are required to clean up any pollution for which they are responsible. Warning signs have been installed at Guadalupe Beach and Avila Beach to alert the public of possible health risks from pollution there. Pismo is one of the last places on the West Coast where it is legally permitted to rip through the tortured sea of sand dunes in dune buggies or 4x4 trucks.

SLO is shark territory. The coastline surrounding San Simeon, like San Mateo County's Año Nuevo State Reserve, is one big, fat elephant seal rookery. White sharks and killer whales love to pop these things into their mouths when the mood strikes, so wherever the elephant seals are, so are the hungry sharks and killer whales. Keep that in mind. Try not to look like a seal.

The earliest-known pioneers of SLO's surf breaks were Santa Barbara surfers Tom Bellow and Dick Willett, who surfed the Palisades and Pismo Pier in 1955. Bellows in turn inspired Sehon Powers and other locals, who started surfing Shell Beach in 1959-60 and St. Andrews in '61. It's been a slow, steady growth ever since, with the realities of the limited local surf venues (and the area's relatively small population) keeping the number of surfers relatively small.

Today's SLO surfers are generally a friendly breed reflecting of all walks of life and all forms of wavecraft, but don't be alarmed if you do happen to run across the odd misanthrope or myopic local at somewhere like, say, Hazard Canyon or San Carpoforo Creek. However, the beachbreaks of Pismo, Morro Bay, Cayucos, and Cambria are generally not good enough to warrant negative localism, and if you do sneak into the water around San Simeon, anybody else out there just might be jazzed to see you. After all, more people means better odds with the sharks.

You could compare the surf at Pismo to a famous pier like Huntington, only the water's about ten degrees colder, the shape isn't as good, and scantily clad sunbathers are nonexistent. What was once one of California's premier breaks for witnessing violent localism, Hazard Canyon has become a relatively passive, crowded arena with endless Cal Poly University students and others reflecting the increasing population of the entire area. This is not to say that aggressive tactics are unheard of in or out of the water, but your chances of being confronted are slim

GLENN DUBOCK

unless you screw up somebody else's wave or just plain act like a kook. A fair number of women get in the SLO water these days, and that's often a welcome damper on any spot's testosterone level.

On the whole, the Cayucos crew is laid-back and cruisy, and a lot of the locals are into windsurfing and kitesurfing. Since Pico Creek is easily accessed and lies near a small population center, a contingent of Cambrians and San Simeonites frequent the reef during the winter and the beachbreak during the summer. There's always the odd surfer who's just passing through, but, for the most part, the guys you'll surf with out here are year-round residents. Since many spots are small, ten guys can make them seem crowded. The beachbreaks are just the opposite since you can simply strut further down the beach if a certain peak has too many guys on it for your taste. Contests are staged regularly at Pismo Pier, Cayucos, and Cambria, and several exceptionally talented surfers have emerged from the county, notably David Parmenter, who now lives and shapes at Makaha.

The northern portion of the Santa Barbara coast offers spectacular scenery which continues into the ranch.

San Francisco County

1. Fort Point

A quality left that breaks out in front of the old fort directly beneath the south end of the world-famous Golden Gate Bridge, best during large winter swells on low tide incoming. Sheltered from most winds, it's a good, clean hideout when the ocean beaches are too big and/or junky.

Beware of rocks in the line-up, also getting sucked out with the tide into San Francisco Bay. Due to its location close to downtown San Francisco it will be crowded when it's on. Plenty of spongers. Free parking, with toilet facilities.

Fort Point

ROB GILLEY

2. Deadmans

A semi-consistent thick, rocky lefthander, which only starts working at 6ft (2m) during big winter swells on a low tide.

Sharks, rips and rocks in the line-up. Park your car at the overlook on top of the bluff, where it will be relatively safe from hostile locals.

3. Kelly's Cove

A couple of large rock formations below the historic Cliff House provide some shelter from afternoon NW winds at the north end of Ocean Beach. This SW-facing nook picks up S swells, which can produce typical Ocean Beach thumpers at any tide, but with generally more reliable peaks and shape.

Because it's relatively sheltered and easily accessible, there's a much higher concentration of surfers here than further south. Large parking lots right alongside the beach accommodate heavy tourist traffic on weekends and summer days. Restrooms, showers, telephones, and other amenities abound.

4. Ocean Beach

Three miles (5km) of some of the best and heaviest beachbreak on the planet, similar to Mexico's Puerto Escondido. Simply called 'The Beach' by locals, it picks up all swells and can hold virtually any size – as it gets bigger, it just breaks further out and becomes nearly impossible to paddle through. A dropping tide increases the hollowness, but the random, shifting peaks remain makeable.

Parking can be found at the ends of streets like Sloat, Taraval, and Lincoln. At head high, you might find some 300 guys spread along the entire beach; head further south out of town to find more secluded peaks. At quadruple overhead, take your pick if you can make it out. In 2000, an estimated 15,000 cubic yards of sand and boulders were dumped along Ocean Beach as erosion protection. The city fathers want to armor the place with seawalls and quarry-rock revetments to save the Great Highway, but local residents and surfers have kinder, gentler ideas. In 2001, the mayor created a task force to look at issues affecting Ocean Beach, and two Surfrider chapter members were included.

Ocean Beach

ROB GILLEY

Sharp Park
PATRICK TREFZ

San Mateo County – North

5. Sharp Park

Two miles (3km) of heavy beachbreak fronting Pacifica, similar to San Francisco's Ocean Beach. Picks up any swell from N, W, and S and can hold up to tow-in size. Lower tides work best. The north side of the pier often boasts a quality sandbar that holds size.

There are parking spots overlooking the beach with restrooms nearby. Gets crowded when it's small.

6. Rockaway Beach

A good option during storms since S winds are offshore. Peaky reef/beachbreak set-up favoring rights on a NW swell during low tide. Big righthanders at both ends in large swells, but currents in the cove can be extreme.

Occasionally crowded.

7. Lindamar (Pacifica)

A stretch of rather mushy, flat-bottomed beachbreak mixed with boulders and rocks at the south end, flanked by cliffs. Best about head high at high tide with straight offshore SE wind. Mellow spot for beginners and longboarders.

There's a large parking lot right by the break. Watch out for the rips and the large longboard crew that frequents this spot when it's on. San Pedro Creek discharges at south end.

Lindamar
PATRICK TREFZ

8. Pedro Point

A gnarly lefthand big-wave reef, best at high tide. A good Mavericks alternative for goofyfooters. Starts working at 8ft (2.5m) and can handle virtually any winter swell up to 25ft (7.5m), as long as it's clean. Offshore during rain storms (S-SE winds).

Located in parkland, there's limited residential or roadside parking above the break.

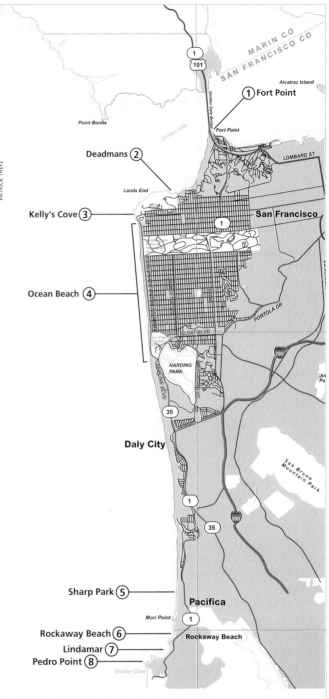

Pedro Point
ROB GILLEY

Mavericks

ROB GILLEY

San Mateo County – South

1. Montara State Beach

Powerful, consistent beachbreak, good during smaller, clean W swells; offshore on an E wind. Sometimes crowded when the Half Moon Bay crew make the trip. Montara can handle a bit of S wind and larger, peaky swells, when getting out can present a problem.

Free parking. Nasty rip currents and undertows.

2. Mavericks

World-famous big-wave reef at Pillar Point for expert big-wave surfers only. Primarily a right, but the lefts have been ridden by a few brave men. An incredibly hollow, jacking take-off in front of a series of house-sized boulders known as The Boneyard is followed by a long, huge wall ending in a deep channel. Starts to work at 12ft (3.6m) and never closes out. One of the biggest, scariest waves in the world. There have been two reported shark attacks here, both non-fatal. Heavy currents and lethal rocks on the inside if you get sucked in. This wave has already claimed the lives of a kayaker and big-wave surfer Mark Foo.

Best access is via boat from Princeton Harbor. Otherwise, park south of Pillar Point and follow the footpath through the James Fitzgerald Marine Reserve past the harbor to a small beach protected by the north jetty. From here, paddle for 40mins around the boneyard to the line-up. Recently, with tow-ins becoming popular at Mavericks, there have been growing claims that jetskis are interfering with paddle surfers and are degrading the marine sanctuary environment. For updates check out www.mavsurfer.com.

3. Princeton Breakwater

Crowded beachbreak peaks off the south jetty, best during large SW swells with N to E wind. Polar opposite of Mavericks. Very protected from big surf and NW winds. Breaks on any swell. Wedgy and hollow.

Watch out for sharp inshore rocks. This is a popular spot with just about everybody in the county, so it gets very crowded. Park along Highway 1 right in front of the break.

4. Francis Beach/
Half Moon Bay State Beach

Average beachbreak in front of the campground. A fairly consistent area, best during high tide with E wind and small, clean, peaky swells. Often maxed-out or blown-out, but when it comes together, Francis Beach and spots to the north go off.

Pay parking keeps the crowds down. Telephones and restrooms available. As with the rest of the central coast, assume that sharks and rip currents are always present. Currently, coastal overdevelopment is threatening all the surf spots in Half Moon Bay.

5. San Gregorio State Beach

Thick beachbreak is best when clean and small; needs mid-high tide with E wind. Exposed to lots of swell, so it's usually best during the summer.

Pay parking with facilities. Rarely crowded.

6. Pomponio State Beach

A good S-swell beachbreak, similar to San Gregario. Only surfable when small and clean. Always has some kind of surf, even on the smallest summer days.

Pay to park atop the cliff.

7. Pescadero State Beach

Two spots here: at the north end is a muscular beachbreak, offering some kind of wave on virtually any day of the year. Best at higher tides with no wind. Can get very peaky and hollow; always juicy and rarely surfed. Park in the lot at the base of the bluff heading north. To the south is Pescadero Cove, a rock-strewn break with peaks aplenty. Best during medium tide going low with SE wind.

Seldom surfed. Can have some funky currents; don't forget about the reality of white sharks.

8. Bean Hollow State Beach

A pocket cove protected by cliffs. Short but sweet lefts break off the south end; there can also be a few rights off the rockpile to the north. Rarely surfed but worth a look during windswell.

Free parking and restroom facilities. From here south to Pigeon Point is deep in the Red Triangle!

9. Gazos Creek

A beautiful beach with pristine sand dunes, home to powerful beachbreak peaks amid scattered rocks. Only surfable when small and clean, maybe a few times a month. Needs a peaky W swell and E wind (morning conditions). Can have very good shape, but is not often surfed.

Very sharky due to its proximity to the stream mouth and sea lion/seal breeding grounds. Free parking and restrooms.

10. Año Nuevo State Reserve

A sheltered cove with a hard-hitting beachbreak, in a pristine natural setting in the heart of the Red Triangle. Swells bounce off the cliff, forming wedging A-frame righthanders, which bowl into the inside. Shortboards only. Very hollow, very powerful, very shallow, and very sharky. Sea lions and elephant seals breed on Año Nuevo Island, just a half mile offshore. Best during peaky S-SW swells, and when the NW wind blows straight off.

A popular spot, expect to find surfers on it, and they will not be happy to see you. It's easy to snap off a fin or get hurt here, so be careful. Park beside the break. Restrooms and telephone nearby.

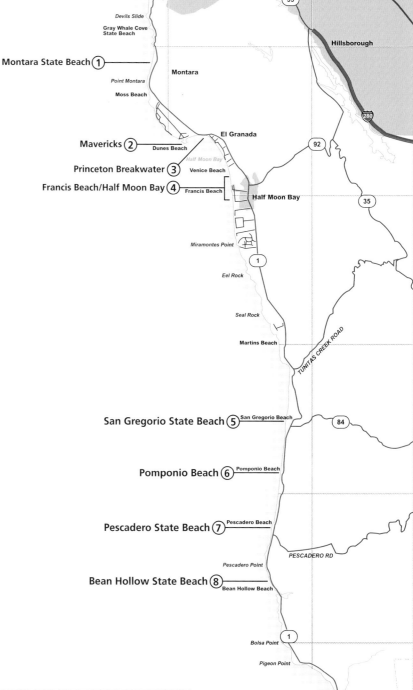

Bean Hollow State Beach

VERN FISHER

Santa Cruz County – North

1. Waddell Creek

Beachbreak peaks with rock shelves to the north; very popular with wind-assisted surfers. Can't handle any size, but offers a lot of small-wave potential during summer and autumn. High tide best; takes any clean, small swell – the peakier, the better.

Intimate proximity to the Año Nuevo food chain. Watch for creek marker along Highway 1 and park in the large dirt lot on the ocean side.

Waddell Creek

Four Mile

2. Scott Creek

A nice beach with occasional good surf. To the north, where the highway climbs the hill, is a thick righthand reefbreak. Several hollow sections during lower tides intersperse the fast, workable walls. It can hold up to nearly triple overhead with a big NW swell, making Scott Creek a consistent winter attraction. The powerful beachbreak towards the south side of the beach is best during summer when small, clean, peaky swells stay hollow through the tide. The whole stretch is easily blown out.

Scott Creek features large, fin-grabbing bull kelp to contend with. The area has a nasty reputation for white shark sightings and attacks. Park by the road bridge where the creek makes its way west from the wetlands to the ocean.

3. Davenport Landing

To the south is a popular, fun, lefthand reef wave best during S swells and medium-low tides. Some tube sections and lots of boils. Gets very crowded with surfers on glassy mornings, crowded with kite and windsurfers on windy afternoons. There is also a mushy righthand reef/point at the north end of the cove, to the right of the restrooms. Needs lower tides and NW swell bigger than chest high.

Park along the road in front of the break. Restrooms are available.

4. Laguna Creek

Wedgy, hollow, whomping beachbreak with wicked backwash at high tide. Surfable during small NW windswells or peaky, clean S swells. Mid outgoing tide is best.

Park in the dirt lot across the highway (watch for creek marker), cross the street and follow the dirt path over the railroad tracks and down to the beach.

5. Four Mile

Crowded, high-quality pointbreak rights. Fast and hollow over the inside shelf. NW winds blow offshore here, making it a popular spot on windy days. Can work on all tides, but medium-low works best.

Located four miles (6km) north of Santa Cruz city limit; park in the rip-off-prone dirt lot on the ocean side of the highway and walk a half-mile down to the beach. If there is any swell, you'll see cars and plenty of surfers standing on high ground craning to see the beach.

6. Natural Bridges State Beach

A heavy righthand reef with a shallow bowl section over the inside rock ledge called The Sidewalk. Dangerous. Not for beginners. Needs a low to medium tide with a clean NW swell and can handle up to a few feet overhead. A high-intensity spot.

Follow the cycle route off Highway 1 to the coast and park at Natural Bridges State Beach. From there you can see the break at the north end of the beach. There are showers and camping nearby.

7. Stockton Avenue

Small, perfect righthand barrel made famous in the surf media as Weasel Reef. The tiny take-off zone and aggressive locals make it nearly impossible for outsiders to get waves. Best during S-SW swells with low tides. Closes out as it exceeds head high size.

Park at the end of Stockton Avenue and look over the bluffs to find the wave in mid-cove.

Waddell Creek ①
Grayhound Rock

Ano Nuevo Bay

SANTA CRUZ COUNTY

17

9

Scott Creek ②
Davenport Landing ③
El Jarro Point Davenport Landing

Laguna Creek ④

San Vicente

1

1

Santa Cruz

Capitola Beach
Seacliff Beach

Four Mile ⑤
Table Rock
Needle Rock Point
Terrace Point
Santa Cruz Harbor
Opal Cliffs
Rio Del Mar

La Selva Beach

Natural Bridges ⑥   ⑦ Stocton Avenue
⑧ Swift Street
⑨ Mitchell's Cove

8. Swift Street

This meaty righthand reef works during large winter swells. Located outside of Stockton Avenue, it needs to be overhead to start working. Doesn't attract the crowds that Stockton does.

Breaking off of a remote-feeling bluff in a residential area, the beach is rocky and rugged, home to seal rookeries and, of course, the landlord.

9. Mitchell's Cove

Classic righthand pointbreak/sandbar set-up best during large, clean swells and low tides. Gets hollow, fast and crowded. One of the best spots in the county when it's on and the sections connect. Any swell, W to N, low incoming tide best.

Watch for shallow reef action on the outside take-off area and a wicked shorepound on the inside sandbar.

Stockton Avenue

PATRICK TREFZ

Natural Bridges

PATRICK TREFZ

Santa Cruz Town – West Side

1-4. Steamer Lane

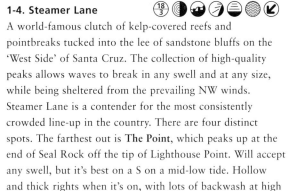

A world-famous clutch of kelp-covered reefs and pointbreaks tucked into the lee of sandstone bluffs on the 'West Side' of Santa Cruz. The collection of high-quality peaks allows waves to break in any swell and at any size, while being sheltered from the prevailing NW winds. Steamer Lane is a contender for the most consistently crowded line-up in the country. There are four distinct spots. The farthest out is **The Point**, which peaks up at the end of Seal Rock off the tip of Lighthouse Point. Will accept any swell, but it's best on a S on a mid-low tide. Hollow and thick rights when it's on, with lots of backwash at high tide. Tight and hyper competitive take-off zone.

The Slot is a wedgy righthander best on W swells and a medium to low tide. A good spot for tube rides or aerials,

Middle Peak, Steamer Lane

PATRICK TREFZ

as it tends to close out a bit. The take-off is close to the cliff, under the watchful gaze of hundreds of onlookers. Straight out from the access stairs and extending out and west towards the channel are several reefs, collectively called **Middle Peak**, then subdivided into First, Second, and Third Reefs. Best during N-NW swells, each reef works at a different size, but each boast heavy elevator drops followed by a softer righthand shoulder. The lefts, however, are usually steeper and hollower, but they can leave you caught inside by the next set coming in off The Slot or The Point. Middle Peak handles any size, although it becomes more challenging to read the line-up as the peaks shift around, keeping the pack on the move.

Further inside the headland, the next peak is the heavily surfed **Indicators**. When swell and tide are perfect, it's a long, classic righthand point wave with a gaggle of speed sections and lips ripe for shortboard tricks, as seen in surf publications and films worldwide. Best with a lined-up W-NW swell and medium-low tide. A great hotdog wave.

On a great day and a great swell, local heroes have been known to rip a few single mythical waves from The Point, through Middles, through Indicators, through Cowells to the shorebreak at Santa Cruz Municipal Pier. On those days you'll see stoked surfers, dripping wet, boards under their arms, jogging back up West Cliff Drive towards the Lane. It's the consistency and sheltered aspect that makes Steamer Lane an extremely crowded proposition with all kinds of wavecraft and talent levels. Wildlife is abundant, and you might find yourself paddling out through the kelp beside a sea otter or seal. There's parking all along the point and out at the Mark Abbott Memorial Lighthouse, which doubles as the Lighthouse Surf Museum.

Steamer Lane

ROB GILLEY

Boardwalk

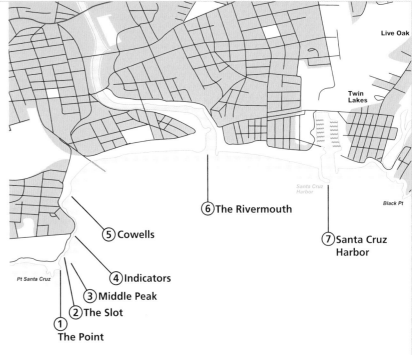

⑥ The Rivermouth

⑤ Cowells

⑦ Santa Cruz Harbor

④ Indicators

Pt Santa Cruz

③ Middle Peak

② The Slot

① The Point

Live Oak

Twin Lakes

Santa Cruz Harbor

Black Pt

PATRICK TREFZ

5. Cowells

A long, slow, mushy sand-bottomed point wave inside of Indicators, suitable for longboarding and beginners. Takes any bigger swell and works on all tides, frequently splitting into subsections that accommodate generous numbers of surfers. The best wave is usually closest to the cliff.

Getting hit by another longboard is probably your biggest worry here. There are a couple of sets of stairs making access to the waves easy for everyone. Restroom facilities.

6. The Rivermouth

The San Lorenzo River divides mid-town from the West Side. The right combination of river flow and swell will occasionally create perfect, hollow sandbar peaks at its mouth. Great rights and sometimes excellent lefts. Check it with a N or W swell and a low-mid tide. Tends to have good years and off years, depending mostly on rainfall in the area.

As with all rivermouths, be aware of rips on outgoing tides and, due to its location in the middle of town, runoff pollution can be bad when it rains heavily. Always crowded when it's on, which is hardly ever.

7. Santa Cruz Harbor

Seriously shallow suckout sandbar barrel breaking off the west jetty and across the entrance to the Santa Cruz Municipal Harbor. On big winter swells rides are possible right across the entrance and past the south jetty.

Broken boards and bodies are common. Experts only. It is illegal to surf here, so proceed with caution. The Army Corps of Engineers created the wave and now must slave to remove it with regular dredging.

Harbor

PATRICK TREFZ

The Rivermouth

BOB BARBOUR

Santa Cruz County – South

1. 26th Avenue

A stretch of beachbreak peaks with a bit of rock reef thrown in for interest, culminating in the rocky reef peak at Little Windansea off the end of Rockview Street. Good spots during springtime windswells and small summer S swells.

Detour around the harbor and head for the coast. Park on any number of side streets all of which emerge onto the beach.

26th Avenue Sandbar

2-6. Pleasure Point

One of the most famous and popular spots in California due to its reliability, expanse, and frequent good shape, groomed as the place is by forests of kelp. Several take-off spots, the first being **Sewer Peak**, a top-to-bottom barrel over a rock shelf. The lefts can be decent, but the rights are generally cleaner and longer. Heavily surfed by excellent shortboarders. Best with S and W swells and low tide.

Next comes **First Peak**, a utility spot. A quality righthander, very predictable and very crowded, because it is surfable on a variety of swell angles and tides. Fun on a big day when it's makeable all the way through to Insides. Moving further down the point, there's **Second Peak**, less of a peak and more of a lined-up wall than First Peak. Not as stellar, but it does have its day. Popular with the grommet pack. Directly out in front of Jack O'Neill's house is **Insides** (a.k.a. Middle Peak), a mushy reef peak occupied with longboarder cruisers and beginners. Some rocks on the inside; best with lower mid tides to minimize backwash but choked with kelp on bigger lows. As the name implies, it is a pleasure to surf here, if you don't mind crowds. There is parking at the top of the point, where you can view the whole mile-long set-up.

Pleasure Point

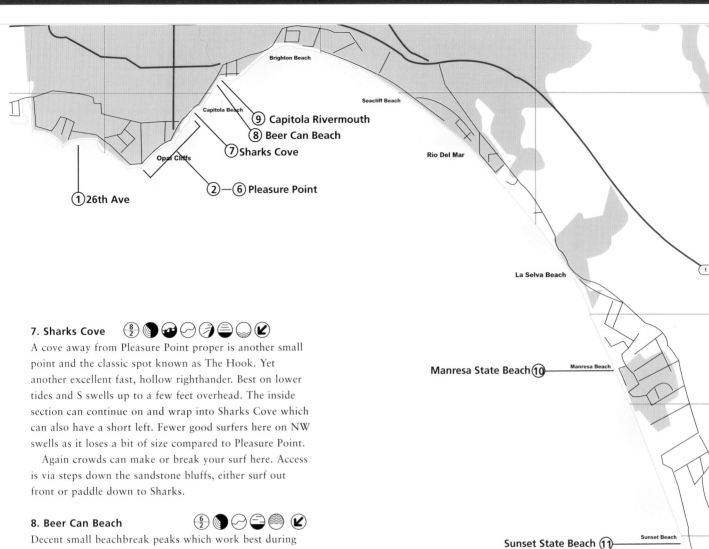

Brighton Beach

Seacliff Beach

Capitola Beach

⑨ Capitola Rivermouth

⑧ Beer Can Beach

⑦ Sharks Cove

Opal Cliffs

Rio Del Mar

② — ⑥ Pleasure Point

① 26th Ave

La Selva Beach

①

Manresa State Beach ⑩ — Manresa Beach

Sunset State Beach ⑪ — Sunset Beach

7. Sharks Cove

A cove away from Pleasure Point proper is another small point and the classic spot known as The Hook. Yet another excellent fast, hollow righthander. Best on lower tides and S swells up to a few feet overhead. The inside section can continue on and wrap into Sharks Cove which can also have a short left. Fewer good surfers here on NW swells as it loses a bit of size compared to Pleasure Point.

Again crowds can make or break your surf here. Access is via steps down the sandstone bluffs, either surf out front or paddle down to Sharks.

8. Beer Can Beach

Decent small beachbreak peaks which work best during small clean, peaky winter swells and high tide.

Gets crowded in the summertime. Take Via Palo Road from Clubhouse Drive; head for the stairway.

9. Capitola Rivermouth

Small, hollow beachbreak peaks which work during huge clean, peaky winter swells or a decent S and low tides.

Rivermouth will bring polluted runoff after rains. Like all Santa Cruz breaks, there is always potential for a crowd.

10. Manresa State Beach

A broad section of excellent and consistent beachbreak that's particularly popular due to the convenient parking lot. The surf can be good (or at least fun) here when the Santa Cruz town spots are flat. Peaks and channels, some current and shorepound action. Typically closes out at a few feet overhead. Mid to high tide with no wind on a peaky, broken-up swell are the primo conditions. Big swell window.

Pay to park; full facilities available.

11. Sunset State Beach

Very similar to Manresa but far less crowded, a little more easily blown out, and stronger currents and rips on bigger swells. Miles of empty beach leading south to the Pajaro River, which marks the county line. Potential for empty,

superb waves, especially with morning offshore winds.

Access is intermittent south of Sunset. The submarine canyon that slices the bay invites the odd larger fish. Camping is available.

Manresa State Beach

PATRICK TREFZ

Monterey County

1. Zmudowski State Beach

Consistent beachbreak waves on wide beach, surfable when small, peaky and clean with a high tide.

No pollution problems but rips and sharks prevalent. Pay to park.

2. Moss Landing State Beach
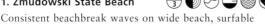

Excellent, extremely powerful sandbars produce some of California's best beachbreak waves, always bigger than anywhere else inside the bay. The Monterey Bay Submarine Canyon funnels swell directly into the beach, so waves are fast-moving and thick, a showcase of quality shape and heavy barrels. NW swells and mid-high incoming tides preferred. Offshore with SE storm winds. The surf down by the jetty is usually smaller than to the north, but is also the most crowded.

Beware of dangerous currents and sneaker sets. Even though there are plenty of peaks to choose from, the locals can be aggressive. There is a toll road for parking by the break. Lock your car. Camping nearby.

Moss Landing

3. Salinas River State Beach

Heavy beachbreak barrels near the Salinas Rivermouth, best with peaky W swells, high tide and SE wind. Similar to Moss Landing. Easy to find your own peak here.

Sharky due to the river outflow; also polluted at times from agricultural runoff.

4. Marina State Beach

Beachbreak barrels similar to Salinas; needs to be peaky and clean with a mid-high tide. E-SE wind is offshore.

Never crowded. Pay to use the car park above the break.

5. Del Monte Beach

Small gentle beachbreak peaks. Needs mid to high tide with small, peaky W-NW swells; a large SW swell may get in.

Accessed via Del Monte Avenue from Highway 1.

6. Lovers Point

Good left pointbreak in downtown Pacific Grove; only breaks with solid winter swells, bigger than head high. Offshore on southerly storm winds, so rainy conditions are the norm for Lovers Point sessions.

Watch out for a few exposed rocks at lower tides and protective locals.

7. Asilomar State Beach

Picturesque crescent beach flanked by two headlands. Three different take-off spots here, each with varying consistency and shape. The beachbreak in the middle of the bay packs a punch, and the reef areas at the north and south ends can get very good. The beachbreak works best on a mid-high tide, while both reefs prefer lows. All spots blow offshore with a SE storm wind.

Southern tip of a bay cruised by sharks. Heavy paddle-outs and currents when big.

Carmel Beach

DON BALCH

Cobblestones

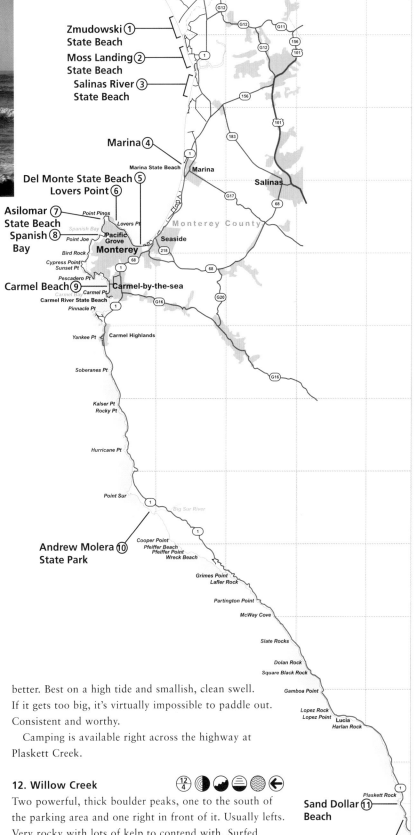

Zmudowski ① State Beach
Moss Landing ② State Beach
Salinas River ③ State Beach

Marina ④
Marina State Beach · Marina
Salinas
Del Monte State Beach ⑤
Lovers Point ⑥
Asilomar ⑦ State Beach · Point Pinos · Lovers Pt
Spanish ⑧ Spanish Bay · Point Joe · Pacific Grove · Monterey · Seaside
Bay · Bird Rock
Cypress Point · Sunset Pt
Pescadero Pt
Carmel Beach ⑨ Carmel Bay · Carmel Pt · Carmel-by-the-sea
Carmel River State Beach
Pinnacle Pt

Yankee Pt · Carmel Highlands

Soberanes Pt

Kalser Pt · Rocky Pt

Hurricane Pt

Point Sur
Big Sur River
Andrew Molera ⑩ State Park
Cooper Point
Pfeiffer Beach · Pfeiffer Point · Wreck Beach

Grimes Point · Lafler Rock

Partington Point

McWay Cove

Slate Rocks

Dolan Rock
Square Black Rock

Gamboa Point

Lopez Rock · Lopez Point · Lucia · Harlan Rock

Plaskett Rock
Sand Dollar ⑪ Beach

Willow Creek ⑫

8. Spanish Bay

Another scenic seascape, a.k.a South Moss Beach. Three spots here, all offshore with SE storm winds: the northernmost break is called **Dunes**, consistent righthanders over a reef/sand bottom. South of Dunes is a beachbreak commonly referred to as **Cobblestones**, despite the lack of any reef, surfable when small and clean; a powerful wave. Then there's **South Moss**, at the far south end of the bay – peaks that bomb on the outside then mush through to the inside. Works best with lower tides.

Pay to access through the Spanish Bay Golf Course & Resort. Reachable by paying the toll to drive onto the exclusive, golf course-rich 17 Mile Drive.

9. Carmel Beach

Decent sandbar peaks up and down the beach. Best with medium-high tides and small, clean, wedgy swells. Lots of room for everyone. There is an extremely rocky point at the southern end, which is occasionally rideable and gets crowded. Rocky Point a half mile south serves up the best waves amid ample portions of local attitude. Offshore with E wind.

Accessed at the end of Ocean Avenue through Carmel; park on the road by the picturesque beach. Famous for sunsets, the Pebble Beach golf course, Clint Eastwood, and exorbitant prices.

10. Andrew Molera State Park

Fast, thin righthand lines at the Big Sur Rivermouth; blows offshore with the prevailing NW wind, so it's a good call on swell days that are blown-out elsewhere. Needs a bigger W or S swell and lower tides to eliminate backwash. Semi-point set-up. Shallow gravel bottom. Beautiful spot.

Accessed by walking nearly a mile from the dirt lot at the park's entrance. Cheap camping here. Can get somewhat crowded with surfers and large sealife.

11. Sand Dollar Beach

Incredibly scenic white sand crescent beach, sometimes crowded with surfers and sunbathers. The north end is rarely surfed but offers some decent sandbar peaks. The south end, in front of the stairs, is predominantly a left peeling into a deep channel with a handy rip current to take you back out. Some rights, but the lefts are usually

better. Best on a high tide and smallish, clean swell. If it gets too big, it's virtually impossible to paddle out. Consistent and worthy.

Camping is available right across the highway at Plaskett Creek.

12. Willow Creek

Two powerful, thick boulder peaks, one to the south of the parking area and one right in front of it. Usually lefts. Very rocky with lots of kelp to contend with. Surfed frequently. Best with a glassy, peaky W swell, it can handle up to several feet overhead. Medium tides work best. The southernmost spot on the Big Sur coast.

Look for the Willow Creek Picnic Ground. There is a small car park with restrooms adjacent to the beach under the highway bridge.

San Luis Obispo – North

1. San Carpoforo Creek

Thick, powerful beachbreak barrels just below Big Sur. Consistent and usually well-shaped creek mouth sandbars; can be good at any tide, but mid-high is best. Blows out and closes out readily, making it a summer, smaller swell location.

Scant parking along the road above the beach, follow trail (obscure) down to the beach. Sometimes crowded.

2. Lighthouse/Cadis

Heavy-duty, hollow beachbreak on the north side of Point Piedras Blancas. Picks up all swells and can be good on any tide. Consistent and uncrowded. Very powerful.

Accessing the spot requires trespassing across a field from Highway 1.

Cayucos

Lighthouse/Cadis

3. Arroyo Laguna

Famous windsurfing spot, but occasionally gets good for surfing. Out front is a shallow beachbreak set-up, fast and hollow. Often closed out. At the south end of the break is a rock outcropping where a hollow right occasionally spins off at low tide. A good S swell nook

Watch for the creek marker along the highway. Park in the dirt lot on the west side of Highway 1 in front of the cattle gate and hop it to access the beach. Beware of huge elephant seals lounging onshore.

4. Pico Creek

Fun reef/sandbar right at the creek mouth to the north of San Simeon. Peaks on the outside before reforming into a speedy inside section leading into a nasty shorepound. Peaky beachbreak to the south with scattered submerged rocks.

Both spots work best with a clean SW swell and mid-high tide.

5. San Simeon Creek

Hollow beachbreak in front and to the south of the State Park campground. Frequently closed out. Needs a small, peaky swell with medium tide. A reef at the south end can produce some shapely lefts.

Park along Highway 1 in the dirt lot opposite the campground turn-off.

6. Exotics

Classic but somewhat rare lefthander at the very north end of Cambria. Hollow and fast. Needs a SW swell and high tide to break properly.

Located around the point from Leffingwell Landing. Check it from Highway 1 and park in the lot above the break off Moonstone Beach Drive.

7. Leffingwell Landing

A long righthand reef wave requiring big winter swells to break. Some sections, lots of boils, and not too hollow. Easy paddle out. Good when it's on; check here when everywhere else is maxed out. The local boys will be on it.

Located off Moonstone Beach Drive.

8. Santa Rosa Creek/Moonstone

Hollow, sectiony beachbreak best with smaller, peaky swells and medium tides. E wind is offshore. A consistent spot popular with shortboarders and bodyboarders.

Easily accessed from the paved car park above the beach. Restrooms here.

9. Cayucos Pier

Fairly reliable, hollow beachbreak, the best wave being the fast, thin right on the south side of the pier when the sandbar is properly shaped. Although often a close-out, can handle up to a few feet overhead with peakier swells. The lefts can get really good with summertime S swells. Blows offshore on a N wind, making the pier a popular surf spot in spring.

Shoreline structures (seawalls) appear to be threatening the surf around the Cayucos beaches. Parking nearby the break with all facilities.

10. Studio Drive/Old Creek

Flat sand and rock bottomed beach with average surf. Mushy. Closes out often but usually has something to ride.

Park in the dirt lot at the bottom of Studio Drive (traffic light on Highway 1).

San Carporforo Creek ①
Ragged Point
San Carporforo Creek
Breaker Point 1

Point Sierra Nevada
La Cruz Rock

Arroyo Laguna

Oak Knoll Creek

Lighthouse ②
Point Piedras Blancas

Arroyo Laguna ③

San Simeon Point

Pico Creek
1

Pico Creek ④

San Simeon Creek

San Simeon Creek ⑤

Exotics ⑥

Santa Rosa Creek

Leffingwell Landing ⑦

Santa Rosa Creek ⑧
Cambria

46

11. Morro Rock

Good, powerful beachbreak when big; fast and fun when small. Long, mushy lefts off The Rock. This consistent and reliable, W-facing swell-catcher attracts a crowd, however there's lots of room northward to spread out. Can be good on any tide. The entrance to Morro Bay can produce some waves in larger swells and the South Jetty beachbreaks are popular during smaller swells.

Morro Bay has undergone a significant beach nourishment program to counter a lack of natural sand replenishment. Jetskis (PWC) are considered a problem to the marine environment in this area.

Point Estero

1

Cayucos Point
Cayucos

Cayucos Pier ⑨ Cayucos State Beach

Studio Drive ⑩

Morro Rock ⑪
Morro Rock
Morro Bay

Baywood Park

Los Osos

Hazard Canyon

Point Buchon

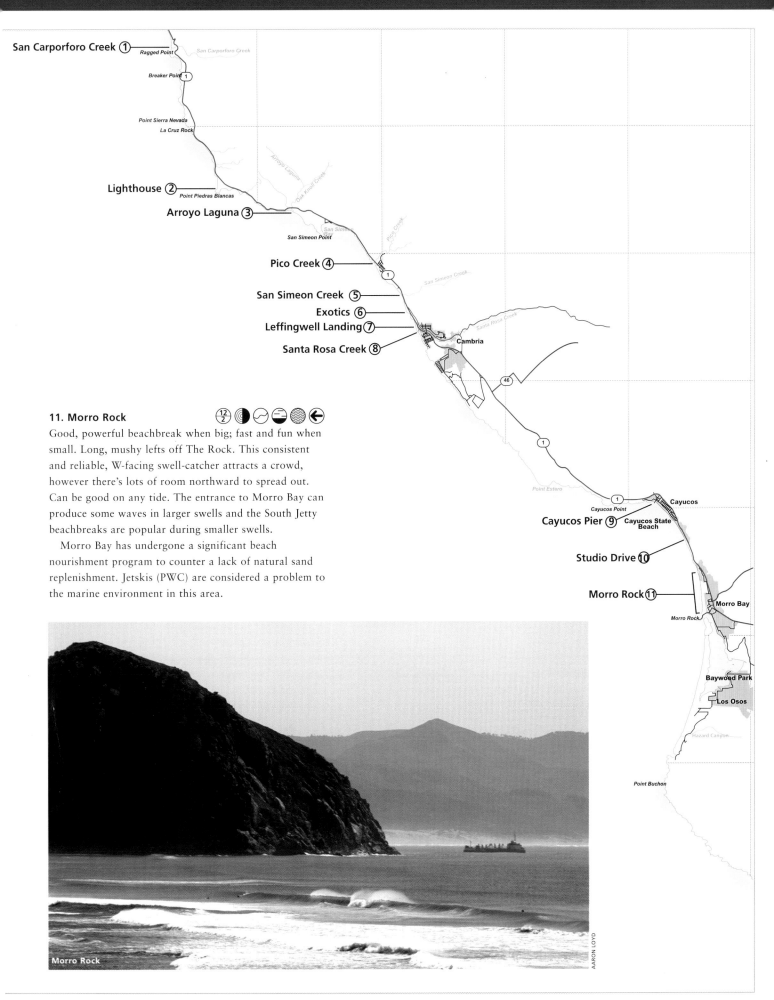

Morro Rock

AARON LOYD

Hazard Canyon

AARON LOYD

San Luis Obispo – South

1. Hazard Canyon

An extremely heavy, dangerous, and unforgiving righthand reef barrel replete with boils, suck-out ledges and wicked currents. The lefts are ridden too, but are far less formidable. The Canyon can be the area's best break when it's on. Glory days are usually mid winter, with overhead NW swell and SE storm wind. Experts only. Do not bring a crowd or your car (or face) will be thrashed. Unfriendly local crew.

Located within beautiful Montana de Oro State Park. Park along the road amongst the eucalyptus groves beside an unmarked trail to the beach.

2. Spooners Cove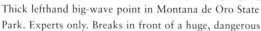

Thick lefthand big-wave point in Montana de Oro State Park. Experts only. Breaks in front of a huge, dangerous

Pismo Beach Pier

AARON LOYD

rock outcropping. Never closes out. A gnarly winter break. Easy to find with a park map.

3. Saint Anne's

Two crowded, mushy reef peaks south of Avila Beach, somewhat protected from NW winds. Better with low to medium tides and needs a big winter swell or strong S swell.

Only a medium consistency break but the crowds appear when it's on. Free roadside parking.

4. Pismo Beach Pier

Decent sandbar peaks up and down the beach, as far as you want to go. Can get hollow. High tides best with smaller, peaky swells from any direction. Tucked ever so slightly into the shelter of Point San Luis, a NE wind is offshore. Consistent and surfed regularly, particularly close to the pier where there's a little more shape.

With its quarter-mile-long illuminated pier and array of shops and restaurants, Pismo is a very popular tourist town during the summer, so expect crowds.

5. Oceano

Miles of beachbreak, wide open to wind and swell. Breaks further out the bigger it gets; the inside reforms are surfed when the outer bars are closing out. Can be rather mushy due the gradually sloping bottom contours. Best during the summer or on small, clean winter swells. High tides work best. Lots of room; crowds are never a factor.

Wicked currents and undertow. Accessed through one of the several parking lots in Pismo State Beach.

Santa Barbara – North

6. Santa Maria Rivermouth/ Guadalupe Beach

Powerful, hollow beachbreak that is never flat. Lots of wind. Sandbars are influenced by the flow of the Santa Maria River. The mouth can have an excellent sandbar following heavy rainfall. Best with incoming tides. Bad currents.

Located at the end of Highway 166 from Guadalupe. The road near the beach is often blanketed with sand.

7. Surf Beach

Isolated, gnarly beachbreak which never goes completely flat. Shapely during peaky swells with SE winds. Very hollow and usually difficult to paddle out. Never crowded, for good reason. Sharky and loads of bad currents. Incoming and high tides work best; harsh rip currents with outgoing tides.

Located at the end of Highway 246. Do not walk north or south of the beach in front of the train station; you will be fined. These areas are strictly off-limits from March 1 to September 30 to allow nesting for endangered snowy plover dune birds. As of February 2002, all public access to Surf Beach has been sealed off by the US Air Force. Quoting September 11 and endangered bird nesting site protection as primary reasons, it's not even surfable by the handful of crewcut surfers on Vandenberg Air Force Base.

8. Jalama Beach County Park

Chunky, shifty beachbreak waves in front of the campground and to the south (known as Cracks). Best with smaller, peaky swells, no wind and high tide. Very popular spot with Santa Barbara surfers and windsurfers. Further south down the beach, the peak at Tarantulas (or T's) is triggered by a rock reef, producing an excellent left peeling into a channel and a decent right racing towards inshore rocks. Jalama catches most available swell, but it's best in the cold morning offshores, since the wind absolutely rips most afternoons.

Located at the end of twisting 14-mile-long (22km) Jalama Road, off scenic Highway 1.

Jalama Beach County Park

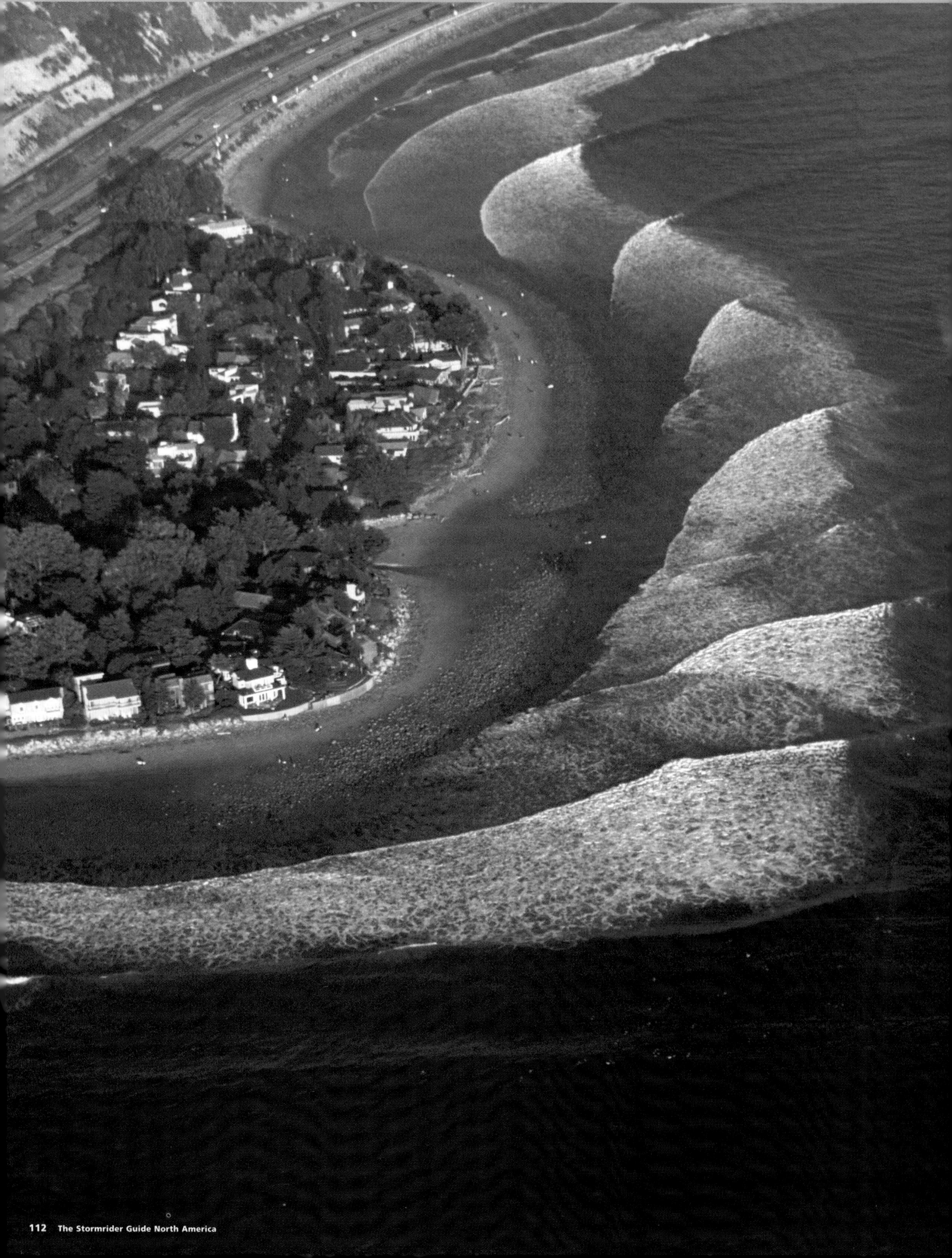

Southern California

Everything you've heard about Southern California is true: ridiculous crowds, plenty of pollution, appalling congestion, hideous strip malls, hundreds of square miles of houses, freeways, lofty living expenses, image paranoia, bikinis, and...relatively weak surf. Although Santa Barbara, Ventura, Los Angeles, Orange, and San Diego counties each boast a handful of heavy surf spots, the general consensus among those who've surfed SoCal all their lives is that the surf really is quite marginal on the West Coast wave scale.

However, consistency is a virtue; there's always somewhere to surf (okay, you may have to use a longboard, but at least it's surfing), as long as the pesky afternoon onshores lay low. Early morning offshore winds are commonplace, especially during winter Santa Ana conditions, but tend to slap down the size of approaching swells.

Here, the concept of a secret spot is an oxymoron. It seems like everybody in SoCal surfs – after all, this is the birthplace of modern surfing and home to most of the sport's industry. Surfing in SoCal is mostly an urban experience until you get into Santa Barbara; a pastoral landscape exemplifying what the rest of SoCal must have looked like before the blitzkrieg of bulldozers and concrete. But if it's mild weather and easy waves you seek, SoCal is still a good place – if you don't mind crowds and high prices. At the very least, you'll feel a part of surfing history.

Morning light at Rincon.

ROB GILLEY

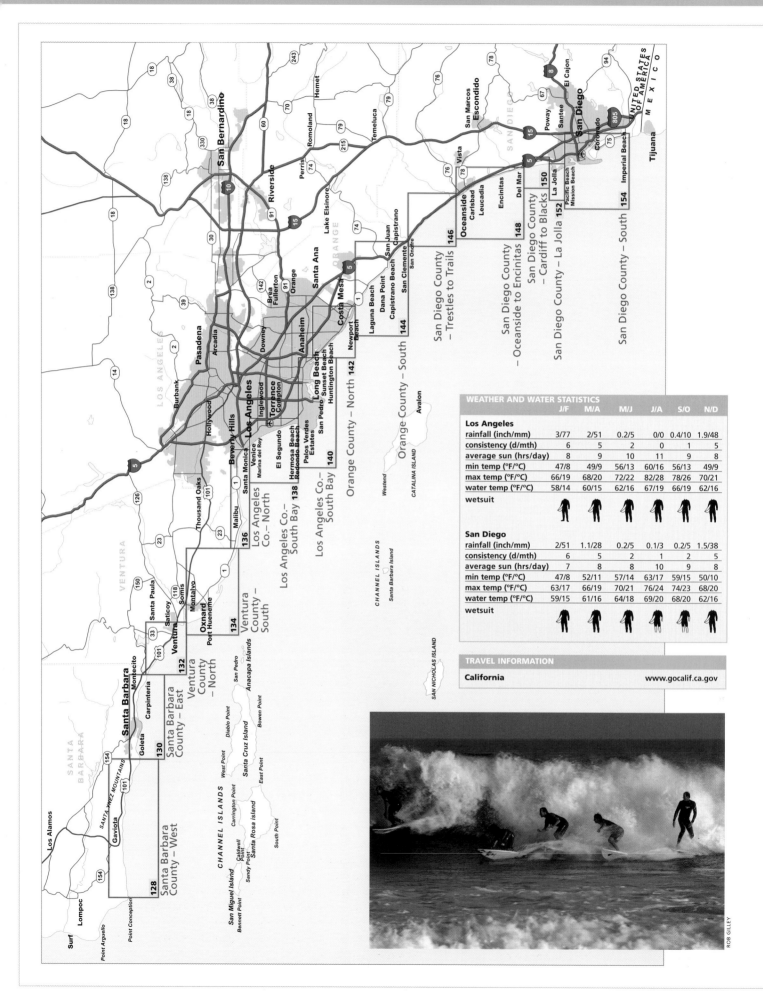

Surf
Los Alamos
Lompoc
Point Arguello
Point Conception

SANTA BARBARA
Santa Barbara County – West 128
Gaviota
SANTA YNEZ MOUNTAINS
Goleta 130
Santa Barbara County – East
Santa Barbara
Montecito
Carpinteria

CHANNEL ISLANDS
San Miguel Island
Bennett Point
Caldwell
Sandy Point
Santa Rosa Island
West Point
Carrington Point
Santa Cruz Island
East Point
South Point
Diablo Point
Anacapa Islands
San Pedro
Bowen Point

Ventura County – North 132
Ventura
Santa Paula
Saticoy
Somis
Montalvo
Oxnard
Port Hueneme 134
Ventura County – South

CHANNEL ISLANDS
Santa Barbara Island
SAN NICHOLAS ISLAND
SAN NICHOLAS ISLAND

Thousand Oaks
Malibu
Los Angeles Co.– North 136
Santa Monica
Venice
Marina del Rey
El Segundo
Hermosa Beach
Redondo Beach
Los Angeles Co.– South Bay 138
Palos Verdes Estates
San Pedro 140
Los Angeles Co.– South Bay

LOS ANGELES
Pasadena
Arcadia
Burbank
Hollywood
Beverly Hills
Los Angeles
Inglewood
Torrance
Compton
Downey
Long Beach
Sunset Beach
Huntington Beach
Newport Beach 142
Orange County – North 142

San Bernardino
Riverside
Perris
Romoland
Lake Elsinore
Hemet
Temecula
ORANGE
Santa Ana
Anaheim
Brea
Fullerton
Orange
Costa Mesa
Laguna Beach
Dana Point
Capistrano Beach
San Juan Capistrano
San Clemente
San Onofre
Orange County – South 144
Avalon
CATALINA ISLAND
Westend

San Diego County – Trestles to Trails 146
Oceanside 146
Carlsbad
Leucadia
Encinitas
Del Mar
San Diego County – Oceanside to Encinitas 148
Pacific Beach
Mission Beach
La Jolla 150
San Diego County – Cardiff to Blacks 152
San Diego County – La Jolla 152
Coronado
Imperial Beach 154
San Diego County – South 154

San Marcos
Escondido
Vista
Poway
Santee
El Cajon
San Diego
Tijuana

UNITED STATES OF AMERICA
MEXICO
SAN DIEGO

WEATHER AND WATER STATISTICS

	J/F	M/A	M/J	J/A	S/O	N/D
Los Angeles						
rainfall (inch/mm)	3/77	2/51	0.2/5	0/0	0.4/10	1.9/48
consistency (d/mth)	6	5	2	0	1	5
average sun (hrs/day)	8	9	10	11	9	8
min temp (°F/°C)	47/8	49/9	56/13	60/16	56/13	49/9
max temp (°F/°C)	66/19	68/20	72/22	82/28	78/26	70/21
water temp (°F/°C)	58/14	60/15	62/16	67/19	66/19	62/16
wetsuit						
San Diego						
rainfall (inch/mm)	2/51	1.1/28	0.2/5	0.1/3	0.2/5	1.5/38
consistency (d/mth)	6	5	2	1	2	5
average sun (hrs/day)	7	8	8	10	9	8
min temp (°F/°C)	47/8	52/11	57/14	63/17	59/15	50/10
max temp (°F/°C)	63/17	66/19	70/21	76/24	74/23	68/20
water temp (°F/°C)	59/15	61/16	64/18	69/20	68/20	62/16
wetsuit						

TRAVEL INFORMATION

California www.gocalif.ca.gov

ROB GILLEY

Left – **With its balmy climate Southern Cal could be mistaken for the South Pacific, were it not for the maddening crowds.** (opposite)

DON BALCH

The Surf, Ocean Environment and Surf Culture

Southern California is the birthplace of modern surf culture and the surf industry. Essentially one massive megalopolis from Santa Barbara to the Mexican border, few people visit here without coming to some sort of conclusion that, hey, this would be a damn nice place to live. Jobs are abundant, the weather's hard to beat, and there's white sand beaches galore. So it is that this mindscape has been romanticized as a Mediterranean Utopia, when in actuality, it's a vastly overpopulated concrete jungle pulsing with rampant development, traffic jams, opulent malldoms, and ever-thickening swarms of surfers. In SoCal, the water's relatively warm, the waves are generally small and forgiving, and there are lifeguards to rescue your lily-white ass should the need arise. Plus throngs of thonged girls on the beach? Yo, this may have been ground zero for the homogenized Beach Boys/Surfin' USA fairytale, but it was also ground zero for Dick Dale and Miki Dora. Virtual light years away from the realities of the Central and Northern shores of the state, this is the zone described by *Surfer* magazine's Steve Barilotti as "the Hollywood of surfing," but that doesn't mean that Hollywood (or local television and newsprint, too, for that matter) has ever understood the peculiar savor of surfing in California.

In summertime, the beaches of Southern California can be a dry sauna stuffed with millions of people, a carnival set appointed with imported desert sand and tired palm trees, sweaty policemen and self-important volleyball squads, uptight and overworked lifeguards, clueless tourist hordes, ageless surgically-reconstructed women, screaming children, skate punks and muscle people, suffocating smog and a concrete river system, endless parking meters, spotless SUVs, intense signage, homeless bums, homeless moms and homeless kids, fast-food trash blowing through trashed ecosystems, toxic bonfires, cigarette butts, broken glass, shit, urine, and stormdrains heading out to sea,

airplanes, traffic helicopters, men with shopping carts collecting aluminum cans in the parking lot, and greasy suntan lotion smeared all over everything.

While more and more Southern California beachgoers pursue the surfing lifestyle, the area's allotment of waves remains (on a good year) static. Meanwhile, the influx continues, keeping developers and merchants in a perpetual frenzy to meet the burgeoning demands of overconsumption. Fortunately and unfortunately, the Pacific Ocean is one of the few escapes from the horrors of society, sort of.

Localism – given broad lip service as the bane of surfing – seems hardwired into the mainframes of human behavior, and down here it's a program that uploads all too often in the line-up. As one SoCal refugee proclaims, it's a matter of "not enough nature to go around" and "too many dogs after the same food." And so, putting on their thinking caps, surfers make it worse with localism. That way, nobody gets to have a nice day. "Too many cocks in the chicken coop," a native San Diegan says, "and there's always someone who wants to rule the roost."

Southern California begins where the coast swings a big right angle bend at Points Arguello and Conception. Here the windy, deep-water Central Coast comes to an abrupt end as the shoreline swings around to face the sun and the warm south. Since prevailing winds along the US West mainland are from the NW, the effect is to reduce that meat grinder of wind and swell to the comfortable beach climate that has spawned a world of lifeguards, movie stars, and glistening flesh.

As one surf scribe put it, "The two worlds clasping weary hands at the tip of Point Conception are as distinctly opposite as if they were separate planets locked in their own respective orbits." As a result, Santa Barbara County is cleaved in two, the north essentially a Central Coast kind of place, the south a pivotal part of Southern California's surf scene.

Santa Barbara County

Santa Barbara County begins at the Santa Maria River, south of which are five miles (8km) of raw, exposed beachbreak, then 35 miles (56km) of publicly inaccessible Vandenberg Air Force Base beaches. Your best option for surfing the county begins at Jalama Beach, a long, sandy beach with some distinct reefs located in the SW-facing saddle between Arguello and Conception (thus neither Central nor SoCal). A portal of consistent swell and hellish side-onshore winds, which have made it California's

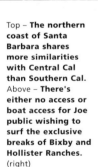

premier wavesailing spot, Jalama is remote, dynamic, and occasionally a good surf spot. Past Conception are the private but notorious Bixby and Hollister ranches, good surf inaccessible to anyone without a good boat or a drive-in connection. Between Gaviota and Goleta,

there are reefs and sandbars but not much access. Nearing Goleta, civilization dramatically increases, but a session in good winter surf is a genuine possibility, you just have to know where to look. Below Goleta, the Santa Barbara shoreline basically consists of a lot of mediocre beachbreaks, a few quirky reefs, and some righthand points (one of them epic), which are well-known and brutally crowded.

Santa Barbara County is similar to Santa Cruz County in terms of geology, microclimates, and surf potential (but for the Channel Islands), only with a chaparral instead of fir trees and no San Jose sprawl just over the hill. Most swells hit north county (in one place or another), and it's rarely flat north of Point Conception, although the area is highly susceptible to adverse winds. East of Point Conception, the Channel Islands do a fine job of denying S swells from this area, except for parts of the Bixby Ranch and a few spots near Montecito. Don't bother coming here in summer unless you're seeking exorbitant hotel prices and plenty of traffic; you probably won't get wet either, unless you've got a longboard or snorkeling gear.

Ah, lovely Santa Barbara! Just whispering the name evokes images of a swank Western Riviera caked with impressive homes, sun-burnt tourists, incessant sunshine, and piles of cash. Santa Barbara certainly has a ladle in the Southern California stew, and the south county rivals areas like Huntington Beach for crowds and congestion. It's been said of surfing here, "you might as well be in Orange County," but that's a mighty stretch. It's different. Although the city of Santa Barbara is affluent and scenic with the old Spanish influence everywhere, especially downtown, where even the malls are done adobe-style stucco amidst genuine historic structures, tiled alleyways, towering palms, and neo-rancho tourist shops, much of this S-facing coast – with the pristine peaks of the Santa Ynez Mountains barricading the north and the Channel Islands guarding the southern prospect – is still raw and undeveloped.

Top – **The northern coast of Santa Barbara shares more similarities with Central Cal than Southern Cal.**
Above – **There's either no access or boat access for Joe public wishing to surf the exclusive breaks of Bixby and Hollister Ranches.**
(right)

The seawall removal at Goleta Beach was a big victory for the Santa Barbara Surfrider Foundation Chapter, but even larger issues include the proposed golf course atop the pristine bluffs at Naples (just west of Goleta) and the preservation of the Gaviota Coast in general, which is threatened by development. In fact, the stretch of beach from Coal Oil Point in the south to Point Sal in the north is basically the last unspoiled coastal area in Southern California. Surfrider and the Gaviota Coast Conservancy want to see the area transformed into a federal park; this stance has drawn both praise and fierce opposition. Many locals don't want the government controlling the land in their backyard; at the same time, they don't want urban development either.

Ocean water-quality is tested weekly at several popular beaches county-wide. The Surfrider chapter continues to oppose the US National Park Service's decision to dump rat poison on Anacapa Island to kill non-native animal species. It also believes the county needs to find a new location for a landfill to replace the nearly-full Tajiguas landfill (a half-mile from the ocean just west of Refugio), which is polluting an adjacent creek. The chapter stages regular beach clean-ups, stormdrain stenciling, and the annual Rincon Clean Water Classic surf contest. Oil pollution is a problem in north county, after an agreement between the county's attorney general and UNOCAL, which stalls clean-up of the Nipomo Dunes at Guadalupe Beach, site of occasionally epic sandbars. The company is appealing court orders to clean up the place after being busted for the biggest toxic spill in California history, to the tune of $42 million in fines and $200-300 million for perhaps a decade of oil clean-up, mandated by a recent Surfrider settlement.

The father of surfing in Santa Barbara was a lifeguard named Gates Foss, who started surfing a plank in 1929, then went south to meet with Pete Peterson to get blueprints for Tom Blake hollow-board construction. Foss pioneered surfing at Three Mile (now called Rincon) back in 1934. He and other lifeguards were also first at Jalama, Refugio, and most of the other Santa Barbara area beaches in the '40s and '50s. Gates (appropriately) had keys to the Ranch gates, and surfed the spots out to Point Conception with his friend Ken Kesson as early as 1957. Story is, El Capitan Beach was first ridden by Paul Hodgert and Tom Lenzie (also Santa Barbara guards) in 1958.

In the mid-1950s, Rincon and the other Santa Barbara spots, become the winter escape for wave-starved Malibu surfers like Mickey Dora, Lance Carson, Dewey Weber, Kemp Aaberg, and Bob Cooper. After glassing boards for Hobie and learning the art of shaping from Velzy, Reynolds Yater came north and opened his Santa Barbara Surf Shop in the fall of 1959. Soon after, Cooper moved up and stayed until highway expansion buried his beachfront house and a surf spot called Stanleys in 1969.

In 1962, a Montecito kid named George Greenough built a 7'8" 'baby' surfboard, but never rode it much, as he took up knee-riding instead. In 1965, he created his first flexible fiberglass spoon (the revolutionary Velo), which he took with him to Australia, where he met Bob McTavish, thus initiating the cross-pollination that led to the shortboard revolution of '67-'68. An asocial, mysto character who flew under the radar, Greenough epitomized an individualistic, non-commercial approach to surfing that inspired other local surfers, as reflected in Santa

DAVID PU'U

Naples Point, Goleta

RON STONER/SURFER MAGAZINE

Barbara's reputation as a 'black wetsuit' zone. It follows then, that SB's most famous competitive surfer, Tom Curren, proved to be one of the most private, low-key champs of all time, with a penchant for riding logo-free surfboards. Another product of Al Merrick's Channel Islands Surfboard dynasty, SB's Kim Mearig was an equally straightforward champion ('83-'84), adding more proof that the area's waves are capable of producing top talent.

Santa Barbara surfers – and therefore the range of surfing experiences here – vary widely. North county surfers tend to be more hardy and prone to ride big surf, while south county surfers are more accustomed to smaller, mellower waves in tamer surroundings. North county is harsh and unpredictable, precisely the opposite of the sheltered south, where the ocean can honestly look like a lake on any given day.

Top – **Removal of the seawall at Goleta has reinstated waves like this, but this whole stretch is still under threat of development.**
Above – **Small right points make up the majority of the spots in SB. Hammonds Reef 1966.**

Ventura County

Significantly more exposed to most swells than Santa Barbara, the scenic Ventura County coast is a haven for summertime S pulses, wintertime NWs, and just about everything in between. Consistent and high quality surf is not uncommon, and there is a diverse wealth of surf spots to choose from on any given day, from pounding beachbreak barrels to slow beginner's waves. Down here, the Channel Islands don't have as prominent a swell-shadowing effect as they do in southern Santa Barbara County, which can be waist high during a big summer swell while Ventura County is double overhead. However, due to the angle of the coast, onshore winds are usually

Top – **Ventura County has world class beachbreak. Silver Strand bomb.** Above – **Ventura is not usually noted for its serene, empty, inviting line-ups. Dawn patrol cruising.**

stronger here than in Santa Barbara, and all Ventura spots blow out fairly easily. Fortunately, strong offshore winds are common, especially during the winter in the Oxnard area, creating classic conditions.

Rincon Point is generally considered a Santa Barbara break, but it's just over the Ventura County line. In fact, there's a series of points and reefs all along the county's northern shores, from Punta Gorda (Little Rincon) to Pitas to California Street. These loosely-populated areas south

of Mussel Shoals along Highway 1 usually offer some sort of uncrowded option for waves. You'll find a much denser pack at Overhead and California Street. From the city of Ventura south, there are some world-class beachbreaks like the Santa Clara Rivermouth and Hollywood-by-the-Sea/Silver Strand. S swells do better at the Oxnard/south county spots like Point Mugu, which is off-limits to anyone without military ID. W swells typically have the most power and are more lined-up at most county spots. The sandbar at the Santa Clara Rivermouth forms after heavy winter rains and can be the best rivermouth break in California. The locals are not nice, however. The best NW-swell spots are at the county's north and south ends – Rincon and County Line. Most waves in the county can been seen from Highways 1 or 101 and are easily accessible. Ventura offers a fun variety of surf and a range of experiences, from extreme localism to good-time camaraderie. Bottom line: whatever you're looking for, Ventura County has it.

The big issue here is the removal of the Matilija Dam on the Ventura River, about 15 miles (24km) upstream of the ocean. Years ago, the Ventura chapter of Surfrider formed the Matilija Coalition to coordinate efforts for the dam's removal because dams accelerate coastal erosion by stopping the natural transport of sediment into the coastal zone. Through dedicated efforts, what was long seen as just a few surfers and fishermen wanting to take down a dam, developed into a real momentum. Surfrider activists believe that removing the Matilija Dam will provide a long-term solution to some of Ventura County's most significant beach erosion problems by restoring the river's natural hydrologic activity and accompanying sediment transport. Another key aspect of dam removal is habitat restoration – improving aquatic and terrestrial ecosystems to benefit fish and wildlife species, particularly the endangered steelhead trout. In October 2000, the chapter's efforts were rewarded when more than 200 people representing both government and citizen organizations converged on the dam, and federal Interior Secretary Bruce Babbitt symbolically tore off a large chunk of the dam with a crane in Ventura County Flood Control District's "demolition demonstration project," which removed some 200 tons of concrete, taught some engineering lessons, and elevated the political momentum for complete removal of the obsolete dam.

Water quality is a primary concern in the county, especially at the mouth of the Santa Clara River, which hosts a world-class sandbar at times, amidst beaucoup toxins, micro-organisms, and other human and inhuman detritus.

Sandwiched between the glitz of Los Angeles and downtown Santa Barbara, mostly-rural Ventura County is a melting pot of SoCal and CenCal surf mentalities – surfers of all ages, races, and sexes, the vast majority

Left – **The north county hosts some heavy point action. Local master Tom Curren hiding from the sun at Supertubes.**
Middle – **Cleaning up an oil spill from a stream in San Jon Road, 1999.**
Below – **Lance Carson and Mike Hynson at Rincon, when development and crowds had yet to engulf the Queen of the Coast, 1965.**

DAVID PU'U

DAVID PU'U

friendly, down-to-earth types. But, as you may have heard, there have been a few bad apples. Territorial enforcement has resulted in near drownings of non-locals, a few cars burned, a number stolen, numerous boards broken or fins busted out, wetsuits ripped off, considerable theft of personal possessions from cars, etc.

Occasionally, this xenophobic Silver Strands mentality oozes onto adjacent beaches. In September 1995, Oxnard's David Ortega head-butted Mark Aaron in the chest, breaking a rib, after claiming Aaron wasn't allowed to surf at Port Hueneme pier. Ortega, then 21, later pleaded no contest to the misdemeanor assault on Aaron, 41, a Santa Monica junior high school teacher.

"We went to Hueneme for the first time," Aaron told the Associated Press. "We pulled over just north of the pier, and we were putting our wetsuits on. Within a few minutes, this guy gets out raving, asking, 'Where are you from? You can't surf here.' We said, 'We're from LA.' He said, 'Get out of here.'"

In May 1996, a Ventura County judge ordered Ortega to five days in jail and banned him from surfing Port Hueneme for three years as a condition of his probation. A few days after the sentencing, Ortega was caught

surfing Hueneme, netting him six months of jail time. Of course, such cases are isolated; although certain spots (like the Santa Clara Rivermouth and Silver Strand) don't put out welcome mats for strangers, you're generally safe anywhere in the county. What you might find lacking in friendliness will most likely be made up in wave quality.

Surfing has come a long way in Ventura County since its breaks were first ridden in the 1930s, Rincon by Gates Foss and other Santa Barbara guys, the Overhead by Santa Monica surfers like Porter Vahn, Joe Quigg, Tommy Zahn, Bob Simmons, Buzzy Trent, and Matt Kivlin, Point Mugu by any number of LA explorers. While Rincon, the Overhead, and C Street had considerable caché in the '50s and '60s, Oxnard attracted notice in 1972, when locals Malcolm and Duncan Campbell invented the "Bonzer" surfboard – a three-fin configuration with twin-concaves in the tail.

RON STONER/SURFER MAGAZINE

JIM RUSSI

Los Angeles County

Los Angeles County's surf is as diverse as its population. From big-wave bays to the most gutless longboard reefs, LA has all the bases covered. The span from Point Mugu to Santa Monica faces almost due S, and its beaches want solid S and W swells to transform them into surf spots (although WNWs do wrap in to some nooks and crannies). W swells generally have no problem in producing quality surf along this stretch of coast. To the south, from Santa Monica to Rancho Palos Verdes, the coast bends into a WSW-facing direction, thus picking up loads more swell than anywhere else in the county. Winter swells are funneled directly into the Palos Verdes peninsula, thanks to a deep-water submarine canyon, thus the large seasonal reef surf here. The Long Beach area is basically shielded from all swells by the peninsula and the gargantuan breakwall.

In the years before the breakwall was constructed, Long Beach was a great place to be a surfer. As a whole, Los Angeles County is as consistent as Ventura and picks up a tad more swell than San Diego and Orange counties, especially in the South Bay and around the Palos Verdes peninsula. However, with the exception of the peninsula and the area north of Santa Monica, most of LA is beachbreak; you can cruise for hours looking for a wave that holds up longer than five seconds. But, summer or winter, you can almost always find a decent wave around the Palos Verdes peninsula, which is essentially the crown jewel of LA surfing, apart from Malibu. Onshore wind is a problem on more westerly-facing beaches, as it usually begins like clockwork at about 11a.m. unless there's a storm.

It's doubtful that many of LA's thousands of surfers have much of a sense of the old history. It probably seems irrelevant, but through the stories of the early pioneers you get a taste of how it was and how much this place has changed. Today, Los Angeles (often referred to as 'Hell-A' or 'Smell-A') is often draped in smog, covered with concrete, and saturated with cars, commerce, and humans (roughly 10 million of them). There's a long stretch of beaches west of downtown LA, which was once a rural haven for scoring abalone and lobster, for sunbathing, surfing, diving, and swimming. Rural no more; most have deteriorated over the years into convenient public sewage outlets, gaudy boardwalks, gang warfare turf, scenes of countless crimes, and, in the case of Long Beach, a brackish basin of calm saltwater, thanks to the Port of Los Angeles' now-useless breakwall. Begun in 1911, the first 8,500ft (2550m) section of the breakwater accompanied a widening of the channel to 800ft (240m) and dredging to 30ft (9m). It was the construction of the 18,500ft

Above – **The Palos Verdes peninsula provides a rocky, big wave forum, courtesy of a submarine canyon.** Below – **LA County has a diverse array of wave types including a few semi-secret reefs.**

DAVID PU'U

DON BALCH

Obviously, the problems in LA are consistent with most overdeveloped areas: non-source-point pollution caused by runoff, elimination of open space and natural filtration and drainage, and a lack of knowledge and stewardship in companies and individuals all contribute to the problem. Meanwhile, California has destroyed more than 95% of its original wetlands, which once provided filtration of runoff waters returning to the sea. In general, as in many urban areas round the world, there is a general lack of environmental laws in LA and a concomitant lack of enforcement of existing laws, including the Clean Water Act.

Aside from the three visiting Hawaiians who may or may not have stood to ride the surf in Santa Cruz in 1885, Los Angeles County is where California surf culture all began. The founding padre of the tribe was George Freeth, the 23-year old Irish-Hawaiian brought to Long Beach by

Left – **Conurbations mean concrete. Runoff discharge is a serious problem for the whole of SoCal.** Below and bottom – **Malibu was as busy in '65 as it is now, but with less regulations back then when the land wasn't owned by film stars.**

(5550m) extension, completed in 1937, that put the kibosh on surfing at Long Beach.

To add insult to injury, over recent decades, the population in the LA-metro area has swollen to some 10 million people. With development came the desire to lay down concrete and channelize the two major rivers of the watershed that empties into the ocean at Long Beach. This created a nightmare, a textbook case of urban runoff. What's left is a body of water (San Pedro Bay) that has little circulation and a steady influx of toxic runoff.

When the US Navy closed its base at Long Beach in the 1990s, it left the breakwater behind. The local Surfrider chapter is promoting a precedent-setting campaign to purposefully reconfigure the breakwater. The general public (and some politicians and bureaucrats, too) has already concluded that the rivers must be cleaned up, and controls are being put into place in ten-year plans. Surfrider expects the LA rivers will meet the present Clean Water Act standard of being fishable and swimmable by the time today's children are in their senior years.

JIM RUSSI

LEROY GRANNIS

LEROY GRANNIS

Above – **Palos Verdes Cove in 1939 had a more sharing vibe than the intimidating modern line-up.** Below – **Saving some strength to haul heavy boards home was always advisable at PV Cove.**

Henry Huntington to wow the crowds at the terminus of his new rail line, Redondo Beach. Tom Blake was a Santa Monica lifeguard in the 1920s and was the first to surf Malibu, along with Sam Reid. Duke Kahanamoku acted in Hollywood and could just as well have been first, since he gave an exhibition of surfboard riding off the Hotel Virginia in 1922 (before a crowd of some 5,000 persons). At the time, Freeth's influence had already spread. "Local boys held their own with the Duke when it came to riding the boards," the *Los Angeles Daily Telegram* reported.

Los Angeles was the seedbed of California surf culture; these were the beaches from which emerged Pete Peterson, Bob Hogan, Bob Simmons, Joe Quigg, Dave Velzy, Greg Noll, Miki Dora and Dewey Weber and a thousand other notables, not to mention the all-but-forgotten discovery generation of the '30s and '40s: Haig Priest, Chauncey Granstrom, Marian Cook, Johnny Dale, Marold Eystone, Mel Crawford, Hoppy Swarts, and Mike Stange. This is where surfers got a look at themselves through the lenses of Doc Ball and LeRoy Grannis, where there were surf clubs and where the first surfboard store was established (Velzy with Hap Jacobs in 1950). The contrast of contemporary Los Angeles with the world these surfers once knew could scarcely be more extreme.

LEROY GRANNIS

By Y2K, LA boasted the largest urban surfing population in the US and was the nation's most populous county. As you might expect, the line-ups in LA are almost always crowded; there are no secret spots. If you're seeking solitude and tranquility, LA is not advised. But if you do surf here, you'll find a most diverse group of surfers, generally all urban folk accustomed to surfing in smoggy air and semi-polluted water at spots with a backdrop of noisy streets, tall buildings, condos, boardwalks, restaurants, dense tracts of beach homes, with the occasional natural outcropping of rock or reef. Tensions run high in many line-ups; longboards and shortboards collide along with the young and the old. Such is the habitat of the modern LA surfer. A few places are particular 'hot spots' for bad vibes – you've got the renowned Lunada Bay, a rocky horseshoe cove on the Palos Verdes Peninsula with a pretty epic righthand reef at its north end. Capable of holding up to 20 feet (6m), Lunada is one of the few bona fide big-wave spots in Southern California, and it's also one of the few places where the local surfers manage to make the six o'clock news. For years, a victim's code of silence protected the already-sheltered 'Bay Boys,' an odd clan of affluent surfers who live in PV Estates, an enclave of affluence in this relative wilderness area. All apparently grown men, they had a reputation for harassing visiting surfers – hurling rocks, waxing windshields, deflating tires, flapping their mouths, and worse. It has generally had the desired effect, causing outsiders to simply surf elsewhere to avoid possible hassles.

After a particularly egregious period of harassment, intimidation, vandalism and physical violence, the South Bay chapter of Surfrider teamed up with the PVE police, the LA County Sheriff's Dept, Surfline.com, and a coalition of surfers and other beach users to make the area safe and accessible to all. The anti-localism effort involves a 'call before you surf' check in with PVE police, a waterproof camera loan program for documentation of incidents, web-camera monitoring, and so on, along with beach clean-ups. The hope is the program will serve as a pilot for other beaches. Pity it's needed.

Orange County

A mixed bag, preferring SW pulses and zero wind, Orange County is more of a small-wave/beachbreak frontier than anything else. Also the hub of the 'surf industry', as it happens, catering to millions of surfers worldwide, and an abundance of surfers right nearby. Too many, in fact. They wait, elbow-to-elbow, noseguard-to-leash plug in the generally mediocre line-ups ... which do get good on occasion, to be sure. Quite good. But, for the most part, Orange County waves are comparatively weak on the global scale, easily disturbed by the slightest onshore breeze, and typically don't last more than four seconds from take-off to close-out. Those big blue 'n sunny Salt Creek barrel photos the magazines have teased you with for the past three decades are actually glorified close-outs – same with Newport and Huntington. It's cruel, but it's true.

Jetties and piers play a major role in determining surf quality from Seal Beach (first spot clear of the LA breakwater) to Newport Beach, which is all fairly consistent beachbreak, home to such wonders as The Wedge, the famous Huntington Pier, and the elusive Newport Point. Down the coast a few more miles are the craggy, fickle reefs of affluent Laguna Beach, the nouveau ritz of Dana Point (harbored to death), and the classic beach city of San Clemente (more beachbreak).

Orange County faces SW, so summer swells have better luck here than in LA or San Diego, occasionally reaching epic status with big waves, warm temperatures. It can seem like the best place in the world at times, but it isn't. Spots that handle the waves and give them decent shape are few and far between, and pesky onshores arrive without warning. Also, it's no secret in California that S swells are as fickle as they come; many spots don't even break without a south. Wintertime W swells do get in quite handily, but due nor'wests tend to approach the coast with less intensity than they do farther north. N-NW swells miss large sections of coast due to the shadowing of Santa Catalina Island, especially during W-SW swells around Huntington. Rideable surf is never huge in Orange County, except for a handful of rare spots and that freak of nature, jetty and backwash known as the Wedge. Still, there's generally something to ride just about every day, be it good, bad, or something in between.

Surfrider Foundation's national office and four chapters are located in Orange County, and maybe that's a good thing, since the county's got a full plate of earth and ocean concerns. Perhaps the two primary issues for surfers are the 240 million gallons of poorly treated sewage that the Orange County Sanitation District discharges into the ocean, a mere 4.5 miles (7.2km) off shore, each and every day, not to mention an estimated 1,300 sewage spills between 1995 and 2000, many due to an aging and inadequate sewage system infrastructure.

Then there's the proposed Jetty-Tidal Inlet at Bolsa Chica State Beach, which conservationists hope will

GEOFF RAGATZ

Above – **Orange County is almost exclusively beachbreak. Hollow perfection or unmakable close-out is usually a matter of photographic timing. Aliso Jetty, San Clemente, surf industry central.**
Left – **Testing take-offs and crowds at the all too infrequent Newport Point.**

ROB GILLEY

RON STONER/SURFER MAGAZINE

Right – **Huntington Pier 1965 with Ironman Chuck Linnen in clean trim.**
Below – **Dana Point in 1937 was already being affected by the dredging of a channel for the harbor.**

LEROY GRANNIS

enhance the Bolsa Chica Wetland, former site of an 80-year old oil field. Other key issues include water pollution from channels like the San Gabriel River in Seal Beach and the Santa Ana River in Newport Beach. The watershed that feeds into the Santa Ana River drains from the San Bernardino Mountains, and all this runoff flows unfiltered into the now-cemented Santa Ana River, out the rivermouth, and into the ocean. Incredibly, all runoff from cars, farms and ranches, city streets, home lawns, and who-knows-what-else is deposited unfiltered into the Pacific. Similarly, the runoff from streets in Newport Beach runs unfiltered directly into its harbor, which is adjacent to the Wedge. Even down in 'pristine' Laguna Beach, some of the beachfront cottages at Crystal Cove State Beach have geriatric septic tanks that send near-shore bacteria levels off the charts in an area that was/is a fertile breeding ground for dolphins and a very popular swimming beach for humans.

Just about the trendiest, flashiest, most image-driven surf culture in California, Orange County is the epicenter of the global surf industry. It's the birthplace of contemporary surf style, ground zero for most of the great surfboard design and technology innovations, and the headquarters of the world's leading surf magazines. *Surfer* magazine was founded by John Severson in 1960 and still collects its mail at the Dana Point post office. *Surfing* (the mag) started a couple of years later and is now headquartered in San Clemente, right across the street from the offices of *The Surfer's Journal*. And *LongBoard* is just one exit down the I-5. In fact, much of what you see in the worldwide surf marketplace comes out of Orange County – the place is the surf biz Mecca of North America.

As with many of America's prime areas, surfing was carried into Orange County on the broad shoulders of Duke Kahanamoku himself, who first surfed at Corona Del Mar on his grand tour of America's beaches following his gold medal performance at the 1912 Olympics in Sweden. In 1925, Duke demonstrated the surfboard's utility as a lifesaving device by rescuing 8 of the 12 survivors from a boat that was capsized by a big set off Corona. The following year, Duke surfed Huntington Beach for the first time, and the locals quickly took up the torch. The first surfing club on the mainland, the Corona Del Mar Surf Board Club, was founded in 1928. The same year, Tom Blake dominated the paddle race at the First Annual Pacific Coast Surf Board Championships (held at Balboa) on his original 1926 Hawaiian Hollow Surfboard. It was Matt Brown, Harrison, and the Corona crew that first surfed Laguna Beach in the late '20s and Dana Point in 1935. When the channel at Corona was dredged to 60ft (18m) deep in 1935, effectively killing the popular surf spot there, San Onofre (just over the San Diego County line) became the getaway of choice for southern Orange County surfers. Fed by the frequent migrations of Harrison and others to Hawaii, San Onofre became the prototypical Polynesian-inspired California bohemian beach scene. Meanwhile, the San O crew explored the cluster of South Orange County pointbreaks to the immediate north – Church, Lower Trestles, Upper Trestles, and Cottons Point, one of the best S-swell spots on the coast. Dana Point – a famed 'big wave' spot – was extinguished (along with Old Man's and a couple of other reefs) when the first phase of the harbor breakwall was completed in 1968.

Today, vacant line-ups are virtually unheard of anywhere in Orange County. What was once a tranquil farming and orchard region with a bucolic necklace of quaint coastal villages is now an unfortunate example of rampant suburbia, cookie-cutter housing tracts, spotless luxury cars, a seemingly endless stream of new residents who come for the business opportunities and undiluted sunshine, and freeways as jammed as the line-ups. If it is serenity coupled with epic surf you seek, you will not find much of it in Orange County. Expect plenty of surfers with rude attitudes, likely due to the hustle-hype pace of the area and the lack of high quality waves. Localism is hard to pin down here, since it's virtually impossible to tell who's local and who isn't. Although it's generally accepted that keeping any spot exclusive and uncrowded is hopeless, many spots have pecking orders, notably the fickle reefs of Laguna. It's easy to blend into Orange County – simply follow the herd, and make sure you bring enough quarters for the parking meters. If nothing else, visit Orange County for its surf history, and for a first person look at what you've been fed by the magazines and videos all these years.

ROB GILLEY

San Diego County

You can find almost any type of wave in San Diego County; from Trestles in the north down to the Mexican border, good surf is a common occurrence, especially during clean conditions in autumn and winter. Like the rest of California, San Diego County has a lot of beachbreak, but it's frequently interrupted by good reefs and semi-points. Although there are no true, classic pointbreaks, world-class sandbar waves can be sussed out at Blacks Beach, Imperial Beach, and Oceanside. Most notably, San Diego's got it covered as far as quality reefbreaks go: Trestles, Swamis, Big Rock, Windansea, Sunset Cliffs, etc. The list goes on – from the longboard sliders of San Onofre to the behemoth lefthanders of La Jolla Cove, San Diego surfers have plenty of options. W swells hit most of the coast with supreme accuracy, though SSWs are favored for the Coronado and Trestles areas. More southerly summertime swells do better up in Orange County, but San

DON BALCH

Top – **San Diego has it all from hollow beachbreaks like Oceanside...**
Left – **...to Pipe style reefs and points. La Jolla Cove, macking.**

Diego gets the preferred wintertime action. Virtually everywhere can be pumping in the winter as long as the size is manageable. Most north/central county spots can't handle anything bigger than a few feet overhead before they close-out. South county reef areas like La Jolla and Point Loma really shine during solid winter swells, but there's a noxious vein of localism at some breaks.

On the whole, San Diego surf varies in power and consistency, but it's safe to say most spots are quite user-friendly and mild on a global scale. Lengthy flat spells are not unheard of, and summer crowds can be stifling, but quality conditions can occur throughout the year. Plus, there's a major resource right next door; it's called Baja.

Water quality is one of San Diego's gnarliest issues, and the county has faced a number of beach closures due primarily to sewage spills (plus ballast-water pollution from cruise ships – the main source for the introduction of destructive invasive species in the coastal zone). An international wastewater plant near Tijuana, was designed

DON BALCH

to treat sewage that, because of ocean currents, might otherwise end up off the coast of San Diego. However, the plant's effluent has failed to meet water-quality standards. Surfrider's San Diego chapter has lawsuits pending, and one was recently settled with the International Boundaries Water Commission regarding its violations of the Clean Water Act at the Mexican border. Camp Pendleton (the large US Marine Corps base in North County) faces a similar action due to numerous alleged violations of the Clean Water Act.

Shoreline armoring is another big county issue. Numerous seawalls, groins, and jetties have been built along the coast, disrupting natural littoral flows and denuding some beaches of sand. There is overwhelming evidence of the destructive impacts of seawalls on San Diego beaches, yet successive city councils have ignored citizen opposition until forced into action by the courts. In reality, it's difficult to let houses fall into the ocean, no matter how short-sighted the homeowners have been in erecting their faux mansions 25 feet (7.5m) from the water's edge. Unfortunately, protective seawalls are so ultimately destructive to San Diego beaches that removing them is the only reasonable long-term option. The public shouldn't have to forfeit a beach because wealthy, arrogant folks have intentionally put themselves in harm's way. The issue is hot in north county, too, where the California State Parks Dept wants to build a 250ft (75m) seawall at North Cardiff State Beach. Designed to protect a parking lot, the seawall will endanger the famous waves at Cardiff Reef, as well as accelerate the loss of sand at the public beach. Surfrider's San Diego chapter is poised to oppose.

Other county environmental issues (as in all urban areas) are stormwater runoff (sometimes resulting in quarantined beaches), a big culprit being non-point source runoff with

Above – **San Diego's landscape and dry climate means that when it does rain it makes sense to avoid the water for several days.**
Right – **The original US palm frond shack at San Onofre, 1963.**

LEROY GRANNIS

virtually undetectable origins, and continuing coastal development – hotels, roads, and commercial and residential structures preventing access to the beach while destroying wetlands and other native habitats. In other words, 'progress.'

The history of surfing in San Diego County is a deep, rich vein, starting in 1916, when Duke Kahanamoku demonstrated the Polynesian rite of walking on water off Ocean Beach in San Diego. It was here that the great George Freeth expired in April of 1919 of influenza, contracted after strenuous lifesaving work in storm conditions off Oceanside; he was just 35. Then in 1933, Bill Sides, Lorrin Harrison, Willy Grigsby, and Bill Hollingsworth checked the waves at San Onofre, surfed all the breaks, and finally settled at the spot where a Hollywood movie crew had built and abandoned a nice palm-thatch shack to set up their perennial surf camp. Other early San O players included Ethyl Harrison, Mary Ann Hawkins and Barney 'Doakes' Wilkes. In 1937, freshly arrived from flying Jennies over Long Island and helping Charles Lindbergh across the Atlantic, Woodbridge 'Woody' Parker Brown III paddled his home-made surfboard out at Windansea in La Jolla and rode the first wave there. Woody also was the first to launch his glider off the wind-blown bluffs of Torrey Pines. In 1947, modeled after San Onofre's, the first palm-roofed shack was built at Windansea, the first luaus are held there, and the San Diego (later Windansea) Surf Club began (Hoppy Swarts was first president). A large storm swept away the first shack in '49, but was soon rebuilt and the luaus resumed, eventually attracting huge crowds. It was here, in June of 1950, that a gang of Malibu guys arrived with their new rockered Joe Quigg balsa boards, which the San Diego guys tagged as "potato chips." About that time, Mike Diffenderfer shaped his first surfboard out of balsa in the street at Bird Rock, because his father wouldn't let him mess up the house. And it was at Windansea, on Sept 26, 1954, that Bob Simmons drowned in good-sized surf. His body was found three days later by Bob Ekstrom. Ten years later, Skip Frye and some Windansea friends made the first documented surf trip to Isla Todos Santos in Baja. In 1966, Nat Young upset the surfing universe with his World Contest win at Ocean Beach on the radical surfboard known as "Sam." The following year, the Windansea Surf Club traveled en masse to Australia and was shocked to discover the Aussies riding short vee-bottom surfboards, thus bringing first word of the revolution back to the States. Five years later, the World Contest returned to town, a miserable event that plunged competition surfing into a malaise. That was about the time 'Rus' Preisendorfer's Canyon Surfboards wanted to "Put a little music in your surfing!" And on and on...yes ...San Diego has surf history.

Even today, this is a great place to be a surfer, as thousands (maybe millions?) have discovered...a great place if you don't mind sharing the water with 50 of your best friends at any given spot during any decent sort of swell. North county especially has seen a sharp increase in surfing population due to runaway development, mostly east of the eight-lane I-5 freeway. Nevertheless, San Diego surfers are typically a friendly breed, many of them newcomers to the area; but there's also a longstanding history of surfers claiming rights to certain spots, notably the Sunset Cliffs area. Still, localism lays quite low save for the random incident.

San Diego County is the essence of Southern California, and flavors of nearby Mexico abound. Surfers are accustomed to drive-up surf spots, with some of the best spots right in front of major roads or housing developments. Much of the coast is shoulder-to-shoulder with expensive homes, as basically all of the county's beach towns are affluent to some degree here, where rain is rare and sunshine is the rule. Cloudy days keep a lot of people away from the beaches, indicative of the SoCal mentality. There are so many surfers in San Diego, it's impossible to tell who is a local and who's not, or who has been living in the county for more than two years, so the traveling board-toting soul shouldn't have a problem fitting in. It's not called "America's Finest City" for nothing.

Top – **The current shack at Windansea, rebuilt after the original was destroyed by a storm in 1949.**
Above – **Skip Frye, Pacific Beach local surfer/shaper who set up S.T.O.P. (Surfers Tired Of Pollution) with his wife Donna.**

Santa Barbara – West

1. Bixby and Hollister Ranches

Publicly inaccessible 14-mile (22km) stretch of private coastline (from Point Conception to Gaviota) containing several inconsistent yet quality points and reefs. The west to east list reads like the roll call of a daydreamer's mindtrip: Government Point, Cojo, Perkos, Lefts & Rights, Rights & Lefts, St. Augustine, Razorblades – it's pretty much bumper-to-bumper spots, but they work on different swells and tides. Strong N swells generally sweep past most of Bixby and nail the Hollister. A good S swell might hit Bixby and be blocked for most of Hollister by the Channel Islands. Full of surprises.

Ranch

Off-limits unless you own a durable boat (or know someone who owns Hollister property) and can motor up from the Gaviota Pier, which is often closed. Outrageous winds, thick forests of kelp, covetous locals, speeding passenger trains, and armed guards have orchestrated some fabulous disasters over the years since the Santa Barbara Surf Club had sole (but limited) legal access. Not for the casual surf tourist.

2. Tajiguas

Various peaks along a small fetch of beach clearly visible from Highway 101, just north of Refugio. Rock and sand bottom. Not really any distinct peak as it has not been very good in recent years. Regularly surfed and usually pretty reliable for some kind of rideable wave. Needs medium-low tide and peaky windswells. Best during the springtime.

Occasionally polluted water after rainfall. Park in the dirt on the ocean side of the road. Two trails lead down to the beach.

3. Refugio State Beach

Mushy righthand sand-bottom point waves favored by beginners and longboarders. Rocks on the outside point area. Needs larger winter swells or the proper direction of W. Sets break out in the kelp beds before reforming into Refugio proper. Usually small and not very good. Rideable at all tides; low best with small swells, high best with big. Rides can be long with a speedy section on the inside; an occasionally good sandbar sometimes forms on the inside that is shortboardable.

Medium consistency and often crowded with longboarders and campers. Nice campground here (closed during winter). Cognoscenti pronounce it Refuffio.

Looking towards Government Point from Augustine Point

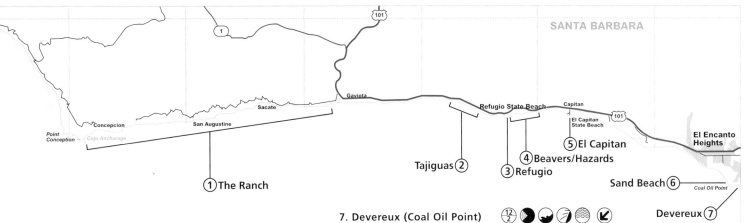

① The Ranch
Tajiguas ②
③ Refugio
④ Beavers/Hazards
⑤ El Capitan
Sand Beach ⑥
Devereux ⑦

4. Beavers/Hazards

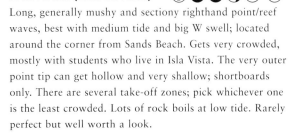

A pocket beach just east of Refugio, clearly visible from the highway. Somewhat mediocre peaks, usually not very good, but it can get fun during windswells. Can't really handle anything over head high. Rock and sand bottom. Needs a low tide; high tide creates backwash. The peak at the east end offers decent, fat, mushy lefts and shorter, hollower rights. Various peaks to the east as well. The peak at the west end is a lined-up right with lots of rock boils. Sectiony and rather mushy but well worth it if the east peak is crowded, which it often is due to the easy drive-by surf check.

Dirt roadside parking is the extent of facilities. Look both ways before crossing the railroad tracks.

5. El Capitan State Beach

Notoriously rare and fickle, hollow, well-shaped righthand point. Extremely crowded with some nasty locals. Tense vibes in the water. Outsiders are easily recognized and are not welcomed. Only breaks during a big, solid W swell and low to mid tide. Can be decent but fat with a high tide during the biggest of swells. There is a rocky beachbreak in front of the parking lot, best with windswells and higher tides. It has not been good in recent years. Rarely surfed.

Pleasant camping is available for the hopeful at this low-consistency gem. If only they'd get those islands out of the way!

6. Sand Beach

A consistent, wide beach west of Isla Vista; usually has something to ride. The rocky area in front of the bluff and bike rack is known as Stu Peak because many UCSB students surf there. Best with a higher tide and peaky windswell. Gets very crowded. Some dangerous rock hazards, especially during low tide. Lots of students on the beach on sunny, warm days. Over toward the slough mouth, sandbars replace rocks, and it can get good and quite hollow. Needs peaky windswells and medium-high incoming tide here too. Low tides create rip currents and close-outs. Blows offshore with a SE storm wind.

Accessed by parking at the west end of Isla Vista and walking a mile or so west across the bluff along the bike trail.

7. Devereux (Coal Oil Point)

Long, generally mushy and sectiony righthand point/reef waves, best with medium tide and big W swell; located around the corner from Sands Beach. Gets very crowded, mostly with students who live in Isla Vista. The very outer point tip can get hollow and very shallow; shortboards only. There are several take-off zones; pick whichever one is the least crowded. Lots of rock boils at low tide. Rarely perfect but well worth a look.

Check it from the very west end of Isla Vista. Access is by parking there and walking across the bluff (same access as Sands Beach). Pronounced DEV-er-oh.

El Capitan

ROB GILLEY

Refugio

DAVID PU'U

DAVID PU'U

Santa Barbara – East

1. Isla Vista

Various mushy reef waves east of Devereux Point breaking a quarter-mile from shore, plus some beachbreak down towards Campus Point. Needs big W swell and low tides or big windswell. Pescaderos, at the end of Pescadero Street, is a fun, peaky beachbreak that blows offshore with NW wind. Needs a lower tide. Gets crowded when UCSB is in session. Depressions is an average beachbreak on the backside of Campus Point below the miniature valley in the bluff. Needs medium tide with smaller, peaky windswell.

All spots are accessible by parking along Del Playa Drive in Isla Vista.

2. Campus Point

Inconsistent right point next to UCSB requiring big W swell. Excellent quality when it breaks correctly. Handles as big a swell as the ocean can provide, the bigger the better. Fast, hollow sections and long rides when it's on; mushy, slow, and weak when it's not. The inner peak is called Poles and is popular with grommets and longboarders. Lower tides are generally best. Always crowded with students.

Access is by parking in the coin-metered lot adjacent to the point (make sure you have coins if you go).

3. The Pit

Consistent beachbreak that responds well to windswell and works best on higher incoming tides. Closes out over head high. Fun peaks, plenty of room for everyone. Gets crowded with grommets after school and during the summer.

The water here becomes very polluted after rainfall, and several surfers over the years have gotten very sick from surfing here. Access is from the car park off Cliff Drive, in front of the restaurant.

Sandspit

DAVID PU'U

4. Leadbetter Beach

Mushy, gentle, long rights off a scenic point boasting great views of the Santa Barbara Harbor and Stearns Wharf. Ideal for beginners and longboarders. Can be really fun with bigger W swells or large windswells. More sectiony and lined-up at low tide, fatter at high tide. Surfers of all abilities crowd the line-up here, but it's almost always all longboards. Good vibes despite the crowding.

Access is by parking along Cliff Drive or La Marina Boulevard, or in the free car park at pleasant Shoreline Park. Take the trail down the bluff fronting the wave.

5. Sandspit

A rare, Kirra-style righthand barrel over an extremely shallow sand bottom, created by the Army Corps of Engineers when the breakwater was built to protect Santa Barbara Harbor. The wave is hard-hitting and dredging, beginning with a huge backwash coming out at an angle to the wave from the breakwater. Gets very crowded and very dangerous – expert surfers with tuberiding experience only. Needs big W swells and low tide. Tom Curren got the all-time longest Californian tube ride here.

A freak that doesn't break very often. Park at the harbor shops and walk out along the breakwater; 90 minutes maximum parking time allowed. On really big swells, rides to the pier are possible.

6. Hammonds Reef

Classic righthand cobblestone reefbreak in the wealthy town of Montecito. Occasional lefts. Well-shaped, lined-up wave with a few punchy sections. Holds considerable size and always offers classic rides on a good day. Medium tides with clean W swells work best here. Big S swells also get in, creating a welcome respite to long, flat Santa Barbara summers.

Almost always crowded, reflecting its high consistency. Accessible by walking up from the small Miramar Beach/Eucalyptus Lane parking area.

7. Miramar

Mushy longboard/beginner's wave. A small cobblestone point just south of Hammonds. Needs winter swell but can get good with a summertime S if it's big enough. Very gentle and well-shaped. Best with a lower tide. Can get crowded.

Limited parking available at the foot of Eucalyptus Lane in Montecito.

Hammonds Reef

8. Tarpits/Carpinteria State Beach

Various reef/sandbar peaks, best with lower tides and smaller, peaky swells. Boils at low tide, vicious backwash at high tide. The beachbreak to the north can provide a lot of elbow room if Tarpits itself is crowded. The beachbreak can be hollow on a mid to low tide. A fun summer spot.

Carpinteria Creek may transport some unwanted pollution into the line-up, especially after rain.

Miramar

Ventura County – West

1. Rincon Point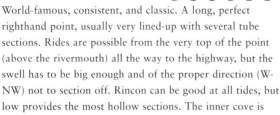

World-famous, consistent, and classic. A long, perfect righthand point, usually very lined-up with several tube sections. Rides are possible from the very top of the point (above the rivermouth) all the way to the highway, but the swell has to be big enough and of the proper direction (W-NW) not to section off. Rincon can be good at all tides, but low provides the most hollow sections. The inner cove is generally a mushier, softer wave popular with longboarders, but it too can be screaming fast on the right day.

Always extremely crowded. Avoid surfing Rincon after heavy rains, when the impact of outdated septic tanks combine with the Rincon Creek outfall to pollute the line-up. While sewage seeps into the ocean from the houses on the point, homeowners block efforts to provide better facilities. Plainly visible from Highway 101, accessed via Bates Road. Free parking.

Rincon

DAVID PU'U

Ventura Overhead

DAVID PU'U

2. La Conchita Beach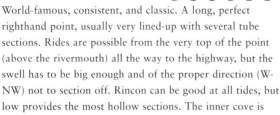

A stretch of fun, peaky beachbreak just south of Rincon, right alongside the highway. Very consistent. A good summertime alternative which can get hollow. Lower tides best with peaky, glassy windswell. High tide creates backwash and fat, mushy waves.

Rarely crowded and plenty of room for everyone. Park along the highway.

3. Little Rincon/Mussel Shoals

Rocky semi-point fronting this small beach community, just south of the oil pier leading out to 'Rincon Island.' Good spot during large winter swells with lower tide. Gets hollow and very fast; speedy sections abound. Less crowded than Rincon but definitely not as good, although it does have its days. Plainly visible from the highway.

Watch out for rock hazards, especially at low tide. Access is through Mussel Shoals, at the north end of Breakers Way and at the west end of Ocean Avenue. Limited parking on either street.

4. Hobson County Park

Fun cobblestone reef peaks; good with any swell and tide. S swells get in here, but the spot is generally best with winter juice. Long, fast lefts off the north peak. Long, sectiony mushy rights off the south peak, which closes out onto an inner sandbar.

Regularly breaks and attracts a crowd. Small campground here. Access is off of old Pacific Coast Highway, just south of Seacliff. Formerly known as Four Palms, but things have changed.

5. Faria Beach

Long stretch of sandbars with cobblestones on the beach, best with incoming tides and small, peaky windswells. Lots of room for everyone. Usually closes out above head high. A good summer spot.

Park along the old PCH, which is a popular (and free) seaside park-up for recreational vehicles and campervans.

6. Pitas Point/Faria County Park

Long righthand cobblestone and rock point hosting several more or less distinct breaks. Requires big W swells and can be the best spot on the coast when it's happening. Lots of room for everyone. Separate take-off areas range from Outsides (fast, hollow waves with power off the outer point) to Insides (slow, mushy longboard waves). A variety of mushy peaks inside the bay spread out into unbelievably slow-moving waves. There is also a left breaking north of Outsides. Sheltered from the prevailing NW wind. Handles any tide except extreme high.

A good alternative to Rincon although the reduction in crowds reflects a much lower consistency. Camping is available and parking is at Faria County Park.

7. Solimar Reef and Beach

Good reef waves a good long paddle offshore amidst thick kelp beds; mostly rights with heavy take-offs. Best with S swells and low tide. There are other easier rights on the inside straight out from the small parking area, best with winter NW swells.

Accessible by walking along pathways on either end of the Solimar community. Park in the dirt area to the south or along the road.

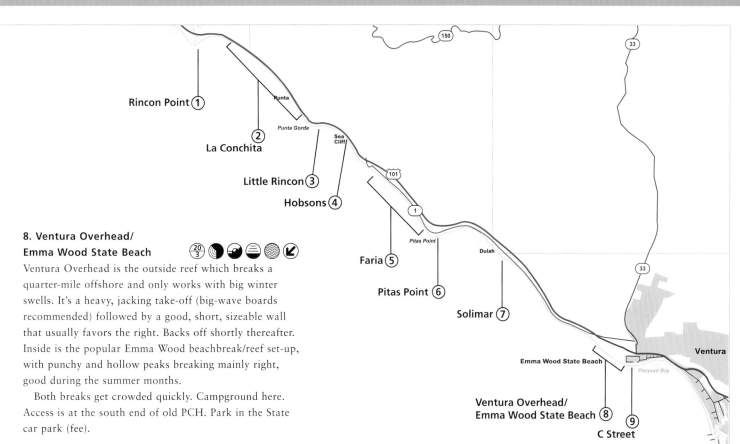

Rincon Point ①
Punta
Punta Gorda
La Conchita ②
Sea Cliff
Little Rincon ③
Hobsons ④
101
1
Pitas Point
Faria ⑤
Dulah
Pitas Point ⑥
Solimar ⑦
150
33
33
Ventura
Emma Wood State Beach
Pierpont Bay
Ventura Overhead/
Emma Wood State Beach ⑧
⑨
C Street

8. Ventura Overhead/ Emma Wood State Beach

Ventura Overhead is the outside reef which breaks a quarter-mile offshore and only works with big winter swells. It's a heavy, jacking take-off (big-wave boards recommended) followed by a good, short, sizeable wall that usually favors the right. Backs off shortly thereafter. Inside is the popular Emma Wood beachbreak/reef set-up, with punchy and hollow peaks breaking mainly right, good during the summer months.

Both breaks get crowded quickly. Campground here. Access is at the south end of old PCH. Park in the State car park (fee).

9. California Street (C Street)

Also known as Ventura Point, a very long right point with several take-off zones. Stables is on the very tip of the point, more consistent and usually bigger than the rest of the point. Fairgrounds is the outer point when the swell is under 8ft (2.5m), breaking with power and speed in front of the Ventura County Fairgrounds. Over 8ft (2.5m) and Outsides breaks on an outer reef right next to a deep paddling channel, up to 12ft (3.6m). Cobblestone and sand bottom. Insides is rather mushy but long and forgiving and can develop great big peaks with rights and a few lefts. Popular with longboarders. Very reliable spot and usually crowded. Paddling out can be difficult during swells over 6ft (2m). Can be good at all tides with all swells.

Beware of water pollution from Ventura River following rains; bad southbound currents when the swell is big. Large car park ($3 fee) fronting the break.

California Street

DON BALCH

New Jetty/South Jetty

DAVID PU'U

Ventura County – East

1. San Buenaventura State Beach

A scattering of small jetties in the Pierpoint area, south of California Street and the Ventura Pier. Various beachbreak peaks, mainly lefts; good with small, peaky swells. Fun during the summertime, the earlier the better since afternoon NW wind blows it out. Never crowded, plenty of room.

Access is by parking at the end of any of the 24 residential streets between Marina Park and San Pedro Street.

2. New Jetty/South Jetty

Good, hollow beachbreak waves below the jetty on the south side of the Ventura Harbor mouth. Good with any swell up to a foot or two overhead.

Known for some unfriendly localism. Accessed via Spinnaker Drive.

3. Santa Clara Rivermouth

One of California's best rivermouth breaks when everything comes together, also one of the most polluted

spots on the West Coast, especially after rain. Then again, perfect sandbars (sometimes called the Star Bar) can form after heavy rains, creating high-quality, A-frame peaks spinning off long, fast walls in both directions. Holds up to several feet overhead. Deep, makeable tube sections.

Bad localism. Gets crowded, but for good reason. Accessed from the south end of Spinnaker Drive.

4. McGrath State Beach/Mandalay County Park/Oxnard Shores

Miles of uncrowded beachbreak peaks between McGrath State Beach and the Channel Islands Harbor. Prefers modest swells and higher tides.

Gets more crowded toward the south end (aka Hollywood Beach/Hollywood by the Sea). Often polluted after rains. Campground at McGrath.

5. Silver Strand

Flanked by the Channel Islands Harbor south jetty and the Port Hueneme north jetty, this popular mile-long stretch of powerful beachbreak is often seen (but not identified) in surf magazines and videos. Always gets some kind of surf with epic barrels during the wintertime, it takes a S nicely too.

Site of nasty localism in years past; beware of potentially sour attitudes in and out of the water. Runoff pollution after rain. Access is via Ocean Drive in Oxnard. Due to history of auto vandalism, park strategically.

6. Port Hueneme Beach Park

Pronounced why-NEE-me. Average beachbreak on the north side of the pier. Can't handle any size. Higher tides and peaky swells work best.

Access is along the west end of Surfside Drive and Ocean View Drive in Port Hueneme.

Santa Clara Rivermouth

DAVID PU'U

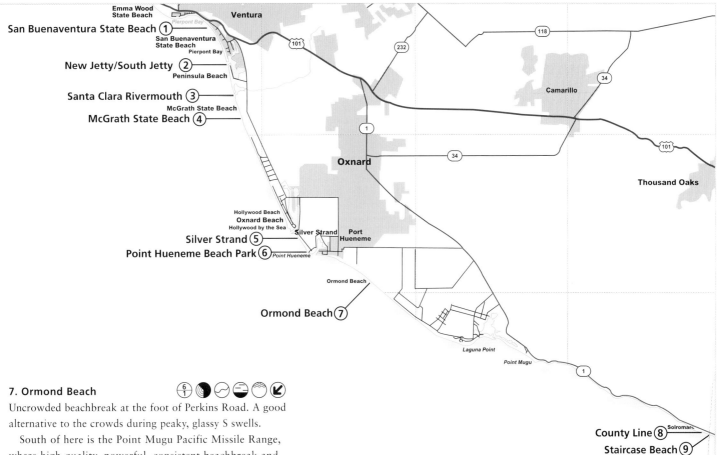

San Buenaventura State Beach ①
New Jetty/South Jetty ②
Santa Clara Rivermouth ③
McGrath State Beach ④
Silver Strand ⑤
Point Hueneme Beach Park ⑥
Ormond Beach ⑦
County Line ⑧
Staircase Beach ⑨

7. Ormond Beach

Uncrowded beachbreak at the foot of Perkins Road. A good alternative to the crowds during peaky, glassy S swells.

South of here is the Point Mugu Pacific Missile Range, where high-quality, powerful, consistent beachbreak and point surf are inaccessible to the general public.

8. County Line/Yerba Buena Beach

Popular, scenic spot with two surfable areas. The rocky north end of County Line is called The Point, mainly rights, though some good lefts are occasionally dished up. Very fun and usually crowded. Kept fairly glassy at all times by thick outside kelp beds. Medium tides work best here, especially on a W swell up to a few feet overhead. To the south is the beachbreak, various peaks lined up on outer reefs, which can get hollow and punchy. Popular with shortboarders. Can be good at anytime.

Undeveloped and a welcome change from the urban surf spots to the south. Park right along the surf on Highway 1 near its confluence with Yerba Buena Road north of the Ventura/LA county line.

9. Staircase Beach

The northernmost undeveloped chunk of Leo Carrillo State Beach. Variable sandbars offering small peaks up to about head high. Must be smallish and glassy with medium tide. Uncrowded and pleasant.

Accessed via a path from the public dirt parking lot of the State Park ranger's residence at 4000 Pacific Coast Highway.

ROB GILLEY

Los Angeles County – North

1. Leo Carrillo State Beach/Secos/Arroyo Sequit

A consistent, fun righthand cobblestone point/reef wave. Likes a mid to low tide and works best with S swells. Kelp forest is too thick to ride comfortably at low tide; sometimes high tide shorebreak can be fun. The take-off zone is just outside of (or next to) the large rock. Prevailing NW wind blows offshore.

State beach campground. Gets extremely crowded with surfers of all ability. Popular with windsurfers too. Lots of movie beach scenes shot just around the point to the north.

Secos

Zuma Beach

2. Zero/Nicholas Canyon County Beach

Hollow lefthand point wave that also likes a mid to low tide. Works on a W swell, but strong S swells are best. Doesn't break very often.

Watch out for heavy shorepound. Once an esoteric hideaway, now located across Pacific Coast Highway from the Malibu Riding and Tennis Club.

3. Trancas Point

The hollow, rocky right point wave at the north end of Zuma Beach. Take-off beside a large rock. Gnarly shorebreak. Good with big swells, the more W the better. Also works during big S swells, but the wave doesn't wrap in as well.

Private property surrounds the break, but there's a public stairway leading to the beach from Broad Beach Road.

4. Zuma Beach County Park

Wide, sandy beach with various sandbar peaks; often very hollow and always powerful. Gets epic during offshore winds, funneled by Trancas and Zuma canyons, and a peaky SW swell. Holds up to a foot or two overhead.

Wicked currents and rips. Use caution. A huge pay-parking lot borders the entire three-mile-plus stretch of beach. It's where all the Valley people come for their beach parties. Think Disneyland-by-the-Sea.

5. Point Dume State Beach/Westward Beach/Drainpipes

Actually the backside of Point Dume itself, which is private and off-limits to the public. Fickle sandbar peaks boasting heavy tubes with the correct angle of S or W swell. Hard-hitting and not for beginners.

Nasty shorepound and bad currents, especially during W swells. Access is through the pay-lot at the south end of Westward Beach Road.

6. Latigo Canyon

Fun, mushy right point, best on some SW swells and a lower tide.

Only medium consistency so a lower crowd co-efficient. Private property on Latigo Shore Drive denies direct access. Walk north from Corral State Beach.

7. Malibu

One of the world's most famous and most crowded righthand pointbreaks. Mainly a summertime spot best on S swells. Three separate take-off zones: Third Point: at medium tide, fast, hollow rides off the northernmost point. Big swells will connect up with Second Point: long, hollow, workable wall at medium tide, unmakeable at low. First Point: the most consistent and therefore the most surfed of the Malibu waves. Can show perfect shape, excellent for any type of surf craft. Works through the full tidal range, getting more hollow as the tide drops.

Mega crowds. One of the worst beaches in the county for beach closures due to bacterial pollution after heavy rains. Construction of a sewage system at Malibu was halted nine years ago amidst protests from local home-owners, who claimed it would lead the way for high-rise beach development. Malibu is home to many big-name environmentalists among the rich and famous – their beachfront homes using outdated, ill-located septic tanks. These leak directly into the Malibu Lagoon and, after heavy rainfall, the line-up, leaving surfers with eye and ear infections, respiratory illnesses and rashes. After 35 years of debate the situation is now at a stand-off, but due to the high profile of the residents the best that can be hoped for is regulation and inspection of the existing systems. There are full-on beach facilities, a small pay parking lot, and free parking along PCH.

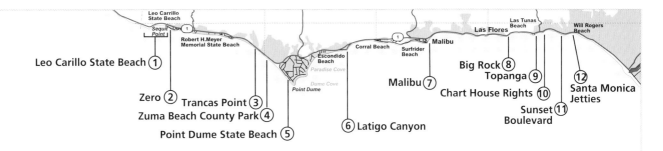

Leo Carillo State Beach ①
Zero ② Trancas Point ③
Zuma Beach County Park ④
Point Dume State Beach ⑤
⑥ Latigo Canyon
Malibu ⑦
Big Rock ⑧
Topanga ⑨
Chart House Rights ⑩
Sunset ⑪ Boulevard
⑫ Santa Monica Jetties

8. Big Rock

Fun little reef wave off a small headland requiring S swells and an outgoing tide, rideable up to a foot or two overhead. High tide creates backwash. A few rock hazards. A summer wave and not surfed very often.

Access via the public stairway (marked by blue-and-white trash cans) about 2mi (3.2km) south of the Las Flores Canyon Road/PCH confluence.

9. Topanga State Beach

Long righthand pointbreak at the base of Topanga Canyon near Topanga Creek; best shape is with a strong W swell and mid to low tide. Some good sections. The outer section is known as Boomers, which is shorter but more powerful than the main wave. Can handle up to double overhead. Not as perfect as Malibu but not quite as crowded either. Still, it can be a high-quality wave.

Site of psychedelic-era experimentation and hedonism, a bit of throw-back localism endures. Pay to park lot off PCH.

10. Chart House Rights

A small, fast, hollow right breaks over shallow reef – where? – in front of the Chart House restaurant, of course. Rock hazards and strong shoreline currents. Needs a small S-SW swell up to about head high. Requires low tide, the lower the better.

Small take-off area, so it can't handle many surfers. Shortboards only. Beware of the shallow reef and use a leash. Access is down the cliff next to the Chart House. They won't let you into the restaurant lot unless you're dining, so park alongside PCH.

Zuma

ROB GILLEY

11. Sunset Boulevard

Large, mushy, user-friendly righthand pointbreak. Likes big W swells and mid to low tide. Highly consistent, but sectiony, so plenty of room for everyone.

Located at the foot of Sunset Boulevard with often stunning views of the Santa Monica shoreline and sunset over Topanga (maybe that's where the name came from).

12. Santa Monica Jetties

Hollow sandbar rights between a few rock jetties. Needs a S-SW swell to fire. Rideable up to about head high. Not the most consistent spots, but good tubes when the conditions are correct.

The Santa Monica region is one of the most polluted seascapes in California, so you may want to look for waves elsewhere. Access off PCH, just north of the entrance to Will Rogers State Beach.

Malibu

ROB GILLEY

Los Angeles County – South Bay

1. Santa Monica Municipal Pier

Mellow, mushy sandbar peaks on the south side. Mostly rights up to about head high with low tide. Never gets big and is somewhat polluted. Best with W-SW swells.

Access is at the corner of Colorado and Ocean Avenues. Pay parking nearby.

2. Bay Street

Surfed since the 1960s, this is 'the beach' in Santa Monica. Small beachbreak waves, best with peaky windswells and low tide. Needs to have holes in the sand bottom, caused by water flow from the creek after rains.

One of the more popular spots around Santa Monica, but still somewhat polluted. Located at the foot of Bay Street.

3. Rose Avenue

Mundane beachbreak, can get good with smaller windswells on any tide. Closes out above head high. Good summer spot and never crowded.

Highly consistent. Located at the foot of Rose Avenue in Santa Monica.

El Porto

4. Venice Breakwater and Venice Jetty

Hollow, somewhat fickle wintertime sandbars, good up to 1-2ft overhead (2-3m). Needs outgoing tides and larger W swells. Plenty of board-snapping potential. Definitely not for beginners.

Unfriendly local crew. Strong rip currents when a good swell is running. Access through downtown Venice.

5. Toes Over

Small, hollow rights off highly-polluted Ballona Creek's south jetty. Needs a head high SW swell with mid tide. Fun summer spot if you can brave the dirty water.

Free on-street parking along Esplanade and along Ballona Creek.

6. Ballona Creek/The Jetty

Polluted but shapely lefts off the end of the jetty just south of Toes Over; requires a low tide and a small W-SW swell. Better for longboarding, as it is quite mushy.

Access is same as Toes Over.

7. D&W

Steep, fast, hollow, long rights off a jetty when it's on, best with a larger NW swell and mid tide. Not real consistent but worth a look if there's a clean swell running. Can be sectiony, but ideal for shortboarders. Broke better in years past, but still gets good.

Access is via fee parking lots along the beach.

8. New Jetty

Short, hollow sandbar rights off the south side of the jetty just north of El Porto. Needs a W swell with lower tide; also works with a small SW. Fairly consistent spot, a bit sheltered from NW because of the jetty. The north side of the jetty is called Hammerland and features big, steep close-out barrels during big winter swells.

Accessed via the pay lot at El Segundo Beach, at the western end of Grand Avenue in El Segundo.

9. El Porto Beach

Crowded, consistent, good beachbreak barrels when it's firing. Always bigger than the spots to the north and south. Several peaks up and down the beach. Can be good at all tides; handles up to a few feet overhead. Blows out easily.

Easy parking, but bring your quarters for the meters. Poor water quality.

10. Manhattan Beach Municipal Pier

Popular beachbreak peaks on either side of the pier. Takes any tide except extreme high. Closes out during large, lined-up swells, so peakier swells are the go, especially SW.

An historic seedbed of surf culture, the place where Dale Velzy's first put ten toes over the nose of his surfboard in 1951. Still consistent but crowded, with nasty commercial pollution, thanks to nearby industries. Access is at the foot of Manhattan Beach Boulevard; metered parking nearby.

11. Hermosa City Beach/ Hermosa Municipal Pier

Mundane beachbreak peaks handling up to about head high. Best with early morning offshores and small, peaky swells combined with medium tides. Close-outs are common during large swells, although they can make for some spectacular barrels.

The waves may be mundane, but they often get crowded. The first Velzy-Jacobs shop was located nearby, and there are numerous surf shops in the vicinity. This is the heart of the South Bay. Access is west of The Strand, a pedestrian walkway, all the way down to Pier Avenue.

Manhattan Beach

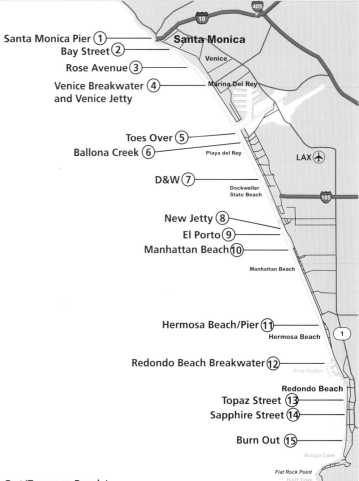

Santa Monica Pier ①
Bay Street ②
Rose Avenue ③
Venice Breakwater ④
and Venice Jetty

Toes Over ⑤
Ballona Creek ⑥

D&W ⑦

New Jetty ⑧
El Porto ⑨
Manhattan Beach ⑩

Hermosa Beach/Pier ⑪

Redondo Beach Breakwater ⑫

Topaz Street ⑬
Sapphire Street ⑭

Burn Out ⑮

12. Redondo Beach Breakwater

An excellent, powerful big-wave left wedge. Needs sizeable W-NW swells; breaks up to triple overhead. Experienced surfers only; big-wave boards are a must. Can get fun on smaller days but really comes alive when it's big. Gets extremely crowded and competitive. Lots of moving water and strong currents. The wave ends in severe shorepound. Usually some bad backwash, especially on high tides, so it's best with a low. One of the county's few big-wave arenas. Never closes out.

Located in front of the Chart House restaurant, on the north side of King Harbor. Park at the Chart House (pay) or along a nearby street.

13. Topaz Street

Sandbar lefts on the north side of the jetty. Picks up most any swell (except a straight S) and is sheltered from S storm winds, so it's a good call when there's rain and some winter swell action. Needs lower tide and swell up to about 1-2ft overhead (2-3m).

Access is at the foot of Topaz Street in Redondo Beach.

14. Sapphire Street

Sandbar rights on the south side of the jetty. Picks up far less swell than Topaz Street, but its location deems it a good option when NW wind is blowing out other spots in the vicinity. Good during the spring. A relatively safe spot; low tide works best, with larger W-SW swell or big windswell.

Access is at the foot of Sapphire Street in Redondo Beach.

15. Burn Out/Torrance Beach/RAT Beach

Beachbreak peaks at the south end of Torrance County Beach; mostly rights. Good with peaky W-NW swells and higher tides; fairly consistent and ridden regularly, especially during the summer. Gets hollow with outgoing tide; bad rip currents. RAT Beach is often surfable when the beachbreak to the north is too big.

Access is through Torrance County Beach, along Paseo de la Playa in Torrance.

Los Angeles County – Palos Verdes

1. Rat Shit

Fun reef peak, best mainly during the winter. Gets crowded. Best with NW swells and low tide.

Access is via a path next to the Roessler Swim Club.

Palos Verdes Cove

2. Haggertys

Named after the old Haggerty estate, classic and thick wintertime lefts off the rocky headland officially called Malaga Cove. Site of some of California's earliest surfing days. Three separate take-off zones here: furthest inside is Lower Hags, a slower left working best on W swell. Haggertys, the main peak at the base of the church parking lot, starts breaking at 4ft (1.2m). Lots of shallow rocks near the take-off; expect blatant drop-ins. Best with NW swell. South of the church, Upper Hags has very long walls. Starts

working at 6ft (2m); a mistake here will mean a trip over the reef. Best on big W swell. Paddle up from Haggertys.

Always plenty of takers at these high-consistency spots. Access is via a trail in the 500 block of Paseo del Mar at Via Chino, leading to the southern end of Malaga Cove.

3. Palos Verdes Cove/Bluff Cove/ Paddleboard Cove

One of California's first surf spots, boasting four separate quality reefbreaks. At the cove's north end is Ski Jump, a mushy righthander, slow and thick, breaking in front of Flat Rock Point. Handles up to 15ft (4.5m) at high tide. Only starts to work over 8ft (2.5m); it can be deceptively powerful and dangerous. Just inside of Ski Jump, North Reef dishes up fast walls – mainly rights with some lefts. High tide works best with W swells. Can't handle much size. The Cove's premier break is Middles, long, slow rights and lefts favored by longboarders. Needs W swells, good with some N. Watch out for clean-up sets and rip currents when it's big. Tends to close out at low tide, when the lefts get better. Boneyards is a juicy, rocky, shallow left on the south end of the cove. Gets hollow, works from mid tide up.

Middles is where Doc Ball shot many of his classic Paddleboard Cove photos in the 1930s. The Cove is now a Marine Preserve protected from development; good bird-watching, plenty of sealife including dolphins and the kelp beds make for glassy sessions. Access is via a broad dirt path at Flat Rock Point.

4. Indicator

A well-known trio of thick, rocky, powerful and somewhat hazardous reef waves off the south tip of Bluff Cove. All break from 4ft (1.2m) and up, best with medium tide and big NW winter swells. Challenging waves that are

Lunada Bay

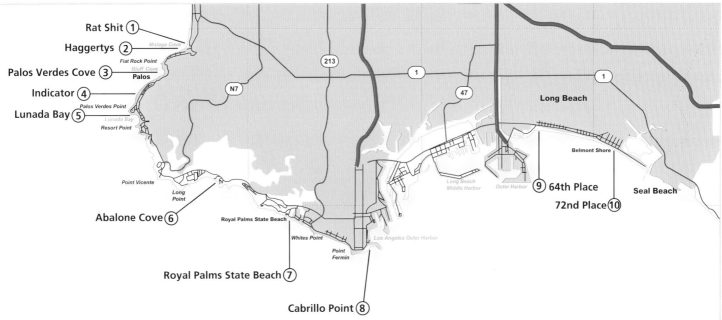

Rat Shit ①
Haggertys ②
Palos Verdes Cove ③
Indicator ④
Lunada Bay ⑤
Abalone Cove ⑥
Royal Palms State Beach ⑦
Cabrillo Point ⑧
64th Place ⑨
72nd Place ⑩

localized, so beware. The spots are too bumpy at extreme high tide, too shallow and rocky at extreme low tide. The innermost section of the point is called Lowers, a hollow, shifty reef wave. Middles lies just outside Lowers, a meaty, shallow left, good up until a few feet overhead. The outermost segment of the point is called Uppers, an unpredictable serious big-wave left only when the conditions are working in its favor. Often mushy and hollow on the same wave. Experienced surfers and big-wave boards only. Never closes out.

Access is via a sheer path off Paseo del Mar.

5. Lunada Bay
Famous big-wave reef infamous for nasty localism and thick, world-class righthanders. One of the few bona fide Southern California big-wave spots. Needs big W-NW swells and any tide. Perfect shape and very powerful with strong currents to match. A horseshoe-shaped bay. Starts at 6ft (2m) and never closes out.

Rocky and unfriendly. The locals can (and probably will) make you feel most unwelcome. Fights and fractured bones are commonplace, as arrests and lawsuits have been in recent years. Not a recommended surf spot for outsiders. Access is via a dirt parking lot and steep trail off Paseo del Mar.

6. Abalone Cove Beach
Decent, rocky lefts off the southeast end of scenic Portuguese Point. Needs S swells or a huge W. Handles up to about head high.

Access is via a steep path from the dirt parking lot (pay) on Palos Verdes Drive South, west of Narcissa Drive.

7. Royal Palms State Beach
Two spots here: the rocky right point is called Palm Point; it works with any W swell up to a foot or two overhead, but it's best with SW swells and low tide, when the wave lines up better. The Jetty is a popular peak best with higher tides and small to medium-sized SW swells. Both breaks get crowded quickly.

JIM RUSSI

Access is off Western Avenue and Paseo del Mar; mostly pay to park, but limited free parking on the bluff.

8. Cabrillo Point
Quality right point requiring large S swells to work. Long rides are possible; can be either fat or fast, depending on the tide. Can get really good.

Access is via Pacific Avenue in San Pedro.

9. 64th Place
Inconsistent, mushy, weak artificial reef wave requiring big S swells to break. Breaks both ways. Longboards only; somewhat polluted.

Access is at the foot of 64th Place in Long Beach.

10. 72nd Place
This mellow, funky beachbreak peak needs a huge S or SW swell to break but works on any tide. Can get good, just not very often.

Access is at the foot of 72nd Place in Long Beach.

Newport

ROB GILLEY

Orange County – North

1. San Gabriel Rivermouth

A.k.a. Power Plant, The River, Ray Bay, Seal Beach Jetty. Soft, fun sandbar peak between the jetties, right in the rivermouth. Needs peaky S-SW swells and lower tides. Can't handle any real size. The neighboring peak off the south jetty is Crabs, a small righthand sandbar wave.

Beware of numerous sand sharks and stingrays (step lightly). Water is warmer here than at surrounding spots, so consider increased likelihood of pollution after rain. Access is at the south end of Ocean Avenue in Seal Beach.

2. 7th Street

Hollow sandbar left tube requiring S or SW swells to work. A summer spot. Bad currents during large swells. Crowded when it's working.

Access is at foot of 7th Street in Seal Beach.

3. Seal Beach Pier

Average beachbreak peaks on both sides of the pier. Doesn't have the form of the peak at 13th Street, nor can it handle anywhere near the same size.

Beware of currents when it's big. Located at the foot of Main Street in Seal Beach. Home to a huge summer annual sandcastle building contest.

4. 13th Street

A beefy, unpredictable sandbar left that breaks during the winter on big W and NW swells. Steep and hollow; epic rides are possible. Crowded when it's on. Gnarly currents and shorepound. Not the most consistent spot in the county. Low tide preferred. Holds bigger than double overhead.

Access is at the foot of 13th Street in Seal Beach.

5. Dolphin Street

Very similar wave to 13th Street; long rides requiring large W and NW swells to break.

Access is at the foot of Dolphin Street in Seal Beach.

6. Surfside Jetty

The best wave at Surfside is the right bomb, which breaks off the jetty at the north end of the beach. Check it during a big W swell and low tide. Heavy waves with heavy currents. Fairly inconsistent.

Access is by walking up from Anderson Street to the south.

7. Surfside/Sunset/
Bolsa Chica Beaches

Six miles of average beachbreak; easy to find your own peak. Needs small SW swells with low-medium tide and NE wind.

Bolsa Chica State Beach fronts a scenic 300-acre wetland preserve, a sole reminder of what much of Southern California's coastline used to look like.

8. Huntington Cliffs

More beachbreak, generally better than beaches to the north. Still mushy and forgiving. Takes a low tide and W-SW swells. Lots of room, and lots of company.

Limited metered parking along Pacific Coast Highway, on the bluffs above the waves.

9. Huntington Pier

Check out the Huntington Pier area for a deep hit of Southern California surf culture. One of the world's most famous surf spots, site of many contests and a lot of history over the years, HB is predictably jammed, especially during the summer. The north side can handle big winter swells, sending often excellent rights peeling towards the pier. The south side works best on SW swells, showcasing frequently good lefts that wall right through the barnacle-encrusted pilings (this is the spot that made 'shooting the pier' famous). Both sides can work at any tide, though medium is usually best. Check further north for peaks where the service ramp hits the beach, also around the terminus of Golden West Street.

Very reliable and consistent on both sides of the pier. Blows out easily about the time surfing is 'blackballed' in

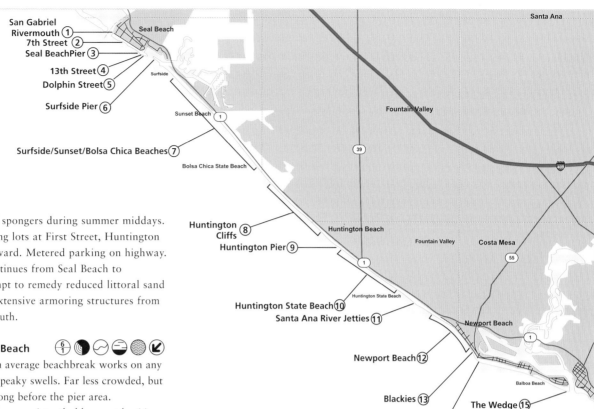

San Gabriel
Rivermouth ①
7th Street ②
Seal BeachPier ③
13th Street ④
Dolphin Street ⑤
Surfside Pier ⑥

Seal Beach
Santa Ana

Surfside

Sunset Beach

Surfside/Sunset/Bolsa Chica Beaches ⑦

Bolsa Chica State Beach

Fountain Valley

Huntington
Cliffs ⑧
Huntington Pier ⑨

Huntington Beach

Fountain Valley

Costa Mesa

Huntington State Beach ⑩
Santa Ana River Jetties ⑪

Huntington State Beach

Newport Beach

Newport Beach ⑫

Balboa Beach

Blackies ⑬
Newport Point ⑭

The Wedge ⑮

favor of swimmers and spongers during summer middays. Access is via pay-parking lots at First Street, Huntington Street and Beach Boulevard. Metered parking on highway. Beach nourishment continues from Seal Beach to Huntington in an attempt to remedy reduced littoral sand movement due to the extensive armoring structures from the Long Beach area south.

10. Huntington State Beach

Two miles of better than average beachbreak works on any tide, but favors smaller, peaky swells. Far less crowded, but closes (and blows) out long before the pier area.

All Huntington beaches consistently blow out by 11am. Access from pay parking lots along the beach. Metered parking on highway too.

11. Santa Ana River Jetties

Consistent, hollow peaks between the two jetties at the rivermouth. Needs a lower tide and any SW swell. Shallow sand bottom.

Polluted and extremely crowded when it's on. Limited parking on the Newport side, pay to park on the Huntington side.

12. Newport Beach

Long stretch of beachbreak interspersed with several short, rock jetties. Popular sandbars lie at the ends of 36th, 54th, and 56th Streets. Hollow, peaky, and very crowded. Holds up to a few feet overhead. Best during summertime S swells, but can be good at any time of the year.

Park anywhere you can find a spot, which is very difficult during the summer, weekends, or periods of good swell.

13. Blackies

Occasionally epic, long wintertime sandbar lefts north of Newport Pier, in front of Blackie's Bar. The rights do exist but pale in comparison. Better with lower tides, a due W swell and a Santa Ana wind blowing.

Definitely always crowded when it's on, since it is a rare and attractive occurrence.

14. Newport Point

Rare sandbar left renowned for producing world-class Pipeline-style barrels during large S swells and Mexican hurricane pulses. Needs a low tide.

Extremely crowded when it breaks. Located at 18th Street.

15. The Wedge

World-famous freak wave dominated by bodysurfers and bodyboarders, although surfers do enjoy some degree of success. Needs big S swells to work. Waves refract off the west (northside) Newport Harbor jetty, amplifying the swell and creating a ridiculous wedging peak, primarily a left, which explodes over a treacherously shallow sand bottom. Broken bodies are routine. Gets giant.

Extremely hollow and crowded. A real scene when it's working. Very dangerous spot, for experts only. Park in Corona del Mar or in West Jetty View Park.

The Wedge

ROB GILLEY

Orange County – South

1. Corona Del Mar Jetty

Quality, long sandbar rights, only during solid S swells, break off the east (southside) jetty of Newport Harbor. Needs low tide. Consistently offshore.

Gets epic and crowded. Access is via pay parking lots at Corona Del Mar Beach, Ocean Boulevard and Iris Avenue.

2. Morro Beach

Rocky, fast left off a small headland, requiring S swells and a medium tide. Not a very long wave but provides a rush. A summer spot, ridden regularly.

Access is via the PCH.

Morro Beach

3. Rockpile/Heisler Park

Hazardous, rocky Laguna Beach righthander best during bigger SW swells. Take-off behind large rock. Needs high tide.

Unfriendly local crew. Dangerous spot. Access is via pay lots at the park or metered parking along nearby streets.

4. Laguna Beach

A series of fickle reefbreaks, notably at the ends of Thalia, Oak, and Brooks Streets. Can get good but very crowded when it is. Best during medium-sized winter swells. Brooks Street can be a great left.

Needs a bit of size to start breaking, so it only rates as medium consistency. A high-quality wave. Free but limited parking on the residential streets.

5. Agate/Pearl Street

Rocky, shifty peak best during smallish-medium W swells and mid tide. Not a stellar break but good enough on its day. Rock hazards and mellow crowd.

Access at foot of Pearl Street.

6. Salt Creek Beach Park

A small, rocky point and a long, sandy beach frequently seen in surf magazines and videos. Three classic surfing areas. At the south end is The Point, a S swell left that gets epic, holding up to double overhead. In front of the restrooms is Middles, a consistent peak that can get good on any swell – sand and rock bottom, very competitive crowd. To the north is Gravels, a shallow, grinding righthand barrel, often closes out but provides great tube views along the way – good lighting and action for surf photographers; sand and rock bottom, takes any swell.

Gets very crowded with surfers and tourists as well. Located below the hotels and the bluffs off Ritz-Carlton Drive. Pay to park.

7. Doheny State Beach

Gutless righthand cobblestone reef waves, ideal for beginners and longboarders. Slow and mushy; any tide and swell. Crowded. Polluted after rains. Campground here.

Access from pay parking lot at Doheny State Park.

Rockpile

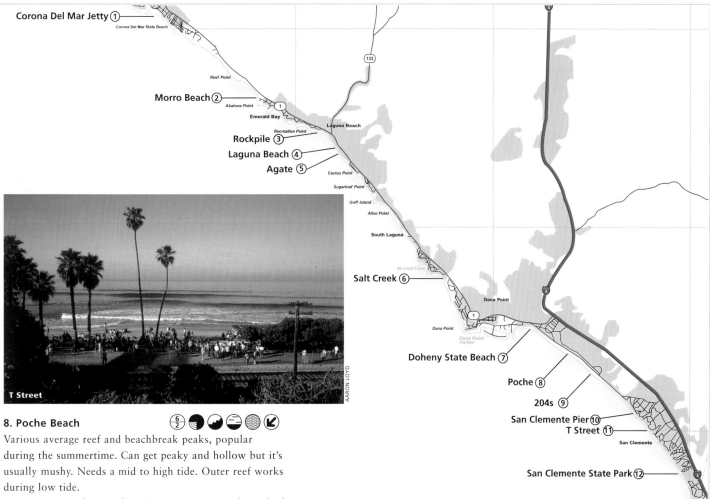

Corona Del Mar Jetty ①
Corona Del Mar State Beach

Reef Point

Morro Beach ②
Abalone Point

Emerald Bay

Laguna Beach

Recreation Point

Rockpile ③

Laguna Beach ④

Agate ⑤

Cactus Point

Sugarloaf Point

Goff Island

Aliso Point

South Laguna

Mussel Cove

Salt Creek ⑥

Dana Point

Dana Point

Dana Point Harbor

Doheny State Beach ⑦

Poche ⑧

204s ⑨

San Clemente Pier ⑩

T Street ⑪

San Clemente

San Clemente State Park ⑫

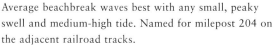

T Street

AARON LOYD

8. Poche Beach

Various average reef and beachbreak peaks, popular during the summertime. Can get peaky and hollow but it's usually mushy. Needs a mid to high tide. Outer reef works during low tide.

Access via underpass from the gas station at the end of Camino Capistrano, below PCH and the trail tracks to the beach.

8. 204s

Average beachbreak waves best with any small, peaky swell and medium-high tide. Named for milepost 204 on the adjacent railroad tracks.

Access is via dirt trail between private property. Ask the locals where.

10. San Clemente Pier

Crowded, mediocre sandbars on the pier's north side can sometimes get good. Typical beachbreak peaks, longer lefts, sectiony and often hollow. No wind protection, but any tide is fine. Fun during the summertime.

High school scene keeps it crowded. Longboard legend Rich Chew has been head guard here forever.

11. T Street (Trafalgar Street)

The main spot in San Clemente; early stomping grounds for many professional surfers of the 1980s, actually located at the foot of Esplanade. There's a rock reef on the outside and beachbreak on the inside; fun peaks best with S swells; lefts are usually better. Mushy with high tides, fairly hollow with low tides.

No surfing 11-6pm in summer and 10-6pm on weekends. Spongers rejoice!

ROB GILLEY

Salt Creek

12. San Clemente State Park

Hollow beachbreak peaks at the foot of Avenue Calafia; rock and sand bottom. Sectiony, mostly lefts. Good during the summer.

Campground on the bluffs. Access is via the pay lot at the foot of Avenue Calafia.

San Diego County – Trestles to Trails

1. Cottons Point

Excellent lefthand walls off the backside of San Mateo Point can get sizeable during solid S and SW swells. A great cobblestone summer wave. Can be fast and somewhat hollow; crowded when it's on. Needs a larger swell to work, and the wave ends in gnarly shorepound. Mid tide preferred. An easy paddling channel follows the northern breakline.

Located in front of President Nixon's old estate. Access is by walking north from Trestles or south from San Clemente State Park.

Cottons Point

ROB GILLEY

2. Trestles
(San Onofre State Beach North)

One of the world's most famous waves, seen in countless magazines and videos. Two breaks here: Uppers is a cobblestone mini-point featuring quality rights, often hollow and fast. Lower tides best with W swells up to double overhead. Generally less crowded than Lowers to the south. An often stellar cobblestone peak, Lowers provides occasional hollow, zippering lefts, but is more known for its long, fast, bowling rights. Best with SW swells up to double overhead. Can be good at any tide.

Pull up on the freeway exit overlooking the break as the sun rises, and there will already be 50 bodies in the line-up. Always super crowded. Park at or near the Carl's Jr. restaurant on El Camino and walk/bike in via the paved foot/bike path found at the Cristianitos Road freeway exit/overpass. Follow the path until it goes under the railway trestle and onto the beach, and you're there.

3. Church

Further south of Trestles is another sand/cobblestone point set-up. Mostly all rights (there's an occasional left off the north end of the trestle), very reliable, consistent, and semi-hollow during low tides.

Accessed by parking and walking north from San Onofre or slogging south from Trestles.

4. San Onofre State Beach

Famous, mushy longboard wave. Seedbed of California beach culture and site of some of California's earliest surfing contests and events. A great place for beginners; a family beach with mellow vibes. Old Man's is the premier cobblestone reef peak at San Onofre, a summertime spot best with lower tides. The Point is just north,

Lower Trestles

JEFF DIVINE

Cottons Point ① San Mateo Point
Trestles ②
San Onofre State Beach
Church ③
San Onofre State Beach ④
Trails ⑤

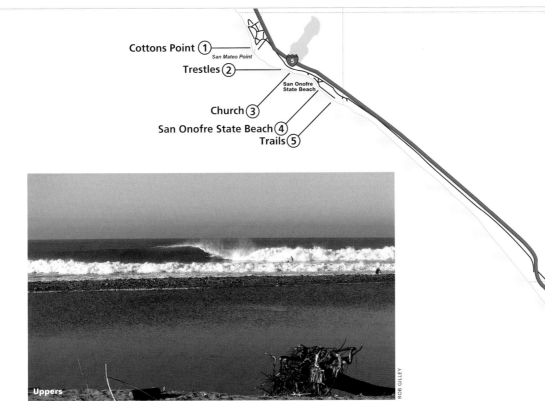

Uppers

ROB GILLEY

predominantly a righthander with occasionally good lefts.

Park entrance is accessible from Basilone Road. In summer and at weekends there are line-ups for parking right from first light, and the surf is just as busy. If you intend to visit often, ask about a yearly pass, good for both San Onofre and Trails.

5. Trails

About three miles (5km) of various beachbreak waves at the bottom of the bluffs west of trails Interstate 5;

secluded by San Diego standards. The closest thing to 'wilderness' in these parts. Trails 6 and 4 offer up the best prospect for favorable waves. Needs peaky SW swells with lower tides; can't handle any size.

Continue south along Basilone Road past the nuclear generating station to the entrance to the Campground/RV park. The hike down the bluffs keeps the crowds down. Surrounded inland and to the south by the Camp Pendleton Marine Corps Base, where several miles of publicly inaccessible beachbreak keep military surfers happy.

Oceanside

San Onofre

JEFF DIVINE

San Diego County – Oceanside to Encinitas

1. Oceanside Harbor

To the north of the parking lot is North Jetty (the south seawall of Oceanside Harbor) with long, consistent sandbar peaks. In front of the lot is South Jetty – mostly rights in a N swell, lefts in a S swell. South of this are more shapely peaks. Better with higher tides and peaky swells up to a few feet overhead. Can get hollow; always crowded. Usually bigger than spots to the south.

Attracts plenty of beach users; pay to park.

Big Rock

ROB GILLEY

2. Oceanside Beach

Decent beachbreak peaks at the Oceanside Pier and down the beach to the south. Hollower at low tide, mushburgers at high. Best with a peaky S swell.

Various access points along The Strand. Crowds, unfriendly locals, and a high crime rate may put you off.

3. Carlsbad City Beach

Stretch of mundane beachbreak, best with small, peaky swells and no wind; higher tides best. Rarely crowded and occasionally quite good, though it will mostly likely be better elsewhere.

Access via the ends of Christiansen Way, Grand Avenue, Elm Avenue and Ocean Street.

4. Tamarack Avenue

One of the better spots in Carlsbad, a sand/cobblestone reef peak best during summer swells up to a foot or two overhead. Very crowded. Any tide. Decent beachbreak to the north and south as well.

Camping available nearby. Down the beach by the power plant is Warm Water Jetty, a decent right sandbar when it works.

5. Terra Mar

Fat, slow, longboard wave. Shifty and usually not very good. Holds size but lacks power. Lefts off the north end, rights off the south end, and variable degrees of quality between. Gets crowded.

Access is off Highway 101, just south of Cannon Road. Park in the dirt on the ocean side of 101 and walk down the path.

6. South Carlsbad State Beach

At the northern end of the Carlsbad campground, just north of Poinsettia Boulevard. A free parking lot on the ocean side of 101 overlooks average beachbreak waves, best with small, peaky swells and no wind with medium tide. A good summertime alternative. Popular with tourists.

7. Ponto

Used to be a reliable stretch of beachbreak at the south end and on the reef at the north end, which was always the better area. But nowadays, the south end is the best spot, with semi-hollow, shifty sandbar peaks. Directly in front of the jetties, at the lagoon mouth, is a hollow, shallow righthand sandbar. Lots of currents, but it can be a fun spot; popular with young shortboarders. There has

Swamis

ROB GILLEY

recently been a perfect left breaking off the north jetty during S swells.

What was once a high-quality reefbreak at the north end has been ruined with the installation of two small jetties in the middle of the beach. The reefbreak is now beachbreak. Located alongside Old Highway 101 between the southernmost end of the Carlsbad campground and Leucadia. Park on the ocean side of the road.

Beacons

DON BALCH

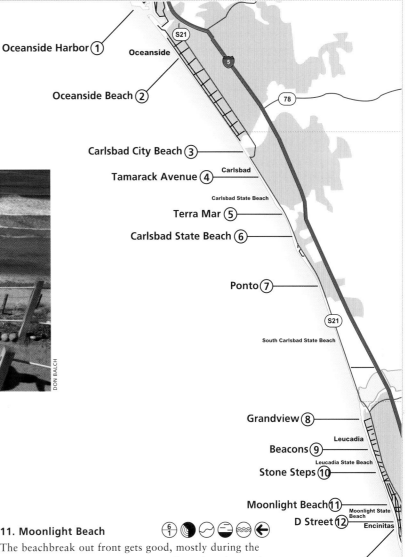

Oceanside Harbor ① Oceanside
Oceanside Beach ②
Carlsbad City Beach ③
Tamarack Avenue ④ Carlsbad
Carlsbad State Beach
Terra Mar ⑤
Carlsbad State Beach ⑥
Ponto ⑦
South Carlsbad State Beach
Grandview ⑧
Leucadia
Beacons ⑨
Leucadia State Beach
Stone Steps ⑩
Moonlight Beach ⑪ Moonlight State Beach
D Street ⑫ Encinitas
Swamis ⑬

8. Grandview
 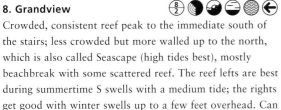

Crowded, consistent reef peak to the immediate south of the stairs; less crowded but more walled up to the north, which is also called Seascape (high tides best), mostly beachbreak with some scattered reef. The reef lefts are best during summertime S swells with a medium tide; the rights get good with winter swells up to a few feet overhead. Can line up quite nicely. Variable peaks down the beach as well.

Park in the lot (free) at the northernmost end of Neptune Avenue and walk down the stairs.

9. Beacons

The peak in front of the bluff trail is the main spot; a good, lined-up left and shorter, mushier right. Has recently lost quality due to human-induced sand build-up on the beach as a money-wasting ploy to attract tourists. Best with W swells up to a foot or two overhead. Needs a lower tide with smaller swells, higher tide with larger swells. Caters to everyone. Gets very crowded. Sandbars at the middle of the beach lead up to Bamboos, a fun righthand reef/sandbar combo in front of the bamboo patch in the bluff, under the houses.

Park in the narrow-paved blufftop lot (free) along Neptune Avenue at its confluence with Leucadia Boulevard.

10. Stone Steps

Variable beachbreak peaks at the bottom of the cement staircase off Neptune Avenue at South El Portal. Gets hollow and fast. Some sections of reef to the north. Medium tides best with small, peaky swells from any direction. No beach here at high tide.

Relatively uncrowded for north San Diego County. Site of the infamous beer-fueled Stone Steps surfing contest.

11. Moonlight Beach

The beachbreak out front gets good, mostly during the summertime with peaky, smaller swells and medium tides.

Developed sandy beach popular with tourists in the summer. Snack bar, volleyball courts, lifeguard tower, etc. Surfing restrictions enforced during the summer months.

12. D Street

Fairly good beachbreak just south of Moonlight. Sometimes hollow and powerful; usually has some kind of rideable surf when all else is flat. Best with medium tides and peaky SW swells. Very crowded. Blows out easily.

Access is at foot of D Street. Park along surrounding streets.

13. Swamis

Famous, high-quality righthand reef that handles big swells (up to triple overhead) better than any spot in the vicinity. The outer peak has been compared with Oahu's Sunset Beach – a big peak and a hollow, thick wall which lines up through a fast inside bowl over the inner shelf. Larger W swells work the best, with lower tides increasing the hollowness. A performance wave. The best spot in Encinitas, always worth a look.

Extremely crowded and competitive. Located down the long staircase below the Self-Realization Fellowship's small parking lot. Check it from the road south of the break.

San Diego County – Cardiff to Blacks

1. Pipes/Campgrounds
Several flat reefs along the length of the San Elijo State Beach campground. Some are square barrels, others are sectiony mushburgers. Low tides produce many boils and suck-up sections. Peaks like Traps, Turtles, Muffs, and 8560s can't handle much size but offer fun, punchy rides during smaller, peaky swells. Best direction is from the W to SW with mid-low tide.

Gets super crowded. Access is by parking along the inland side of 101 and (dangerous) running across the road, or in the pay lot in the campground, which is now open year-round.

Cardiff Reef

2. Cardiff Reef
Three high-quality reef waves are soft during summer months but come alive with winter swells. The reef to the immediate north of the lagoon mouth is called Tippers, primarily a hollow, fast left and shorter, mushier right. Gets crowded. Just south is Suckouts, a hairball righthand barrel over a very shallow reef (like a miniature Shark Island). Easy to get hurt here. Experts/shortboards only. Then there's the more mellow South Peak in front of the parking lot – long, quality rights peeling into the channel. Difficult to make it out during big swells. Some hollow sections; really lines up during low tide.

You can almost always find something to surf at Cardiff Reef, but it will always be crowded. Access from the pay lot in front of the break, right off the 101.

3. Sandbox
Average beachbreak directly in front of the restaurants. Needs mid tide with small, peaky swells. Can be really fun. Good summer option.

Park along 101 near the stoplight at Las Olas Mexican restaurant.

4. Georges
About a mile of beachbreak right alongside Old Highway 101, between the restaurants in Cardiff and Seaside Reef.

Needs small, peaky swells with lower tide to alleviate backwash. Has regained some of its previous quality with recent beach sand nourishment. Hardly broke for years because of sand loss. Never crowded.

Park along 101 and find your own peak.

5. Seaside Reef/
South Cardiff State Beach
Quality deep-water reef peak, lefts dominating. Outside is a thick, hollow, ledgy take-off after which the wall backs off in the middle before reforming on the inside. Needs big W swells with mid tide. High tide creates backwash. Highly competitive crowd.

Access is via large paved parking lot off 101.

6. Pillbox/Fletcher Cove Park
Decent sandbar peaks up and down the beach. Small, peaky swells with mid-low tide work best here. No beach at high tide except right in front of the parking lot ramp. Popular summertime spot.

You can get a recorded surf report for Pillbox when you dial 858-755-2971. Located in Solana Beach off South Sierra Avenue.

7. Del Mar Rivermouth
Although not a consistently epic rivermouth break by any standards, it can get quite good, especially following heavy rainfall (somewhat of a rarity in SoCal) with a smaller W swell. Usually an average beachbreak.

Access is via parking in southernmost Solana Beach (and walking down) or in northernmost Del Mar (and walking up).

8. Del Mar Beach
All beachbreak from the rivermouth down to 15th Street. Average and cannot hold size. Needs smaller, peaky swells and incoming tide. Plenty of room for everyone, though, and some good sandbars do exist. Shifty and uncrowded.

Access is at the ends of the seaside streets of Del Mar.

9. 15th Street
Primarily a fun lefthand reef with adjacent beachbreak peaks. The most popular and consistent spot in Del Mar, it likes a WSW swell and light E wind. Any tide will do, although extreme highs tend to make the surf too fat and mushy, while lows can get hollow. 8th Street is another popular break, a slow and mushy peak. Mellow.

Site of Del Mar longboard contest. The lifeguards here offer a daily recorded surf report at 858-259-8208. Access is on-street pay parking around 15th Street.

10. South Del Mar
Decent right reef that usually has something to ride. Takes any small to medium-sized swell and any tide with no wind or morning offshores. Rather mushy but fun.

Access is by walking north from Torrey Pines State Beach.

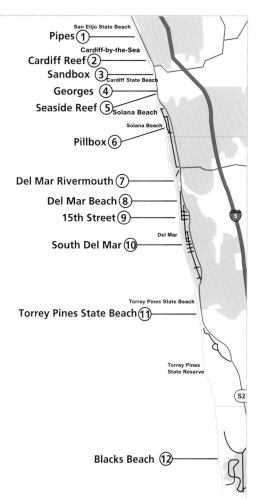

Pipes ① San Elijo State Beach
Cardiff Reef ② Cardiff-by-the-Sea
Sandbox ③ Cardiff State Beach
Georges ④
Seaside Reef ⑤ Solana Beach
Solana Beach
Pillbox ⑥

Del Mar Rivermouth ⑦
Del Mar Beach ⑧
15th Street ⑨
South Del Mar ⑩ Del Mar

Torrey Pines State Beach
Torrey Pines State Beach ⑪

Torrey Pines State Reserve

S2

Blacks Beach ⑫

11. Torrey Pines State Beach

To the north of the parking lot, about a mile of average beachbreak peaks fronted by sheer sandstone bluffs. Best with small winter swells and high tide. The beach is crowded with tourists during the weekends and summer months.

Beach access and the main parking lot are at the North Beach area adjacent to Los Peñasquitos Lagoon. Check out the nearby Torrey Pines State Reserve, site of the only natural continental habitat for the world's rarest pine, the Torrey.

12. Blacks Beach

Also known as Torrey Pines City Beach, this is a famous, high-quality half-mile stretch of beachbreak, known for its consistency and power. Usually the biggest spot around. The La Jolla Submarine Canyon funnels swells directly into Blacks, which features three distinct spots: South Peak, a heavy, perfect left; Middle Peak, a two-way affair with the lefts usually being better, and North Peak, a brief but exciting righthand barrel. Blacks holds huge swells, but be prepared for lots of severe rip currents, sneaker sets, and long hold-downs. Very painful if you get caught inside. Gets very crowded.

Located at the south end of Blackgold Road, off of La Jolla Farms Road. Nudist beach for those who wish to surf naked. Access is via a very steep and rocky pedestrian path down the bluffs (even the nudists wear shoes).

Blacks Beach

La Jolla Cove

ROB GILLEY

San Diego County – La Jolla

1. Scripps Pier/La Jolla Shores

Wide sandy beach with peaks breaking on both sides of the pier, the south side usually being better. The Shores, fronting the parking areas to the south, can be excellent. Best with a medium tide; blows offshore during rare wintertime SE winds.

Home of the Scripps Institute of Oceanography (researchers love the deep waters of the canyon). The Shores becomes very crowded during the summer. Very friendly beach. Access via La Jolla Shores Drive.

2. La Jolla Cove

When La Jolla Cove is breaking, most everywhere else will be closed out, and there will be hundreds of spectators here. A long, big-wave left, which only works during the biggest winter NW swells. Very thick and powerful, but not very hollow. Great drops. Mid-low tide works best. Southerly storm winds blow offshore here. Gets crowded when it's on.

Simmons Reef

JEFF DIVINE

Scripps Pier and La Jolla Shores

ROB GILLEY

Use caution and good timing when entering and exiting the water; very rocky and rough with caves in the cliff face. Experts only. Located off Coast Boulevard, east of Girard Avenue.

3. Horseshoe

Strong W swells produce this ledgy, high-quality peak. Shallow, jagged reef with little room for error. Edgy locals. Mid tide with a solid swell works best.

Not very consistent but well worth the wait. Heavy spot, experts only. Walk north from Marine Street.

4. Rockpile

Good reef peak during S and W swells; quality walls during ideal conditions – medium tides and no wind.

Can get crowded with it's on. Access is via Sea Lane in La Jolla.

5. Little Point

Fast summertime left, steep and hollow. Crowded. High tide only and shortboards preferred. Breaks off the small point just north of Windansea.

Walk north from Windansea.

6. Simmons Reef

Thick, barreling righthander over shallow reef. Not a consistent spot but high-quality when it breaks. Broken boards and bodies are common. Low tide only with solid W swells working best. Also takes NW.

Named after Bob Simmons, the early surfing innovator who drowned at Windansea in 1954. Walk north from Windansea.

7. Windansea Beach

Famous reefbreak firmly entrenched in the annals of surfing history. Powerful, thick peak with a long, tapering right and a shorter, hollower left. Either can hold sizeable swells. Best with summer SW swells and any tide; usually bigger than other spots around.

Gets very crowded and has a competitive atmosphere. Accessed from the end of Vista de la Playa and from Vista de la Playa at Fern Glen, and by stairways along Neptune Place, south of Fern Glen.

8. Big Rock

A Pipeline-style barrel to the south of Windansea, also called Moids or Lobster Lounge. Very heavy, very shallow, very hollow; holds up to several feet overhead – expert tuberiders only. W swells work best. Only rideable at mid to high tide.

Dangerous rocks and a tight take-off zone means lots of aggression in the line-up.

South Bird Rock

DON BALCH

9. South Bird Rock

Fun, small summertime reefbreak best during outgoing tides and peaky SW swells. Backwash at high tide.

Located at the end of Bird Rock Avenue.

10. Tourmaline

Popular, mellow peaks best with SW swells and higher tides. Good spot for longboarders and beginners. Gets crowded during summer. Pacific Beach Point is the sectiony right reef just north that only really works with straight W swells. Worth a look if that is the case.

Park in the free lot at the end of Tourmaline Street.

Big Rock

ROB GILLEY

Tourmaline

DON BALCH

Scripps Pier/La Jolla Shores (1)

La Jolla Bay

La Jolla Cove (2)

Point La Jolla

Horseshoe (3)
Rockpile (4)
Little Point (5)
Simmons (6)

La Jolla

Windansea Beach (7)

Big Rock (8)

South Bird Rock (9)

False Point

Tourmaline (10)

Crystal Pier

DON BALCH

San Diego County – South

1. Crystal Pier/Pacific Beach

Decent beachbreak in the heart of Pacific Beach. Works best with small, peaky SW swells and higher tides. Gets hollow. Lots of room.

Located at the end of Garnet Avenue.

2. Mission Beach

A mile of mundane beachbreak from Santa Rita Place to the Mission Bay entrance channel. Only surfable when small, clean and peaky at high tide. South Jetty at the south end of the beach can get good, with shorter rights ending in a channel and longer lefts with a harder paddle back out. Gets crowded.

A paved promenade runs along the beach.

3. South Jetty/Dog Beach

Decent sandbar peaks; can be good with any tide and peaky swell up to a foot or two overhead. Punchy sections and some tubes. Consistent.

Usually crowded. Watch out for dog shit on the beach. Located at end of Voltaire Street.

South Jetty/Dog Beach

DON BALCH

4. Ocean Beach Jetty

Small, variable beachbreak waves. Needs small, peaky swells and no wind. Regularly surfed; almost always has something to ride. Blows out easily, so catch it early or late during the summer.

A popular spot and often crowded. Access via Ocean Beach Park.

5. Ocean Beach Pier

Fun beachbreak peaks on the either side of the pier (the longest pier on the West Coast – 2,100ft/700m). Nice paddling channel for the rights on the north side. Occasionally gets hollow.

Always crowded. Located at the end of Niagara Avenue. Loads of surf shops nearby.

6. Sunset Cliffs

There are several excellent reefbreaks along Point Loma, site of unfriendly locals and stellar waves at the base of sheer cliffs. Steep, unsafe trails lead from the road down to the water. Best during the winter on lower tides when W swells set the reefs firing up to triple overhead. Top spots include (from north to south): Luscombs, a thick peak with fast sections; Rockslide, more thick peaks; North and South Garbage, consistent rights and lefts; Abs, a long, chunky left custom-built for performance; New Break, a hollow, zipper-fast right with protective locals – the jewel

Ocean Beach Pier

ROB GILLEY

Sunset Cliffs – Abs

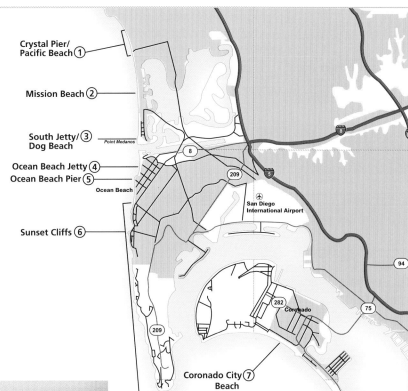

Crystal Pier/
Pacific Beach ①

Mission Beach ②

South Jetty/ ③
Dog Beach   Point Medanos

Ocean Beach Jetty ④

Ocean Beach Pier ⑤
                    Ocean Beach

Sunset Cliffs ⑥

San Diego
International Airport

Coronado

Coronado City ⑦
Beach

Point Loma

Silver Strand State Beach

Imperial ⑧
Beach

Sunset Cliffs – Rockslide

of Sunset Cliffs, and Chasm, a tapering left across the channel from New Break.

All spots are accessible by parking along Sunset Cliffs Boulevard or in the lot off Ladera Street.

7. Coronado City Beach/ Coronado Shores Beach

Long fetch of powerful beachbreak, best with peaky summertime S to SW swells. Very hollow and unforgiving when it's firing. High tide works best. Blows offshore with a N wind.

Unfriendly local crew.

8. Imperial Beach

Consistent, high-quality, powerful wintertime beachbreak where good sandbars can form around the pier. Often back-breakingly hollow and never crowded. Long, reeling rights and lefts; difficult paddle-out when sizeable.

Water is often polluted. Located west of Ocean Lane, between Carnation and Encanto Avenues.

Imperial Beach

Baja

For over half a century, the Baja peninsula has held an unique place in the psyche of Californian surfers. For some, 'Lower California' represents the promise of immediate escape from the madness of Stateside crowds, a place to troll the coast or hole up in front of an isolated pointbreak and live the simple surfer's existence. For others, it's a party trip – heading across the border in a car full of friends hoping to score a couple of days of fiestas and barrels. Then there's the crew that flies down to Cabo for an easy two-week getaway, enjoying all the comforts an inflated dollar, warmer water, and (hopefully) good waves can bring.

However you go, the one common factor is quality surf. This wildly wave-rich desert, heavily stacked with righthand points, can truly be recognized as one of the world's great surf zones. Throw in an exuberant Latino culture, good food, and cheap living costs, and it's little wonder that Baja is a perennial favorite with American surfers.

There are some dangers (not least the roads, which can lead to a perfect point or to the middle of nowhere, shaking many a vehicle to death along the way), but rest assured that, for the intelligent and friendly surfer, Baja is a worthy surfer's destination.

Shipwrecks, Cabo.

DON BALCH

The Surf, Ocean Environment and Surf Culture

Rosarita (above) **and Baja Malibu** (below) **are both located within an hour of the US border.**

Baja California is a 1,200km (750mi) finger of rock and desert bounded by the Pacific Ocean on the west and separated from mainland Mexico by the tranquil Gulf of California (a.k.a. Sea of Cortez). Its rugged coastline of hidden coves, sandy beaches, and rocky bluffs is an indisputable extension of Southern California's surfing consciousness. For decades, Baja has remained an essential desert surfari destination for mobile surfers looking to escape the pressure-cooker atmosphere and crowds of SoCal's modern surf scene.

Plate tectonics created Baja's separation from the mainland over 5 million years ago (the notorious San Andreas Fault runs the length of the Gulf), and the peninsula continues to drift northwesterly an inch or two every year. The first maps, drawn up by Spanish explorers in the 16th century, depicted the peninsula as an island, rumored to be rich with gold, which ignited a struggle for control of its mineral wealth. In the early 1800s, the United States offered to purchase Upper and Lower California for $25 million. Mexico's refusal resulted in the Mexican War (1846-8) ending in a peace treaty. In subsequent negotiations, the US offered $15 million for both the Californias; Mexico again refused, but a compromise gave Upper California to the US, while Mexico kept Baja.

Much of Baja is a sparsely-populated desert wilderness, but the Mexican government is trying to make some changes they think will attract more tourist dollars. Environmental impacts are difficult to assess here, but it's certain that coastal development is on a crash course with a number of excellent Baja surf spots. Increasingly, coastal access is blocked by private condo developments using armed guards to patrol perimeters, sealing off beaches from non-owner surfers. Meanwhile, many top-quality surf breaks are under threat from a proposed string of harbor developments running the length of Mexico's Pacific Coast.

Swell Forecasting

Baja is famous for surf and sunshine, thanks to its fortunate positioning on the fringes of the major weather systems to the north and south. The winter Aleutian storms deliver strong NW swells, bringing consistent surf to the entire coast. As this swell source fades in spring, the summer cycle begins to pump from the south – long range pulses from Roaring Forties storms along with more local tropical disturbances or hurricanes, known as chubascos.

The northern and southern regions of Baja have different climates and ideal surfing seasons, but on the whole Baja is a genuine year-round surf destination. As an extension of the Upper California coast, Northern Baja, with its S-angled beaches, is well-suited to the winter pattern of NW to W swells and northerly winds. Even so, some good northern breaks work only on strong southerly swells, which has led to the belief that Baja is a summer destination. This is true of the Cabo region, which receives less energy from North Pacific swells. Here, those W and NW winds blow offshore at the tip and around into the Gulf of California, where any strong swell with S in it will bring waves to some part of this more developed coastline.

The conditions of dirt roads is greatly affected by rain and whether they have been recently graded.

JIM RUSSI

The Trans-Peninsula Highway (Mex Highway 1) snakes the length of Baja, alternating coasts, sometimes tracing the peninsula's midline. The northern third of Baja has a strong California influence, and surfers are targets of the burgeoning tourist industry. Paid campsites just off Highway 1 offer beach access, cold showers, and holiday crowds for $5 per vehicle. Exploring further south requires a bit more perseverance, but the rewards more than compensate – free camping on sandy beaches, at a procession of uncrowded right points.

A good, sturdy vehicle will get you to the best-known surf spots, but heading off the beaten track requires 4WD and a self-sufficient stash of water, gas, and food. South of Ensenada, services get sparse, and it's 800km (500mi) of bad road ahead. But from La Paz down to Cabo San Lucas, it's a developing new world, with all the trappings of tourism lining the southern shore of the vastly warmer Gulf of California. This return to civilization comes complete with 5-star hotels and smooth, paved roads.

WEATHER AND WATER STATISTICS	J/F	M/A	M/J	J/A	S/O	N/D
Tijuana						
rainfall (inch/mm)	2/51	1.1/28	0.2/5	0.1/3	0.2/5	1.5/38
consistency (d/mth)	6	5	2	1	2	5
average sun (hrs/day)	7	8	8	10	9	8
min temp (°F/°C)	47/8	52/11	57/14	63/17	59/15	50/10
max temp (°F/°C)	63/17	66/19	70/21	76/24	74/23	68/20
water temp (°F/°C)	59/15	61/16	64/18	69/20	68/20	62/16
wetsuit						
Cabo San Lucas						
rainfall (inch/mm)	0.6/15	0/0	0.1/2	1/25	5.7/150	0.7/20
consistency (d/mth)	1	0	0	2	6	2
average sun (hrs/day)	9	9	8	7	8	9
min temp (°F/°C)	54/12	55/13	62/17	72/22	70/21	59/15
max temp (°F/°C)	75/24	84/29	91/33	95/35	91/33	81/27
water temp (°F/°C)	74/23	74/23	77/25	82/28	82/28	79/26
wetsuit						

TRAVEL INFORMATION	
Mexico	www.mexonline.com
Baja	www.bajaexpo.com

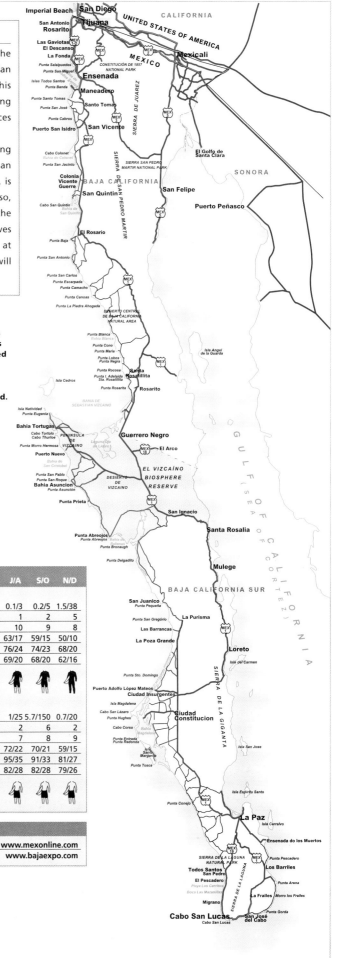

JEFF DIVINE

Both Salsipuedes (right) and San Miguel (bottom) are famous Ensenada points.

The Surf

The following areas represent both geographical and psychological differences that separate Baja into five distinct zones:

Tijuana to Ensenada – The most crowded part of Baja is between the US/Mexico border and Ensenada. Expect very little in the way of the 'true Baja' experience here; instead, it's easy road access and mass tourism with crowded waves at a variety of good breaks. Beyond the average beachbreaks of Playas de Tijuana and the subsequent private condo developments, Baja Malibu is a powerful and consistent peaky beachbreak that takes any swell from S to NW and is best from low to mid tide. It's very easy to find and will always be crowded. Rosarito, a few miles further south, has a long stretch of exposed beachbreak scattered with reefs and rivermouths. It's a crowded party town and has good facilities, including a surf shop and a hospital, but the water can be polluted.

Distance markers in kilometers are used to name breaks like K-38 and K-38.5 which get California-crowded thanks to easy access and quality waves. These spots break year-round; they work best on a S but will handle a big W or NW. Spots like K-40, Las Gaviotas, Raul's, and others offer above-average waves, but can get crowded too.

Campo Lopez (K-55) is known for powerful, tubing beach peaks with some lefts off the rocks; very consistent, but new development will severely restrict access. La Fonda (K-58) has good rivermouth-fed sandbars that keep the beachbreak waves hollow and punchy. Salsipuedes (reef) and San Miguel (slick cobble) are legendary Baja right pointbreaks. The area has some sharky breaks, like 3M's, near the canneries and fish-processing plant. The metropolis of Ensenada is the jumping-off point for Baja's most famous wave, Killers, which bombs onto the reefs off Islas de Todos Santos 20km (12mi) offshore. This is a world-class big-wave spot where any available winter swell is focused and magnified. (Rental boats are available from Ensenada; 6 people with guns for $100).

Ensenada to El Rosario – South of Ensenada, true Baja surf missions begin where the highway leaves the coast and strays into the beautiful and barren inland. There's still plenty in the way of 'civilization' all the way past San Quintin and on to El Rosario, which is sort of a halfway house between the crowded tourist reality north of Ensenada and the remote and challenging country below El Rosario, where the winds get stronger, the water gets colder, and the waves are less crowded away from the well-known spots.

Past Ensenada and the military checkpoint at Maneadero is the little village of Santo Tomas. Head west from here along one of the unpaved tracks and you'll arrive at Punta San Jose or Punta Cabras. Both have great point, reef, and beachbreak waves, and the kelp helps keep 'em glassy in this wind-challenged area, but they're only five hours or so from the border, so they can be jammed with San Diego weekend warriors. There's a rare signed and paved road that leads straight to the reefs and beaches of K-181 and the well-stocked town of Erendira. Access south of there gets difficult until San Telmo de Abajo signals a string of kelpy, righthand points from Cabo Colonet down to Punta Camalu. Name breaks like Quatro

TOM DUGANESM

Casas (Punta San Telmo) are often crowded with longboarders who relish the forgiving waves and camping scene overlooking the break. Freighters (Rincon de Baja) is located at Punta San Jacinto, where surf-camp clients enjoy long, mellow rights.

The coast west and south of San Quintin is an abundance of sand interspersed with volcanic reefs. Problems with tough access and strong NW winds are offset by minimal crowds and great sport-fishing. The empty beachbreaks sheltered by Cabo San Quintin are great on a S swell, with more of the same stretching for miles down to El Rosario.

El Rosario to Guerro Negro – About 8-12 hours from the border, Highway 1 sweeps inland, heralding the first of many long, slow, dirt tracks that don't always make it to the coast and rarely link up. Rest assured, you will find few day trippers or weekend surfers here. Expect to get lost. Punta Baja is the first and easiest in a procession of classic righthand points that include the infamous Seven Sisters. There are more than seven puntas, but surfing them all will require returning inland to the highway and choosing another bone-shaking track with no guarantees at the end. Punta Santa Rosalillita is a sheltered spot looking for a decent W swell to dish up perfect long pointbreak rights when elsewhere is too big (Santa Rosalillita is one of the waves threatened by Mexico's harbor-development plans). When the swell is smaller, try the right and left reefs at Punta Rosarito. There are loads of other good (even excellent) spots, but finding them is tough work.

Guerro Negro to Todos Santos – South of Guerrero Negro Highway 1 veers to the Gulf side, so this is the least explored section of Baja's west coast. Although (just like you) NW swells have trouble getting in, S and W swells can morph into world-class waves along this stretch of beach where N winds blow offshore and the water temperatures rise. The only well-known spots are the insanely hollow beachbreaks off the east coast of the island of Natividad and the points at Scorpion Bay (Bahia San Juanico). Isla Natividad's world-class beachbreak, Open Doors, provides some serious grinding barrels; swells come out of deep water and hit the sandbars with board-snapping power. Access problems and costs keep crowds down as the only options are luxury fly-in trips or boat access-cum-feral camping.

Down the coast, more scalloped, S-facing bays funnel the afternoon trades into offshores at a series of puntas, freckled with reefs and beachbreaks. Punta Abreojos faces almost E, which has put its long righthanders (breaking over the razor-sharp reef) on the endangered-by-harbors list. Much further south, the headland at Scorpion Bay boasts seven righthand points reached by 48km (30mi) of gravelled washboard road. On a precise S swell, the third point breaks top-to-

bottom like a machine, while the second is a sheltered nursery for novices. However, the bay can be flat for weeks, so that's a concern. Rumors of all seven points connecting into a 5km (3mi) ride can not be discounted. It's about 14 hours straight driving from the border.

The next 420km (262mi) can only be described as 'out there'. Apart from exclusive surf tours to Isla Magdalena, empty beach, reef, and points are probably waiting for those willing to go the extra, arduous miles.

Cabo San Lucas – The Tip of Baja is washed by warmer waters and offers a 200° swell window, from NNW around to SE. There's a decent road system and a growing abundance of seaside resorts. This area is one of the most popular destinations for Californian surfers; you'll either love it or loathe it.

On the Pacific side, Todos Santos is an oasis of civilization, fueled by a long-established artist community that attracts tourists and, more recently, developers. Playa San Pedrito continues the oasis feeling with its scattering of palm trees overlooking decent beachbreaks and even a rare lefthand point on a S swell.

BOOTS MCGHEE

The rights at the Pescadero reefs are close to shore and get the maximum out of the swells; surf in the morning to take advantage of the clean conditions. Cerritos is well-protected by its northern headland, which shapes nice rights, especially in a NW swell. The long beach to the south consistently works on all swell directions and is a favorite all-abilities zone. Further down, Migrino has a similar righthand point set-up; the closest west-side spot to Cabo, it is earmarked for development.

Cabo San Lucas proper is always flat; the closest good wave is Monuments, a spectacular left that picks up extra swell along an offshore submarine canyon. It's a short wave with no room for a crowd, it picks up a wrapping W swell. Various pockets of beach and reef lead through Chileno, past the excellent, easy-access rights of El Tule. Punta Palmilla is a bay that is full of resorts and condos; it

The desolate central Baja landscape is constantly buffeted by winds.

takes a big swell to ignite the rights that break out off the point. Costa Azul is the main surf center on the south shore with three main breaks, beginning with the mellow longboard section of Acapulcito. More crowded is The Rock, a wave that surges through a minefield of smaller rocks before mushing out onto the shore. The third and final section is the superfast right wall known as Zippers, the most famous and crowded wave in Cabo. Don't be surprised to encounter vibes from the locals, who wait for magical days when all three sections link up.

The luxuries of Cabo recede as typical Baja washboard track leads into the deserts of the East Cape and a series of right pointbreaks on the edge of the Gulf of California. The further east you drive the less consistent the surf becomes and the more important it is to time your trip with a big chubasco swell from the S or, better still, SE. Shipwrecks is a major landmark, along with Nine Palms; both offer long rides. There are more reefs and points to scope out in this wind-sheltered area. Los Frailes is one harbor with a reef worth checking. Live coral reefs begin to appear south of Punta Arenas, which protrudes into the Gulf to pick up local storm waves out of the N as well as very strong S swells.

Cabo region.
Below – **Monuments, a rare left in a sea of rights.**
Bottom – **Shipwrecks is a S swell only spot on the East Cape.**

The Environment

While at least 65% of Baja is desert, the peninsula is subject to strong wind and rain from the E and S, especially when summer disturbances hit the south coast. Flash floods and short-term chaos are compounded by impassable, washed-out roads. Pacific storms can wrack Northern Baja with similar torrential conditions in winter, when heavy rains transport huge amounts of sediment to the rivermouth sandbars, frequently through narrow arroyos and across already challenging roads.

The Trans-Peninsula Highway is a shoulderless ribbon of road, used by meandering mules and livestock, assorted beat-up vehicles, and tequila-fueled long-haul truck drivers. Cattle trigger a large proportion of the road deaths, but driving at night is the biggest killer. The local warning system for an approaching hazard could be as obscure as a strategically-placed white-painted rock, branch, or tire...meaning 'slow down.' Detailed topographic maps are essential for navigation; vehicles should carry tools, a tow-rope, and a shovel.

Water temperatures vary hugely from north to south and so do wetsuit needs. In Baja's northern waters, winter temperatures hover in the mid-50s (13-14°C), calling for a 4/3 or 3/2 steamer plus boots. South of Vizcaino, winter temps gradually rise until you round the tip and enjoy the East Cape's 65°F (18°C) water. Summer is generally springsuit weather up north, unless you're surfing the cold upwelling between Ensenada and El Rosario. Trunks are all you'll need around Cabo, but some light rubber might still be useful for west coast dawn patrols.

The burning environmental issue in Baja is the planned string of 22 marina/resort complexes along the west coast. Citing preposterous projections of nautical tourist numbers and commencing construction without any Environmental Assessment (EA), observers fear the outcome will be a whole herd of white elephants. Intense pressure from experienced environmental campaigners has forced the government to make a concession and commission some form of EA, which range from superficial to all encompassing. Proposed sites are almost all protected righthand pointbreaks like Cabo Colonet, Punta San Carlos, Punta Canoas, Punta Abreojos, and Scorpion Bay.

Shoreline development in Northern Baja and the Cabo area has put many breaks behind the walls of private condo and hotel developments. This trend is set to continue as SoCal population pressure grows and coastal real estate prices soar, while the Mexican government continues to chase the high-end, unsustainable tourist dollar.

Inadequate (or no) sewage treatment facilities are the rule throughout Baja, particularly in the coastal city of Tijuana, where poorly-treated sewage has long plagued surfers.

DON BALCH

JEFF DIVINE

ROB GILLEY

Surf Culture

Although a few pioneers made surfing forays into Northern Baja in the 1940s and '50s, larger numbers of SoCal surfers began making the pilgrimage south in the 1960s. While a few Mexicans started to surf on boards they got from visitors, only recently have significant numbers of locals joined the mainly gringo line-ups in the north and down in Cabo.

Even before WWII, surfers rode the Tijuana Sloughs; known as the best big-wave venue in SoCal, these peaks just north of the border attracted many of the best surfers around. Back in the 1950s, a few pioneers ventured south into Mainland Mexico. In '57, while delivering a small yacht back to the US, Phil Edwards and Whitey Harrison stumbled across perfect, peeling waves on a small desert island off the coast, where an old board was stuck in the sand proclaiming, "Mel Ross surfed here. The surf was 10 feet." Greg Noll made the long drive to Mazatlan in '58, but with no Trans-Peninsula Highway to help explore Baja, he only got a look around Cabo when he and wife Beverly crewed a yacht through the area. Cabo resident Mike Doyle recalls that, "when I was about 13 [c. 1955], a guy named John Thurston rowed the whole coast in a dory without (or with little) provisions."

Surfers began to trickle over the border in the early 1960s, congregating at the name spots like K38 1/2, San Miguel, and 3M's. In 1963, Bill Fury and Mike Hynson explored the surf for some 120km (75mi) south of Ensenada. Skip Frye and other Windansea Surf Clubbers made the first documented surf trip to Isla Todos Santos in

1964. Steve Bigler checked out Cabo and environs in '67. MacGillivray-Freeman Films was first to showcase some of Baja's new discoveries in the 1968 film, *Free and Easy*.

In 1966, Mike Doyle met Nacho Felix (Ignacio Cota) in Ensenada's notorious Long Bar. "He was Ensenada's first surfer," says Doyle. "I helped him put on the first contest at San Miguel with Hoppy Swarts and the whole deal. The Mamas and Papas were there along with Jimi Hendrix, and the police wanted to bust them for smoking grass, but Nacho's father warned against it, because they were so popular in the US that it would be bad for tourism." Directed by Nacho (a '66 World Contest competitor in San Diego), the Baja Surf Club Invitational was held at San Miguel from '66 to '69, and most top California surfers made the scene.

Once the two-lane Trans-Peninsula Highway opened in late '73, California surfers started making longer, more in-depth Baja forays; new discoveries included Abreojos and Scorpion Bay, both first-rate pointbreaks. Then, on February 5, 1987, World Champ Tom Curren, along with Dave Parmenter and a crew of other hotties, motored out to Isla Todos Santos off Ensenada to surf the biggest waves yet photographed on the West Coast, shaking Hawaii's pre-eminence in the big-surf arena. In recent years, California crowds have mushroomed and, slowly but surely, Baja's breaks have been found and ridden. Mike Doyle quotes Mama Espinosa, who had a place at Rosarita Beach where the paved road ended and everybody stopped in the old days: "The bad road brought the good people, and the new road brought the bad people."

Punta Abreojos faces east, offering natural protection, which puts it on the list of proposed harbor development locations.

Nova Scotia

Northeast of New England, arcing off into the North Atlantic, are Canada's Maritime Provinces – lands of rugged, windswept terrain, chill waters, fog, and sometimes good waves. The most surf-rich of these provinces, Nova Scotia, is as large as Vancouver Island even without adding in Cape Breton Island, its rugged northeastern territory.

This predominantly southeast-facing arc of coast is in a good position to gather up a wide range of swell pulses, and its complex, sawtooth shoreline provides an ideal set-up for bending swells and creating wind-sheltered pockets. Pointbreaks, an assortment of reefs and plenty of beachbreaks bring a wide range of wave choice to surfers in Nova Scotia, where crowds are rarely an issue. Away from the established breaks near the cities, there is obvious potential for lonely sessions in quality waves. But icy cold water and harsh northern seasons make it an uncomfortable place to surf, which is fine with the small group of hardcore locals.

Nova Scotia has a seemingly endless coastline with enormous untapped possibilities. Get ready for long drives, frustrating searches, and the occasional happy payoff…and bring plenty of rubber!

DAVID PU'U

Rudy's Head.

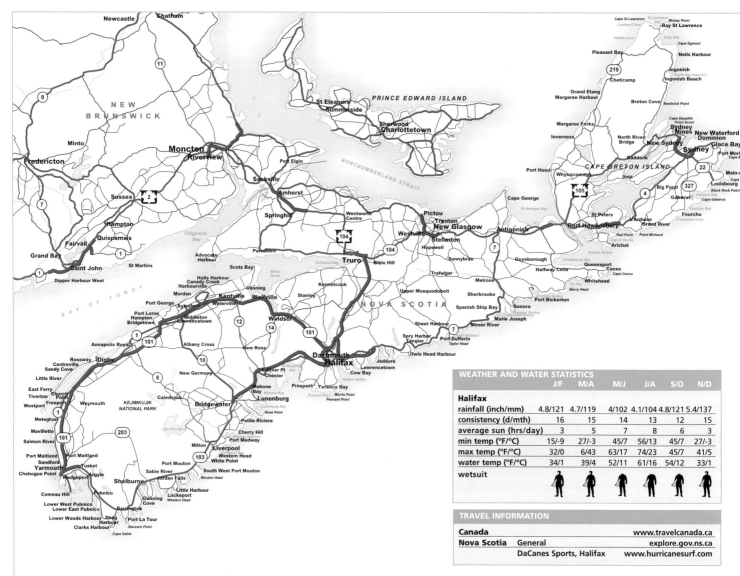

WEATHER AND WATER STATISTICS						
	J/F	M/A	M/J	J/A	S/O	N/D
Halifax						
rainfall (inch/mm)	4.8/121	4.7/119	4/102	4.1/104	4.8/121	5.4/137
consistency (d/mth)	16	15	14	13	12	15
average sun (hrs/day)	3	5	7	8	6	3
min temp (°F/°C)	15/-9	27/-3	45/7	56/13	45/7	27/-3
max temp (°F/°C)	32/0	6/43	63/17	74/23	45/7	41/5
water temp (°F/°C)	34/1	39/4	52/11	61/16	54/12	33/1
wetsuit						

TRAVEL INFORMATION		
Canada		www.travelcanada.ca
Nova Scotia	General	explore.gov.ns.ca
	DaCanes Sports, Halifax	www.hurricanesurf.com

The Surf, Ocean Environment and Surf Culture

The bulk of Nova Scotia is bucolic, but access to the coast is straightforward.

Nova Scotia is a 580km-(360mi) long peninsula-cum-island (Cape Breton) surrounded by four bodies of water – the Atlantic, the Bay of Fundy, the Northumberland Strait and the Gulf of St Lawrence – with a tortured topography that has been gouged and shaped by numerous glacial advances, the last of which reached its height about 20,000 years ago. With an average width of only 130km (80mi), you're never far from the sea. With a mosaic of rugged headlands, serene harbors, and ocean beaches, the irregular coastline of Nova Scotia stretches some 10,500km (6,500mi), highlighting the surf potential of this northeastern outpost.

People of the Mi'kmaq First Nation inhabited Nova Scotia for thousands of years before the first European explorers arrived. Norsemen are believed to have visited the region in the early 11th century, but the cycle of Western European exploration didn't begin until around 1500. The French were the first to settle in NS, which (along with parts of New Brunswick, Quebec and Maine) they named Acadia. France and Britain feuded over the area for sometime before Acadia was surrendered to the British in 1713. In 1867, Nova Scotia (named after Scotland) was one of the four provinces that composed the new federation called the Dominion of Canada. The province was known for its shipbuilding, lumber and fish trades. Its chief city and capital, Halifax, was an important naval port during the First and Second World Wars.

MEZ/ESM

DAVID PU'U

MEZ/ESM

The population of Nova Scotia is just under a million, approximately a quarter of them of British decent, with significant percentages of French and other Europeans. Smaller proportions of the population are of native, black, Asian, or Middle Eastern origin. Close to 400,000 Nova Scotians live in the Halifax metropolitan area. Some of the other major towns include Yarmouth, Kentville, Bridgewater, Truro, and Sydney. Almost half of the province's population still resides in rural and coastal areas.

Although there are some environmental issues, it is difficult to discuss surfing in Nova Scotia without the conversation turning to temperature. This is the main concern of Canada's East Coast surfers, who brave the coldest ocean water in North America. The bulk of the surfing population is based in Halifax, riding the popular and consistent breaks of Lawrencetown. Surfers from south of the Canadian border first discovered the empty waves of Nova Scotia over a quarter century ago; since then there's been a steady growth of summer surfers as well as year-round hardcore riders.

Swell Forecasting

While often unpredictable, hurricane season (especially late summer and early fall) offers the best potential for the combination of relatively warm water and quality surf. If you're lucky enough to catch a solid hurricane swell from the south, you could score overhead surf with good power. This is also the time of year that North Atlantic storms start winding up, bringing consistent swells to the east coast. Wave heights in the fall range from 1-3m (3-10ft) with water temperatures generally between 12-18°C (54-64°F).

Summer surf in Nova Scotia consists of small locally-generated wind swells, arriving at various angles from the NE around to the SW with wave heights ranging from 1-1.5m (3-5ft), while water temperatures usually fluctuate between 10° and 18°C (50°-64°F). Early season hurricane swells are uncommon but not unheard of, while occasional North Atlantic low pressure systems relieve the summer doldrums with overhead surf.

Springtime can produce some quality surf, too, but water temperatures remain very cold into the early summer – ranging between 3°-6°C (37°-43°F). The occasional late season nor'easter can generate quality groundswell, but most waves come via locally generated windswell.

As might be expected, Nova Scotia receives consistent surf in the winter months, as nor'easters and other deep North Atlantic low pressure systems repeatedly pound the coast. Unfortunately, heavy snowfall and storm-force winds often accompany the waves. Meanwhile, water temperatures drop near the freezing point, while air temperatures plunge as low as -20°C (-4°F) when the offshores rip out of the NW. With recent advances in wetsuit technology more Nova Scotian surfers are braving the cold and scoring good surf, but it's grueling.

Above – **Minutes, Cow Bay. One of the quality pointbreaks close to Lawrencetown.**
Left – **For those wishing to look further afield there are endless possibilities along the fjord like coastline.**

The Surf

The convoluted coastline of Nova Scotia provides for a multitude of perfect set-ups. Although the East Coast, with its Atlantic exposure, is the only part of the province that receives semi-consistent swell, the options are prolific. The surfable coastline can be broadly divided into three regions: the South Shore, the Eastern Shore, and Cape Breton.

The South Shore of NS is largely untapped in terms of surf potential having countless set-ups with varying levels of accessibility. There are plenty of point and beachbreaks in the Yarmouth and Lockeport areas, but the most popular breaks on the South Shore are around Liverpool. White Point Beach is a relatively consistent beachbreak, while nearby Western Head is a reef and pointbreak that offers more power on a good groundswell. To the northeast of Liverpool are a number of beachbreaks, such as Cherry Hill and Hirdles, and many infrequently surfed points that are yours to explore.

The Eastern Shore, although often more crowded, offers numerous point, reef, and beachbreaks. Lawrencetown Beach is the most consistent beachbreak in the region, but it rarely gets good and starts to close out at about 1.5m (5ft). During larger swells, the points in this region start to light up, offering a variety of lefts and rights that provide shelter from the various wind directions. During the winter and on larger summer swells, the points and reefs of Cow Bay can also get good. Martinique (about an hour east of Lawrencetown) is another consistent beachbreak that is surfed regularly in the summer.

Cape Breton Island is another largely untapped surf region in Nova Scotia. There are only a handful of locals in Cape Breton, but the area has been explored and has unlimited potential. Some of the more well-known surf areas include south-facing Michaud Point, Kennington Cove, and the exposed NE area of Ingonish, on the fringe of the Cape Breton Highlands National Park.

Top – **Nova Scotia experiences more than 100 foggy days in a year.** Below – **Unlike the US East Coast, Nova Scotia has plenty of left pointbreaks.**

MEZ/ESM

Ocean Environment

The Nova Scotian climate is driven by the sea, which surrounds most all of the peninsular province, moderating seasonal temperatures. In the spring, stubborn cold ocean temperatures postpone the arrival of summer, while in the fall relatively warm water from the Gulf Stream delays the onset of winter. Summers are cool compared to the rest of Canada, with July temperatures averaging 17.5°C (63°F), but 30°C (85°F) daytime highs are not uncommon. Winds prevail from the SW in summer, which is onshore at most of the main surfing beaches. Winters are moderately cold with an average January air temperature of -4.5°C (24°F) and the occasional -18°C (0°F) day. Prevailing winds in the winter are from the NW – offshore at most breaks, but straight from polar bear territory. On average, Nova Scotia receives 1500mm (60in) of precipitation per year (10% of it snow), which peaks in late fall and early winter when storms are more frequent. The interaction of the warm Gulf Stream and the cold Labrador Current south of Nova Scotia produces extensive fog, which can engulf coastal areas for long periods in spring and early summer. Halifax is foggy more than 100 days per year.

Water temperatures fluctuate dramatically with the seasons, ranging from near 0°C (32°F) in late winter to 20°C-plus (68°F+) in late summer/early fall. Consistent sub zero air temperatures and tenacious offshore winds set the scene for the winter months, resulting in frigid water temperatures that rarely break the 4°C (40°F) barrier. Although the air warms significantly when spring arrives, water temperatures remain cold at 3°-6°C (37-43°F) into early summer. By mid-to-late summer, water temperatures have caught up with the air, generally ranging between 10°-18°C (50-64°F). The warmest waters occur in late summer and early fall when temperatures hover around 15°C (59°F), but occasionally reaching 20°C (68°F) or more when warm core rings reach the coast after breaking off the Gulf Stream. This wide range of water temps means Nova Scotia surfers need to have a good variety of (thick) rubber.

MEZ/ESM

On the northwest coast of the peninsula, the Bay of Fundy is famous for the biggest (up to 17m/50ft) tides on the planet. Twice a day, approximately 100 billion tons of water move in and out of this 270km-long (170mi) straight-sided, somewhat funnel-shaped bay where even normal tides rise and fall 9-13m or (30-40ft). When the moon is new or full, the range can be as great as 18m (53ft)! Each day as the tide comes in, the tidal bore charges across the mud flats and up into the bay's coves and rivers, creating tidal bores as the channels narrow. The largest bore in the Bay of Fundy occurs on the Petitcodiac and Schubenacadie rivers, where thousands of summertime tourists ride the bore waves in inflatable craft, a boon to the local economy. Fortunately, Nova Scotia's eastern seaboard is less radical in range, where the semi-diurnal tides max out at a mere 2m (6ft) allowing most breaks to be ridden on all tides if there is enough swell. Water quality at most of the surf breaks is good due to the lack of coastal development, however some of the harbors, especially Halifax's, are very polluted due to a lack of sewage treatment facilities and the presence of heavy marine traffic.

The continental shelf south of Nova Scotia (Scotian Shelf) was once amongst the most biologically productive fishing grounds in the world. Unfortunately, centuries of overfishing resulted in the collapse of the once lucrative fishing grounds in the early 1990s. More recently, the offshore oil and gas industries has expanded, introducing another threat to this already degraded ecosystem.

Nonetheless, marine life is still relatively abundant in the coastal zone, especially on the South Shore, where whales, porpoises, and seals are encountered on occasion. Shark sightings are rare, and interactions with humans are virtually non-existent.

When the pointbreaks get good in the Eastern Shore region (especially in and around Lawrencetown), it is important to respect the locals. There is an influx of Americans with each hurricane season, and this has spawned some physical confrontations and acts of vandalism in the past. Cameras are discouraged by the heavier locals, who have been described by traveling Americans as "hockey-playing construction workers." Beyond the Lawrencetown-Cow Bay area, localism is virtually non-existent. Instead, expect welcoming grins and generosity from the locals.

The Lawrencetown area is about an one-hour drive from Halifax International Airport, which is three hours from the South Shore and 4-5 hours from Cape Breton. Renting a car is almost essential, since the surf spots are spread out along the rural, fjordlike coastal terrain, where getting from point A to point B is seldom direct. For real searching (e.g. in the Cape Breton region), a 4x4 may be an asset, although many breaks are easily accessible.

The historic capital city of Halifax, 30km (19mi) from the Lawrencetown area, offers an energetic nightlife with one of the highest ratios of bars per capita in North America. Hotel rooms can be hard to find in the city, especially during summer and early fall. For this peak tourist season, booking a room ahead of time is a good idea. Bed and breakfasts are an option outside of the city, but they can be expensive. A cheap summer solution is to use the numerous campgrounds scattered throughout the province.

Surf Culture

The first surfers to explore Nova Scotia's waves were adventurous Americans, who followed hurricane swells up the coast about 25 years ago. Several of these explorers liked what they saw in the Lawrencetown area, so they stayed. The idea started to spread amongst the local residents and ever since, the surf community has been slowly growing. Even so, by the late '80s there were probably no more than 100 surfers in the province.

At present some 400 regular summer surfers enjoy the Eastern Shore region of Nova Scotia. A much smaller core group of about 50 endure the frigid winters. The level of surfing is average at best, but the locals are keen, and recent advances in wetsuit technology have led to rapid progression over the last few years. Most local surfers are between the ages of 20 and 35, but there is also a prominent group of 40-plus veterans that show up when the points start to work. The surfer population outside the Eastern Shore region probably doesn't exceed 50.

You won't find a prototypical surf town in Nova Scotia; most of the beaches are outside major urban centers and protected by strict coastal development restrictions. The surf scene in NS has a low profile. Surfing is still a relatively new sport in the province, and boards on the roofs of cars still attract curious looks. There is, however, a prominent skateboard community and an associated music scene, which naturally overlaps with the surf crowd. A few surf shops (like DaCanes Sports in Halifax) sell equipment tailored to the harsh local conditions. They'll be happy to see you.

While much of the coast has been explored it still remains relatively unridden.

New England

New England, the cluster of six states occupying the extreme northeast corner of the United States, is fabled for its fiercely cold winters, yet it is situated on about the same longitude as southern France. Four of these states touch on the Atlantic Coast and have surfable waves: Maine (ME), New Hampshire (NH), Massachusetts (MA) and Rhode Island (RI).

In fact, New England boasts the American East Coast's best surfing areas. Further to the south, a broad, smoothly sloping continental shelf drains incoming swells of much of their wave energy, but here the offshore waters are deep and swells sweep into shore with plenty of punch still left in them. New England's four surfing states are the only places in the east where you're likely to encounter rocks in the surf. Pointbreaks and reefs, consisting of boulders, pebbles, or fingers of rock, provide a contoured base for some killer waves. Complimented by a scenic landscape of forested hills and a twisting coastline, New England is a beautiful and laid-back place to check out.

Hospitable people, plenty of history, unique architecture, and autumnal colors, are just some of the attractions for the millions of tourists who flock here in summer and fall. But, if it's surf you're after, then any season other than summer is going to be your best bet, which means thick rubber, thick skin, and hopefully some thick waves. Respectful travelers will find the hardy locals friendly and accommodating, unlike New England's winter conditions, which can be extreme.

The Point at Ruggles, Rhode Island.

MEZ/ESM

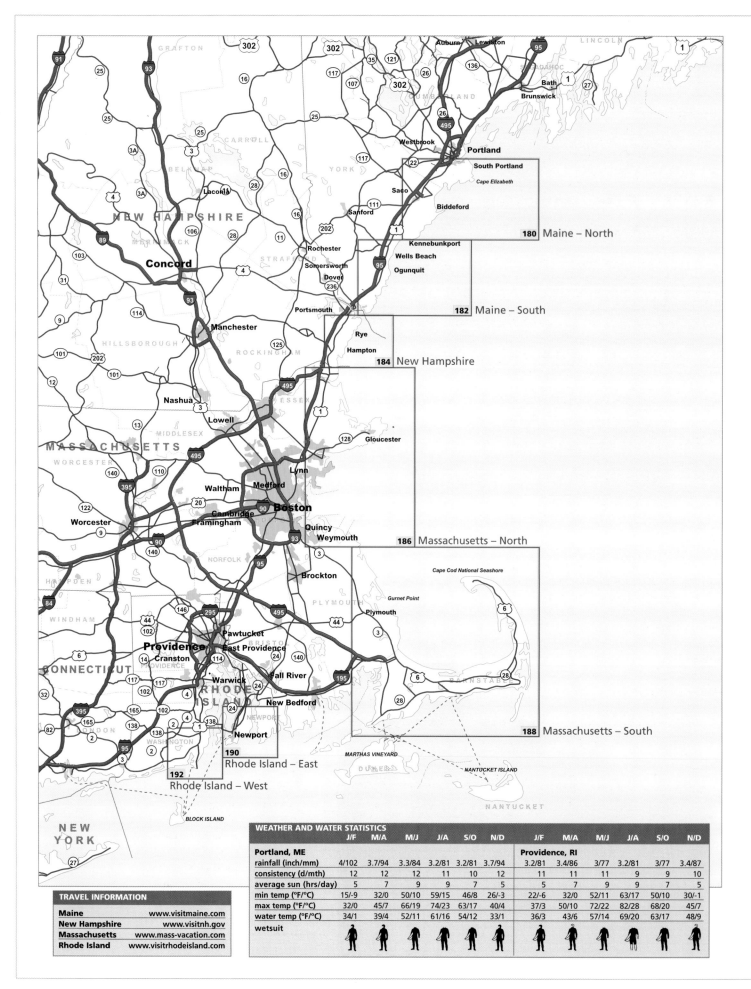

WEATHER AND WATER STATISTICS												
	J/F	M/A	M/J	J/A	S/O	N/D		J/F	M/A	M/J	J/A	S/O	N/D
Portland, ME							**Providence, RI**						
rainfall (inch/mm)	4/102	3.7/94	3.3/84	3.2/81	3.2/81	3.7/94		3.2/81	3.4/86	3/77	3.2/81	3/77	3.4/87
consistency (d/mth)	12	12	12	11	10	12		11	11	11	9	9	10
average sun (hrs/day)	5	7	9	9	7	5		5	7	9	9	7	5
min temp (°F/°C)	15/-9	32/0	50/10	59/15	46/8	26/-3		22/-6	32/0	52/11	63/17	50/10	30/-1
max temp (°F/°C)	32/0	45/7	66/19	74/23	63/17	40/4		37/3	50/10	72/22	82/28	68/20	45/7
water temp (°F/°C)	34/1	39/4	52/11	61/16	54/12	33/1		36/3	43/6	57/14	69/20	63/17	48/9
wetsuit													

TRAVEL INFORMATION

Maine	www.visitmaine.com
New Hampshire	www.visitnh.gov
Massachusetts	www.mass-vacation.com
Rhode Island	www.visitrhodeisland.com

BRIAN NEVINS

The Surf, Ocean Environment and Surf Culture

New England can lay claim to being the best surfing area on the East Coast for a number of reasons. Whereas the eastern seaboard to the south is virtually devoid of any coastal geological variation other than sandy barrier islands, New England provides a whole range of permanent surfing substrata. From Maine's cliffy, craggy coast of reefs, rivermouths and islands through New Hampshire's boulder-strewn points and slabs of submerged granite, right down to Rhode Island's cobblestone reefs and rocky protrusions, New England has the goods – a welcome relief from those endless shifting beachbreaks.

On top of the obvious geological advantages, New England tends to receive the lion's share of non-hurricane swell from North Atlantic depressions, plenty of hurricane swell when it is around (particularly for the south and southeast), and parts of it boast the widest swell window on the East Coast. Add to this a distinct lack of crowds and a welcoming vibe from the remarkably laid-back bunch of

GIB... / PAUL KENNEDY

hardcore locals who brave the extremes of winter, and New England becomes the definitive locale for quality East Coast surf.

While New England presents a beautiful natural backdrop to many lightly populated surf locations, the history of environmental pollution in the region makes for less attractive reading. Possibly because of the harsh winter weather conditions, recreational ocean users have been a voiceless minority and, until recent years, have not been considered by the government or industry. Surfrider Foundation chapters are now active in most New England surf states and are providing the catalyst for changing attitudes within the state and county bureaucracies, as well as among the surfing and non-surfing communities.

The history of New England surfing centers around Rhode Island, which has always been the most accessible for surfers and surf. The other three states have had a similar chronological history, albeit on a smaller scale.

Above – **The Wall is New Hampshire's most consistent and accessible break. Even in conditions like this with winter water temperatures getting down to 33°F (1°C) there will still be some takers.**
Below – **New England's favorite seafood.**

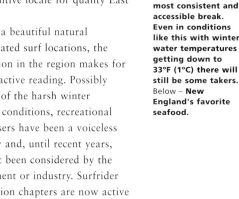

Maine

Maine gets the frontiersville tag if you're looking at surfing north of Portland. From the capital south to New Hampshire, Ogunquit is the main focus; this is where the bulk of the surfing population either live or hang out. Winter northeast swells provide the most consistent source of sizable waves since the Maine coast can find itself eclipsed from some hurricane swells by Cape Cod to the south.

Winter water temperatures can plunge below freezing with the ocean 'slushing' in places, but recent years have seen milder temps prevail, possibly linked to the global warming phenomenon.

Maine should be high up the clean-and-green meter, but the truth is quite the opposite. Industrialization, insensitive industries, archaic treatment facilities, and a general attitude of apathy have conspired to make it less pleasant (and safe) to surf in Maine than it should be.

Maine is one of the few states that have stopped building any hard stabilization structures, such as jetties, piers, or seawalls, but no erosion information is available for the state. Overfishing in the Gulf of Maine has led to rotating bans on fishing for cod within 30 miles (48km) of shore, but this seems a token gesture for just one of many species being squeezed to extinction. A recent victory involved breaching a dam that had prevented many fish species from accessing their spawning grounds.

Human access issues in Maine are coming to the forefront, particularly in towns where residents-only permits or expensive lots are the only parking options, where private land is a barrier to the coast, and where mindless bureaucracy has banned surfing, even in a State Park like Short Sands. Surfing permits are rearing their ugly heads in some counties, where the owners of coastal land feel the general public should have to pay for the

MIKE BAYTOFF

PAUL KENNEDY

Above – **Add a strong, cold offshore, just to remind you it is Maine. Moody Beach right.**
Right – **Nasty looking brown foam, Costellos, New Hampshire.**

The massive natural harbor of Portland has seen recent oil spills threaten parts of the coast and decimate concentrated areas of marine habitat. Fishing has always been a backbone industry in Maine, but is undoubtedly the source of much of the flotsam and jetsam found washed up on many of the southern beaches. Poor sewerage treatment means that the Ogunquit River is used to transport the town's sewage directly into the line-up. Although a mile-long outfall pipe deals with the primary treated waste, it drifts straight back to the beaches in onshore conditions.

Rivers flowing from inland also bring plenty of unknown elements to Maine's 230 miles (370km) of coast, particularly in the spring months when water levels are high. Stormwater treatment in the state is either non-existent or at best, rudimentary. Where does that colored foam come from?

Maine's municipal governments have begun water-quality monitoring (at least once a week) at East End Beach in Portland, Old Orchard Beach, Willard Beach, Ogunquit Beach, and Wells Beach, and beach closures do occur.

privilege of enjoying the short stretches of coast still in the public's possession (only about 5%). Access is further encumbered by the fact that some beaches are privately owned between the low and high tide lines, which restricts lateral movement on dry land.

Surfer Crow is the name that always crops up when you ask about the history of surfing in the northeast corner of The States. A colorful, easily identifiable character who's always seen out in the line-up at Ogunquit wearing a scruffy old canoeing helmet, Crow had a small shop in town during the 1960s, when he shared the line-up with just a handful of locals. Other than that, there was an old lady who ran a classic shop from her basement in York, which she stocked each year on a winter van trip to California with her husband.

Maine enjoyed the latter days of the pre-shortboard surfing boom, but followed the rest of New England into the dead 1970s. Only the core kept surfing year-round here; most of them are still scattered through the line-ups, among a new breed of Maine surfer, who has only known the comfort of modern wetsuits and drysuits.

New Hampshire

New Hampshire only has 17 miles (27km) of coastline, but it's probably the most action packed stretch of surf on the whole East Coast. The Wall is a super consistent and powerful beachbreak, but it's the surrounding reefs that are the real challenge. The concentration of rock-bottomed breaks makes it possible for experienced surfers to ride a range of wave types from walled-up right points to hollow left reefs, with or without some company.

Summer can be a bummer for any sizable swell, but winter will always throw up some heavy lines for the small crew of big wave junkies.

Wave size may be less consistent than the frequent offshore winds of spring and fall, but there are sure to be a few classy days during these months.

New Hampshire appears to have fewer environmental problems than its neighbors, largely because of the diminutive length of its coastline. The main problem areas are centered around estuary water and salt-marsh outflow, which is particularly noticeable at spots like Costellos. Plus, there are the unknown effects of having the nuclear plant, which is located within sight of the main tourist town of Hampton Beach. As yet, there is no Surfrider Foundation chapter operating in New Hampshire.

One access note: the popular reefbreaks around Rye and Foxhill are almost devoid of parking places; this is also a problem if you are surfing the Seabrook area to the south during the summer.

A surfboard appeared on the tiny New Hampshire coastline as early as the 1950s, but, as with the rest of New England, the scene didn't kick off here until well into the '60s. Dewey Weber pioneered the rights at Rye On The Rocks, and many West Coast luminaries of the period (like Mike Doyle and Greg Noll) made annual East Coast runs to promote surfboard sales.

By the time the boom was over in the '70s, the state was devoid of shops, and surfers had to make a trip to Maine or Rhode Island for equipment, and equipment was a major issue when it came to handling the extreme cold of the best surf seasons. Things remained seasonal here until the era of the beavertail jacket disappeared and 5mm front-zip Victory suits hit the market, via Kevin Grondin's garage, in the late '70s. Even then, the groms were always waiting on the beach trying to borrow any available rubber, but it was a small closed community until summer came around again. Surf shops appeared again around 1984, and the surfing population has been growing organically and steadily ever since.

Above – **One of the first New Hampshire reefs to be surfed. Rye on the Rocks showing some form.**
Below – **Looking down the New Hampshire coast at rocky reefs and pockets of sandy beach, which make this tiny coast a big New England attraction.**

PAUL KENNEDY

Above –
Boston Skyline.
Right – **Plenty of
summer restrictions
around the big city.**

Massachusetts

North of Boston appears to be well set up, with potential reefs and points everywhere, but they never seem to deliver the quality waves that this coastline suggests. There are a few fickle secret spots, tucked away, while places like Deveraux attract a dedicated crowd.

South of Boston, the beachbreaks of Hull and the breaks around Scituate offer a haven for the city surfers. Cape Cod is a bit of a weird one; it's one big crescent of sand, producing shifting beachbreaks of variable quality. These hard-breaking, sand bottom waves can reach epic size, by East Coast standards, way out to sea, in an area that is regularly blighted by thick ocean fog. Summer gets crowded on the Cape but it does tend to pick up any swell from the east and has the right aspect to pick up some hurricane swell too.

The islands of Massachusetts – Martha's Vineyard and Nantucket – are the state's real gems, with wide swell windows and few surfers, but access and localism are apparent problems.

Massachusetts or, more to the point, Boston, has suffered the worst ocean pollution in the northeast, courtesy of a turn of the century sewage treatment facility, which was only decommissioned in recent years. So ancient was the system that many a museum was interested in acquiring its old pumps, which were perfect specimens of Victorian engineering. The late 1990s brought an improvement in water quality, both north and south of Boston Harbor, courtesy of a new treatment works. However, this could merely be diluting the problem, as outfall pipes have simply been extended further out into Massachusetts Bay.

Other major concerns are stormwater runoff, beach debris and access issues.

NO SURFING 10AM TO 5PM MAY 15th TO SEPT.15th

NO PARKING ANYTIME

PAUL KENNEDY

While most of the state's coastal communities have regular water-quality monitoring programs, Surfrider Foundation members have been mapping the stormwater drains and collecting data to help pinpoint the origin of pollutants. Cigarette butts are top of the heap in the beach debris tables, since they can travel from urban zones to the beach quite easily. Commercial and industrial pollution levels will be more closely monitored and hopefully enforced via the BEACH legislation, allowing Surfrider to concentrate on issues such as access, beach clean-ups, and the grassroots education program, Respect the Beach.

In order to improve water quality on Cape Cod, ex-president Bill Clinton asked for federaly managed beaches there, where an overburdened infrastructure in summer leads to problems with septic tanks, of which 25% of the existing installations failed to meet state and local standards. The Governor of Massachusetts has passed an historic bill that requires comprehensive testing and monitoring of coastal waters, the results of which will be readily available for surfers to assess the state of their local breaks. Another large environmental concern on the Cape is the heavy erosion that has been eating into the crumbling, sedimentary cliffs.

Through the data collection for the Beachscape Project, the most shameful fact to emerge is that 73% of the Massachusetts coastline is privately owned with access restricted. This includes the crucial low tide to high tide strip.

As with Rhode Island to the south, surfing was huge around Boston in the 1960s. The seawall at Nantasket Beach bristled with new boards, even though half the Hobies, Hansons, and Webers didn't get wet and were just there to score points on the poseur index. Many's the board that was used once before the owner realized that a plank on the loose in the whitewater could deliver a good whack; a lot of these early fiberglass boards were consigned to the garage.

Four Massachusetts shops (the big Cal names plus a Challenger East shop) lasted until the shortboard rang the death nell for the longboard scene. A handful of guys (Buddy Horsely, Stevie Wall, Billie Graham [not the evangelist], Mike McFarlane, and a few others) longboarded through the metamorphosis of the '70s. Then the mid '80s saw a shop called the California Surf Company go down the fashion road until Cory Wells opened Hard Corps in 1989, which was the center of the Boston/Nantasket scene until it closed in 2001.

Rhode Island

Rhode Island has a lot of quality beach, reef, and pointbreak surf in a relatively small area. Ruggles attracts as much attention as the surrounding grandiose architecture on the Newport side, which is less accessible and surfer-friendly than the west side, where Narragansett provides easy access to a full menu of tasty breaks. Cobblestone reefs are an unusual feature that groom lines of swell into nice defined peaks, one of which resembles its famous Californian namesake.

Rhode Island's twisting coastline allows for a multitude of wind options, but the predominantly southern aspect means northeast swells have a long way to wrap around from Cape Cod. This southern exposure is good news for hurricane swells, however, making Rhode Island the most consistent, year-round New England destination.

Block Island is the icing on the cake, but, as with Nantucket and Martha's Vineyard, its fruits are jealously guarded by part-time or would-be locals.

Connecticut lies to the west, tucked up north of Long Island. It gets the occasional wave but is so marginal that we are not covering it here. Long Island blocks out all the swell from the south, and if a rare due-east swell hits, the surf will be far better in neighboring Rhode Island or elsewhere on the New England coast.

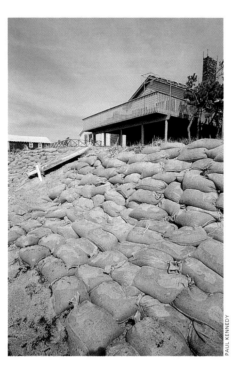

PAUL KENNEDY

The environment seems fairly clean and green, however, even this smallest of US states has not escaped environmental disasters altogether. In January 1996, a tugboat towing a fully laden barge lost power and drifted aground spewing almost 1,000,000 gallons of heating oil onto the beaches just west of Point Judith. This spill destroyed a wide range of local wildlife, including thousands of lobsters, seabirds and clams. The government's huge clean-up effort took two days to mobilize into action and finally contain a 12 mile (19km) oil slick which threatened the unique habitat of Trustom Pond, which some 74,000 birds and untold rare plants call home. The effects of such a spill will take years to come to light and monitoring continues to build up a strong case for new and increased safety legislation.

Left – **The last line of defense for shoreline properties at Matunick, RI. While sandbags buy some time, the inevitable answer is to pull back from shoreline development.**
Below – **Narragansett has been the focus of west side surfing in Rhode Island since the 1960s.**

PAUL KENNEDY

MEZ/ESM

Right – **Block Island Sunset.**
Right – **Crisp right at Point, Matunuck with Block Island in the background.**

PAUL KENNEDY

Despite the often harsh conditions, the waves of New England have been ridden for quite a long time. Postcards depicting people aquaplaning (an ancient form of bodyboarding) were circulating as early as 1902. However, the Northeast missed out on the pre-World War I demonstrations of Duke Kahanamoku and the Tom Blake hollow paddleboard era of the 1930s. By all accounts, it wasn't until 1962 that Don 'Crashboat' Johnson returned to Rhode Island from California, bringing the first modern surfboard to New England.

Rhode Island's Surfrider Foundation chapter cites stormdrain stenciling and implementing the Blue Water Task Force program as its main priorities. Surfrider is currently paying for water testing and analysis at ten surf spots in an effort to build up a reliable water-quality database. Rhode Island is also one of only four states that prohibits the construction of hard structures for beach stabilization. Access issues are immediately obvious around the elitist suburbs near Ruggles in Newport. This is also a factor in The Comptons area, and beach clubs can make it difficult in summer at many of the western beaches. Once again, privately owned coastline is a reality and rights of way can involve a fee.

The following year heralded the Beach Boy California surf music phenomenon, and the first surf shop soon appeared, opened by Howie 'Goldie' Goldsmith, 25 miles (40km) from the coast in Cranston, Rhode Island. Top West Coast surfboard brands like Gordon & Smith, Weber, and Hansen were sold in numbers until demand forced Goldie into local production. By 1965, his board factory was pumping out as many as 24 sticks a day, building models with names like Lahaina, Keokea, and Kailua.

That same year, the first contest was held in New England, at Narragansett Town Beach, where all the big East Coast teams showed up for a crack at the big prizes, which included automobiles and motorbikes. Goldie, who organized the

MEZ/ESM

JOE MCGOVERN

contest, recalls: "The first year (1965), the town was unprepared for the thousands of surfing fanatics that came to watch the contest. The town actually ran out of food at all the restaurants and gas at the two gas stations!"

By 1967, there were three main pockets of surfing in RI, with five shops in Cranston, six in Narragansett, and two in Newport, along with a couple at the popular surf spot, Matanuck. Hobie had three different retail locations, and the respective teams enjoyed a fierce rivalry among their riders, which continues to this day between Newport and Narragansett surfers. Some of the standouts of this competitive era were Bill Bolenda, Brad Stoner, Bill Charboneau, Will Needs, Dan Sassey, and Cindy Palmer from Newport, while Narragansett was represented by Pat McNulty, Peter Pan, Charlie Johnson, Dennis Tully, Jerry Judge, Paul Buchannan, Frank Garceau, Ed Logee, Janice Chronley, and Sue Lloyd.

The surfing rage had peaked and was declining by 1969, due in part to the introduction of the shortboard. Many of the talented longboarders could not adapt to the new equipment and, consequently, dropped out of the scene. Things had come full circle

by 1972, when there were no surf shops open in Rhode Island. Fortunately, Sid Abruzzi opened The Surf Store (now called WaterBros) in 1973, and Peter Pan opened The Watershed in Narragansett by 1975. Both stores are still going to this day.

Surfing's relatively recent resurgence is very apparent in New England, with swelling year-round ranks dotting the line-ups from Portland to Newport once again. Enough quality surf shops in the main areas provide local access to surf supplies, with the occasional locally-produced board displayed among a wide choice of Californian and southern East Coast imports. Mid week in mid winter it can be difficult to find a surf shop open away from the cities, but they're usually there on weekends.

New England's Eastern Surfing Association (ESA) districts hold regular local and regional contests for the competitive types, including a large contingency of modern longboard revivalists. The main thing to remember when surfing in New England is respect. Respect the gnarly conditions, the waves that occur because of them, and, most of all, the hardy crew that rides them.

Above – **One of many hidden gems located on the islands off the south coasts of Massachusetts and Rhode Island.**
Left – **Rhode Island legend Peter Pan struggles to get out at Point Judith.**

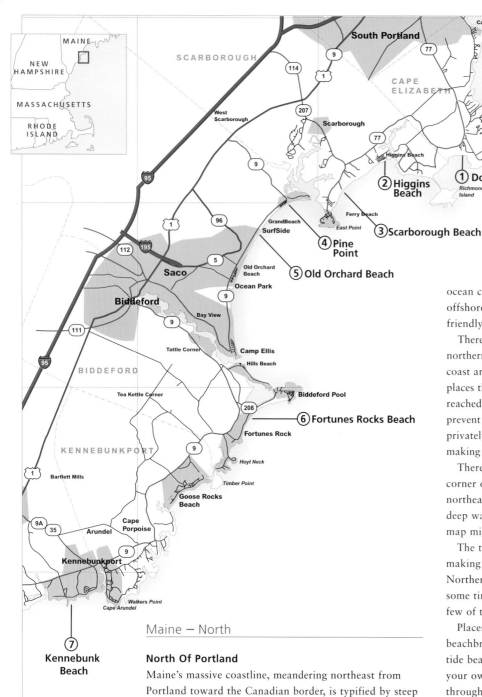

MAINE

NEW HAMPSHIRE

MASSACHUSETTS

RHODE ISLAND

Cape Cottage
Cape Elizabeth

South Portland

SCARBOROUGH

CAPE ELIZABETH

Pebbles Point
Trundy Point

Pond Cove
Hunts Point
Staples Point

West Scarborough

Scarborough

Higgins Beach

② **Higgins Beach**

① **Doc Browns**

Richmond Island

Ferry Beach

East Point

④ **Pine Point**

③ **Scarborough Beach**

GrandBeach
SurfSide

Old Orchard Beach

⑤ **Old Orchard Beach**

Saco

Ocean Park

Biddeford

Bay View

Tattle Corner

Camp Ellis

Hills Beach

BIDDEFORD

Tea Kettle Corner

Biddeford Pool

⑥ **Fortunes Rocks Beach**

Fortunes Rock

KENNEBUNKPORT

Hoyt Neck

Timber Point

Bartlett Mills

Goose Rocks Beach

Cape Porpoise

Arundel

Kennebunkport

Walkers Point
Cape Arundel

⑦ **Kennebunk Beach**

Maine – North

North Of Portland

Maine's massive coastline, meandering northeast from Portland toward the Canadian border, is typified by steep ocean cliffs, a rugged tapestry of granite outcrops and offshore islands. This is primordial terrain, no gentle, friendly stretch of shore.

There are many difficulties associated with surfing northern Maine, but greatest of them is access. Roads to the coast are limited and require long driving distances between places that are close as the crow flies. And, once you've reached the coast, cliffs and other shoreline features may prevent access to the waves, or, more likely, the roads are privately owned, as is most of the state's coastal real estate, making it legally impossible to get to the high tide mark.

There are definitely some surfable spots in this remote corner of the world, but Nova Scotia blocks out north and northeast swells, and a lot of the land drops straight into deep water, so such spots are far rarer than a look at the map might suggest.

The tidal range increases markedly as you head north, making for extremely transient optimum conditions. Northern Maine is a frontier that will stay that way for some time to come, leaving a few hardy locals to surf a few of the known spots by themselves.

Places to check are Small Point Beach (low tide beachbreak, hike in) and Popham Beach State Park (high tide beachbreak, small swell). North from here, you're on your own. Always ask for permission to access the ocean through private property.

Scarborough

RICHARD SPIES

Pine Point

RICHARD SPIES

1. Doc Browns

A fickle lefthand pointbreak that is generally half the size of open beaches in the area. It's only surfable around high tide and needs to be at least chest high to be clear of the rocks. Workable open faces, which aren't steep or critical, provide a perfect longboard forum.

Sometimes crowded at this small cove spot, particularly if there is a summer hurricane swell. Locals are protective because it doesn't break often. Limited roadside parking with no facilities. Mild pollution possibilities from the stream outlet and estuary water from Portland Harbor.

2. Higgins Beach

Higgins is well protected from N winds, but consequently doesn't receive any swell from the north either. Handles decent size, particularly if it's a SE swell, which can make for shapely and powerful peaks. Stops breaking at high tide.

High consistency means Higgins is often crowded. Rips are common, and locals report occasional whiffs of residential sewage. Parking in summer is limited to pay car parks or resident permits, while winter is free on the roadside.

3. Scarborough Beach

Situated inside the Scarborough Beach State Park, this pristine, sandy, southwest-facing stretch of beach can provide some good peaky waves. Optimum conditions are very similar to Higgins, but Scarborough will still break at high tide on larger swells.

Less crowded than Higgins because the peaks are more spread out; plus, it costs money to get through the gates to go surfing.

4. Pine Point

A crescent beach leads around to a rivermouth sandspit where the Scarborough River flows into Saco Bay. Here you'll find average, all tides beachbreaks; however, in certain conditions, an extremely long lefthander can run down the western side of the sandspit. Low tide only, a SE swell between 4-6ft (1.2-2m), along with any northerly winds should make for some long, fun, point-style waves without the rocks.

Medium to low consistency means you'll be lucky to ever see it work, but if it does, you'll probably be on your own. Free roadside parking in winter and pay car parks in summer.

5. Old Orchard Beach

Similar conditions to the beachbreaks north of here. All tides, but preferable on low incoming, and when there's some west in the wind. Open to a bit more swell, but NE swells will still have trouble getting in. The pier can help to hold the sand in place and occasionally gets classic.

No summer surfing from 10-5pm. Stormwater pipes can pollute the line-up after heavy rain.

6. Fortunes Rocks Beach

Pounding, sucky beachbreaks that crash close to shore on a high tide. Short, hollow rides with thick lips that'll pummel the careless.

Scattered rocks in the line-up. Often attracts a crowd, mostly from Portland. Hassley permit parking in summer, and the closest you'll get to facilities is the odd porta-potty.

7. Kennebunk Beach

Although it faces almost due south, a NE swell still manages to wrap around Cape Arundel, which is a bonus if the wind is also NE, making it dead offshore for Kennebunk. Needs at least 3ft (1m) to start breaking, but it'll handle as big as it gets. Big, brown, heavy, smokin' lefts and rights with critical drops, especially on a low incoming tide.

The crowds can be as thick as the lips because it's only a medium consistency spot. The strong rips combine with a mixture of residential, stormwater and estuary effluent. Residents-only parking in town in summer. Free parking in winter, which is when it's most likely to break anyway.

JIM READY

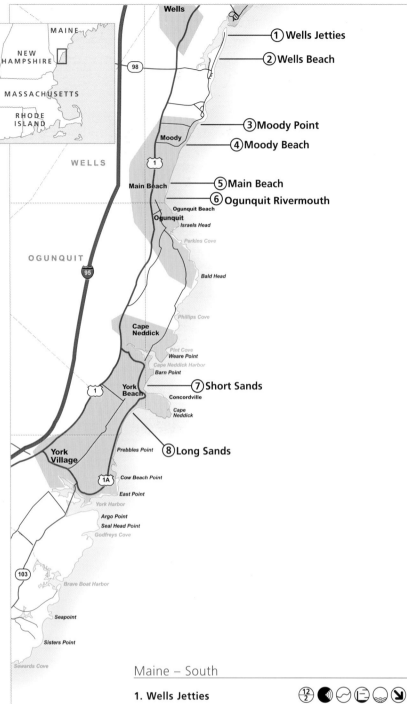

Maine – South

1. Wells Jetties

There's a jetty on either side of the Webhanner River, and the southern side builds up a nice sandbank directly off the tip. A low tide only peak, it breaks in any swell direction and deals with plenty of size. Short, steep, fast, and round.

Only sometimes crowded because everywhere else will also be working. Strong currents in the harbor entrance, which can be busy with fishing and pleasure boat traffic. Estuary drainout and boat pollution.

2. Wells Beach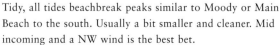

Tidy, all tides beachbreak peaks similar to Moody or Main Beach to the south. Usually a bit smaller and cleaner. Mid incoming and a NW wind is the best bet.
High consistency, rarely crowded, a few rips, no pollution, and pay parking.

3. Moody Point

It's got to be a big swell and tide before Moody Point will consider breaking. This submerged boulder reef shapes rights and lefts, which are both hollow and powerful. From the critical, steep take-off, there are a few barrel sections, which depend on swell direction to work. The rights like a SE swell and are easier to make than the lefts, which generally close-out because a right breaks into it from further down the beach. Easy paddle-out.

Tight take-off area means a half dozen surfers is a crowd. A sewer pipe discharges into the line-up along with some stormwater from the salt marshes behind Moody. Parking absolutely sucks.

Moody Point

JIM READY

4. Moody Beach

A great wave from mid to high tide with plenty of push and some top-to-bottom waves. Tolerates a bit more north in the wind than Main Beach.

No pollution or hazards, and it's rarely crowded because it is a so-called 'private beach'. There is no lifeguard to call you out of the water, but 'moody' local residents have been known to try. There is a pay car park in Moody or you can walk from Main Beach.

5. Main Beach (Ogunquit)

Any swell from NE to SE will see rideable peaks throughout the tidal range. High tide can stop the outside bars from breaking, but it will form up on the inside. Mid gives the best choice of outer and inner breaks, with some steeper reforms closer to shore.

Rarely crowded as strong rips disperse surfers over a wide area. There is a non-surfing area roped off in summer for the swimmers, but the lifeguards won't bother you if you avoid this area. The further you go from the rivermouth, the cleaner the water gets.

6. Ogunquit Rivermouth

The focal point of Maine's surfing scene for decades, this rivermouth right has the potential to provide quality rides in various conditions. A SE groundswell with a WNW wind on an incoming tide from low create the primo conditions, however the shifting sand in the flow of the rivermouth is the real quality controller. Very finicky these days, since they dredged the river to build up the beach dunes, resulting in sand being pushed back into the river from the break. The huge currents also play their part in sweeping the sand around. When it does break well, it starts from in front of the rocks and peels fast across the rivermouth onto the inside banks, where zippery walls and barrel sections can be found. A shorter left reforms and breaks into the river flow and is consistent on smaller swells.

Summer brings always crowded conditions with up to 50 surfers competing for waves. Rip currents are consistent in strength but not in direction. The river used to carry the town's sewage out to sea, but now there is a pipe running a mile out, so it can be shared over a larger area when the wind turns onshore. Unfortunately, this hasn't changed the fact that the river carries some pollutants, especially after heavy rains and spring thaws. Parking out at the point is a lottery for one of the dozen or so free spaces, so walking from the Main Beach pay car park is the main deal.

Ogunquit Rivermouth

Long Sands

7. Short Sands

Short Sands is short on swell direction options, but when a decent NE swell hits, this is one of the most powerful beachbreaks in Maine. It used to be a high tide only spot, but the sand is very susceptible to change, and it could be working at any stage of tide. Refraction off the surrounding rocks causes a real wedgy peak to jack up, giving short rights and longer barreling lefts into the beach. A difficult wave that always punishes the unwary.

Although Short Sands is in a State Park, there is a total blanket ban on surfing at this beach in summer. Winter, they are less interested in ticketing your car or calling the Coastguard to remove you from the line-up. Because of this, and its medium consistency rating, there is rarely a crowd here, but there is always a current, plus the possibility of stormwater runout.

8. Long Sands

Long Sands, as the name suggests, is a wide open west-facing beach that's well protected from the wind by its northern headland, Cape Neddick. Plenty of peaks to choose from, which never get top-to-bottom but can peel off fast. Great for longboards or beginners.

Plenty of stormwater pipes and strong rip currents are the main hazards at Long Sands. No surfing 10-5pm in summer, which is when the parking meters click in.

Short Sands

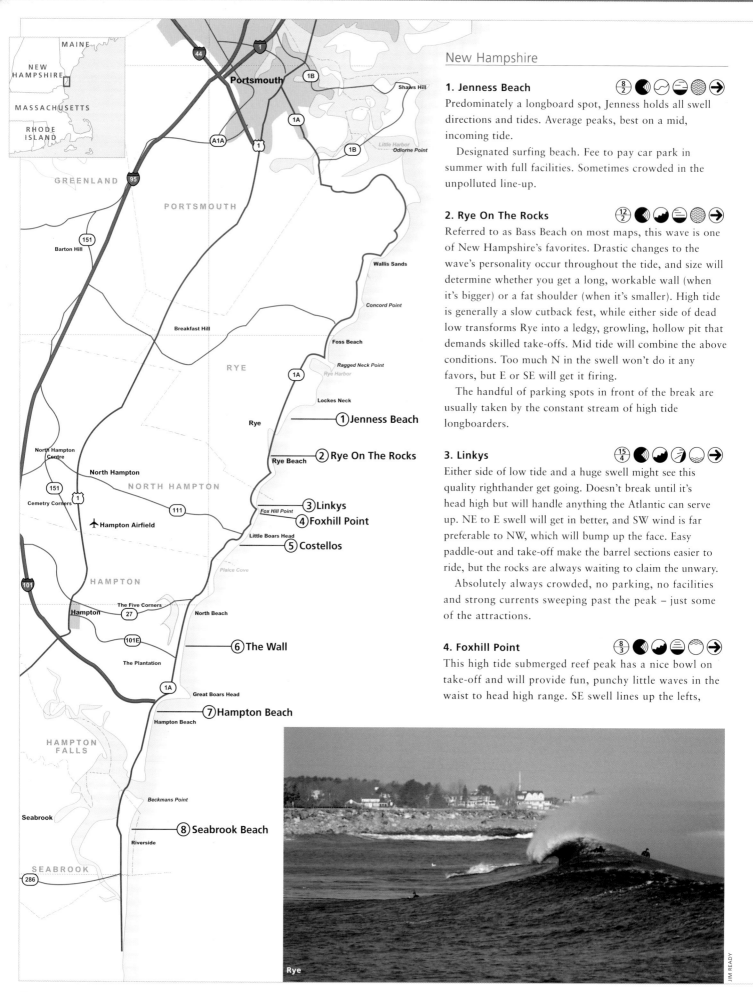

MAINE

NEW HAMPSHIRE

MASSACHUSETTS

RHODE ISLAND

Portsmouth

Shaws Hill

GREENLAND

PORTSMOUTH

Little Harbor
Odiorne Point

Barton Hill

Wallis Sands

Concord Point

Breakfast Hill

Foss Beach

RYE

Ragged Neck Point
Rye Harbor

Lockes Neck

Rye

① Jenness Beach

North Hampton Centre

NORTH HAMPTON

Rye Beach

② Rye On The Rocks

North Hampton

Cemetry Corners

③ Linkys

Fox Hill Point

④ Foxhill Point

Hampton Airfield

Little Boars Head

⑤ Costellos

Plaice Cove

HAMPTON

The Five Corners

Hampton

North Beach

⑥ The Wall

The Plantation

Great Boars Head

⑦ Hampton Beach

Hampton Beach

HAMPTON FALLS

Beckmans Point

Seabrook

⑧ Seabrook Beach

Riverside

SEABROOK

New Hampshire

1. Jenness Beach

Predominately a longboard spot, Jenness holds all swell directions and tides. Average peaks, best on a mid, incoming tide.

Designated surfing beach. Fee to pay car park in summer with full facilities. Sometimes crowded in the unpolluted line-up.

2. Rye On The Rocks

Referred to as Bass Beach on most maps, this wave is one of New Hampshire's favorites. Drastic changes to the wave's personality occur throughout the tide, and size will determine whether you get a long, workable wall (when it's bigger) or a fat shoulder (when it's smaller). High tide is generally a slow cutback fest, while either side of dead low transforms Rye into a ledgy, growling, hollow pit that demands skilled take-offs. Mid tide will combine the above conditions. Too much N in the swell won't do it any favors, but E or SE will get it firing.

The handful of parking spots in front of the break are usually taken by the constant stream of high tide longboarders.

3. Linkys

Either side of low tide and a huge swell might see this quality righthander get going. Doesn't break until it's head high but will handle anything the Atlantic can serve up. NE to E swell will get in better, and SW wind is far preferable to NW, which will bump up the face. Easy paddle-out and take-off make the barrel sections easier to ride, but the rocks are always waiting to claim the unwary.

Absolutely always crowded, no parking, no facilities and strong currents sweeping past the peak – just some of the attractions.

4. Foxhill Point

This high tide submerged reef peak has a nice bowl on take-off and will provide fun, punchy little waves in the waist to head high range. SE swell lines up the lefts,

Rye

JIM READY

Boarshead

The Wall

This summertime designated surfing beach always attracts a hefty crowd. Plenty of roadside meters and full facilities at the northern end.

7. Hampton Beach

The north end of Hampton Beach offers some decent protection from a NE wind, and the whole stretch can have some nice peaks, particularly on a mid to high tide. The lefts that run down the southside of Great Boars Head are fast, hollow, and shallow with no room for error, so "experienced surfers only" applies.

It's rarely crowded because everyone is probably surfing The Wall, plus the fact there is a summer surfing restriction, daily from 9-5pm.

while a NE swell favors the rights, which both diminish in size as you ride down the line. Any wind with a sniff of west is good, and the higher the tide the better.

Foxhill is often crowded, which makes the chances of finding one of the virtually non-existent parking spots impossible. Surfers' cars have been known to be towed, even in the depths of winter.

5. Costellos

A short wave with a steep take-off plus the odd dry rock popping up in the face. Looks like a potential goer but doesn't really do it. High tide only. Plaice Cove to the south can get some very decent beachbreaks on occasion.

Estuary runoff from the salt marshes does show some pollution, and minor ear infections are on the cards if you surf here. Pay parking at North Hampton State Beach.

6. The Wall

New Hampshire's most consistent spot, works on all tides and swells. Best around mid tide in a due W wind, it'll handle a bigger swell and usually keeps good shape. South of here there may be some waves breaking over various boulder reefs, but they are fickle, have difficult access, and require some local knowledge to score them when they're on. Best left to the locals.

Foxhill Point

8. Seabrook Beach

Beachbreak peaks that work on all swell directions. Handles up to double overhead, but you'll have trouble getting out the back. Constantly changing sandbars can shape powerful hollow waves or slow mushy shoulders, plus the position of tide is crucial to this tricky spot.

No access problems in winter, but in summer it can be near impossible to park in the area. Posted signs say no surfing. No hazards or crowds.

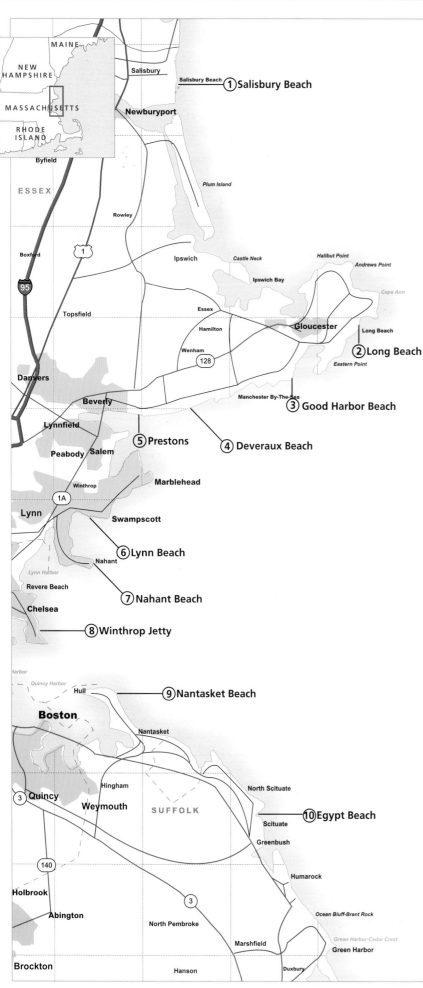

Massachusetts – Boston Area

1. Salisbury Beach

Salisbury Beach faces NE and will pick up any swell from the north. Even a S wind blows offshore here, and the place breaks on all tides. The ideal conditions formula would be head high NE swell, SW wind, and mid to high tide for some nice sucky, powerful wedges.

There is bound to be some drift in a north swell. Crowds are rare, even in summer, when 9-5pm surfing restrictions apply. There is camping in the Salisbury Beach State Reservation, just south of the main access road to the beach.

2. Long Beach

Probably the most powerful beachbreak in northern Massachusetts, Long Beach consistently attracts the maximum available swell and magnifies it onto the low tide sandbanks. The southern corner has a hollow left breaking into the rocks, which is less likely to close-out than the rest of the beach.

The most crowded spot in the Cape Anne area, which isn't saying much. Parking is sketchy.

3. Good Harbor Beach

Needs some angle in the swell direction to avoid closing-out; shape is also helped by higher tides. Rarely gets as good as the set-up suggests, but the rivermouth may groom some decent banks that can have some power.

Rarely crowded, easy parking, full facilities, but questionable water quality from the river runout.

Salt Island

4. Deveraux Beach

A steep shorebreak in front of the car park can get good, but most surfers come here for the submerged reef peak. Classy, hollow, and powerful with long workable walls on an E or NE swell. Remains offshore in the winter NE winds and needs low tides to prevent it from closing-out. Needs to be head high to break and continues to hold it right up to the biggest swells that Massachusetts receives.

More than half a dozen in the line-up is a crowd, which is usually the case at this average consistency spot. This makes the locals more protective than usual.

5. Prestons

Often talked about but rarely deserves the attention. Like all the breaks south of here, a SE swell doesn't really get in, so it relies on an E or NE swell to throw up some average all tides beachbreaks. The legendary pointbreak here is more of a fairy tale than a legend based on fact.

Public beach where the public won't find a place to park in summer, unless you're a local resident.

6. Lynne Beach

A big nor'easter can wrap around Swampscott and hit this long, flat beach, which is indistinguishable from Nahant Beach. A few more surfers up at this end, particularly up near Kings Beach if there are strong NE winds. Offshore can be anything from W to N. Weak but lined-up swells produce fat, crumbly peaks.

Only just qualifies for weekly (high) consistency, rarely crowded, and less polluted than the breaks to the south

7. Nahant Beach

This curving stretch of beach only offers average beachbreaks that seem to be more popular with windsurfers than surfers. The south end offers some protection from southerly winds. If the swell gets giant from the NE, then Nahant Island will probably be hiding a few waves.

Consistent spot, all beach facilities, and easy parking. The crowds are usually holding on to something to stand up.

8. Winthrop Jetty

A large jetty at the southern end of Winthrop Beach is the closest surf spot to the center of Boston. From mid to high tide, an E to NE swell with any type of W wind should see predominantly righthanders breaking close to the jetty over the cobblestone bottom. Low tide causes it to break on outside shoals, which knocks down the size of the reforms considerably.

Only a medium consistency spot, so it rarely gets crowded. Kinda polluted is a bit of an understatement, especially after rain, but things have improved in Boston Harbor since they decommissioned the oldest working sewage plant in the world and replaced it with a new secondary-treatment works.

Long Beach

9. Nantasket Beach

The curve of this long beach catches the full swell window because the southern end faces NE and the northern end almost faces SE. This means SW to NW winds will be offshore depending which end you're at. All tides are possible although dead high will do it no favors. Optimum conditions would be W winds, a NE groundswell, and four hours before high to produce longer rides from further outside, which can be fast, steep, and hollow, then slow, fat, and mushy, along various sections of the wave all the way to the beach. Best described as a variety pack.

Consistent wave magnet that only gets crowded when everyone hits the same peak in front of one the many pay car parks in Hull. Minor northerly drift, occasional stormwater runoff, and inconsiderate tourists' trash.

10. Egypt Beach

Consistent beachbreak with a bit of punch as long as it's lower than mid tide. SW wind is fine, overhead swell is not.

Often crowded because it's consistent. Resident Parking Permits or a few meters are the sad choice. More snaking for a parking place than a peak.

Nantasket Beach

Massachusetts – South

1. Scituate Harbor

A long left pointbreak over boulders on the south side of Scituate Harbor. Easy and slow outside, a little steeper and occasionally hollow inside. Miserable at high tide, but it will handle maximum swell along with some nearby rare but good spots. A SE swell will sneak around Cape Cod, but a due north tends to march right past. NW wind and a big E swell on a low incoming tide is the go.

Good rips, swirling currents, and some estuary outflow, plus a sometimes crowded scene. Summer parking sucks because of a scarcity of meters.

2. Wrexham

Beachbreak peaks which can get good on small swells from a northerly direction. Over 8ft (2.5m) faces and high tide are bad news for Wrexham, but a low incoming should see some hollow sections.

A bit inconsistent because it relies on the N swell, so it's rarely crowded and has good water quality. Pay car parks or meters, full facilities and summer lifeguards.

3. Fieldstone

Open beachbreak that can be fun without being challenging. All tides, SW winds, and a good E swell.

A bit more consistent than the breaks south of here, but still rarely crowded.

4. Brant Rock

Brant Rock has random peaks breaking over a mixture of sand and rocks. Short rides, steep faces, but not really a hollow wave. Doesn't handle much swell, which needs to be from the north.

Low to medium consistency, low crowds, and no current.

5. Marshfield Jetty

The north side of Green Harbor inlet needs SW to W winds, lower tides and a N swell. Steep take-offs followed by fun performance walls.

More consistent than Green Harbor and handles way more size. Limited roadside meters.

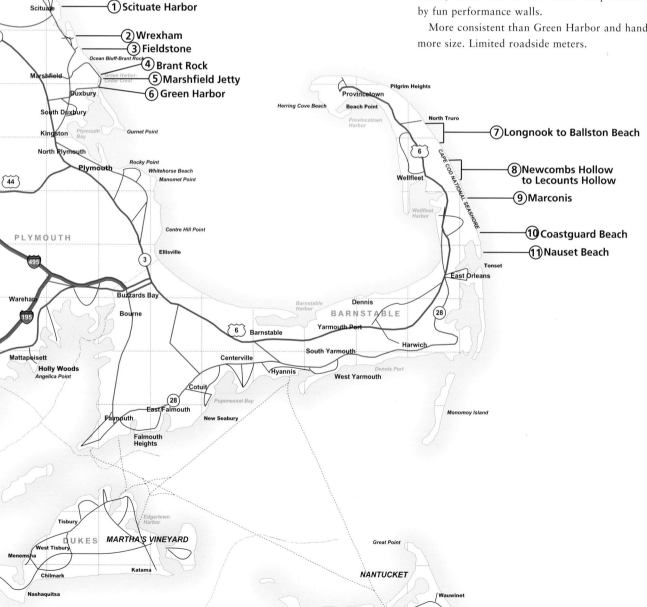

6. Green Harbor (Duxberry)

One of the few places in Massachusetts Bay that is offshore in a NE wind. Big NE to E swell will wrap around a jetty giving mainly lefts and peaks further down the beach at mid tides. Sloppy shoulders and lots of cutbacks.

Moderate to low consistency means sometimes crowded conditions. Estuary water flows out here into the surf which can get rippy.

7. Longnook to Ballston Beach

The curve of Cape Cod prevents any decent SE swell getting in from Longnook to Ballston. It is also badly affected by the regular and strong NW winds. Low tides, SW winds, and the weaker, lumpy NE wind swells may produce some decent conditions on the less battered sandbars. North of here, take a windsurfer. Smaller and more manageable in big SE swells.

Extreme currents intensify nearer the northern tip of Cape Cod. Rarely crowded, clean water. Early arrival in summer to snag a pay-to-park spot.

Cape Cod

BRUCE CHRISNER

8. Newcombs Hollow to Lecounts Hollow

Includes the designated summer surfing spot at Whitecrest (Four Mile Beach). Consistent bars along a ENE-facing length of beach. Less power and ability to handle size than breaks to the south. Lecounts Hollow will take a big swell and be more manageable, with easier paddle-outs and fatter, crumbly walls.

Sometimes crowded as there are various pay car parks on the cliffs. Plenty of drift to contend with alongside regular pea soup fogs that roll in with monotonous regularity.

9. Marconis

The Marconi Station area has good beachbreak peaks at the base of tall cliffs and dunes. Needs some NE or SE swell angle to provide the hollowest, gnarliest pits on the Cape. Will accept SW winds but not high tide. From here to Nauset Beach has the potential to handle triple overhead on a sandbar, way out from the usual low tide break.

No paddle-out channels and strong currents at this rarely crowded open stretch. Cape Cod National Seashore area is where the first transatlantic radio transmission was made, hence the name. Fee-to-pay parking and all facilities.

Four Mile, Cape Cod

JOE MCGOVERN

10. Coastguard Beach

Nausett Light to Coastguard Beach experiences heavy cliff erosion that washes cobblestone and rock into the line-up. This helps sand build up in well-defined bars for short periods. Low tide on a SE groundswell will make the rights link up through to the beach. Hollow and powerful until higher tides create mushy shoulders.

Sometimes crowded, currents, and the odd VW Beetle-sized rock in the water. A shuttle service operates from a large pay car park to the beach in summer.

11. Nauset Beach

The first easily accessible beach from the west. Usually short, fast and really, really hollow in an offshore westerly. Dead low and high make it shut down or turn into a big shoredump, so around mid incoming and outgoing are the pick.

Surfer lifeguards will oblige by not putting the swimming area at the best sandbar. Rarely crowded, with plenty of peaks to choose from, but strong rips with size.

Wellfleet, Cape Cod

MEZ/ESM

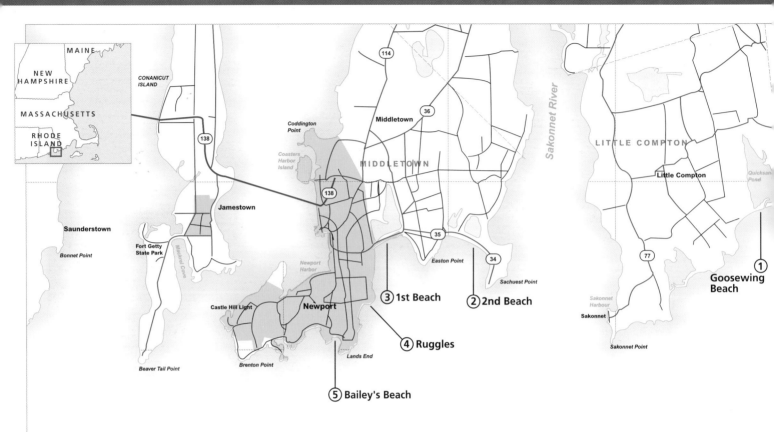

Rhode Island – East

1. Goosewing Beach

The only easy access points in the Little Compton area are Goosewing and South Shore Beach. A mixture of beach, reef, and pointbreaks are found in a large bay. Trailer Park has steep rights next to hollow beachbreaks, plus a right and left in front of a little creek runout that breaks over boulders. All tides, up to 10ft (3m). SE to SW swell. Many other reefs and pointbreaks on this peninsula (including an occasional wave up in the Sakonnet River), but access is minimal.

Pay to park on the beach in summer. Consistent with lower crowds but some current.

Little Compton

1st Beach

2. 2nd Beach (Sachuest Beach)

Also known as Sachuest Beach, this bay faces SW, catching all the sea breeze windswell. It will handle a bit of size, especially at higher tides. Bigger and better shaped peaks than 1st Beach. At the eastern end, a protected left pointbreak called The Dumps cranks up when both the swell and an E wind picks up.

Seaweed is the biggest problem here in the summer designated surfing area along with some jellyfish. Good access and facilities in this National Wildlife Refuge.

3. 1st Beach (Eastons Beach)

NE to NW winds and mid incoming tides for this soft beachbreak. A long, gently-sloping, shallow bay causes things to break up outside as it gets over 6ft (2m). Best on a SE swell.

The closest beach to Newport with all facilities and huge parking lots. Plenty of beach users but not that many surfers.

Old Harbor, Block Island

4. Ruggles

At the end of Ruggles Avenue a series of reefs line a point in the rocky coastline. Regular Ruggles is The Point, Bobbies and Stupid Spot in the middle, and Around the Corner at the end. All are rights except for a short left off The Point in a SW swell. A quality wave in large swells when it can link up long and strong without being really hollow. A SE swell hits dead on, but lower tides with NW winds are needed for Ruggles to live up to its reputation.

Parking in this historic, tourist-trampled neighborhood is the main hazard. There are a few side streets some distance from the break, which are plausible in winter.

Average consistency along with above-average crowds and currents.

5. Bailey's Beach

All tides and any wind from NW to E for this hollower beachbreak. Mid tide on a SE swell can get good up to head high. Usually only breaks on stormy easterlies.

Not very consistent and nasty parking equals low crowds. Private beach once frequented by the Kennedys. One end is public, but parking is a long walk away in unposted side streets. No surfing in summer when it hardly ever breaks.

Ruggles

Ruggles line-up

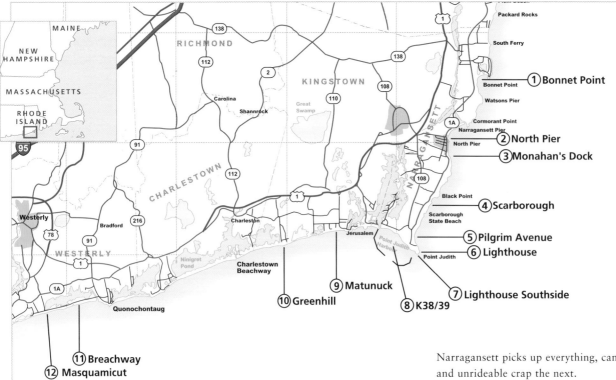

MAINE
NEW HAMPSHIRE
MASSACHUSETTS
RHODE ISLAND

RICHMOND

KINGSTOWN

Great Swamp

Carolina

Shannrock

CHARLESTOWN

Charleston

Jerusalem

Point Judith Harbor

Point Judith

Charlestown Beachway

Ninigret Pond

WESTERLY

Westerly

Bradford

Quonochontaug

Packard Rocks

South Ferry

① **Bonnet Point**
Bonnet Point
Watsons Pier
Cormorant Point
Narragansett Pier
② **North Pier**
North Pier
③ **Monahan's Dock**
Black Point
④ **Scarborough**
Scarborough State Beach
⑤ **Pilgrim Avenue**
⑥ **Lighthouse**
⑦ **Lighthouse Southside**
⑧ **K38/39**
⑨ **Matunuck**
⑩ **Greenhill**
⑪ **Breachway**
⑫ **Masquamicut**

Rhode Island – West

1. Bonnet Point

A big south swell is needed to get these very long lefthanders to run down Bonnet Point. The cliffs provide good protection from NE winds, and all tides are surfable when it's overhead. A short tube section, but generally a performance wave with plenty of time to perfect turns.

Sometimes crowded at this fickle spot, usually when elsewhere is hurting from the wind. A rip will help get out the back on the long return paddle. Tight roadside parking, or use the private beach club lot in winter or after hours.

Monahan Dock

BRUCE CHRISNER

2. North Pier

This is the area of Narragansett Beach that can be surfed year-round. E swell gets in the best, combining with W winds and lower tides to give some good beachbreaks. Further north along the beach there are rights off a sunken barge, lefts off old pier pilings, peaks in front of The Dunes private beach club, and a rivermouth left at the end.

Narragansett picks up everything, can be unreal one day and unrideable crap the next.

Highly consistent and crowded, with occasional currents and jellyfish. Full facilities and pay car park.

3. Monahan's Dock

State Pier #5, Tucker's Dock, or Monahan's Dock are all used to describe this rock construction. The submerged reef peak has some crumblier lefts, which occasionally produce, but the rights are where the good stuff happens. Low tide, top-to-bottom, thick barrels with a critical take-off right in front of the dock. High tide is an easier take-off walling into a bowly end section. The dock claims plenty of boards and bodies that don't make the wave. Some other reefs in the vicinity are equally powerful and dangerous, such as Rincon, Pigs, and 40 MPH. Handles everything. Experts only.

Always crowded – because six is a crowd in the tight take-off zone. Medium consistency with very little current, even when it's huge. Free car park or roadside parking.

4. Scarborough

This fickle wave will only break good when there's a S swell, W wind, and low tide. Head high is the max size it'll handle.

Rarely crowded because although it picks up E and S swell, it's always better somewhere else. Full facilities and a huge car park at this state beach.

5. Pilgrim Avenue

Pilgrims is the best of the waves named after the streets that run to the cliffs NW of Point Judith. Will handle the howling SW'ers, big swells, and all tides at this right point. Generally a mushy, slower wave, conducive to longboarding. Conant, the next wave north, is even mushier.

Not much drift to contend with, but it's crowded sometimes. Not much parking above the break means walking from the lighthouse car park.

6. Lighthouse

This lengthy righthand point can supply endless walls all the way 'round to Pilgrim Avenue when a strong S swell is running. A few hairy sections at low tide get better at mid incoming. A classic pointbreak with steep fast sections followed by a cutback section, but rarely a tube. Three take-off peaks when it's small become one lined-up wall when it's big. Handles triple-overhead and W-NW is offshore.

The year-round free parking at the Point Judith lighthouse gets rammed in summer, as do the consistent waves. Currents.

7. Lighthouse Southside

The south side of Point Judith will line up better and have more powerful sections on a south swell. This lefthand point gets longer as it gets bigger, filling in the holes between the three peaks that appear on smaller days. A few short rights into the rocks here and there. Not noted as a barreling wave, there can be a hollow section off the first peak in an offshore NE wind.

There is a rock on the inside, which has a long steel bar sticking out of it. Less crowded than the right and the same parking deal.

8. K38/39

The longest left on the East Coast breaks over a mussel bed reef inside the breakwall of the Point Judith Harbor of Refuge. Known as 'The Ks' these two deep-water peaks provide long, workable walls on the lefts and shorter, steeper rights at K39's more eastern take-off point. No barrels, even when it's as big as it gets, making it a favorite for longboarders and cruisers. S or SE swell only, lower tides, with winter NE'ers being just enough offshore.

The third-largest fishing port on the East Coast means motorized traffic, including jetskis. No parking at the busy commercial port, so parking at the lighthouse and walking almost a mile along the breakwall is the best bet. Average consistency at best.

9. Matanuck

This concentrated area of quality waves is one of the focal points of Rhode Island surfing. Three main peaks start with Deep Hole to the east, Trestles in the middle, and The Point to the west. Deep Hole is essentially only a left that is fast and sectiony at low tide. Trestles, like its California cousin, is a shapely peak with hollower rights and down-the-line lefts at lower tides. The Point is a peak with a short, bowly right and a long workable left, which can link into The Bar at higher tides, making for a long wave to practise cutbacks. All these waves break over cobblestone/boulder reefs, and they all handle good size. High tide still has good shape, but it makes the walls slower and fatter. Swell-wise, SE makes The Point line up, E is best for Trestles and Deep Hole, but they all still work on a due S.

Guaranteed always crowded including kayakers and jetskis. Rip currents and difficult paddle-outs when big. Year round free parking lot.

Point Judith

10. Greenhill

This solid beachbreak barrels off close to shore with defined lefts and rights. Low tide with N to NE winds on a due southerly swell. There is also a longer left off the point, which will break at high tide.

Rarely crowded because this is a private beach. Public access is provided, but absolutely zero parking in summer. Watch out for the rock at the end of the righthanders!

11. Breachway

These inlet jetties won't handle much size or higher tides. Longer rides than the surrounding beachbreaks, with hollow lefts forming over the inlet sandbars.

Public beach access beside the private beach club. Sometimes crowded, rip currents and jellyfish.

12. Masquamicut

Masquamicut State Beach needs a S swell to be any good, even though E will get in there. N winds and lower tides should see some decent beachbreak peaks. Some rocky outcrops to the east and west can hold some waves in bigger swells.

Rarely crowded with surfers. Summer 9-5pm restrictions and pay to park.

Matanuck

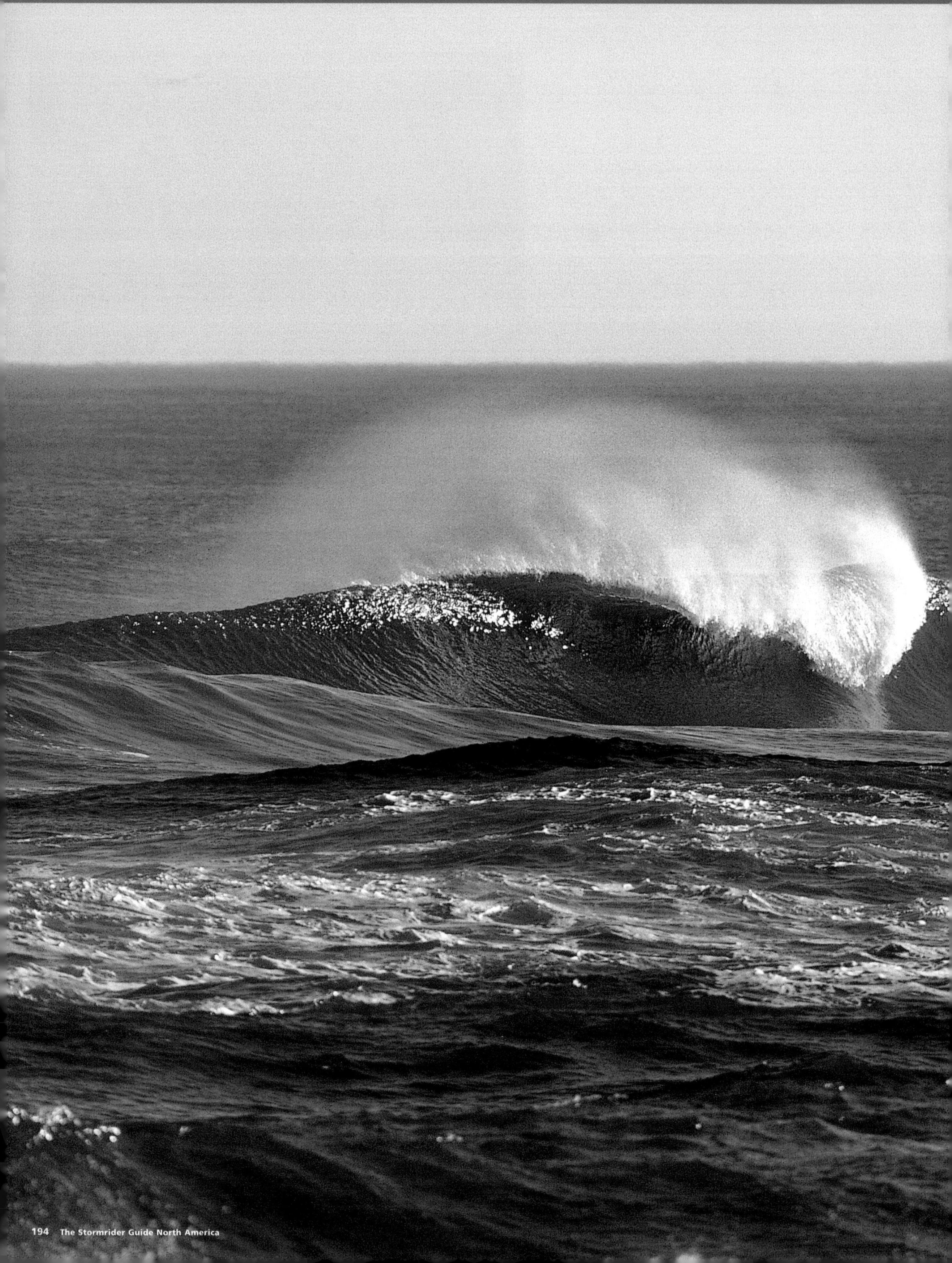

Mid Atlantic

The Mid Atlantic surfing states include New York (NY), New Jersey (NJ), Delaware (DE), Maryland (MD) and Virginia (VA). In the global surfing consciousness, these locales might not automatically conjure up images of epic surfing conditions, but the fact is, they are home to an abundance of good quality, hard-breaking beachbreaks. Endless man-made structures litter the coast in the form of piers, jetties and breakwalls providing plenty of options and some organized sandbars.

This area of the eastern seaboard is full of sharp contrasts, where miles of deserted white sand beach may be a short drive from a sprawling metropolis, like New York, Philadelphia, or the nation's capital, Washington DC. Deeply rooted in the complex history of the most powerful nation on Earth, these Mid Atlantic states encompass all aspects of modern American culture.

As with most of the East Coast, the best time to find consistent waves along this Atlantic shoreline is right before, during, and just after the winter season. The only hope during the warmer months is to luck into some summertime hurricane action. Even so, you won't get lonely. There will always be other surfers at the main breaks, and they can be both friendly and competitive when sharing their waves with the large number of travelers and vacationers that flock to these shores every summer.

RAY HALLGREEN

Juicey New Jersey pier wave.

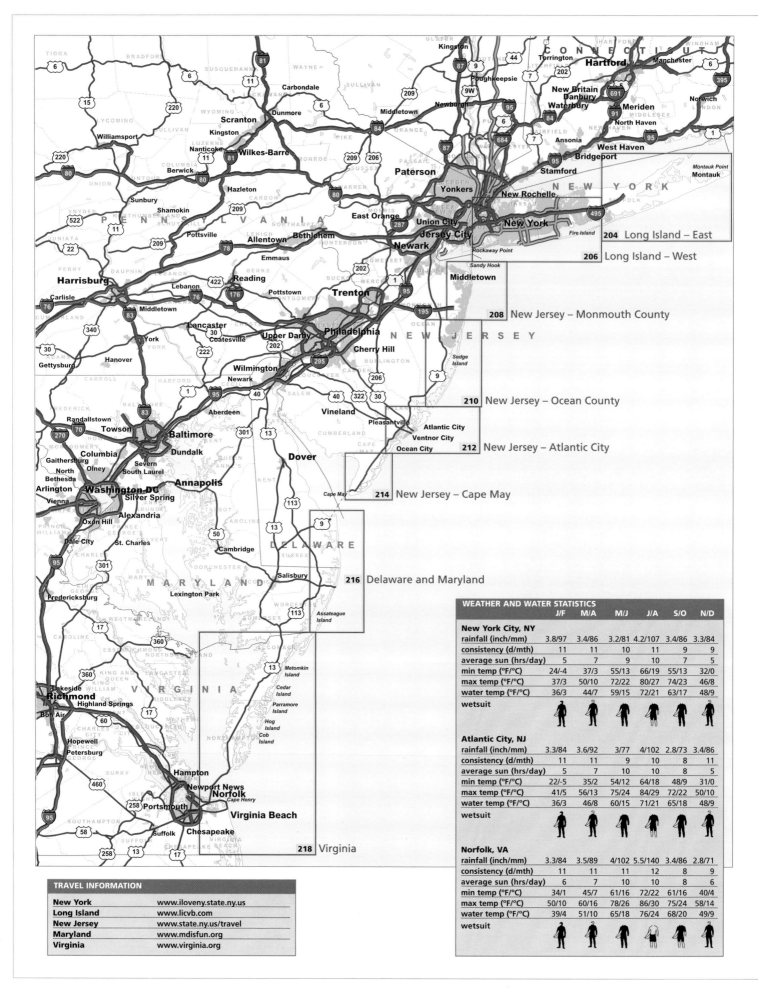

204 Long Island – East
206 Long Island – West
208 New Jersey – Monmouth County
210 New Jersey – Ocean County
212 New Jersey – Atlantic City
214 New Jersey – Cape May
216 Delaware and Maryland
218 Virginia

WEATHER AND WATER STATISTICS

	J/F	M/A	M/J	J/A	S/O	N/D
New York City, NY						
rainfall (inch/mm)	3.8/97	3.4/86	3.2/81	4.2/107	3.4/86	3.3/84
consistency (d/mth)	11	11	10	11	9	9
average sun (hrs/day)	5	7	9	10	7	5
min temp (°F/°C)	24/-4	37/3	55/13	66/19	55/13	32/0
max temp (°F/°C)	37/3	50/10	72/22	80/27	74/23	46/8
water temp (°F/°C)	36/3	44/7	59/15	72/21	63/17	48/9
wetsuit						
Atlantic City, NJ						
rainfall (inch/mm)	3.3/84	3.6/92	3/77	4/102	2.8/73	3.4/86
consistency (d/mth)	11	11	9	10	8	11
average sun (hrs/day)	5	7	10	10	8	5
min temp (°F/°C)	22/-5	35/2	54/12	64/18	48/9	31/0
max temp (°F/°C)	41/5	56/13	75/24	84/29	72/22	50/10
water temp (°F/°C)	36/3	46/8	60/15	71/21	65/18	48/9
wetsuit						
Norfolk, VA						
rainfall (inch/mm)	3.3/84	3.5/89	4/102	5.5/140	3.4/86	2.8/71
consistency (d/mth)	11	11	11	12	9	9
average sun (hrs/day)	6	7	10	10	8	6
min temp (°F/°C)	34/1	45/7	61/16	72/22	61/16	40/4
max temp (°F/°C)	50/10	60/16	78/26	86/30	75/24	58/14
water temp (°F/°C)	39/4	51/10	65/18	76/24	68/20	49/9
wetsuit						

TRAVEL INFORMATION

New York	www.iloveny.state.ny.us
Long Island	www.licvb.com
New Jersey	www.state.ny.us/travel
Maryland	www.mdisfun.org
Virginia	www.virginia.org

Left – **Paddler's eye view of a Seaside Heights peak.**
Below – **The Atlantic City casinos now overlook the birthplace of East Coast surfing.**

RAY HALLGREEN

The Surf, Ocean Environment and Surf Culture

From New York to Virginia, then all the way to Miami, a string of barrier islands bear the brunt of the Atlantic's waves. Separated from the mainland by the ribbon of blue that is the Intracoastal Waterway, these sandy, fragile, and somewhat temporary oases of terra firma have been shifting for millennia under the influence of wind, waves, tide, and now the rising sea levels associated with global warming. As a result, literally thousands of man-made structures (and ruins) litter the coastline from Montauk to Virginia Beach, representing a futile human effort to defy nature and temporarily halt the erosion. Ironically, it is this collection of jetties, groins, and piers, which tend to retain and shape the shifting sands and give Mid Atlantic surfers some well-shaped wave formations.

If there is an area in the US where you would expect environmental problems and pollution, the Mid Atlantic states would probably spring to mind. Huge populations concentrated in sprawling cities and suburbs obviously exert huge pressures on the surrounding environment. Historically, these pressures have been manifested in the form of blatant, large-scale pollution, with private industry and government generally treating the streams, bays, and ocean as cheap and easy dumping grounds. Flying into New York not so long ago, you were likely to see a dark, brown slick of sewage emanating from lower Manhattan and snaking through the already heavily polluted Hudson River, heading out to sea. Barges piled high with the waste of tens of millions of people would sail through this slick on their way out to an offshore dumping ground between Long Island and New Jersey. Added to this were industrial and commercial pollutants,

including ships jettisoning filthy payloads of dangerous medical wastes. It wasn't until thousands of hypodermic needles were washing up on the beaches of New Jersey, creating a huge health scare, that action was taken. Recent improvements in inshore water quality have been achieved through advanced treatment processes for residential waste, plus tighter legislation for commercial waste management. However, the fact remains that a large percentage of the nation's population lives in or around this area, so there is always going to be a heavy environmental impact to monitor, control, and (if you're a surfer) avoid.

Surprisingly, surfing made its East Coast debut in New Jersey in 1912. Duke Kahanamoku had just set a new world record, winning the gold medal for the 100

PAUL KENNEDY

meter swim at the Olympic Games in Stockholm, Sweden. On his return to the States, Duke took time to demonstrate the Hawaiian art of surfboard riding on the waves near the old steel pier in Atlantic City. Twenty years later, Tom Blake's "genuine, approved" hollow surf/paddleboards (called 'water sleds' or 'cigar boxes'), manufactured by the Thomas N. Rogers Company of Venice, California, become the ubiquitous tools of surf-lifesavers everywhere, including these same Mid Atlantic states.

New York

The surf in New York is different from the lower portion of the Mid Atlantic coast; Long Island juts due east out into the ocean, giving its south-facing beaches an excellent hurricane swell window and the ability to pick up some SW wind swells. This however means that regular wintertime NE swells can't get into most spots. There are even a few rock-bottomed reef and pointbreaks, at the southern boundary of New England's geology (found at Montauk, on the eastern tip of Long Island). This is where most New York surfers would choose to be on just about any given set of conditions, but it can be a long and grueling drive for residents of the Big Apple. There are plenty of beachbreak and jetty options much closer to the city – from the mad city scenes of Rockaway Beach to the spacious and audacious wealth out at The Hamptons.

'New York' conjures visions of urban chaos, with the denizens of densely-populated neighborhoods fighting for space in crowded streets amidst overflowing trash cans, gangs, and drive-by shootings. In fact, most of the surfable coastline of New York State is far more rural and undeveloped than the global city image would suggest. Even so, the city has a long reach in terms of inshore water pollution. In sheer volume of discharge, NYC is off the charts, graphically illustrated by its recent request to discharge 500 million gallons of untreated sewage into the East River, while workers repaired a sewage-treatment facility. Add to this the history of offshore toxic dumping, busy shipping channels, and large-scale non-specific-point pollution from the concrete jungle's stormwater system, and you won't be surprised to find New York's surf zones a bit dirty.

TOM DUGAN/ESM

PAUL KENNEDY

Top – **Ditch Plains, NY: summer and winter – the only difference is about 5mm of rubber and less people to share with.**
Bottom – **Hither Hills, NY**

PAUL KENNEDY

While the cobblestone reefs seem clean enough, the threat from the Millstone nuclear power plant on Long Island Sound is a real one. The affluence of Long Island towns doesn't necessarily translate to a better treatment infrastructure, and legislation lags behind the citizen health concerns. Although the state does require regular water quality tests and forces counties to publish sewage-discharge figures, no stormwater runoff figures (or plans to monitor its volume) are currently available.

All this underlying reality might conflict with the impression visiting surfers get as they check out the long sandy beaches far from the city or out toward Montauk. Long Island (which is now technically classified as a peninsula) is as full of surprises as it is, well...long – over 100 miles (160km) long. Rural and bucolic, much of it doesn't look much different than it did a hundred years ago. In fact, not far from the city, Deep Hollow Ranch, established in 1658, was the first cattle ranch in North America and remains relatively undeveloped.

For New York surfers, access is always a critical issue, particularly in and around exclusive areas like the Hamptons. Here, gated tracts of lavish beachfront mansionettes prevent the public from any easy access to the mean high tide mark, thereby creating millionaire-only beaches. Private beaches exist alongside community beaches, some of which charge non-residents for the privilege of getting sand between their toes. Summer parking restrictions (or no parking at all) help perpetuate the imbalance of privilege. Predictably, many areas enforce a beach tag/permit system.

Members of the new Surfrider Foundation chapter are currently implementing the Respect the Beach and Blue Water Task Force Programs into New York schools.

The summer of 1934 saw Tom Blake on Long Island, teaching the children of a wealthy businessman to swim. He met up with the lifeguards at Jones Beach who were already pro surfboards being used as lifesaving equipment and were stoked when Tom showed up with the latest model hollow paddleboards. Charlie Bunger started shaping out of his garage back in 1962, then opened Long Island's first surf shop in Copiague the following year. Other notable shapers early on included Jack Hand and Bob Hawkins, who shared the empty line-ups with a crew that included George Fisher, Billy Shelton, Rowly Eisenberg and Eric Eastman. These lucky locals had it to themselves until things got really busy in the mid-1960s, when popular Californian imports became available alongside the local boards. The huge population of nearby NYC provided plenty of customers for the expanding surf industry, which spread out towards Montauk. But the arrival of the shortboard era really took its toll on the public's interest in surfing here, as beginners became easily frustrated with the small, unstable boards. Although some big companies, like Surfjet, flooded the market with boards in the early 1970s. The scene stayed fairly quiet and predictable right through the twin- and tri-fin eras until the modern mal resurgence saw a marked increase of surfers in the line-ups of New York.

New Jersey

Pronounced "Joisey" by the locals, it boasts the most powerful, challenging beachbreaks on the East Coast. Long, straight barrier islands, punctuated by frequent inlets or jetties, are home to one of the largest East Coast surfing populations. Extending south from Sandy Hook, hundreds of jetties focus swells into classy waves for the hordes of beach culturists who live in this largely built-up area. The deep-water entrance to Manasquan Inlet, generally regarded as the most testing and tantalizing wave on the eastern seaboard, can focus and handle the biggest swells thrown at it. Seaside is a circus of humanity with excellent waves to boot, while Long Beach Island has a reputation for grinding barrels and protective locals. Atlantic City is where the casinos meet the coast and where you can also bet on finding some decent waves. The southern tip of Cape May provides shelter from the howling winds of the winter nor'easters and attracts a big contingent of Jersey surfers when conditions dictate.

Below – **New Jersey speed blur.**
Bottom – **Ocean City regularly replenishes beaches with massive sand pumping programs.**

MIKE MESEROLL

DOUG GOTTHOLD

New Jersey also plays host to just about every conceivable type of environmental problem that occurs in North America. Apart from pollution, access is the main issue at the top of the Surfrider Foundation's agenda here.

MIKE MESEROLL

New Jersey is one of the few states in the USA, where members of the public have to pay for the privilege of using the beach in the summer. Beach tags are enforced by local councils or other authorities that control the recreational use of coastal areas. Costs fluctuate and resident tags are available, but at the end of the day, you have to pay to go surfing in summer.

The arrival of hypodermic needles on New Jersey beaches only confirmed the stupidity of allowing various dangerous and toxic payloads to be dumped offshore by ships that had been allowed to 'pay to pollute' for years.

Incredibly, one such shipment was dioxin-contaminated mud, dredged from a Newark river after an Agent Orange factory caught fire. Dioxins are among the most toxic substances in existence and easily infiltrate the ecosystem and food chain.

Even so, the Army Corps of Engineer has plans to dump 90,000 tons of toxic mud off the coast of New Jersey, a practice theoretically outlawed since 1997; but the Army Corps claims this mud is clean, even though its own documents prove otherwise. The Corps wants to cap off an old toxic dump with this new toxic mud.

Right – **Mid Atlantic beachbreaks can get thick and powerful.**
Below – **Womens division, 1965 ESA event at Seaside Heights.**

RON STONER/SURFER MAGAZINE

The same Army Corps of Engineers is responsible for dredging rivermouths like Manasquan Inlet and vainly trying to create hard structures to reduce the coastal erosion that affects all Mid Atlantic states. New Jersey has hundreds of jetties and piers in all shapes and sizes; some produce good wave forums, others destroy them. Sand pumping and beach replenishment are temporary measures that sometimes have a very negative effect on sandbar formations, and many a reliable surfbreak has disappeared when the engineers have redistributed the wealth.

The good news is that the New Jersey departments of Health and the Environment conduct water-quality testing at most beaches, and stringent standards are enforced, meaning beach closures occur before ocean users suffer. New Jersey is also home to the East Coast's most experienced and active chapter of the Surfrider.

Glittering casinos now dominate the shoreline around Atlantic City's Steel Pier area, where the Duke treated beachgoers to that surfing exhibition back in 1912. Subsequent "swimming tours" during the roaring 1920s brought Johnny Weissmuller (of Tarzan fame) and other great swimmers to these beaches. Summertime visitors enjoyed various forms of wavecraft at the state's crowded resort until, by 1939, surfing was banned at many of the most popular locations where one too many solid wood boards or sharp, thin belly boards had taken out the legs of an unsuspecting citizen, wading in the shallows.

Surfing remained generally taboo in New Jersey until 1963, when Cecil Lear and several other surfers banded together to form the Jersey Surfing Association and asked permission to hold a surfing contest. Permission was granted, and the club began meeting and organizing competitions with other surf clubs up and down the coast.

Charlie Keller and Bill Yerkes were pioneers in the East Coast surf rep scene, filling their station wagons with surf gear and accessories and traveling up and down the coast from their base in Lavallette. They weren't alone, since West Coast heavyweights – like Hobie, Bing Copeland, Dewey Weber, Greg Noll, and Hansen – were heavily flogging the East Coast market for surfboard sales by the mid-1960's. Even *Surfer* magazine started covering events on the Atlantic shore, following leading surfers like David Nuuhiwa and Jeff Hakman when they came back to compete in the major contests.

No history of Mid Atlantic surfing could pass without a mention of Dan Heritage who made his first surfboard after seeing an ad in *Popular Mechanics* magazine, circa 1962. Although the resulting stick only lasted half an hour in the shorebreak, Dan went on to become one of Jersey's most influential shapers and a surf-industry stalwart. He established Little Waves (an early East Coast surfer's joke) in Sea Isle in 1964, then changed the name to Heritage Surf and Sport in the 1970s. The Heritage family continues to run a string of Jersey surf shops, despite Dan's untimely death in 1997, just after his induction by Greg Noll into the inaugural East Coast Legends' Hall of Fame roster.

Delaware and Maryland

The coasts of Delaware and Maryland occupy a common peninsula that extends from the mouth of Delaware Bay to Chesapeake Bay. This is not the East Coast's most illustrious wave zone. Even so, Delaware is less consistent, has fewer breaks, and receives less swell than its southern neighbor. A swell-stifling shelf extends out from Delaware Bay, making the southern part of the coast the only decent surf option in the state. The Indian River Inlet attracts good waves on both sides, and the beachbreaks to the south are very similar to those found only 10mi (16km) away in Maryland, where Ocean City has a concentrated stretch of short jetties along a heavily developed coast. Crowds swell in summer by 1000%, but the surf usually doesn't, so winter is the

PAUL KENNEDY

Above – **A bigger board can help offset the thick rubber required to surf during winter.**

time to catch some hollow, punchy waves with the blue-lipped few. One way of escaping the bustle is to search the wild expanses of Assateague Island, where endless 4WD beachbreaks beckon.

The District of Columbia chapter of Surfrider has the unenviable task of keeping an eye on the politicians responsible for getting legislation through the proper channels between close-out sets and making sure the powers that be are aware of the issues that the Foundation champions. It was the Capitol chapter's role to follow the BEACH (Beaches Environmental Awareness and Coastal Health Act of 2000) Bill on its journey through the House of Representatives and Senate, following which, on October 11, 2000 it was signed into law by President William Jefferson Clinton.

Calling the BEACH Bill "the most sweeping legislation ever regarding national ocean-water-quality testing," Surfrider's Executive Director Chris Evans said, "Surfers have become the indicator species and this is a personal achievement that our members and beach users in general will benefit from. After all, we wear that water every day."

Delaware is an environmental newcomer, joining the Surfrider Foundation flock in August of 1998. Its short stretch of surfable coastline merges seamlessly with the equally brief stretch of Maryland's Ocean City beachbreaks to the south. Delaware's coast may be small, but they have worked extremely hard and some big issues

PAUL KENNEDY

the summer with hundreds of thousands of people arriving to frolic by the sea. Cross over the inlet and the virtually virgin landscape of Assateague State Park gently curves down to the Virginia border. Miles of beachbreaks are allowed to naturally shift without the concentration of hard structures that typify the coastline from Ocean City to Delaware. Since these jetties and groins aren't effective enough on their own, sand is pumped up onto beaches to counteract inevitable erosion. Reserves of sand for beach replenishment are running ominously low, and fresh supplies are needed to maintain the beach width of 100ft (30m).

Surfrider's Ocean Beach, Maryland Chapter is relatively young, too, but has already managed a couple of significant precedents. They will be working directly with the EPA (Environmental Protection Agency) to instigate a 15-year plan, which targets septic tanks, agricultural runoff, sewage plant infrastructure, preservation of open

are coming to light, particularly in the area of sewage treatment and discharge. Reports of events involving raw sewage being pumped into the Indian River and making it into the primo Delaware line-up of the same name are the

PAUL KENNEDY

Top – **The Army Corps of Engineers are partly responsible for Delaware's premier spot at the mouth of the Indian River.** Above – **Typical Ocean City, Maryland beachbreak**.

result of an outdated treatment plant infrastructure. Testing is high on the list of priorities to bring pressure on the polluters to raise their game. Delaware does have a summertime testing program, but it collects samples only 5 times a month. Phosphates and nutrients are generally at high levels, providing a strong platform for pfiesteria to form, which has been detected in Delaware waterways.

The southern border with Maryland positively bristles with short jetties and groins designed to combat an annual 2-4ft (0.6-1.3m) of sand erosion. Millions of dollars are spent on beach-nourishment programs, justified by predicting a downturn in tourist numbers if the beaches aren't maintained at a particular width.

A tale of two distinct and essentially opposite coastal environs exists in Maryland. Ocean City is exactly that in

space and other important influencers of coastal water quality. Maryland will also become the first US state to receive a federal seal of approval on a state 'coastal non-point pollution control plan' to reduce untreated runoff, the number one source of water pollution.

Historically, Delaware and Maryland have lagged behind neighboring states in maturing a population of surfers and, thus, surf advocacy. Nevertheless, a large contingent were regularly hitting the Indian River and Ocean City waves by the late 1960s. Skip Savage ran Surf Shop East during the 1960s attracting large crowds of longboarders to Rehoboth Beach. Since then, Ocean City has become the focus, providing a home for many modern surf shops and the year round crew are always ready for action regardless of the conditions.

Virginia

The surf is notable because, apart from the extreme north and south of the state, there is little or no access to the plethora of offshore islands that dot the coastline. These islands undoubtedly hold some quality waves and a few privileged locals make forays into this wilderness by boat. Chincoteague National Wildlife Reserve is a continuation of Assatague Island, offering miles of unspoiled beaches and waves similar to those north of the border in Maryland. Virginia Beach, or "Va Beach" as the locals say, is another highly developed seaside resort of urban dimensions. While Va Beach isn't necessarily associated with great surf, it does have its share of days, both in 'town' and at the nearby Camp Pendleton spots. Even so, a large number of Virginia Beach surfers spend more time surfing on North Carolina's Outer Banks spots than at their local beaches.

The Chesapeake Bay catchment area is the largest estuary in the US. The bulk of Virginia's accessible waves are on the coast along the southern entry to the estuary, the beach water-quality is greatly affected by this huge estuarine environment. Hundreds of rivers and streams feed into the bay and many are carrying phosphates, nutrients, and pollutants from agricultural and industrial runoff. This puts too much nitrogen and phosphorus in the water and the resulting algae blooms rob the water of dissolved oxygen consequently decimating the marine life by suffocation. This problem now affects a third of America's coastal areas. An estimated half million fish have died in just two waterways on the Virginia/Maryland border. Officials are mistakenly blaming a drought for the fish-kill event (saying that the drought has made the runoff concentrations higher than normal), though the problem lies squarely with agriculturally polluted runoff.

All the usual problems are apparent around Virginia Beach, including the hard structures associated with shoreline armoring, contribute to erosion (Virginia has been replenishing its main beaches for longer than any other state on the East Coast), stormwater runoff from the built-up coastal area, and complex access issues. In fact, between Chincoteague Island and the Chesapeake Bay Bridge, there is virtually no access without a boat (not to mention military activity in the Pendleton area). This tends to concentrate surfers in Virginia Beach, where

surfing is not allowed within casting distance of the piers (ever see ol' Bob cast 300 feet?). Summer restrictions on surfing exist at most beaches.

During the 1920s and 1930s, a few solid surfboards, made of redwood or mahogany, arrived on the Atlantic coast from places like Hawaii and California before the Tom Blake paddleboard era arrived in the late 1930s. Tom Smith and Babe Braithwaite were notable Virginia beach locals, responsible for introducing the first solid board to Florida pioneers, Bill and Dudley Whitman. Some teenagers got to stay at home and surf through WWII, but things were pretty quiet until about 1951, when the first balsa boards started to filter through from Hawaii and the West Coast. The most popular spot in Virginia was the Steel Pier, which was located at Rudee Inlet; modern-day feuds with fishermen were as yet non-existent, and shooting the pier was a common pastime.

Bob Holland opened Virginia Beach's first surf shop in the early 1960s, stocking Jacobs, Webers, Hansens, and Hobies, but the shop closed soon after, partly because people thought the logo T-shirts in the window were actually undershirts, not street wear. Surf fashion was in its infancy! But the late 1960s surf explosion brought surf clubs, competitions, local board manufacturers, and crowds to the line-up. Virginia then followed the rest of the East Coast into the stale 1970s and anonymous 1980s before the 1990s brought renewed interest and the desire of local governments to embrace and expand surfing within the state. A large amateur competition scene has grown up in the Mid Atlantic states, and over the years a few notable surfers from Virginia (including Wes Laine and Todd Holland) have made the transition to the professional ranks and the world's liquid stage.

Above – **A couple of historic images from Bob Holland's shop in Virginia Beach, early 1960's.**

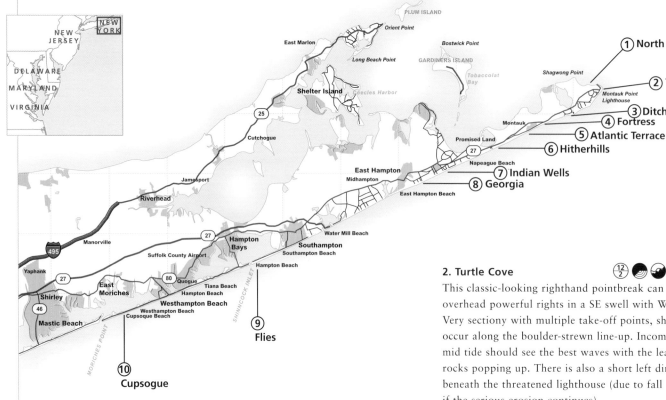

Long Island – East

1. North Bar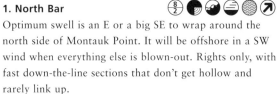

Optimum swell is an E or a big SE to wrap around the north side of Montauk Point. It will be offshore in a SW wind when everything else is blown-out. Rights only, with fast down-the-line sections that don't get hollow and rarely link up.

This medium consistency spot is sometimes crowded when conditions are right. As with all Long Island spots, there can be jellyfish in summer, and the current here gets strong. Parking inside the Montauk Point State Park costs unless it's a winter weekday. Parking anywhere else will result in a ticket or towing. The heated restrooms are a sub-tropical, wetsuit-changing refuge.

RICHARD QUINN

2. Turtle Cove

This classic-looking righthand pointbreak can hold double overhead powerful rights in a SE swell with W-NW winds. Very sectiony with multiple take-off points, short barrels occur along the boulder-strewn line-up. Incoming around mid tide should see the best waves with the least dry rocks popping up. There is also a short left directly beneath the threatened lighthouse (due to fall into the sea if the serious erosion continues).

A strong, constant current often helps disperse the crowds that come to surf here. Camp Hero Air Force Base has been added to the Montauk Point State Park providing less crowded surf if you're willing to make the long walk to the southwest.

3. Ditch Plains

This mushy left with its workable wall and longer rides is a favored longboard spot. Occasional steeper rights, plus a few faster lefts further to the east. Between here and the lighthouse, there are some more rocky reef spots, which require a long walk.

Main hazards: absolutely always crowded, with some large rocks in the line-up to the east. The dirt car park is restricted in summer, meaning an expensive town parking permit. The Ditch Witch rules in summer for munchies.

4. Fortress

A submerged reef of boulders makes for some fun, walled-up sections. Favors rights on a SE swell at all tides, but won't handle much size.

Often crowded with the local grommet crew. The town car park fills up quickly with permit holders making access difficult. Good facilities for this underdeveloped area.

5. Atlantic Terrace

Mainly sand with a sprinkling of boulders along this stretch of beach in the town of Montauk. Breaks closer to shore with occasional good shape until high tide kills it completely.

No parking near the beach without a town permit, which costs $150+ a year. Even so, the place is often crowded with locals and vacationers staying in the numerous beachfront hotels.

Turtles

BRUCE CHRISNER

6. Hitherhills

This average beachbreak has a wide swell window, with SE on an incoming tide being the pick. The sand gets chopped up by winter swells but sorts itself out through the summer.

Full facilities at this State Park make it an easy option during the crowded summer months.

7. Indian Wells

Open beachbreak that occasionally gets good in winter. No rocks to contain the shifting sandbars. Low incoming on a S swell is the best chance.

Rips, average crowds, expensive parking.

8. Georgia (East Hampton)

SW swell is optimum for hollow rights when sand builds up on the east side of the jetties. Will handle all tides but not too much swell.

Consistent waves and crowds, with more difficult, expensive parking.

9. Flies

Average beachbreak from East Hampton through Southampton down to Shinnecock Inlet. The eastern jetty gets longer rights on a SW swell, while a SE swell can produce some hollow wedges. The other side of the inlet gets good waves only in bigger swells.

Exclusive suburbs make parking and access difficult in summer. More town tags required to park.

10. Cupsogue

From Shinnecock Inlet to Moriches Inlet, shifting sandbars can produce good waves, particularly at the West Hampton jetties. Cupsogue Beach Park has the long inlet jetty which provides some protection from the W winds. Needs a bigger swell to break near the jetty, but there will be peaks further up the beach if it's small.

Very little access on this barrier island. A couple of town-sticker parking lots and 4WD beach access. Crowds sometimes congregate at certain spots along with local rip currents. Walking up or down the beach should provide empty waves.

Hampton

BRUCE CHRISNER

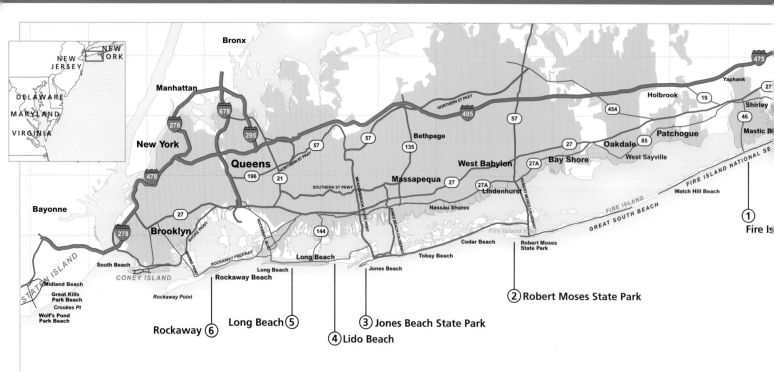

Lazy Mans

Long Island – West

1. Fire Island

This notorious but pristine barrier island stretches for 30 miles (45km) with one access point, at the eastern end. A 4WD is a must to explore the endless breaks that can get hollow and powerful. NW is offshore and it will break on all tides, but low incoming is best. Optimum swell direction depends on which part of the island you're at, but it generally breaks on all swells.

Rarely crowded due to the large scope of choice. Lots of rips and currents. Annual 4WD vehicle passes are about $150. Renting a 4WD is much cheaper outside the NY metropolitan area.

Looking south from Manhattan towards the city's closest surfing beaches.

Lido Beach

2. Robert Moses State Park

On the curved end of Fire Island, this State Park has the easiest access and parking in the city area. Broken into 4 'fields', #4 picks up the most swell on the east side. Field 1 faces more south meaning it will be smaller but the curve of the beach can line up the lefts quite well. It always breaks close to the beach with hollow thumping sections.

Often crowded in spots with plenty of current to contend with. Full facilities at each large car park.

3. Jones Beach State Park

From Fire Island Inlet to Jones Beach, 10 miles (16km) of unstabilized beach can produce some decent sandbars on the right day. High tide is no good because it amplifies the trough of deeper water between the outside and inside banks. The Gilgo area is generally the most consistent.

Large car parks make access easier at points, but walking is the way to escape the consistent crowds. Long distances between facilities.

4. Lido Beach

This due south facing stretch of beach needs a N wind and a SE swell to be at its best. Low to mid tide will have the hollowest waves.

Picks up a bit more swell than Long Beach and gets just as crowded. Some area residents offer parking in their driveways or yards during summer madness, usually for a reasonable fee.

5. Long Beach

Long Beach faces a bit SW, allowing it to handle the NE winds better. When the rest of Long Island is maxing out,

Long Beach jetties will be organized but smaller. Can get hollow and perfect at lower tides.

Just above medium consistency, it's often crowded and suffers from rips. More suburban parking problems.

6. Rockaway

The closest surfing beach to NYC, the crowds are more challenging here than the waves. Average beachbreaks that need a sizable swell to make it in here with big E swells bringing some decent lefts.

Always crowded with surfers who are as aggressive as Yellow Cab drivers. Parking spots can be found a few blocks back from the beach, where rip-offs are common.

Cedar Beach

Sandy Hook

① The Cove

Gateway National
Recreation Area
Sandy Hook Unit

Atlantic Highlands

②1st Parking Lot

Highlands

Highlands Beach

Sea Bright

Red Bank

36

Shrewsbury

Monmouth Beach

③ Presidents Street Park

Oceanport

Long Branch

West Long
Branch

71

Deal

Oakhurst

④ The Wedge

Allenhurst

Loch Arbour

Ashbury Park
Ocean Grove

⑤ Bradley Beach

Neptune City

Bradley Beach
Avon-By-The-Sea

⑥ 'L' Jetty

⑦ Belmar Fishing Pier

Belmar

South Belmar

Spring Lake

⑧ Belmar to Sea Girt

Spring Lake Heights

Sea Grit

⑨ Manasquan

Manasquan

Masaquan River

Brielle

New Jersey – Monmouth County

1. The Cove

The Cove at Sandy Hook picks up and handles swell from all directions. Better than 1st Parking Lot, a natural point here creates mainly rights and occasional short lefts when the wide section breaks. Low to mid tide on a southerly swell is going to provide longer right walls on a bigger swell. The lower the tide, the higher the quality.

Often crowded, especially in summer when they limit the number of cars/people into the park. All facilities, no restrictions. Due to proximity to New York Harbor, commercial pollution is a strong possibility. The water is more turbid than the rest of Jersey. Nuclear sub base 5 miles (8km) from here.

2. 1st Parking Lot

The Hook gets really good on maxing S swells even if it's blowing S. Always smaller than more famous spots to the south, these rights off the jetty and lefts towards it can be picture perfect when it's low incoming and due W wind. South of here, the beach diminishes and the seawall causes backwash at higher tides. There are some waves, but only locals have the time to work out when and where.

Same deal as The Cove.

3. 7 Presidents Street Park

The Monmouth Beach to Long Branch stretch has some good waves in amongst the tight jetties and old pilings, but it suffers from difficult access and inconsistent

Belmar

sandbars. This means that 7 Presidents County Park is the best place to go for smaller, varied jetty waves that take all swell directions at lower tides.

All facilities and no restrictions once you pay the minimal fee.

4. The Wedge (Allenhurst)

The stretch from Long Branch down to Loch Arbour through the ritzy and architecturally-diverse suburb of Deal provides some good jetty surf. The left at the Cove in Allenhurst has steep, bowly sections on a NE swell at low.

Always crowded in the tight take-off zone, despite a complete lack of parking in the area. Try the main street, half a mile away. Has a private swim club feel in summer.

5. Bradley Beach

From Ocean Grove to Avon, concentrated jetties can provide hollow waves. Fickle, shifting sandbars are usually smaller than breaks south of here, but it copes well with a moderate swell.

The jetties break up the drift and paddle-outs are easier.

6. 'L' Jetty

A generally softer wave that needs SE or E swell up to overhead to produce rights breaking in front of the L part. No room for error at this wobbly, backwashy, low tide spot.

Blackballed (no surfing) between 10-5pm during summer at this guarded, tagged cove.

7. Belmar Fishing Pier

The south side of Shark River Inlet between the jetty and the battered pier can get powerful and hollow, but very shifty. Only NE or E swell along with lower tides.

Easy check from the car at the metered roadside parking along the seawall. Rarely crowded because it's rarely good. Tags and pier restrictions. Some submerged objects from old jetties.

8. Belmar to Sea Girt

The jetties are consistent, but the access isn't. Around New York Boulevard in Sea Girt is the most popular area. Accepts a full north New Jersey swell window and can work well on any direction. High tide doesn't do this stretch any favors, but with a W wind and a head high swell, there will be some barrels.

Hazardous old stormwater drains lurk in the line-up. Often crowded, tags, and a rotating designated surfing area.

Sea Girt

RAY HALLGREEN

9. Manasquan

A S/SE swell, a W wind, and the bigger the better for this famous jewel of 'Joisey'. Deep water leading to the inlet, a beefy jetty and good sandbars conspire to provide long barreling righthanders. Low to mid and closer to the beach if it's smaller, when the tall jetty will provide some protection in a southerly wind. Will handle whatever the Atlantic can throw at it without shutting down. People have been known to paddle out the inlet in huge conditions. Generally regarded as the best wave in Jersey, this grinding board-snapper regularly gets as good as the photos. There are also good waves off the shorter jetties further up the beach.

Always heavily crowded with plenty of attitude out in the water until it gets big enough to thin out the pretenders. Lots of currents and drift to contend with. Free roadside parking in winter, but summer brings meters and tags.

Manasquan

MEZ/ESM

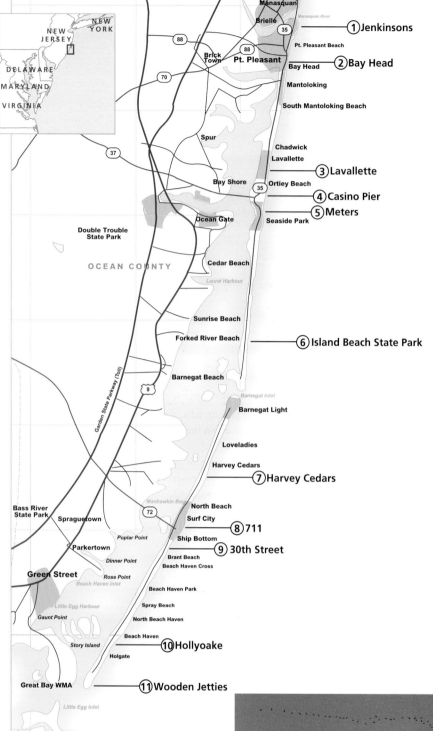

Manasquan
Brielle
88
Brick Town
88
Pt. Pleasant
①Jenkinsons
Pt. Pleasant Beach
Bay Head
②Bay Head
Mantoloking
South Mantoloking Beach
70
Spur
Chadwick
Lavallette
37
Bay Shore
③Lavallette
Ortley Beach
35
④Casino Pier
Ocean Gate
⑤Meters
Seaside Park
Double Trouble State Park
OCEAN COUNTY
Cedar Beach
Laural Harbour
Sunrise Beach
Forked River Beach
⑥Island Beach State Park
Barnegat Beach
Garden State Parkway (Toll)
9
Barnegat Inlet
Barnegat Light
Loveladies
Harvey Cedars
⑦Harvey Cedars
Manahawkin Bay
North Beach
72
Surf City
⑧711
Bass River State Park
Spraguetown
Poplar Point
Ship Bottom
⑨30th Street
Parkertown
Brant Beach
Dinner Point
Beach Haven Cross
Green Street
Rose Point
Beach Haven Inlet
Beach Haven Park
Little Egg Harbour
Spray Beach
Gaunt Point
North Beach Haven
Beach Haven
Story Island
⑩Hollyoake
Holgate
Great Bay WMA
⑪Wooden Jetties
Little Egg Inlet
Brigantine Inlet

New Jersey – Ocean County

1. Jenkinsons (Point Pleasant)

The south side of Manasquan Inlet only works on a NE or E swell. Once again, the deep water offshore here focuses the swell, which throws up a powerful wedge that barrels for a short distance before the shoredump. Mainly lefts that need lower tides, will handle a SW wind.

Often crowded, including lots of bodyboarders. Privately-owned boardwalk enforces tags. Private guards generally don't let surfers out in the water in summer, which is when it generally doesn't break.

2. Bay Head

The jetties are a bit longer in the Bridge Avenue area than the ones to the south. When the sand is in position and a good southerly swell is running, fast, hollow, ruler-edged rights will break in shallow water. Handles size and mid to high tide is usually best.

Sometimes crowded, but well dispersed over a mile-long stretch. Tags and 10-5pm restrictions. Free roadside parking can be a hassle in summer, particularly if you get caught towel-changing in this prudish residential area.

3. Lavallette

A series of short jetties from Lavallette Beach through to Ortley doesn't protrude enough to provide anything other than average beachbreak peaks. An E swell should throw up some A-frames on all but high tide.

Sometimes crowded, which gets worse when all the surfers are funneled into a few areas for June, July, and August. The jetties can be a dangerous obstacle depending on where the sand has collected. Rips and tags.

4. Seaside Heights/Casino Pier

One of the premier waves in NJ, breaking either side of a huge pier, which hosts a roller coaster, mini-golf course, plus all sorts of family amusement and fairground-style attractions. Picks up just about any swell, which will break on a low tide bar right in front of the pier. Fast, hollow rights and lefts squeeze past the end pylons and can grind

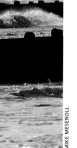

Bay Head

MIKE MESEROLL
Jenkinsons

on down the beach in bigger swells. At higher tides on a NE swell, the south side will have a high-performance, bowly right, breaking back into the pier. This is mirrored by a less intense left on the north side in a southerly swell. The wide mass of tight pylons offers excellent onshore or sideshore wind protection.

An absolute circus in summer with hundreds of thousands of people cruising the cheesy boardwalk. The waves are as consistent as the crowds, along with plenty of drowning swimmers if the swell is on. Meters everywhere, but very few of them will be vacant.

5. Meters
A fun, snappy beachbreak with barrels and steep, workable walls just south of Casino Pier. High tide will kill it in smaller swells.

Often crowded, particularly in summer, due to the sheer weight of people who holiday here and the miles of metered parking. Designated surfing beach with tags required and a charge to use the restrooms or showers.

6. Island Beach State Park
Favors rights on a SE swell. Gets hollow on lower tides, and there is an endless selection of peaks all the way down to the jetty at the southern end. 4WD or Herculean hike required.

Early arrival necessary in summer, before they close the gate to protect this pristine but sensitive area. It is possible to camp for up to 3 nights on the beach, if you have a 4WD pass and an intention to fish. Pluses include consistent and rarely crowded waves, no tags and no dress code. Minuses are currents, jellyfish, and entrance fee.

7. Harvey Cedars
From Barnegat Lighthouse State Park through Loveladies, Harvey Cedars, and on to North Beach, this stretch is home to a good percentage of Long Beach Island's heavy beachbreaks. A good NE or SE swell will come out of deep water and slam on the bar at lower tides. Sand-dredging, wide-open barrels created along a 4mi (6.5km) stretch of groins make for a punishing paddle-out, particularly in winter.

The power of the surf is the main hazard, along with some rips around the groins. Rarely crowded because there is always another jetty just as good up or down the beach. Citations for towel-changing in the roadside residential parking area.

8. 711
The closest stretch of beach to the only causeway connecting LBI to the mainland. Accepts any swell direction but rarely produces anything other than an average beachbreak at lower tides.

Often crowded with all types of surfcraft. Close to the SevenEleven (obviously) and free roadside parking, as opposed to the beach, where you have to pay (tags) to park your butt in summer.

9. 30th Street (Ship Bottom)
More straight beachbreak. Ship Bottom is a decent option in summer, even though surfing restrictions apply. Lots of groms without cars to take them somewhere better.

Average crowds. Will break if there's any swell about. Tags required. Free parking but no facilities.

10. Hollyoake
An E or NE swell will produce long punchy lefts, which are hollow on take-off and in sections down the line. S or SE closes out. Low incoming tide is best.

A strong north-to-south drift means a constant paddle to stay on the tight take-off area. Entering on the north side of the jetty and walking back up after a wave helps to spread the concentrated crowd of dialed-in locals. Limited residential roadside parking, which the police patrol heavily. Tags loosely enforced by lenient lifeguards who surf.

11. Wooden Jetties
Situated in Holgate Wildlife Reserve on the southern tip of LBI. A slight bend in the coast gives Wooden Jetties the capacity to hold the biggest NE swells. It will break on all tides, but low will be smaller and high will make it full, so mid is the pick. Lefts only, which seem to break below sea level with plenty of punch.

A big slab of steel submerged on the inside and severe currents are the main hazards. Pay to park in summer but no tags.

R. HALLGREEN
Harvey Cedars

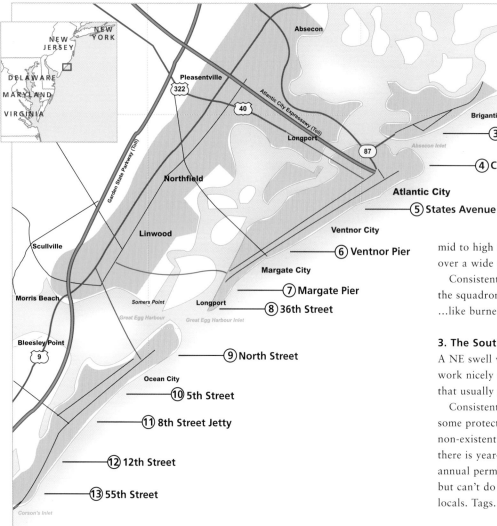

① Kirbys Point

② The Castle

③ The South Jetty

④ Crystals

⑤ States Avenue

⑥ Ventnor Pier

⑦ Margate Pier

⑧ 36th Street

⑨ North Street

⑩ 5th Street

⑪ 8th Street Jetty

⑫ 12th Street

⑬ 55th Street

New Jersey – Atlantic City

1. Kirbys Point

Average beachbreaks along a stretch with short jetties. NE swell and higher tides.

Jellyfish and greenhead flies in summer.

2. The Castle

The pier used to have a bar and surf shack on it until a 'colorful' local businessmen converted it into a Disney-style attraction. After a few years of business it burnt to the waterline and can now be called stumps. Takes the full swell window with lefts working best on a nor'easter at mid to high tide. Fatter, mushier longboard waves spread over a wide area.

Consistent and rarely crowded, which could be due to the squadrons of giant greenhead flies. Submerged objects ...like burned-out pilings.

3. The South Jetty

A NE swell will be a mess here, but E to S swells will work nicely at mid to high tide. A fun summertime wave that usually gets chest high peaks.

Consistent and sometimes crowded, as the jetty offers some protection from S winds. Parking in the summer is non-existent in the surrounding residential streets, but there is year-round 4WD beach access if you have a $100+ annual permit. The lifeguards keep the swimmers away but can't do anything about the rabid fox that bites non-locals. Tags.

4. Crystals

This shallow beachbreak forms up close to shore on all tides. Popular with bodyboarders looking for the steep, short rights that occur here. NE swell best, but it won't handle as much size as the breaks just south of here.

Free parking here may end up more costly, as this is a depressed downbeat neighborhood and rip-offs are common. Less crowded and usually no tags needed.

5. States Avenue

Also known as Gas Chambers, this is Atlantic City's premier wave. Between the old Gardens Pier and the Steel Pier, very powerful, top-to-bottom peaks will break close to the beach on a SE swell at low to mid tide.

This is one of the beaches where the Duke first surfed in 1912. It is now overshadowed by huge high-rise casinos and apparently rates as America's favorite playground. Often crowded, strong currents, and nightmarish parking problems. Sometimes valet parking in some of the casinos is the best option.

6. Ventnor Pier

A popular break that lines up well with some longer, peeling waves.

Often crowded, high consistency, pay to park and surf (tags).

Crystals

States Avenue aka Gas Chambers

DOUG GOTTHOLD

7. Margate Pier

Good summer wave that gets hollow at low tide. Not too heavy. Handles swell but always has a strong drift.

Stay 300ft (100m) from pier. Less crowded and the northernmost free roadside parking on Abescon Island. Tags.

8. 36th Street

Basic beachbreak surf that favors lefts in a NE swell. Occasionally hollow but never heavy.

All facilities are further north at 32nd Street. Surfing beach in summer. Tags.

9. North Street

All the Ocean City breaks focus on the short jetties, breaking closer to shore at all sizes. North Street is the closest to the inlet and receives plenty of sand, which builds up at the north end after a summer of S swells. Takes all swells up to 10ft (3m) on both sides of the jetty. Lower tides on the south side then the north side starts working after mid, which can have good rights.

The most consistent break around, which is always bigger in size and larger in crowds. Exclusive neighborhood that dislikes seeing surfers' buttocks. Suit up with care in the free roadside parking areas. Full facilities at 2nd Street.

10. 5th Street

The sand build-up here provides a steep sucky left from a critical take-off point just in front of the end of the jetty down towards the next groin at 8th Street. Handles the big NE swells, but a S swell doesn't work on the north side of the jetty.

Hazards include the long, exposed stormwater pipes that stick out in the surf at high tides. Summer surfing restrictions and plenty of taggers.

11. 8th Street Jetty

The only year-round surfing area in Ocean City and one of the best waves in the state. Handles as big as it gets with pitching gnarly waves no further than 150ft (45m) off the jetty. Rights on the 7th Street side in a southerly and long left barrels in a nor'easter.

Timing paddle-outs and reading the rips is essential here when it's bigger. Watch the stormwater pipes at higher tides. Very consistent, therefore it's often crowded. Tags needed. You can't surf the lefts south of the jetty between 10-5pm.

12. 12th Street Jetty

The beach fills in a bit south of here, making 12th Street a more fun, rippable wave. Mid tide rising, NW winds, and only NE to E swells.

Burgeoning boardwalk crowds and 10-5pm no surfing enthusiastically enforced by unsympathetic lifeguards.

13. 55th Street Pier

A shallow bar off the end of a dilapidated pier that may be rebuilt soon. Catches all the sand that's pumped in at Ocean City. SW winds will bump it up a bit, even though a NE swell is best. Hollow, longer rides either side of the pier.

Consistent and clean at this sometimes crowded spot. Year-round, on-beach parking with the Marmora Wildlife Management Area Coastal Wetlands just to the south.

DOUG GOTTHOLD
5th Street, Ocean City

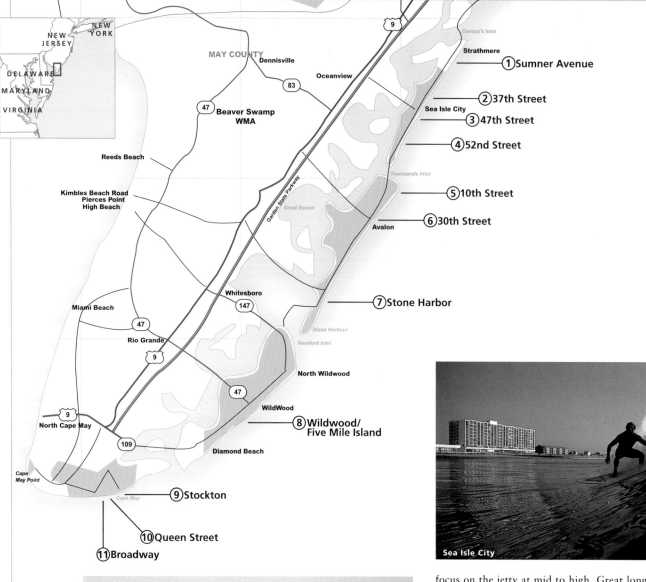

New York

New Jersey / Delaware / Maryland / Virginia

Corson's Inlet

Strathmere

①Sumner Avenue

②37th Street

Sea Isle City

③47th Street

④52nd Street

Townsends Inlet

⑤10th Street

Avalon

⑥30th Street

MAY COUNTY · Dennisville

Oceanview

83

47 · Beaver Swamp WMA

Garden State Parkway

Great Sound

Reeds Beach

Kimbles Beach Road
Pierces Point
High Beach

Whitesboro

147

Miami Beach

47

Rio Grande

9

⑦Stone Harbor

Stone Harbour

Hereford Inlet

North Wildwood

47

WildWood

⑧Wildwood/
Five Mile Island

9

North Cape May

109

Diamond Beach

Cape May Point

⑨Stockton

Cape May

⑩Queen Street

⑪Broadway

Cape May

New Jersey – Cape May

1. Sumner Avenue (Strathmere) ⑧/2

Designated surfing beach. Will break on all tides but
doesn't like dead low. Strathmere is the first break south
of Corson Inlet, which is being allowed to fill in and
return to its natural state. Picks up more of the S swell
than the rest of Sea Isle. Weak at low way outside, it'll

focus on the jetty at mid to high. Great longboard wave.

Very consistent as the inlet channel will attract swell.
Sometimes crowded with hippies and beginners. No
pollution problems.

2. 37th Street Jetty ⑮/2

Lots of sand on the outside bar translates to barrels at
lower tides, which then feather at higher tides before
pitching on the inside. Will handle both the biggest swells
around and some S in the wind.

Rarely crowded since there is such a wide area to choose
from. The Sea Isle City lifeguards are all surfers and will
keep swimmers away from the jetties, which are designated
surfing areas. Tags loosely enforced and Wednesday is free.
No pollution or regular rips.

3. 47th Street ⑫/2

This is where erosion has brought the beach in closer to
the boardwalk, giving the wave a bit of a point like set-up
at mid tide. 300ft (90m) lefts are not uncommon. High
tide will be fat under head high.

Tight take-off area next to the jetty means sharing with
the local boys.

Sea Isle City

DOUG GOTTHOLD

DOUG GOTTHOLD

4. 52nd Street

After blowing S for a couple of days, a right will peel down this stretch of due E-facing beach. Always smaller than everywhere else, and only works on a southerly swell.

Not very consistent, no facilities, tags required.

5. 10th Street (Avalon)

The stretch from 8th Street to 16th Street in Avalon picks up the NE swell and seems to amplify it. Hollow peaks around the jetties.

Summer brings the crowds, beach taggers, and occasional jellyfish.

6. 30th Street (Avalon)

This summer surfing beach can get shapely in a NE swell when the offshore kicks in. Usually better elsewhere.

Very tough on beach tags here. Do some sprint training!

7. Stone Harbor

Part of the Seven Mile Beach that extends from Townsends Inlet to Hereford Inlet. There are more than the usual amount of jetties but no real stand-out waves. Nuns' Beach is a mellow longboard wave right in front of the convent in Stone Harbor. Better on higher tides, this is a good place for beginners as the waves don't usually break off the jetty.

Sometimes crowded with families on all sorts of surfcraft. Beach tags.

8. Wildwood/Five Mile Island

Most of the sand from the rest of Jersey's beach-nourishment program ends up on this 5-mile (8km) resort stretch. All swells and tides, with high not being a problem due to the volume of sand. The US Coastguard owns the island's prime surfing real estate.

Stormwater and summer jellyfish but rarely crowded at this non-tagged island resort. Rollercoasters, a million hotels, and WWII pill boxes contribute to the ambiance.

Cape May

9. Stockton

This is the pick of the Cape May south-facing beaches. Incoming tide on an overhead swell usually means barrels, unless they have recently pumped sand.

Stormwater, rip currents, and a sometimes crowded scenario because the rest of NJ will be onshore when this consistent spot is firing. Beach tags required for all Cape May beaches. Designated summer surfing.

10. Queen Street

These fun, lined-up lefts need a bit of size before they'll break hollow.

Sometimes crowded, stormwater runoff, and currents at this consistent designated surfing beach.

11. Broadway

The southernmost break in New Jersey is one of a series of jetties that has recently developed good bars after a sand-pumping program. Best at mid to high on a building NE swell. Mainly well shaped lefts that can get hollow, plus a few bowly rights.

Highly consistent and often crowded since it handles the NE winds. Some stormwater pollution, currents, and no surfing summer daytimes.

Sea Isle

Delaware/Maryland

1. Naval Jetties

Long rights off the groin on its day. Has potential to get heavy, hollow, and fast without sectioning. Good spot in hurricane swells. Best on S swells and low tides. Holds decent size. Head here when Maryland is getting out of control.

Watch out for submerged tree stumps. Not particularly consistent, and rarely crowded. No pollution.

2. Indian River Northside

Breaks way out producing long, rolling walls that stand up on the inside section. Very popular playground for longboarders. Gets big without becoming heavy.

Sand pumping from the inlet constantly changes the bars. Consistent and often crowded. Occasional sea-lice and potential sewage problems.

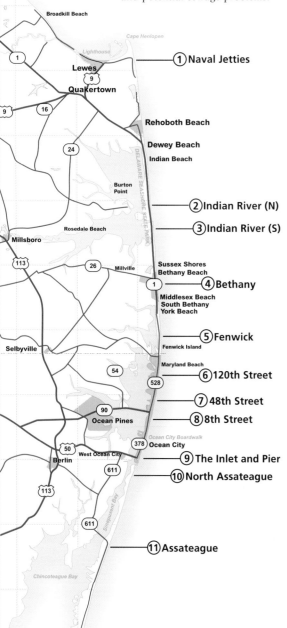

Indian River South

PAUL KENNEDY

3. Indian River Southside

One of the heaviest waves in the Delaware/Maryland area. Known to have snapped a board or two. Longer rights and short lefts offer walls and quick, thick barrels. Bodyboarder central.

Less consistent than other local spots, but often crowded. Some rips if big. Summertime sea-lice.

4. Bethany

Beachbreaks and lefts/rights off jetties. Often small and perfect. Main Street is the best spot. Rights fire off the jetty in a NE to S swell, starting as a barrel then walling up.

Length of ride depends on swell direction. Consistent.

5. Fenwick

Smaller than Maryland and not as powerful. Grooms the swell well. Short and fast with barrel sections. Usually more rights than lefts. Best on low incoming tides.

Consistently small and doesn't get crowded because people usually surf elsewhere. Occasional stormwater runoff.

6. 120th Street

Holds a big swell. One of the best places for hurricane swells. Breaks way out with steep drops. Gets hollow. Mainly long rights. Has big but short, open lefts on a NE swell.

Consistent and sometimes crowded. Rips/currents when it's big.

Fenwick

PAUL KENNEDY

Inlet Pier

7. 48th Street

Usually has the biggest waves in Ocean City. Bowly barrels, both left and right can get absolutely perfect. A safe bet for good waves when the swell is firing. Low tide is best. Good in hurricane swells.

Consistent and often crowded. No pollution. Rips/currents when big make it a long paddle-out.

8. 8th Street

This series of jetties around 8th Street has good waves with longer lefts on a NE swell. Some reasonable power and well-shaped barrels at this popular boardwalk spot. Strong currents make the paddle-out difficult when it gets overhead. Low tide is best and will handle a bit of N in the wind.

Consistent and often crowded in front of surf shop scene. Summer sea-lice.

9. The Inlet and Pier

The most consistent and popular spot in Maryland. Visiting surfers usually end up here. There are three main breaks. Steep, bowly rights off the north inlet jetty are probably the best waves. Second peak is a left and right that's not quite as steep. Peaks either side of the pier. Can be 1-2ft (0.3-0.6m) bigger on incoming tides. Somewhat sheltered from S winds, which means it's often good in hurricane swells.

Consistent. Often crowded. Rips and currents when big.

10. North Assateague

Known as 'The Wedge' this lefthander breaks off the south inlet jetty. Rides of 100 yards (90m) and more are common. Unlike most other local breaks, high tide is required, and a NW wind is still offshore. Half a mile south are outside shoals, but you'll need a boat since they break way out. These shoals can hold a good-sized swell; they break both ways; a good spot in a big hurricane. Can

break on S swells and handles N winds.

North Assateague is a wildlife sanctuary and inaccessible by land. You need to paddle across the inlet from Ocean City's fishing harbor, but strong currents and boat traffic can make this paddle hazardous. Consistent and rarely crowded. No pollution, some sea-lice.

11. Assateague

Potentially powerful lefts and rights can produce long rides on the outside sandbar when it's lined up and big. Getting out can be a problem, as there are no channels and strong rips/currents. Good and fun when smaller. Longboarders surf here as it often doesn't break top-to-bottom. No good on higher tides unless it's big.

Consistent spot and rarely crowded. State Park facilities with campground. Area inhabited by wild ponies, which, as the signs say, will kick and bite.

Inlet Pier

Virginia

1. Chincoteague

The National Wildlife Refuge of Chincoteague is the southern end of Assateague Island and the surf displays all the characteristics of the Maryland waves to the north. If anything, the trench between the shorebreak and the outside sandbar is more pronounced so if the surf is small, pumping and bouncing is obligatory. Gets wild and out of control quickly and doesn't tolerate any E winds. There is the possibility of scoring some longer lefts down at the horseshoe shaped southern point of the island on big NE swells.

Consistent spot and rarely crowded. There's no campground inside the Wildlife Refuge but there's a few in Chincoteague itself. Breaks to the north of the car parks are foot access only while there is an Oversand Vehicle Route south to Toms Cove Hook once you've payed a hefty permit price to avoid the 3 mile (5km) soft sand slog down to the lefts.

Virginia Beach Pier

BRUCE CHRISNER

2. Fishermans Island

At the northern extremity of the Chesapeake Bay Bridge, a small crescent of sand is home to an extremely rare point-style lefthander. The swell has to be coming from a S to E direction and N winds will groom the long, fast barreling walls. Will break on all tides but is more makeable with more water.

So fickle it's not funny. To compound things, there's no access without a boat. No stopping or parking in the immediate vicinity, and no trespassing on the beach. This means that only the most dedicated locals are ever going to surf this spot.

3. North End

The surf off this long stretch of residential blocks north of the main Virginia Beach area is usually smaller and therefore quieter than the town breaks to the south. Feeble in small swells when the outside break fats out over the deep-water trough before the shorebreak. This makes low tide and bigger swells the only way to go.

8th Street

BRUCE CHRISNER

Summer surfing and parking restrictions apply. The adjacent First Landing State Park offers good camping, virtually on the beach.

4. Virginia Beach

Classic example of average East Coast pier surf, warts and all. More rights than lefts on both sides because the winter nor'easters provide a right breaking back towards the pier on the south side. Any W in the wind for offshore conditions plus the side/onshore protection offered by the pylons on the rare occasions you can surf near the pier.

Mad summer crowds compound restrictions like no surfing between 10am-5pm or within 300ft (100m) of a pier full of trigger-happy fisherman. Fight for a meter to park. Highly consistent in its averageness.

5. 1st Street Jetty

This is the home of East Coast surfing competitions and 'the' designated surfing area for Virginia. On the north side of Rudee Inlet, this jetty holds sand and focuses swell that is non-existent at other breaks. Prefers S swells and higher tides, which will form up the rights, which so many people ride – all at once!

1st Street is a menagerie, and you have to be an animal to get a wave. Surfers of all stripes will show up on any given day, vying for anything remotely rideable. A continuous circuit of contests (including a WQS) compounds the crowding. Meter parking is the only option. Close to the inlet means questionable water quality.

6. Croatan

South of the inlet from 1st Street, Croatan lefts should peel strongly down the jetty. The peaky take-off fast gives way to a flabby wall and occasionally faster inside section. High tide on a NE swell is best, while the NE wind doesn't affect it too adversely.

Ridiculous crowds, absurd parking, and anti-surfing residents add to the ambience of this over-rated, average-consistency spot. Park well outside the Croatan parking restrictions and walk in. No facilities.

7. Camp Pendleton

Camp Pendleton offers respite from the cramped surfing areas to the north with a stretch of beachbreak flanked by a massive army training camp. Handles the bigger swells on outside sandbanks that will throw out the odd barrel at low tides. E to S swells are preferable, making this more of a summer and fall break.

Large parking lot with easy access makes this a favorite for blow-ins. Crowds can be huge but spread out over a wide area. The main hazard would be something going horribly wrong with the war games next door!

8th Street

BRUCE CHRISNER

The South

In surfing terms, the South Atlantic includes North and South Carolina and Georgia (Florida gets its own chapter). For East Coast surfers, this region represents both heaven and hell in the beachbreak bible. Heaven being the specks of sand that have congregated up to 30 miles (48km) offshore to form the crescent of slender barrier islands known as the Outer Banks. This is where barrel devotees come to worship from all over the eastern states and where the Atlantic throws up the biggest and most consistent swells year-round. The continental shelf is as narrow as it gets off the Outer Banks, but unfortunately for Georgia, some 400 miles (644km) south, this same shelf is at its maximum swell destroying width. South Carolina shares more surf similarities to Georgia than North Carolina, but any major redemption for this southern coast has to await those big hurricane swells.

Virtually all of the coastal South is unconnected to the mainland. The Intracoastal Waterway isolates hundreds of sandy barrier islands, which are often linked by bridges or ferries. Casting a surfer's eye on the map might conjure up visions of long, sandy pointbreaks at the extremities of these islands, but such set-ups are in reality a rarity. While interference with the natural world can be instrumental in creating or destroying quality surf spots it is in fact the man-made structures which have the ability to shape the eternally shifting sandbars and provide the surfer with the best chance of finding a well-defined wave with any reliability. However, those same hurricane swells regularly take out these structures, just to remind man who's the boss.

DOUG WATERS

Cape Hatteras.

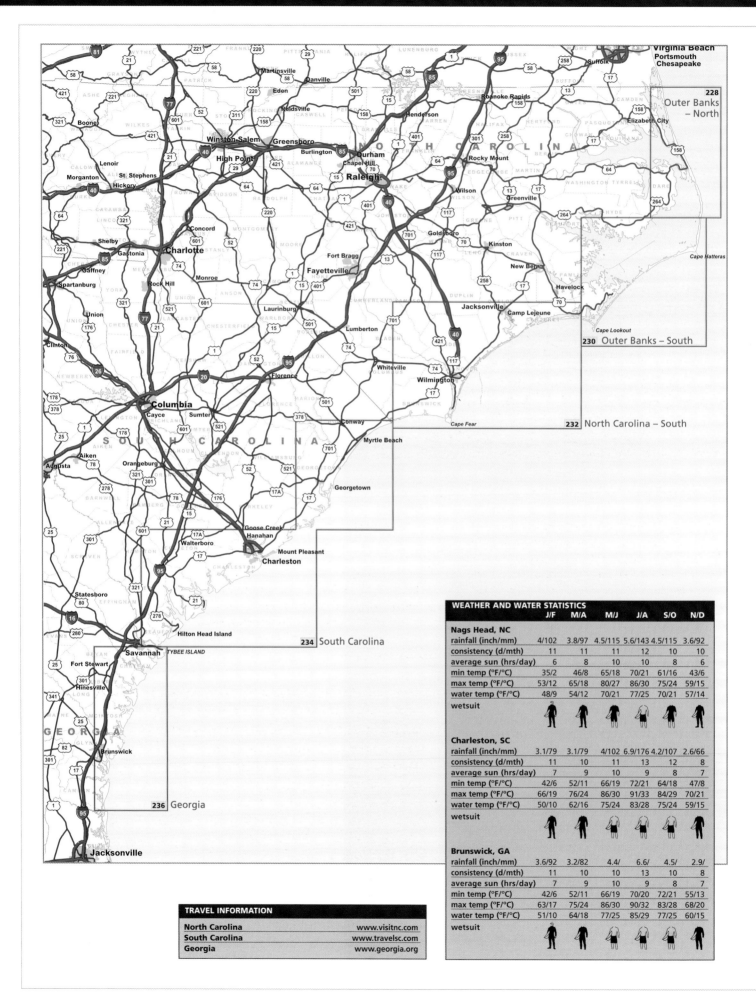

WEATHER AND WATER STATISTICS						
	J/F	**M/A**	**M/J**	**J/A**	**S/O**	**N/D**
Nags Head, NC						
rainfall (inch/mm)	4/102	3.8/97	4.5/115	5.6/143	4.5/115	3.6/92
consistency (d/mth)	11	11	11	12	10	10
average sun (hrs/day)	6	8	10	10	8	6
min temp (°F/°C)	35/2	46/8	65/18	70/21	61/16	43/6
max temp (°F/°C)	53/12	65/18	80/27	86/30	75/24	59/15
water temp (°F/°C)	48/9	54/12	70/21	77/25	70/21	57/14
wetsuit						
Charleston, SC						
rainfall (inch/mm)	3.1/79	3.1/79	4/102	6.9/176	4.2/107	2.6/66
consistency (d/mth)	11	10	11	13	12	8
average sun (hrs/day)	7	9	10	9	8	7
min temp (°F/°C)	42/6	52/11	66/19	72/21	64/18	47/8
max temp (°F/°C)	66/19	76/24	86/30	91/33	84/29	70/21
water temp (°F/°C)	50/10	62/16	75/24	83/28	75/24	59/15
wetsuit						
Brunswick, GA						
rainfall (inch/mm)	3.6/92	3.2/82	4.4/	6.6/	4.5/	2.9/
consistency (d/mth)	11	10	10	13	10	8
average sun (hrs/day)	7	9	10	9	8	7
min temp (°F/°C)	42/6	52/11	66/19	70/20	72/21	55/13
max temp (°F/°C)	63/17	75/24	86/30	90/32	83/28	68/20
water temp (°F/°C)	51/10	64/18	77/25	85/29	77/25	60/15
wetsuit						

TRAVEL INFORMATION	
North Carolina	www.visitnc.com
South Carolina	www.travelsc.com
Georgia	www.georgia.org

The Surf, Ocean Environment and Surf Culture

Although The South undoubtedly has the goods to lure surfers from all over America to its warm-water waves, most East Coasters will make the journey to the Cape Hatteras epicenter at least once in their surfing lives. Many see such a trip as an annual pilgrimage not to be missed. The Outer Banks pick up all available swell and provides a range of exposures to optimize different wind directions, making it one of the more flexible East Coast surfing destinations. Further south, things deteriorate rapidly surf-wise, but there is some rich culture and beautiful natural environment to balance the equation.

Whereas the Mid-Atlantic states armor the coastline with hard structures in a huge battle with erosion, The South is a far more natural coastal environment, where many of the barrier islands are left to follow their nautical migratory paths. There are, of course, exceptions – for instance, where affluent coastal residential developments pump in sand to maintain beach width, but the ironic truth of it all is that where there are jetties and piers, there are usually better waves for surfing. So it is doubly ironic that fishing piers are the subject of another big battle, which pits surfers against other ocean users in a struggle for coexistence. Meanwhile, most water-quality problems here stem from intense agricultural processes, remote from the coast, from which the runoff works its way through an intricate system of rivers that drain into the Intracoastal Waterway.

While the Outer Banks of North Carolina has long been known as a prime surfing area, historical info on South Carolina and Georgia is harder to come by. It seems that the West Coast legends, who repped the big manufacturers during the Sixties boom in equipment, passed quickly through these southern states in their rush to get to the greener pastures of Florida. Nevertheless, certain characters have emerged as industry pioneers in their respective areas.

Top – **Frisco**, one of the many fishing piers in The South where surfers and fishermen regularly clash for rights of the ocean's spoils. Below – **Erosion signs** that are part of the high level of information that most southern states provide on (some) environmental concerns.

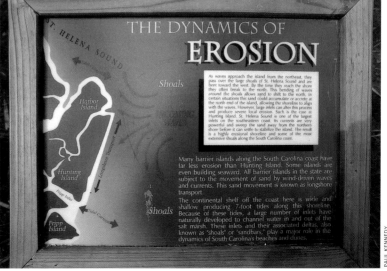

North Carolina

North Carolina has a much longer coastline than the Outer Banks, but the real quality waves are concentrated off these thin ribbons of sand. At Buxton, the recently relocated icon of the Cape Hatteras Lighthouse draws surfers like moths to a flame, and most surfers refer to the Outer Banks as 'Hatteras.' From Easter to Thanksgiving, this means crowds, particularly at the big-name spots. The sheep mentality is always a factor because for every quality peak with a crew at work on it, there is another, empty, quality peak a short walk north or south. This whole area is rife with good beachbreaks, and the only constraints are finding a place to park – unless you have a 4WD to disappear down the beach to your own private peak.

Outside the Cape Hatteras National Seashore, the more developed Kitty Hawk to Nags Head coastal stretch is a stronghold of the East Coast surf industry. All the main players are represented by a plethora of surf shops, while the local pier waves provide a good proving ground for equipment testing by the large population of resident and transient surfers.

The southern half of North Carolina sweeps away to the southwest, increasing the width of the continental shelf and weakening the energy of the waves. Atlantic Beach and Emerald Isle face due south and, consequently, miss out on NE swells; but they light up when there is a good S or a hurricane swell. Access restrictions to a lot of pier-surf areas mean hassles, particularly in summer, but winter brings some good conditions, since the prevailing angle of the coast is perfect for offshores during winter nor'easters.

Wrightsville is one hotspot with punchy waves, where a dedicated crew of shredders competes with the crowds from the large campus at Wilmington. More well-defined set-ups can be found near Carolina Beach before rounding Cape Fear to the sheltered, south-facing areas of Long Beach and Holden Beach.

North Carolina is one of the few states that have a blanket ban on armoring the coast with hard structures. Because the Outer Banks move so rapidly, the state has been forced to come to grips with erosion. Maps are available for every beach showing the rates of depletion and replenishment all the way back to 1942. The most graphic illustration of the speed of the erosion was manifest in the monumental task of relocating the famous black and white barber's pole – the Cape Hatteras Lighthouse. Built in 1870, at the time 1,500ft (450m) from the ocean, by 1935 it was just 100ft (30m) from the high tide line. Decades of erosion-control programs commenced

PAUL KENNEDY

Above – **Winter Nags Head pocket, North Carolina.**
Right – **Getting out when it's big can be a real challenge, especially on the open beaches of the Outer Banks, North Carolina.**

M MCCARTHY

(including thousands of feet of interlocking steel-sheet pile groins, reinforced concrete groins, millions of cubic feet of sand replenishment, gravel-filled polypropylene tubes, rubble walls, and massive sandbagging programs), but to no avail. In 1999, the tallest lighthouse in the USA followed the migratory path of Hatteras Island and inched 2,900ft (870m) westwards over 23 days.

One of the biggest problems for surfers in North Carolina, particularly around the Atlantic Beach area, is friction between fishermen, pier owners, and any surfer who gets too close to the piers. Deliberate casting of lead weights and large hooks at surfers is commonplace, sometimes leading to violent confrontation, which has been known to involve threatening behavior with a firearm. While there are usually clear signs posted, stating the distances that surfers must remain from piers, when disputes have reached the courts, they have usually been dismissed without a judgement.

PAUL KENNEDY

MEZ/ESM

Meanwhile, the State's Division of Coastal Management is creating a fine example for other states to follow by providing a professional website, detailing North Carolina's excellent coastal access, parking and facilities. They also provide location information on stormwater drain locations, but unfortunately no info as yet on the state's more pernicious sewage outfalls. Also, many coastal properties utilize septic tanks, which are prone to overflowing whenever a big, wet hurricane makes landfall. While most surfers pray for these swell-generating storms, hurricanes are also responsible for littering the line-ups with debris, stormwater pollution, and sometimes worse.

MEZ/ESM

MEZ/ESM

It should also be noted that North Carolina is usually runner-up to Florida as the top-scoring shark attack state. Fatalities were unheard of until the recent tragedies on the Outer Banks and just to the north in Virginia. Many surfers reckon that blue fish are responsible for some of the nibbles, but it is an issue, and one of the downsides of surfing so close to the nutrient-rich Gulf Stream.

In the early 1960s, Smith and Holland, along with Govenors Surf Shop, opened in Kitty Hawk. These two surf outlets flanked the Kitty Hawk Surf Club, whose membership was swelled by surfers from the Elizabeth City area, an hour's drive inland. Notable names from this period include the Fearing brothers and Dewey Weber teamster Jimbo Brothers, who transplanted to the Outer Banks from Virginia Beach. Few remnants of those 1960s years survived the 1970s bust. One exception is the Hatteras Island Surf Shop, which opened c. 1971, in the well-named town of Waves.

One of the most enduring chapters in East Coast surfing history commenced a little to the south in Atlantic Beach, where the first district directors for the fledgling ESA were appointed in 1967. Buzzy Trent's sister was penciled in for one of the jobs but was unable to do it, resulting in Betty Marsh taking the post. To this day, Betty remains an ESA stalwart and matriarch to the Marsh family surfing dynasty.

Above – **Shark fishing – Outer Banks. One of the main detractors of surfing so close to the rich ecosystem of the Gulf Stream.**
Middle top – **East Coast rules.**
Middle bottom – **ESA legend Doc Couture's commemorative plaque at Cape Hatteras.**
Bottom – **The long established Hatteras Island Surf Shop and equally long established VW surf mobile.**

KEVIN UPTON

PAUL KENNEDY

South Carolina

South Carolina is afflicted by the vast, gently sloping, shallow continental shelf, which causes the incoming swell to drag, reducing the power of the waves. Nonetheless, Myrtle Beach is a seething cauldron of youth in the summertime, as college students descend en masse to party and hang out at the beach in the hot climate. This puts a stress on very limited wave resources, not to mention ordinances that restrict when and where you can surf along the built-up coastline. Even so, on its day, it can look good here, with clean, hollow waves and no shortage of dedicated year-round locals to capitalize on these infrequent conditions. The Charleston scene centers on Folly Beach where the Washout provides the most consistent waves around. Average to middling until a hurricane swell has everyone scrambling to catch the rare large waves.

Like its northern sister, South Carolina offers good information on the state's erosion statistics, beach armoring and beach-nourishment programs. As the name suggests, erosion is a constant threat to South Carolina's best wave at The Washout. Although new hard structures are banned, there are plenty already in existence, but access is restricted to many islands and gated communities. Apart from the Cape Romain National Wildlife Refuge, there are four small coastal state parks. Water-quality testing is sporadic, and no sewer or stormdrain information is available. The marshy nature of the Intracoastal Waterway has some beneficial filtering properties and thus acts as a diffusion barrier between mainland's non-specific-point pollution and the barrier islands' surf beaches.

Two California airmen were instrumental in kicking off the surf scene in the Folly Beach area around the summer of 1963. They opened a surf shop and got the kids onto boards but disappeared soon after, perhaps transferred to another area. Popouts from department stores like Sears were the sole equipment suppliers until McKevlin's Surf Store opened in 1965. The surfing community grew so quickly that city authorities implemented controls and crammed all surfers into a two-block area. Injuries inevitably resulted, causing surfers to take legal action. Funds were raised, and an attorney took the case to State Supreme Court, where victory resulted in the reopening of all the good spots, providing surfers wore leashes. Ironically, the same lawyer became the attorney for the City of Folly Beach!

A steady stream of Californian servicemen kept drifting into Folly Beach, and they coalesced under various guises, such as the West Coast East Surf Club. They bought their boards with them, which helped keep the local surfers up to date with what was developing on the Left Coast. Local board manufacturing was non-existent and left to traveling reps with Noll, Weber, Hansen, and other boards to sell. West Coast manufacturers were constantly trying to get a foothold in the potentially huge East Coast market. McKevlin's catered to the hardcore kids by stocking boards, wax, and cheese sandwiches, with a place to sit in front of a heater between pre-wetsuit midwinter sessions.

Top – **Folly Beach, South Carolina.**
Above – **More evidence of the rampant erosion that is prevalent in The South. Hunting Island, South Carolina.**
Bottom – **The original McKevlins surf shop that even sold cheese sandwiches to groms between sessions in the 1960's.**

MCKEVLIN ARCHIVE
PAUL KENNEDY

Georgia

Georgia has got to be home to the friendliest crew of surfers on the East Coast. That good ol' Southern hospitality is strong in the surfing community because they rarely have anything much to offer the traveler in the wave department. When there is enough swell to make it in over the shelf, a few spots around Tybee Island and St Simons Island will serve up average-to-good beachbreak surf, occasionally with a little power, but there is very little easy access to the lion's share of Georgia's coastline. Tales of long sandspits and peeling waves off some of the uninhabited islands aren't necessarily groundless. Armed with a boat and a lot of time, discoveries are possible among the wildlife refuges of Georgia's barrier islands, but the fickle nature of the area will deter all but the most intrepid explorers.

Georgia is notably absent from the Surfrider Foundation map of US chapters, but, paradoxically, it has become the first state to provide real-time water-quality data via the Internet, and Surfrider has teamed up with Earth's 911 and the Environmental Protection Agency to begin the first statewide implementation of the BEACH system. This

PAUL KENNEDY

will give nearshore ocean users the ability to "know before they go," providing water-quality information for most popular beaches. The system relies on a consistent testing regime and heralds a new era of public information and observation. In the meantime, local surfers seem to think there aren't too many problems with Georgia's water quality, especially in the southern areas, and the larger inhabited islands have full treatment facilities.

Sharks and jellyfish are common, but jetskis are not because there is a statewide 1000yd (1090m) exclusion zone keeping all motorized craft well clear of the beach. Although Georgia receives less swell than most Atlantic states, erosion is a major problem, with the sea relentlessly marching into the swampy barrier islands. On St Simons Island, foundations of old buildings, reclaimed by the sea, are sometimes found in the line-up. Stumps and tree trunks also litter some of the breaks off pristine uninhabited islands. Erosion is usually the culprit when a surf spot disappears.

Surfers like Carlos Hudson, Mike and Rusty Fleetwood, and Chip Oar were shredding in the Tybee area right through the mid-1960s. During the ESA's infancy, contests would be held at Tybee Island, and East Coast notables like Gary Propper would take on the local crew. The 4th annual Georgia State Surfing Championships, which took place on September 21st 1970, reportedly attracted most all of the surfers in the state – 100 entries. This small population remained static until the early 1980s, by which time a Hawaiian transplant working for the Coastguard, had opened High Tide Surf Shop. There had been another shop in the early 1970s, but a shrinking surf population put it out of business, so for a few years there was no place to buy surf equipment in Georgia. The recent East Coast surfing explosion has extended to Georgia, bringing more industry infrastructure, surf shops and, yeah, surfers.

Left – **Deep South rustic motor home.**
Below – **Tybee Islands 17th Street Boardwalk rates as Georgia's best beachbreak.**

PAUL KENNEDY

North Carolina locator map showing numbered surf breaks:
1 Corolla Lighthouse
2 Kitty Hawk Pier
3 Laundromats
4 Avalon Pier
5 1st Street
6 Nags Head Pier
7 Jennette's Pier
8 Outer Banks Pier
9 Boilers/Ranger Station

Laundromats

TOM DUGAN

North Carolina – Outer Banks North

1. Corolla Lighthouse

The northern tip of the Outer Banks has a more extensive shelf than all the breaks to the south. This means a bit less size and power for the area, but nonetheless, it receives some decent waves when the sand lines up. SE swells are favored plus it will handle a S wind better, as it faces a touch NE.

Throughout the Outer Banks, hazards include sharks, jellyfish, and sea-lice in the summer months. Access can be problematic since most of the ocean frontage is residential. Legal access paths are few, which means it is generally the local builders who score all the waves. This explains the lack of crowds on this consistent stretch of coast. 4WD beach access means you can drive up to the Virginia State line.

2. Kitty Hawk Pier

Kitty Hawk Pier breaks on all swells and handles solid size. Pitching lips have been known to land on the walkway, meaning no fishermen in sight when there's swell. Can be powerful and hollow on all tides with inside and outside breaks.

Attracts a crowd, especially when Avalon Pier is packed out. Free parking lot.

3. Laundromats

Heavy erosion here means you could end up riding underneath a house at high tide. On the outside bar, bigger swells will provide steep, crumbly waves that are easier to get to via the abundant channels and rips. Good, sucky peaks close to shore on small days. Northerly swells and all tides.

Parking is a hassle, which is probably why it is often less crowded than the two piers at either end of this beach.

4. Avalon Pier

Best on N swell and all but the highest tides. Good sandbars form up here regularly, particularly on the south side of the pier, usually providing some good righthanders.

It's often crowded in the busy parking lot south of the pier, which gives easy access to these consistent waves. Hazards include the usual pier fishermen and the odd high-spirited swashbucklers, who congregate here for a few drinks.

5. 1st Street

This popular local spot is always crowded due to above average sandbars. Low incoming with some N in the swell is best.

Watch out for submerged objects from an old shipwreck.

6. Nags Head Pier

Historical hot spot from the 1960s, like all Outer Banks breaks, the sand comes and goes. Looks like it is coming again. All tides and swell.

All facilities available on the beach. The sometimes crowded scenario will increase if the sandbars line up.

7. Jennette's Pier

Full swell window, but NE best. All tides, and it can handle some size. Less crowded than other nearby piers.

Temporary bonus: recent damage to the pier means no aggro fishermen.

8. Outer Banks Pier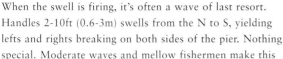

When the swell is firing, it's often a wave of last resort. Handles 2-10ft (0.6-3m) swells from the N to S, yielding lefts and rights breaking on both sides of the pier. Nothing special. Moderate waves and mellow fishermen make this

Jennette's Pier

PAUL KENNEDY

a good spot for beginners. Works on all tides, but it's best at low incoming.

There's a free parking lot in this quieter residential area, where it's rarely crowded.

9. Boilers/Ranger Station

A better big-wave spot found way outside in front of the Ranger Station on Pea Island. A shipwreck has built up sandbars around it, which prefer lower tides and NE swells to get the long walling lefts and short bowly rights working. It also breaks inside on smaller swells that reform after the trough.

A walk over the dunes from the free car park is the only way to check it. There's camping at nearby Oregon Inlet and no lifeguard to tell the ladies what they can or, in this case, cannot wear. Once you're past the white pointers on the beach, keep an eye out for their cousins cruising the shipwreck.

Nags Head Pier

MO DADDY SANFORD

NORTH CAROLINA

SOUTH CAROLINA

GEORGIA

① S Turns
② Rodanthe
③ K.O.A
④ Avon Pier
⑤ The Lighthouse
⑥ Frisco Pier
⑦ Triple "S" Pier
⑧ Bouge Pier
⑨ The Point

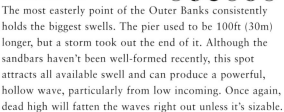

Salvo

North Carolina – Outer Banks South

1. S Turns

This wave has been an object of media attention in recent years, and parallels have been drawn with famous beachbreaks like Hossegor. Similarities exist, like top-to-bottom heavy barrels breaking close to the beach. But all the hype has resulted in serious overcrowding at one spot in the middle of a long stretch of quality waves. As a result, when Rodanthe Pier is not working, this place is a mob scene. Best on S swells with lower tides, if it's small, high tide will kill it.

Heavy paddle-outs with strong drift when it's big. The free roadside parking can trap the careless in the abundant soft sand.

2. Rodanthe Pier

The most easterly point of the Outer Banks consistently holds the biggest swells. The pier used to be 100ft (30m) longer, but a storm took out the end of it. Although the sandbars haven't been well-formed recently, this spot attracts all available swell and can produce a powerful, hollow wave, particularly from low incoming. Once again, dead high will fatten the waves right out unless it's sizable.

Bad summer parking scene. Hazards include an anti-surfing pier owner, who doesn't want you parking nearby or riding within 250ft (80m) of the pier, and aggro fishermen, who can be quite accurate at casting their lead-weighted hooks.

3. K.O.A.

Hollow, powerful waves on the outside sandbar with inside reforms at higher tides. Handles size.

Only sometimes crowded because it's difficult access unless you're camping in the K.O.A. Campground.

4. Avon Pier

This popular spot can develop good sandbars that form steep, fun, crumbly-type waves. Won't handle bigger swells and tides. S swell best.

Various beach on-ramps north and south of here provide 4WD access to endless peaks that simply require a little walking for rarely crowded conditions. Nearby camping.

5. The Lighthouse

This famous break in front of the tallest lighthouse in the US (recently moved a few hundred feet back from the surf) is constantly changing from the heavy erosion at Cape Hatteras. Picks up most swells, NE being the best to line up the longer lefts. The ends of the battered jetties can get dredgy, but it all depends on where the sand is. Barrels one week, mushy the next. All tides, but best on low incoming.

Always crowded because it's always breaking. Hazards include rocks and submerged objects, plus shipwreck debris brought in by storms. Plenty of camping options in the Buxton area.

6. Frisco Pier

Although the sign on the pier says Cape Hatteras Pier, everyone refers to it as Frisco Pier. Protected from N/NE swells by Cape Hatteras, it works best on anything with S in it. A snappy wave with occasional barrels, it's offshore in northerly winds and can handle the bigger swells.

Generally much less crowded than the Lighthouse because it is far less consistent – until a S swell hits, which may pass by a lot of the spots to the north. Easy parking and camping.

7. Triple S Pier

One of the few remaining surfing areas at Atlantic Beach, this break will be particularly good when the swell sweeps up the coastline from the SW. Incoming tide best.

Observe 'distance from pier' laws, in this case 200ft (67m). Apparently, surfers invited the best fisherman to come and see how far they could cast. The longest cast was well shy of 200ft, which resulted in the pier distance restrictions being reduced from 250ft (83m). Facilities include restrooms, showers, camping, telephones, and a lifeguard in summer.

Rodanthe Pier

8. Bogue Pier

This seasonally crowded pier provides easy access to above average waves. Picks up swell from the E, right around to SW and any N in the wind will be offshore.

Keep 250ft (83m) from Bogue Pier and pay to park in summer. Other piers on the island do not allow or tolerate surfing in the vicinity as part of an old and ongoing battle between surfers and fishermen (pier owners). Rules change annually at various breaks, like the Sheraton Hotel Pier, for instance, which is under new ownership and has eliminated public surfing access.

9. The Point

This changeable, predominantly left wave will break hollow in larger swells. Because it faces almost to the SW, a NE wind will clean it up nicely, providing there is some swell coming up from the S.

On the western end of Emerald Isle, this break is rarely surfed because parking is virtually non-existent. This problem is a constant theme on the Isle, where beach-access paths are provided, but no public parking lots. Beware strong currents in this area.

Third Groin, Buxton

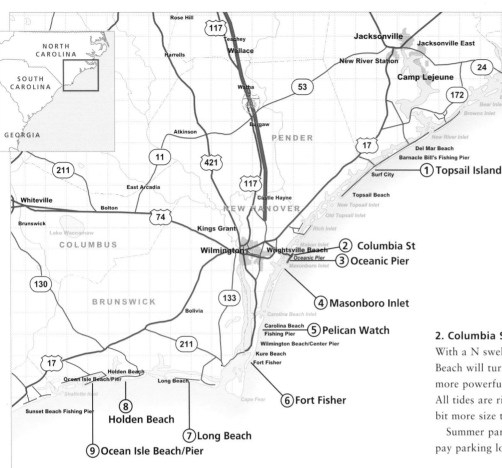

Pier Jump

DOUG WATERS

North Carolina

1. Topsail Island

Topsail Island encompasses Topsail Beach, Surf City and Del Mar Beach to the north. This long stretch of shifting beachbreaks is always changing, so flexibility and lots of surf checks are required. Somewhere is always working at a particular tide, subject to swell direction. Adjacent to the piers is usually best, so check the Topsail Beach Pier (S), The One Eyed Pier (central) and Atlantic Pier (N).

Laid-back place that will only get crowded in the peak holiday season. Average consistency, but nice and clean on this residential island.

2. Columbia Street

With a N swell and a NW wind, this area of Wrightsville Beach will turn on. Incoming tide should see hollower, more powerful waves, which are always heavily utilized. All tides are rideable, but Columbia Street will handle a bit more size than Oceanic Pier.

Summer parking blues for the few roadside meters and pay parking lots. High crowds to match the consistency.

3. Oceanic Pier

This popular consistent pier surf area will accept the north to south swell window and all tides. Best on an incoming tide up to 8ft (2.6m).

Observe distance from pier rules particularly in summer, when all the parking becomes metered.

4. Masonboro Inlet

When it's good, Masonboro Inlet can be one of the best waves on the East Coast. Deeper water off the inlet and a long jetty combine to produce longer, walled-up lefts and short, hollow rights especially on a NE swell.

Situated on an isolated and uninhabited island between Wrightsville Beach and Carolina Beach, it's always crowded with hot locals, who can access this wave by boat, rather than the long tiring paddle required to get across the fast-flowing and busy inlet.

Masonboro

ROBBIE JOHNSON

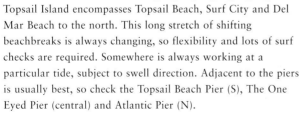

5. Pelican Watch

In front of a hotel/motel by the same name, the sandbars here seem to be improving in recent years. Takes all swells and tides but needs some angle in the swell to keep it from closing out. Breaks hard and close to shore. This popular spot picks up smaller swells.

Always crowded because if it's not breaking here, it's not breaking anywhere in the area. Good camping in the nearby State Recreation Park

6. Fort Fisher

This wave will jack up and expose a steep, workable face with occasional barrels when conditions are on. Low tide incoming on a good NE swell should create some longer lefts until dead high fattens it away.

This quality wave will attract the crowds when conditions dictate, which unfortunately is not that often. There are some boulders and rocks to look out for in the line-up. Camping on the beach is an option.

7. Longbeach

South-facing beach with not much going on unless there is some S swell happening. Average beachbreaks, best at higher tides.

Low consistency meaning rarely crowded. Most of the surfers around here are heading for the ferry to take them to Carolina Beach and the east-facing breaks

8. Holden Beach

Same deal as Longbeach and still no chance of N swells wrapping around Cape Fear. Offshore in any type of northerly wind, it can hold good shape in a summer southerly swell.

Sometimes crowded with summer vacationers and Myrtle Beach surfers when the conditions are good.

Carolina Beach pier break

Carolina Beach beachbreak

9. Ocean Isle Beach Pier

This long stretch of south-facing beach is popular in summer with average peaks from mid to high tide only. After an hour of outgoing, things deteriorate rapidly.

Can attract a crowd escaping from the manic Myrtle Beach area. Some localism in summer.

Fort Fisher

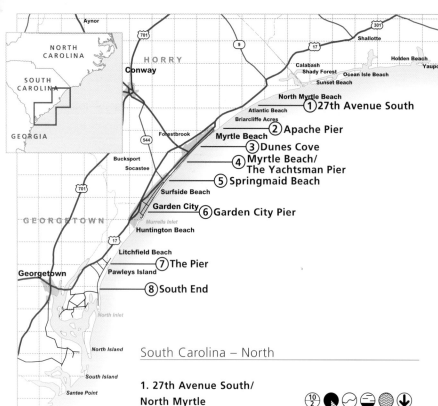

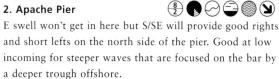

South Carolina – North

1. 27th Avenue South/
North Myrtle

Takes a bigger swell than the rest of the area. Hugo removed the pier, but a recent beach nourishment has resulted in a good low tide outside bar and a high tide shorebreak. Longer rides when it links up.

Always crowded at this average consistency, county-designated surfing area. Stormwater outfalls bring pollution after rain.

2. Apache Pier

E swell won't get in here but S/SE will provide good rights and short lefts on the north side of the pier. Good at low incoming for steeper waves that are focused on the bar by a deeper trough offshore.

Situated in front of a campground, Apache Pier tends to be grommetsville. Always crowded, high consistency and rips in the stormwater-tainted line-up to contend with.

The Washout, Folly Beach

3. Dunes Cove

Probably the best break in Myrtle Beach, just out front of the Dunes Country Club. The swash here creates a definite sandbar, which breaks both ways into the rivermouth, giving longer rights on a SE swell. A hollow, top-to-bottom punchy wave.

Consistent and uncrowded with surfers but packed with fish that bite. Exclusive residential streets with no legal parking means a one mile hike in. Stormwater and estuary runoff can affect water quality.

4. Myrtle Beach/
The Yachtsman Pier

One of the better and more consistent breaks in the area. Works on lower tides and a SE swell.

Limited access and parking along this hotel strip. No surfing between 9-5pm in summer. Lots of locals plus plenty of floating non-surfing tourists to slalom around in the line-up.

5. Springmaid Beach

Just north of the good campground in Myrtle Beach State Recreation Park, this non-restricted all-day surfing beach and pier usually gets crowded in summer. It's more of a shorebreak since hurricanes have cleared out the sandbars. Swell direction dictates whether the lefts or rights are better, which can break powerfully and close to shore.

Can be heavily affected by stormwater outfall and estuary water. Access may change when beachfront hotel and condo development is finished. A 300ft (100m) 'distance from pier' law is in force in summer.

6. Garden City Pier

Best on a S/SE swell on all tides except high outgoing. Average crumbly pier surf.

Pollution from stormwater and inadequate residential drainage can be a factor. Good public access and parking means it's always crowded at this designated surfing area. Off-season beach parking.

7. The Pier

Longer lefts on a NE swell at mid to high tides. Gets better on the incoming tide because it generally doesn't break at low. Shuts down if it gets overhead.

Surprisingly crowded for an average-consistency spot. The pier does little to cut the drift.

8. South End

With the right conditions, there can be longer workable rights that reform on the inside. Occasionally hollow, but generally very inconsistent.

Restrooms are as far as the facilities go at this uncrowded break.

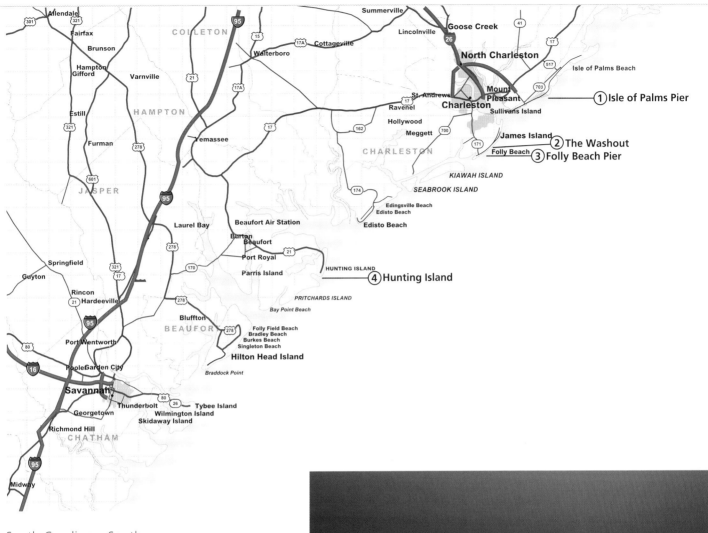

South Carolina – South

1. Isle of Palms Pier
This long, wide, sandy beach is more popular with tourists than surfers. A big hurricane swell at low tide is the best reason to surf here.

Low consistency and crowds. Free parking in winter; meters appear with the summer crowds.

2. The Washout
The most popular and consistent spot in southern South Carolina. Semi-submerged short groins every 300ft (91m) are a hazard at higher tides, but generally the sandbars are farther out. Can hold the larger swells. Mid incoming can deliver powerful, hollow waves.

Besides the rips and submerged chunks of jetty, there are also sharks, jellyfish, and territorial locals to watch out for.

3. Folly Beach Pier
Occasional long lefts off the southern side of the pier on a NE swell. Mid tide incoming will see steeper, hollower, shifty peaks that will get a bit mushy at dead high if it's not very big. Low tide will close out over 4ft (1.3m).

Restrictions include no surfing within 200ft (66m) of the pier and no surfing from 10-6pm in summer. The hazard list includes jetskis and jellyfish, plus stormwater runoff.

The Washout
PAUL KENNEDY

4. Hunting Island
This pristine beach is rapidly disappearing as the ocean is now making it into the sub-tropical forest at high tide. Either side of high tide, walled up peaks will appear, offering occasional barrels when it's offshore. The area in front of the lighthouse, which had to be moved due to the erosion, is generally best.

Beware strong currents at either end of the island, also many underwater tree stumps and the odd floating palm tree in the line-up. Even if it's flat, Hunting Island State Park is worth checking out. Full facilities include a good campsite.

Windchop hop at Sugar Shack

Georgia

1. North Jetty

The best wind for the next few breaks is onshore! Without it, there will be no waves. The banks at the North Jetty are a fair way down the beach. Same deal as Sugar Shack and 2nd Street. Crumbly, mushy, fat waves that might wall up on the inside.

As with all of Georgia, consistency is a problem – but crowds usually aren't. Expensive parking.

2. Sugar Shack

Sugar Shack needs a strong NE wind to start supplying average peaks, similar to 2nd Street. The main difference between these two onshore spots is the tide, which makes Sugar Shack a mid to high spot. Steeper outside, it fattens out before hitting the suckier inside.

Rarely breaks, rarely crowded, and rarely any good!

17th Street, Tybee Island

3. 2nd Street

This crumbling wave has a little less power than 17th Street to the south. It needs a 20mph NE wind to break, so it doesn't get hollow, but it has a good workable face. High tide results in a nasty backwash.

Across the state, sharks, rips, and jellyfish can be found in the line-up.

4. 17th Street Boardwalk

Since the construction of a new pier, the waves here have improved. This short top-to-bottom wave produces rights and lefts a couple of hours before and about an hour after high tide. Lower tides, forget it.

Although it is one of Georgia's best breaks, it still doesn't rate in the weekly high-consistency stakes. Since it only breaks sometimes, its crowd rating is similarly described. Pay parking right in front of the break. All facilities nearby.

5. Goulds Inlet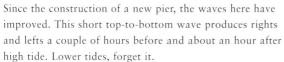

Located off the southern tip of Sea Island, Goulds is only accessible by paddling from the northern tip of St. Simons. The most consistent wave in the area, it will break at mid tide incoming. Fun but fickle peaks with occasional long lefts back towards the rivermouth, where there can be some very strong currents.

The crowd record for this break is 60 people! Stay below the high tide line to avoid arrest by the private police force employed by affluent Sea Island residents.

6. Coastguard/St Simons

This wave used to break until the residents of Sea Island dredged out the sand to replenish their private beaches. However, sand is now returning and this spot has started to break again. It looks like the long left is back at high tide.

Big car park in the East Beach area. Not as consistent as Goulds Inlet but a better bet than the breaks to the south.

7. 5th Street/7th Street

There used to be a decent left here until erosion, problematic throughout this part of the coast, all but destroyed the surf. A virtually non-existent grommet, longboard, or bodyboarding wave.

Submerged objects include old house foundations, while other hazards include sharks, man-o-wars, and rip currents. Consistency is barely in the average category, meaning you may get wet a little more than monthly.

8. Comfort Inn/Jeckyll Island

Gutless is the word to best describe these typical Georgia beachbreaks. High tide only. Bring a longboard.

The good news is that it's rarely crowded; the bad news is that it rarely breaks. Plenty of parking and facilities.

PAUL KENNEDY

17th Street, Tybee Island

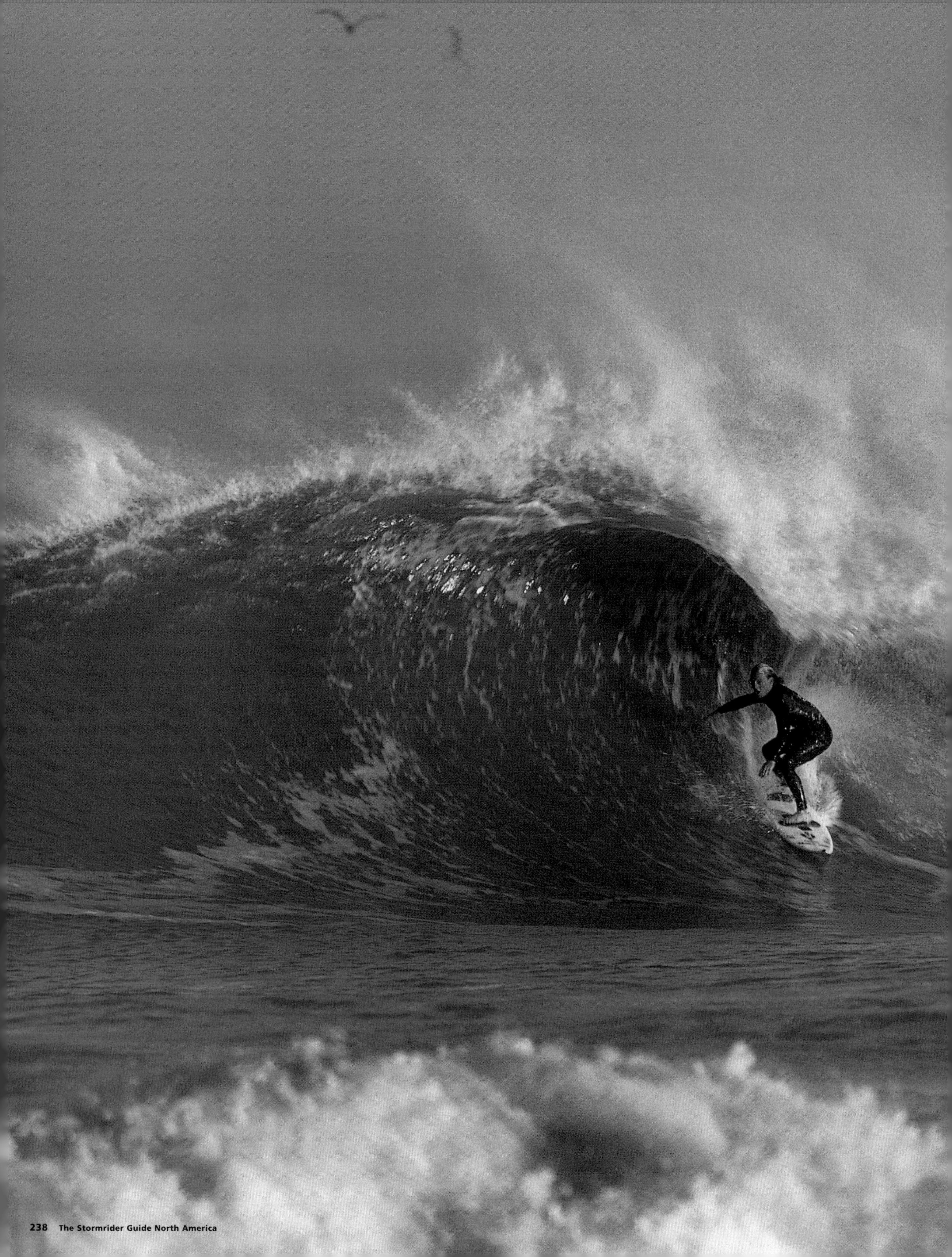

Florida

Florida encapsulates the East Coast surf scene unlike any other Atlantic State. The most southern point on mainland USA conjures up visions of warm weather, sub tropical water temperatures, and a whole year round, beach life environment, that even California has problems equaling. While this is true in the south, where the warm Gulf Stream current kisses the coastline near Miami, Florida hides a much more complex persona than the stereotyped image of sun and surf. The barrier island theme continues the length of the coastline, and the only interruption to the predominantly NE facing coastline is the huge tract of off limits land at Cape Canaveral. Florida is also home to the most prolific surfing champions, in both the men's and women's divisions of international surfing competition.

While West Coast surfers sneer at the absence of regular ground swell and sizable wave challenges, the average Florida surfer continues to make the most of what is available, which can range from 1ft windchop to 20ft faces in a hurricane swell. While the danger from hurricanes is real, surfers still prey for their late summer arrival to bring some respite from the small summer conditions. Once again, it is the man-made structures that provide the best line-ups, sprinkled along the extensive Atlantic seaboard.

Sebastian Inlet.

MEZ/ESM

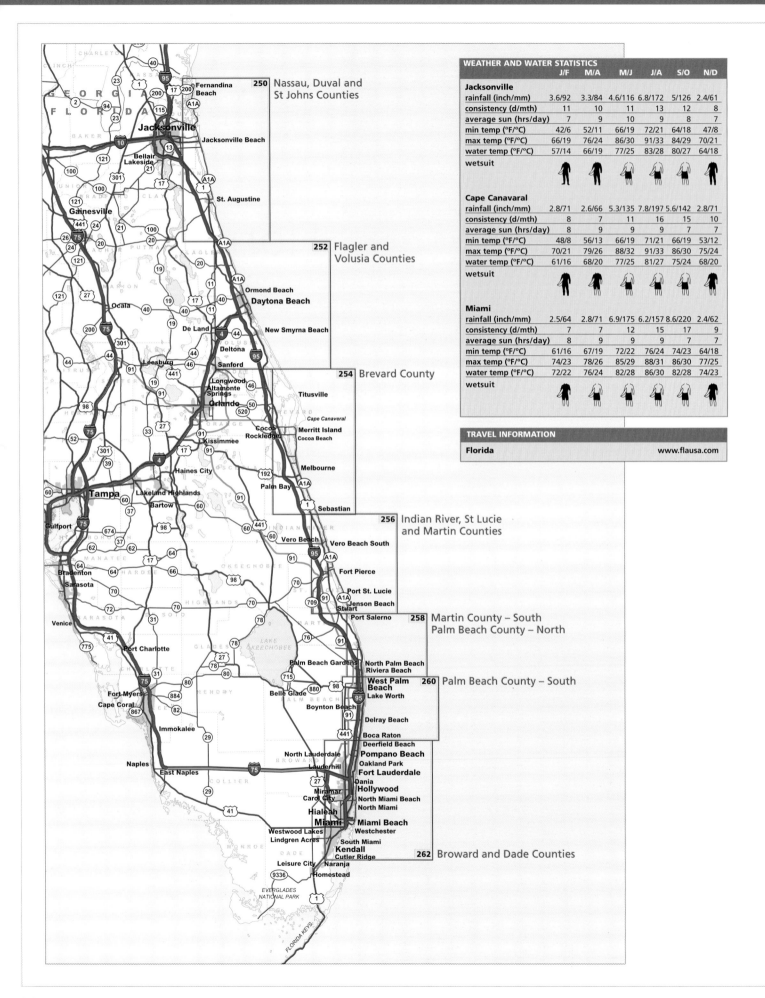

Nassau, Duval and
St Johns Counties **250**

Flagler and
Volusia Counties **252**

Brevard County **254**

Indian River, St Lucie
and Martin Counties **256**

Martin County – South
Palm Beach County – North **258**

Palm Beach County – South **260**

Broward and Dade Counties **262**

WEATHER AND WATER STATISTICS

	J/F	M/A	M/J	J/A	S/O	N/D
Jacksonville						
rainfall (inch/mm)	3.6/92	3.3/84	4.6/116	6.8/172	5/126	2.4/61
consistency (d/mth)	11	10	11	13	12	8
average sun (hrs/day)	7	9	10	9	8	7
min temp (°F/°C)	42/6	52/11	66/19	72/21	64/18	47/8
max temp (°F/°C)	66/19	76/24	86/30	91/33	84/29	70/21
water temp (°F/°C)	57/14	66/19	77/25	83/28	80/27	64/18
wetsuit						
Cape Canaveral						
rainfall (inch/mm)	2.8/71	2.6/66	5.3/135	7.8/197	5.6/142	2.8/71
consistency (d/mth)	8	7	11	16	15	10
average sun (hrs/day)	8	9	9	9	7	7
min temp (°F/°C)	48/8	56/13	66/19	71/21	66/19	53/12
max temp (°F/°C)	70/21	79/26	88/32	91/33	86/30	75/24
water temp (°F/°C)	61/16	68/20	77/25	81/27	75/24	68/20
wetsuit						
Miami						
rainfall (inch/mm)	2.5/64	2.8/71	6.9/175	6.2/157	8.6/220	2.4/62
consistency (d/mth)	7	7	12	15	17	9
average sun (hrs/day)	8	9	9	9	7	7
min temp (°F/°C)	61/16	67/19	72/22	76/24	74/23	64/19
max temp (°F/°C)	74/23	78/26	85/29	88/31	86/30	77/25
water temp (°F/°C)	72/22	76/24	82/28	86/30	82/28	74/23
wetsuit						

TRAVEL INFORMATION

Florida   www.flausa.com

The Surf, Ocean Environment and Surf Culture

Florida is the southeastern extremity of the United States and, while not the largest state (it's only one-third the size of California), Florida boasts the nation's longest coastline (some 1,350 miles [2,160km], over 8,000 [12,800km] if you count all the shorelines of its bays and islands!). For information on the western coast of Florida, see the Gulf of Mexico chapter. We have divided Florida's Atlantic Coast into three areas, which (while they may not be geographically distinct) represent subtle differences in these surf zones not evident when scrutinizing a map of the state.

Florida is home to some great winter waves, but summers of discontent are the surfer's lot here, and it gets worse the further south you go. Between May and September, swell-producing weather systems are completely unreliable, and flat spells are often measured in months, not days. Summer high pressure systems bring weak wind swells from the east, while extremely hot inland temps assure the presence of plenty of company in the line-up – even if it is only 'triple over ankle.'

Hurricanes can appear on the scene as early as June, but September is more likely to deliver some salvation swells from these tropical storms. In general, fall is the best time of year; that's when the first cold fronts and low pressure systems begin to appear off the northern East Coast, pumping N to NE swells down to Florida.

Route A1A runs right along the beaches from Georgia to Miami (apart from a brief detour around the off-limits areas of the Kennedy Space Center at Cape Canaveral), which makes navigation on Florida's Atlantic Coast very simple for surfers. Even so, proximity to the beach doesn't always guarantee you'll get sand between your toes at all beaches in Florida, where public access tops a long list of environmental concerns.

Much of Florida is a low-lying marshland of waterways and barrier islands, but the state is home to a range of ecosystems, with more diverse flora and fauna than any other eastern state. However, human pollution, erosion, coastal armoring, greenhouse-associated problems (rising sea levels and temperatures), coral reef depletion, and diminishing habitat for some of Florida's unique, and

endangered wildlife are also critical issues. Sharks are ever-present in Florida's waters, which makes the state a perennial leader in the global shark-attack league.

Florida surfing's rich cultural heritage dates back to the 1930s, when the Whitman brothers – Bill and Dudley – of Miami Beach crafted their own Hawaiian-replica solid-wood surfboards. During the postwar era, Daytona Beach became extremely popular as a beach-style destination, and with the '60s came the music-fueled surfing craze, when Cocoa Beach and Sebastian Inlet moved into prominence. But it is not these famous breaks alone which are fueling the rapid growth of Florida surfing.

Top – **Birds eye view of Brevard County. Most of Florida's Atlantic Coast is developed, leaving few natural beachscapes.**
Bottom – **The A1A navigates the coast religiously, effortlessly conveying surfers up and down the shoreline. If you lose the A1A, you've lost the beach.**

PAUL KENNEDY

Right – **North Florida has its' fair share of barrels, albeit at a far lower temperature in winter. Jax Pier juice.**
Middle – **Beach parking at New Smyrna saves a long hike to the inlet jetties. Look both ways when crossing the sand.**
Below – **Kona Skate Park in Jacksonville is a legendary seventies relic that caters for all types of skaters. A collection of concrete ramps, bowls and snake runs provide unreal flat day fun. BS snakin' one.**

Northern Florida

Northern Florida from Jacksonville to Cape Canaveral includes Nassau, St Johns, Flagler, and Volusia counties.
There are plenty of well-defined waves courtesy of numerous piers and jetties. The large breakwaters of the St Johns River, St Augustine, and Ponce inlets are real focal points for quality surf, attracting large surfing populations from inland cities like Gainesville and Orlando. Fishing piers are strategically located, albeit with the usual keep-your-distance laws, and some areas of Northern Florida allow beach driving, helping surfers access less crowded peaks along long stretches of beachbreak. This coastline is far less developed than further south; the State Park system is a welcome respite from the hotels perched on the high tide line, blockading the beaches. Jacksonville, St Augustine and Daytona Beach are the big population centers, which also describes their typical summer line-ups. New Smyrna is reputedly the most consistent break in Florida, and the summer crowds attest to the fact. Winters can be really good, but Northern Florida does not support the general misconception that Florida is blessed year-round with balmy land and sea temperatures. From November to April, colder, darker water here means fullsuits, booties, and sometimes even gloves and hoods in the far north. Meanwhile, down Palm Beach way, they may still be wearing boardshorts.

PAUL KENNEDY

TOM DUGAN/ESM

Many of the environmental hazards found off the massive littoral expanses of the Sunshine State come in the most natural forms possible and apply to surf spots statewide. Florida is the shark-attack capital of the world, but in the nicest possible way – fatalities are rare. Smaller species like sand, spinner, lemon, and black-tip sharks join the more traditionally nasty mako, thresher, bull, and occasional tiger sharks to chase the schools of small fish that congregate in the warm, shallow waters, especially between spring and fall. The nutrient-rich Gulf Stream ensures the attractiveness of the area for these potentially ferocious selachian fish, which unfortunately leads them straight into the surfer's habitat, particularly in South Florida.

Most attacks involve an exploratory taste followed by instant rejection and a spit of disgust as the shark realizes it has a bony foot and not a succulent sardine. Volusia County has the highest incidence of unprovoked attacks in the state (and therefore the world), not so closely followed by Brevard and then Palm Beach, reflecting a complex Atlantic distribution. The Northern Florida shark hotspots are usually the inlets around St Johns River, Matanzas, and Ponce, making for a real conflict with surfers, since these spots have the best surf.

Recent fatalities, particularly children, reinforce the need to exercise caution. Consider advice from the International Shark Attack File (see boxed info).

It is worth noting that another scourge of the Florida surf zone is lightning, which is far more likely to kill or maim than a shark. In fact, alligators have accounted for more deaths than sharks over a 50-year period recently ended; luckily for surfers they stay out of the line-up.

Overfishing of some shark species has become a concern, along with the recent phenomenon of shark feeding, whereby dive tour operators hand-feed marine predators, thereby altering the natural behavior patterns of both species.

Beyond bites of sharks and bolts of lightning, jellyfish and sea-lice are actually more common, if somewhat less life-threatening, natural hazards. Once again, their distribution is statewide; they are most likely to invade during summer sou'easters.

Man-made environmental concerns include significant pollution from the St Johns River, which flows through urban Jacksonville. The diminishing coastal dune ecosystems between Jacksonville and St Augustine are coming under heavy pressure from developers and proponents of beach-nourishment schemes, while the natural inlet at Matanzas is being dredged to ensure easy Intracoastal Waterway access for the huge fleets of pleasure boats. While most North Florida surfers consider the water quality to be fine, recent increases in monitoring may bring to light a slightly less rosy reality.

Daytona Beach had a budding surfriding crew in the '30s, led by East Coast Hall-of-Fame inductee Gauldin Reid. These guys built their own hollow surfboards then attacked the surf at Main Street Pier, providing an unusual spectacle in the growing tourist resort town. These few dozen locals were regularly visited by the Miami pioneers

the Whitman brothers who attended the University of Florida, sharing their board building skills and blazing the well worn trail from the campus to the beach. The war temporarily halted surfing's growth until the '60s exploded into the mainstream surf scene.

The Daytona Beach Surf Shop was one of the earliest East Coast retailers, opening on A1A near Ormond Beach in 1961. The business was started by Viola Horner and her son Albert Salvatore, who soon moved to their present location on Main Street after the meat market next door complained about resin fumes permeating their meat! While 90% of boards sold were West Coast imports, local shaper George Miller (he married Viola's daughter) built boards too, first as Millers and then Kahunas before settling for the Daytona Beach Surf Shop label. Due to the shop's strategic location (amidst a lot of people who wanted to buy surfboards), the shop got attention from notable visitors and locals alike, including Greg Noll, David Nuuhiwa, Gary Propper, Claude Cogden, Dana Brown, Jim Heath, and George Warren, to name just a few.

Daytona Beach Surf Shop has a long history and some historic longboards racked up out the back.

Main Street competition sprang up when local suntan-lotion entrepreneur Paul Burke launched two surf shops, one grandly dubbed 'Surfboards Galore.' Demand for equipment remained steady in Northern Florida with a definite upturn as the shortboard era arrived, which opened the door for more local shapers and cut through the brand name fever that was feeding the sale of West Coast imports.

Ormond Beach local Mimi Monroe was one of very few women chosen to ride on the national Hobie team; she had excellent ability and an unusually strong style, even as a young teenager. This same area has produced two of the most successful women surfers in history, Frieda Zamba and Lisa Andersen, both four-time World Champions.

In the '60s and '70s, few surfers visited the New Smyrna area because of its natural isolation. With no bridge over the Ponce Inlet and the natural barrier of the Canaveral National Seashore to the south, most people stayed on US1 and headed south. The close-knit community of New Smyrna surfers included Jack Riley, Dave Coffee, Dave and Dan Nichols (who opened the first New Smyrna surf shop), Charlie Baldwin, Ross Pell, Randy Richenberg, plus a lot of core guys who all still surf.

Advice from The International Shark Files

- Always stay in groups – sharks are more likely to attack a solitary individual.
- Do not wander too far from shore – this isolates the individual and places him or her farther from assistance.
- Avoid being in the water at night or during the morning and evening twilight hours when sharks are most active – they're competitive and have a significant sensory advantage.
- Do not enter the water if you're bleeding from a wound or while menstruating – a shark's olfactory ability is acute.
- Don't wear shiny jewelry in the water – the reflected light resembles the sheen of fish scales.
- Avoid waters with known effluents or sewage and those being used by sport or commercial fishermen, especially if there are signs of bait fish or feeding activity (diving seabirds are good indicators).
- Sightings of porpoises do not indicate the absence of sharks – both often dine at the same restaurants.
- Use extra caution when waters are murky, and avoid uneven tanning and bright-colored clothing – sharks see contrast particularly well.
- Refrain from excess splashing and do not allow pets in the water because of their erratic movements.
- Exercise caution in the deeper areas between sandbars or near steep drop-offs – both favorite hangouts for sharks.
- Do not enter the water if sharks are known to be present, and evacuate the water if sharks are seen.
- Finally, and obviously, do not harass a shark if you see one!

Central Florida

Exactly where Central Florida begins and ends is a matter of conjecture, but we have set our boundaries as **Cape Canaveral in Brevard County in the north down to St Lucie County**. Anywhere south of Jupiter Island in Martin County, the shadow of the Bahamas prevents east or southeast groundswells from arriving at the South Florida beaches. It might be argued that Fort Pierce is the cut-off point, but its mid-county position and water temps (it can be radically colder than 40 miles to the south) point towards Hobe Sound and the St Lucie Inlet as being the more user-friendly line of demarcation.

Brevard County epitomizes the Florida surf scene in three of its most important beaches. Cocoa Beach has a reputation for small waves, the biggest surf shops, and being home to the consummate surfing professional, Kelly Slater. Indialantic/Melbourne Beach has become a surf industry hotspot, lorded over by Eastern Surf Magazine, the voice of the right coast surfer. At the southern boundary of Brevard Co. is a beach that has built its reputation on quality waves, small or large, and is the proving ground for all Florida surfers. Sebastian Inlet is the most revered East Coast surf spot thanks to the wedging rights that peak and peel off the long north jetty.

Between Cocoa and Sebastian, there are a few more quality waves, some of which break on coquina reefs, a commonplace geological phenomenon in central and southern Florida. These formations (soft limestone sandwiches of shells and dead coral) create stable launching pads that trip larger swells, transforming small, mellow beachbreak waves into large, fast, challenging screamers that peel like freight trains along the shelf. RC's is the most notable of these reef breaks in Brevard County,

but it requires some N in the swell, so hurricane swells are not always the best, as a more E swell direction causes many of the breaks to close out.

Indian River County and St Lucie County are flanked by more illustrious surf zones that remain under the radar of media attention, which is just fine for the local crews. Coquina reefs provide some stability and reliability to the surf at places like Stuart Rocks, while the inlet breakwater at Fort Pierce is a real swell magnet. Access in this area is far better than in the exclusive and exclusionary world of the gated beachfront communities and condos that dominate the coast in South Florida, and there are plenty of beachbreaks to escape the concentrations of able surfers at the main spots.

Hurricanes are seasonal depressions that only form in sub-tropical latitudes (10°-30°) when the contrasts between sea and air temperatures are at their greatest. East Coast surfers become amateur meteorologists when it comes to tracking these counter-clockwise spinning storms, but even the professionals on the Weather Channel find it difficult to predict their erratic paths

Central Florida has excellent exposure to these storms that spin through the hurricane alley from the West Africa coast to the Caribbean, where they will either cross into the Gulf or swing N and head up the East Coast of the continent. Surfers must temper their prayers for these swell producers against the possible havoc they can wreak if they make landfall. Provider and destroyer in one package, hurricanes are a two-edged sword responsible for accelerating erosion, damaging hard structures (mainly piers), causing massive stormwater problems, overloading

Top – **Florida's surfers have always performed well on the global stage and none more so than Cocoa Beach maestro, Kelly Slater.**
Opposite top – **Walton Rocks nuclear power station discharges cooling water directly into the line-up, which surfers say make it a pleasurable winter surf spot. Hopefully the brown unidentified foam doesn't go with it.**
Below – **Well lined-up, large lefts are usually the result of a hurricane tracking north of Florida. Coquina shelves like RC's usually handle the juice.**

PAUL KENNEDY

outfall systems, sewage, and agricultural holding tanks, plus generally filling the line-up with debris.

Florida is home to more boats than anywhere in the States, a situation responsible for bringing plenty of pollution to the Intracoastal Waterway and its adjoining inlets, often the areas with the best surf. It is estimated that these 'pleasure craft' (including PWC) are responsible for the death of one manatee per day, on average. Additionally, many marine engines, particularly two strokes, pump as much as 25% of their unburned fuel directly into the water.

Many Central Florida surf breaks are spoiled by jetski traffic, particularly around inlets. Monster Hole and Stuart Rocks are especially noisy, smelly places to surf. A Surfrider Foundation-backed initiative to legislate against these so-called 'personal water craft' is part of a worldwide protest by surfers unhappy with the presence of jetskis in the line-up.

Another downside of the Florida surfing experience is tension between surfers and fishermen, a longstanding problem at Sebastian Inlet, for instance, where "fisherman beats up surfer, surfer throws fisherman off jetty" stories are not unheard of.

Florida has seized on the Beach Bill legislation and implemented a water-quality testing program that provides a cohesive example for other states to follow. This is not surprising considering that Florida's thousand miles of sandy beaches sustain a year-round recreational population far in excess of its 10 million coastal-area residents. Testing has resulted in fewer temporary closures but an increase in permanent ones.

Some 147 miles (235km) of Florida's sandy beaches have been armored, and restrictions on further construction have recently been relaxed. Provided the Department of Environmental Protection agree that a structure is vulnerable to erosion, and that access isn't compromised and sea turtles nesting sites are not disturbed, then permits can be granted. This generally permissive scenario has affected the surf at Wabasso, where seawall construction has led to legal action by the Sea Turtle Survival League.

Surfrider Foundation is active in Florida as a surf spot-survival campaigner through its Beachscape project, but it seems that surfers have less political clout than turtles when it comes to conservation of habitat. Although easy access to some breaks in Central Florida (like Spanish House) is threatened, on the whole, the region fares well in this department.

The growth of surfing in Central Florida was a little slow in the pre-World War II years, with what activity there was

MEZ/ESM

TOM DUGAN/ESM

concentrated in the Miami and Daytona areas. By the late '50s, Cocoa Beach was becoming a focal point, and the surf industry took its first tentative steps when Jack Murphy (a.k.a. Murph the Surf) opened the first retail outlet in a cabana at a beachfront hotel. He quickly outgrew that beachhead and moved to a factory in Melbourne, feeding boards to his new shop at Indiatlantic. Other board manufacturers like Jim Campbell and James O'Hara sprung up as Murph lost control of his business and moved on to an illustrious career of "other endeavors."

Dick Catri entered the picture in the early '60s after a tour of duty in Hawaii (as the lifeguard at the Officers'

Middle – **A Sebastian Inlet wedge, trying its best to be twice the swell size courtesy of some serious refraction off the long, curving jetty.**
Above – **Looking down on Monster Hole in the foreground and Sebastian Inlet beyond the fast flowing inlet channel. Great surf and fishing, but the two groups have never comfortably co-existed.**

gained an enormous amount of notoriety for its almost invincible competitive record and unbridled talent. Teamsters included Gary Propper, Mimi Monroe, Mike Tabeling, Fletcher Sharp, and Bruce Valluzzi among a host of other gifted surfers.

By 1965, Catri's success was noted by Hobie Alter and the team changed brands, but it continued with its concerted efforts to raise the East Coast profile among the traditionally exclusionary West Coast media. When Mike Tabeling's win at the Laguna Masters in California was branded a fluke, little did the California establishment realize that East Coast surfers would become the most dominant force in international surfing competition right up to the present day. Even in the late '60s, sales of Hobie's Gary Propper signature model made Propper the highest paid surfer of the 1960s. Propper's rivalry with Claude 'CC Rider' Cogden was legendary at the Cocoa Beach Pier, setting the competitive tone for the continuous stream of talented groms emerging from Cocoa Beach High School.

Surfing exploded into the public's consciousness in the mid-'60s, surging into popularity right alongside the development of the space-program infrastructure at nearby Cape Canaveral. In fact, before NASA moved in, there were great waves to be had out at the fast peeling breaks of False Cape.

Although surfing competitions had been held up and down the East Coast for some years (including Cocoa Beach), it wasn't until the formation of the Eastern Surfing Association in 1967, that a cohesive contest circuit began. Dick Catri became the ESA's first district director, coordinating the entire state of Florida.

1967 was also the year the big jetty was constructed at Sebastian Inlet. They were halfway out when the quality wedges suddenly appeared. The local surfers were straight onto it and had it to themselves until the completion of the jetty brought the fishermen and ensuing years of conflict. Fortunately (and rather incredibly), state intervention has resulted in Sebastian Inlet becoming a designated surfing area.

One of the most notable Sebastian locals has been Jeff Crawford, who continues to live close to the Inlet and surf it regularly. After solid showings at the East Coast and United States Surfing Championships (Huntington Beach, California), Crawford made a name for himself at the Pipeline. In the early '70s he was very much in a class with

Above and right – **Typhoon Lagoon is Disney's present to the land locked Orlando surfer. Working like a large toilet cistern, it drops massive amounts through a series of gates which can be programed to create a left, right or peak. To surf Typhoon Lagoon you must have a very thick wallet or be a pro-surfer like Kalani Robb. Lessons are also available for a (large) price.**

Club Pool, Pearl Harbor) and opened up Shaggs surf store on the boardwalk of Indiatlantic. Representing the Surfboards Hawaii label for the entire East Coast, Catri went about the marketing and promotion of the label and began building a competitive surf team of local riders. The Surfboards Hawaii Surf Team (later the Hobie team)

Rory Russell, Brian Bulkley, and a handful of others who were almost as good as Gerry Lopez. Jeff won the Pipe Masters in 1974 and was twice top-16 on the international pro tour ('76 and '78).

Following the shortboard transition in the late '60s, Florida surfers embraced the change. Fact was, shorter boards worked great in Florida's waves. Dick Catri started his own label and introduced early examples of the fish piloted by team riders like David Nuuhiwa. These were the early years for local shapers like Rich Price and leading epoxy proponent Greg Loehr; both have become modern shaping gurus, particularly for the Central Florida performance surfers. Claude Cogden now shapes longboards for a large number of customers who want more foam for when the summer surf gets marginal.

Southern Florida

Southern Florida or more specifically **Palm Beach County** may be a playground for the rich and famous, but there's plenty of natural wealth here too on the southern side of the 'Treasure Coast.' There are many jewels to be found in this area where the Gulf Stream rubs against the continent, and her tropical warmth caresses the beaches. The surf here can be overhead when barely 60 miles (100km) to the north it is 1ft slop. Palm Beach County catches swell that other states, or even other parts of Florida, don't get a sniff of. This is because Palm Beach County is the most easterly point of the USA mainland south of the Outer Banks, making it well-situated to receive swells from the north. The Gulf Stream current also seems to be a swell corridor, even though it flows against swells coming out of

Another Cocoa Beach icon is the sprawling 2-acre vastness of the Ron Jon 'One of a Kind' Surf Shop. Opened in 1963 by New Jersey transplant Ron DiMenna at Canaveral Pier, it has become the world's largest surf shop and trades 24/7/365.

Despite its perceived weaknesses in wave quality, Florida has remained at the forefront of surfboard development over the past three decades, and the ability to ride Florida's often gutless surf, has created a long line of successful professional surfers. The most notable so far has been Cocoa Beach local Kelly Slater, the sport's only six-time World Champion, who developed under the philosophical paradigm that if a surfer can do three maneuvers in five seconds on a 2-foot wave, then it just gets easier in bigger, longer waves. Today's top-16 Floridians – including 2002 World Champ C.J. Hobgood – might well agree.

the north. Reef Road is the obvious diamond here, but there are plenty of other jewels in this particular crown. The new pier at Juno and Lake Worth Pier are super consistent and therefore super competitive, with threatening locals (and local authorities) ready to reprimand those who upset the status quo.

Fort Lauderdale and Miami (Broward and Dade counties) somehow miss out on receiving waves of the caliber that converge on Palm Beach. Offshore shoals and, more importantly, the shadow of the Bahamas mean that almost any swell either gets broken up or doesn't get through to these average beachbreaks at all. SE winds will produce some rideable windchop and, of course, hurricanes will liven up the area, but on the whole, Miami is not the best surf zone in Florida. The exception is South Beach, where powerful, quality peaks are jealously worked

Above – **Stuart Rocks, one of the few reef and sand set-ups in a state of beachbreaks.**
Opposite bottom – **Dick Catri and some old sticks from one of the oldest continuous surf outlets in Florida, Shaggs.**

PAUL KENNEDY

Above – **The tropical vibe comes easy in the Florida Keys, but waves do not.**
Below – **When Southern Florida's beachbreaks come alive, they can be worth the long wait. South Beach, Miami.**

over by a large local crew that has to wait a long time for conditions to synchronize and produce the best waves in the area. The crystalline blue-green water color gives Southern Florida a unique feel, and a tropical photogenic look rare on the mainland. The Florida Keys to the south are waveless on all but the biggest swells, although the extraordinary natural beauty and varied ecosystems make it a worthy place to visit.

Like the diverse array of animal species that live and breed in the state, humans too have been attracted to Florida, spawning the archetypal modern tourist capital of the USA. Inevitable conflicts arise between man and nature, but people as well as animals may find some areas difficult to access. South Florida boasts the most expensive oceanfront property on the continent and developers continue to try to stake their exclusive claim to stretches of this sandy shoreline. Money talks louder than reason and, while Florida doesn't prevent lateral beach movement between the high and low tide mark, exclusive gated communities, commercial developments, and privately-

owned beachfront properties can make access challenging. Palm Beach Shores, Reef Road, south of Lake Worth Pier, north of Boca Raton inlet, and plenty of isolated areas between Fort Lauderdale and Miami Beach are diabolically difficult to park near or even make it to the water's edge, let alone get away with a surf without a hassle.

Pressures like this ensure that crowds are inevitable at all of the name spots, not least because the South Florida surfer has to wait longer than most for good local conditions. But when it happens, the biggest surf in the state is usually found here, in the Palm Beach area.

The usual physical threats are just as prevalent in South Florida, but seem even more acute, perhaps because the lower part of the state is on the frontline when storms come, being in the most regular hurricane path. Also, there's a visibly large shark population hanging around just offshore; when a bait fish run is on, it's possible to see feeding frenzies from the beach involving all manner of large fish. In reality, lightning is a far greater danger and will clear the line-up as quickly as the swarms of man-o-wars that compound the surfer's summer misery.

The Florida Keys are threatened by the effects of the increasingly-accepted theory of 'global warming,' which would see rising sea levels envelop the fragile reefs and beaches. Property loss is probably the biggest incentive for the local population to try to combat the problem, but so long as the USA continues to produce about a quarter of the World's greenhouse gases, the Keys will remain at risk, along with 42 other island nations that barely rise above sea level.

Rising sea surface temperatures are also a growing worldwide threat, and huge tracts of coral reef are being bleached by what seems like a trivial increase of 4°F. This graphically illustrates how hypersensitive the reefs are to their environment, let alone the impact of humans; even the rubber soles of reef walkers are contributing to the genocide as surfers trample the delicate coral. The US Government also accepts that inland sprawl and non-coastal generated pollution is affecting the nation's coral reefs, some of which are found off Florida. The proposed reef-protection legislation would ban fishing from 20% of all US reefs. This is a seemingly small

DOUG WATERS

proportion of the habitat, and it deals with just one of the destructive forces contributing to coral reef decimation around the world, but it represents a step in the right direction.

Surfing began in Florida in the 1920s with the arrival of Tom Blake in Miami to double for Ramon Navaro in the Rex Ingram film, Where the Pavement Ends. He fell in with a bootlegger, was a lifeguard at the Roman Pools, and came across a surfboard one of the Hollywood crew had left behind. He "got fooling around on it" and was the first to surf here. When he returned in the early '30s with his patented hollow rescue board, there were still no other surfers – almost.

In Miami Dudley and Bill Whitman were into bellyboarding. Bill, the elder Whitman, was good with his hands and shaped the boards. In 1932, two Virginia Beach surfers (John Smith and Babe Braithwaite) passed through with a 10ft Hawaiian surfboard – the standard redwood model of the period. Inspired, Bill crafted a similar board from locally-available sugar pine. This was the first surfboard built in Florida.

Dudley Whitman started on his own board-shaping project at the tender age of 13, using spruce instead of pine. A year later (1933), Tom Blake was touring Florida with his hollow boards and paddled up the coast to look for 'the Whitmans.' Bill spotted Tom and was blown away by the speed of the Blake board and immediately altered his boardbuilding approach. The resulting hollow boards, based on plans in Popular Mechanics magazine, were tweaked and arguably improved by softening the sharp nose and tail as well as substituting screws for wooden dowels in the assembly process. It was these finely-executed details that opened the door to Dudley's lifetime membership in the Outrigger Canoe Club in Waikiki. By 1935, the brothers were surfing with their Daytona counterparts, like Gauldin Reid, who was building 40lb hollow boards on a $3 materials budget. The Whitmans continued to push design boundaries by patenting the first underwater camera and inventing the slalom water-ski.

In the 1940s, pioneer waterman Pete Peterson happened across a surfboard washed up on a beach in Hawaii. The size and shape of the mysterious find were roughly the same as his own, but it was blond-colored and weighed only 30-40lbs. Apparently the surfboard had been made in Florida from a South American wood called balsa. Virtually unknown in Hawaii at the time, this lightweight wood was difficult to obtain, but because of their proximity to the source, Florida's surfboard builders had access to the material that Californians didn't.

The post-war years were quiet down Miami way, with only the well-off having the means to purchase a board. Dick Catri and Jack Murphy were acrobatic divers at South Beach when one day Murphy showed up with a

Velzy Jacobs balsa board to while away the days while they were waiting for clean conditions to dive. Even with the Whitmans, there were barely a dozen boards on the beach in 1958.

West Coast East was the first surf shop in Miami, but the growth of surfing was hampered in Southern Florida by draconian laws that completely banned surfing in counties like Palm Beach to placate anti-surfer sentiment among the residents of the elitist beachfront communities. It wasn't until the ESA lobbied Palm Beach County to change the local laws on the grounds that it had regulated surfing out of existence, which was unconstitutional. The county conceded, paving the way for surfers like Dr John McCranels, who became US Grand Masters Champion.

The modern scene has come full circle from the uncrowded days of the '50s to severe zooing at breaks like South Beach and Reef Road, which attract surfers from far and wide when conditions are right. Equipment is easy to come by these days, with some large chains operating in Southern Florida along with some quirky, long-established, independent shops.

Top – **Maintaining sea defences is a full time job. Jupiter Inlet.**
Above – **The modern skyline of Miami is a million miles from the bucolic backdrop that greeted Tom Blake and the Whitmans in the early '30s.**

Nassau, Duval and St Johns Counties

1. Hooks

A hard-breaking beachbreak with no outside bar makes this high tide only spot very hollow and powerful. The lefts are at their best in a NE swell.

A fairly consistent break, which is sometimes crowded. As with all of Florida, the sharks are never far away and summer swarms of man-o-war are always a distinct possibility.

2. Main Beach

As with Hooks, there is no outside sandbar here to intercept swells making this a more powerful beachbreak at higher tides. Peaks break close to the beach, short rides.

Often crowded conditions. Easy access with full facilities.

3. Fernandina Beach Pier

Long lefts or rights will break off either side of this private pier, depending on the swell direction. All tides. Same conditions also apply to the beachbreaks south of here.

Less consistent than Main Beach, so generally a smaller crowd. The pier cuts the swell drift a bit, but the line-up still suffers from some hefty currents. Access along the high tide mark via the parking lots north and south of the condo development.

4. Little Talbot Island

Located inside Little Talbot Island State Park, a long stretch of pristine beach holds any swell direction as long as it's low tide. A long walk to the north, there's a left that is usually bigger, more powerful and will break on either side of low.

Lots of sea life and currents here, a beautiful location that attracts plenty of surfers and beach-goers alike.

5. North Jetty

This mile-long jetty blocks any average swell from a southerly direction. Anything with north in it can give some long righthanders and shorter lefts. Wedgy waves are formed from mid incoming through high tide. Experienced longboarders dominate the peak; younger rippers dominate the scraps, leaving some tasty crumbs for well-behaved visitors.

Although it is right at the rivermouth, locals report no real pollution problems. North Jetty is always crowded, and the longstanding local pecking order demands respect. Parking is right on the beach, which can cause problems at high tide. There is a campground directly behind the beach.

6. Hannah Park/Mayport Poles

This stretch of beach is south of the extremely long jetty that protects the southern entrance to St Johns River. This is part of the Mayport US Naval Station, which uses the inlet side of the jetty as safe harbor for destroyers and aircraft carriers. Parking lots 1 - 6 in Hannah Park are closest to the break called Mayport Poles. Guards once prevented you from walking north to the better breaks, but now it's open access unless there's a war on. There are a few other named breaks here, like Lighthouse and Officers Club, but the waves are all pretty much the same. As you get closer to the jetty, the waves get smaller if it's a N/NE swell – but also get cleaner in onshore winds. Handles a big swell from any direction but prefers a N/NE either side of low tide. These hollow peaks can provide longer lefts and shorter rights, both with plenty of power.

The wide area can handle the consistent crowds. Hazards include rip-offs, rips, plenty of sharks, and naval base pollution, which includes a nasty incinerator.

7. Jax Beach Pier

On a N/NE swell, this pier can produce long lefts on the south side, with plenty of shorter rights as well. This is the opposite on the north side, which is generally less crowded. Very consistent on higher tides with occasional barrels and good shape.

Easy parking north and south of the main parking lot in front of the pier, which used to be off-limits unless you were fishing or using the pier facilities. Fortunately, Hurricane Floyd devoured the end of the pier and ended the fascist fisherman-only laws. Unfortunately, some of the local surfers have taken on the enforcer attitude in the always crowded conditions.

8. Ponte Vedra
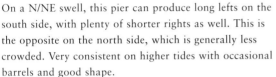

This low tide break needs a good 6-10ft (2-3m) swell to break on the outside coquina shelf. Requires some swell angle to be any good, so a S hurricane or a winter N/NE are ideal. Low tide incoming or outgoing can produce good peaks and fast walls. Occasionally will form a surfable high tide shorebreak along the miles of coast south of Jacksonville Beach. Always affected by shifting sandbars.

Average consistency so it's only sometimes crowded. The large parking lot is a favorite for thieves, who obviously don't come from the surrounding affluent area. Other problems include jetskis and estuary runout, which in turn attracts more than the usual amount of sharks.

9. Vilano Jetty

So much sand has built up near the short north jetty of Anastasia Inlet that finding good waves here is becoming a rare occurrence. Occasional good bodyboarding in the shorepound is the norm these days. However, there is some protection from a SE wind at either side of high tide when smaller swells get through the deeper inlet water and pitch on the shallow banks close to shore.

The consistency and crowding of Vilano has dropped considerably in recent years unless you're a bodyboarder or skimboarder. On-beach parking for 4WD.

10. Middles

North of Blowhole, where the sand dunes build up, is the locals' favorite low tide spot. These bowly horseshoe

Mayport Poles

peaks break both ways, giving super-hollow and long lefts on a N/NE swell.

There's a designated jetski area north of Middles, so a session here could be both noisy and smelly. Once you have paid to go into Anastasia State Recreational Park, there are all the facilities such as restrooms, showers, camping, telephones, and a lifeguard in summer.

11. Blowhole

This is the first break found 1/2 mile north of the beach-access ramp inside Anastasia State Recreational Park. It used to be an inlet but has completely filled in. Consistently larger than nearby breaks, it prefers an E to SE swell and a low tide incoming. Will break at higher tides on bigger swells, which will mean fewer people make the long walk along the diminishing beach.

If there is any swell around, there will definitely be a crowd to dodge along with some submerged tree stumps. Vehicles are no longer allowed to make the drive north along the sand.

12. FA's

Just north of the St Augustine Pier (which rarely breaks well due to recent massive beach erosion) is a little protrusion in the coastline called FA's. Peeling rights, especially on a S swell at higher tides, break off a rock jetty up to about 8ft (2.5m).

Watch out for rocks on the inside, especially at high tide. Fairly consistent and often crowded.

13. A Street

A Street is a consistently good high tide break that is mushy on the outside but stands up on the inside. Takes all swells but prefers S. Handles larger swells than surrounding breaks because it's always a bit smaller.

A finite amount of roadside parking can be a hassle in summer, but a post-surf munch in the Beachcomber at the end of A Street makes up for it. Absolutely always crowded, all year round.

Flagler and Volusia Counties

1. Matanzas Inlet
This is the last remaining natural entrance to Florida's Intracoastal Waterway. Lack of jetties means the sand moves around a lot, and the currents run strong. Check from the bridge to figure out which side is working best on any given day. If the sand lines up, long rides are possible.

Crowds of surfers aren't the problem, but the crowds of 'men in gray suits' could be. There is also a fair amount of motorized traffic. No facilities.

2. Flagler Pier
Above average pier surf that can wedge up and barrel. Bigger swells will break through to high tide, otherwise it's a shorebreak. Best on low incoming, but the good sandbars are usually within the 150-yard no-go area on either side of the pier.

Often crowded, reflecting this spot's consistency. Best place to surf with 4-time world champ, Frieda Zamba.

Flagler Pier

TOM DUGAN/ESM

3. Ormond Beach Pier
This damaged and disheveled pier can get good on its day. Tide depends on swell size and the usual north-side-on-S-swells, south-side-on-N-swells scenario. Usually best around head high at low incoming.

Watch out for submerged pylons, etc. Ormond Beach is home to another 4-time world champ, Lisa Andersen.

4. Main Street Pier
This used to be the hot spot back in the '60s and '70s but the crowd has drifted south to greener pastures. Same deal as Sunglow, except there is a chair lift along the length of the pier. Pity it doesn't drop you out the back when it's big.

If you want to surf Main Street in summer and park on the beach, get there early, otherwise it will be expensive meter parking. Beware: focal point of midsummer college revelers.

5. Sunglow Pier
Another pier break that takes all swells and tides. Best at high on the opposite side to the swell direction. Will handle some size, but the bigger the swell, the stronger the current. Hot young local crew.

Always crowded when it breaks, which is not as often as the inlet to the south.

Map locations:
- ① Matanzas Inlet
- ② Flagler Pier
- ③ Ormond Pier
- ④ Main Street Pier
- ⑤ Sunglow Pier
- ⑥ Ponce Inlet
- ⑦ The Inlet
- ⑧ Flagler Avenue
- ⑨ Bethune

6. Ponce Inlet

This popular spot on the north side of Ponce de Leon Inlet is another consistent wave when swells come up from the south. The long jetty creates rebound, destroying anything from the north, but a southerly of any size can peel off right for long distances. Will break on all tides, but generally high is best and the spot handles it as big as it gets.

Plenty of good, no-nonsense local surfers. As with most inlets, sharks aplenty. Pay parking.

7. The Inlet (New Smyrna)

Surfers travel for miles to surf this super consistent area. A short jetty juts out at the north end of New Smyrna Beach, protecting the southern side of Ponce de Leon Inlet. As a result, the long stretch of beach south of the jetty has good sandbars, which spreads the usually heavy crowds around. An outside bar called Shark Shallows provides quality waves in most swell conditions, which always seem a couple of feet bigger than nearby areas. These outside bars take the sting out of the swell at low tide so higher tides are usually better. Very occasionally, rights peel down the north side of the jetty into the estuary looking like long, fast, point-style waves.

The usual hazards – sharks, man-o-war, and possibly polluted estuary runout. There is motorized traffic in the water and on the beach, which is the best place to park if you don't want to make the long trek along the boardwalks and through the pristine dune environment from the pay lot. Hectic crowds in the water – from dialed-in locals to clueless tourists.

The Inlet

8. Flagler Avenue

Right in front of the lifeguard tower is usually the pick of the waves at this very consistent all tides break. Incoming to high tide is generally better, especially with a N/NE swell, but it will be smaller than The Inlet.

There is always someone surfing here, but it's hassle-free until the summer months, when the lifeguards prohibit boarding from 10-5pm.

9. Bethune

The spot in front of the seawall can have its days when swell, tide, and wind conspire to create outside peaks at low and shorebreak peaks at high. Usually better at high when the backwash of the seawall can make it jack up more than usual.

The locals have it wired, but many take-off areas spread the occasional crowd.

The Inlet

① Playalinda

Playa Linda Beach

Gate

Gate

False Cape

JFK SPACE
CENTRE (NASA)
No Public Access

Courtenay

3

CAPE
CANAVERAL
AIR FORCE
STATION
401 No Public Access

Cape Canaveral

Gate

Port Canaveral
Jetty Park

Artesia

② Jetty Park

Cape Canaveral

Canaveral Pier

Merritt Island

Sheppard Park

520

Sidney Fisher Park

Cocoa Beach ③ Cocoa Beach

3

South Cocoa Beach

Georgina

Bonaventure

A1A

Pineda

404

3B

1

513

South Patrick

Satellite Beach ⑤ Satellite Beach

5

Pelican Beach Park

509

Indian Harbour Beach

Eau Gallie Beach ⑥ Canova Beach

518

Paradise Beach Park

Eau Gallie

Indialantic ⑦ The Boardwalk

192 500

Melbourne Beach ⑧ Melbourne Beach

Melbourne

Spessard Holland Park

A1A

509

Malabar

Palm Bay

514

Valkaria ● Melbourne Shores

Floridana Beach

Grant ● Evans Pines

95

⑨ Spanish House

9

1

5

⑩ Chernobyl

Micco

A1A ⑪ Sebastian Inlet

Sebastian Inlet

④ Patrick Air Force Base

Melbourne Beach

TOM DUGAN/ESM

Brevard County

1. Playalinda

Inside Canaveral National Seashore and in the shadow of Kennedy Space Center, this long stretch of beachbreak can get good. Best on N swells and an incoming tide.

Consistent and rarely crowded because of the sheer scale of the beach. Watch out for sharks, gators, nudists, and spaceships.

2. Jetty Park

On rare occasions, waves can be surfed inside the channel entrance, but more likely, the south side of the jetty will break in big S or SE windchop. Lefts and rights on all tides. North of here the Coastguard will prevent people poaching the obviously good waves peaking along the coast of the Kennedy Space Center on Cape Canaveral.

Low consistency, often crowded, estuary pollution, and large commercial shipping carrying the odd rocket or space shuttle fuel tank means Jetty Park isn't high on the Brevard County hit list. If you see a large, dark gray shape in the water, you may have spotted one of the few remaining manatees that live in the Canaveral National Seashore.

3. Cocoa Beach

Cocoa Beach is home to Kelly Slater and the biggest surf shop in the world. This is quite surprising due to the lack of quality waves here. Cape Canaveral shields the best of the N and a long, gently-sloping sand shelf cuts the power. Cocoa Beach Pier, formerly known as Canaveral Pier, is the best bet on SE wind chop or a big nor'easter. Higher tides will produce longer rides with reforms on the inside.

The main hazard is trying to score waves if Kelly Slater and his mates are out. That's if you can find a parking spot, which always costs something.

4. Patrick Air Force Base

Various breaks opposite the large AFB with names like Missiles, Hangers, Second Light, First Light, Officer's Club, and Patricks. There is some coquina shelf, however Cape Canaveral starts to affect the size and power of N swells. All tides and swells mean the consistent crowds have a choice of spots.

To avoid being towed by the Air Force, park only in designated parking areas, some of which have no facilities. Plenty of noisy air traffic. Area will be off limits in times of war.

5. Satellite Beach/RCs

Satellite Beach consists of broken coquina shelf and sand. One of these reefs can produce long, well-defined and hollow lefts when a decent groundswell hits. RCs, on the north corner of the Ramada Inn, is the locals' favorite and has been ridden with 20ft (6m) faces. Takes all swells but prefers a N/NE at mid tide. There are other reefs up and down the beach, but RCs has the goods. Only the most experienced surfers can get out when it's really big because there is so much water moving.

Shallow, rocky, big rips, and locals, plus a complete lack of parking in the immediate vicinity. There are a few clandestine parking spots, but you'll need inside information and a bit of luck to avoid being towed.

6. Canova Beach

Situated at the end of Eau Gallie Causeway, this average beachbreak prefers lower tides on a NE groundswell, although with size it will break inside on higher tides. The best of the Indian Harbor Beach stretch.

Only average regularity means only average crowds.

7. The Boardwalk

Beachbreak barrels coveted by a swarm of hot groms. Close to shore, high tide action up to head high. Home of Florida's first surf shop, Shaggs, which is now one of many in the area.

The crowds are more consistent than the waves, and you'll always have to pay to park.

8. Melbourne Beach

Ocean Avenue has average peaks over outside sandbars at lower tides.

Often crowded, possibly due to a large cross-section of the surf industry being based in Melbourne/Indiatlantic area. Home to the voice of 'The Right Coast,' otherwise known as *Eastern Surf Magazine*.

9. Spanish House

On the same stretch of beach as Sebastian Inlet but far less consistent because it needs more swell to break. Short and sweet barrel when it lines up, though.

As soon as there is groundswell, the crowd will swell. From here south to Martin County is probably the sharkiest water in Brevard County.

Spanish House

MEZ/ESM

10. Chernobyl

Similar set-up to Spanish House, expect good lefts on strong N/NE swells. Needs above shoulder height and lower tides to kick in.

Chernobyl can't handle the crowds that often surf here, because it has a limited take-off zone. Average consistency guarantees a crew when it's on, especially if The Inlet is rammed.

11. Sebastian Inlet

Florida's most famous wave is undoubtedly one of its best and most reliable. It is situated on the northern side of the long jetty that protects the man-made entrance to the estuary waters of the Indian River. There are 3 main breaks: First Peak is a righthander that uses the rock-and-timber jetty formation to peel down the line. Side wash off the jetty can make it wedge, jack up, and barrel down towards the Second Peak, which can offer a left, depending on swell direction. Third Peak, further north of the jetty, provides fast, hollow lefts when the swell has some N. Best tide is low to mid incoming, but it will break through to high, unless it's small, in which case the backwash takes over.

Always crowded, which means the Sebastian Inlet State Rec. Area is making money because it costs at least $3.50 to use their large car park, toilets, showers, picnic area, boat ramp, beach café, etc. Hazards include sharks, man-o-war, rocks in the line-up near the jetty, aggressive fishermen on the jetty, and enough talented surfers alongside that jetty to make surfing here a real challenge.

DOUG WATERS

Sebastian Inlet

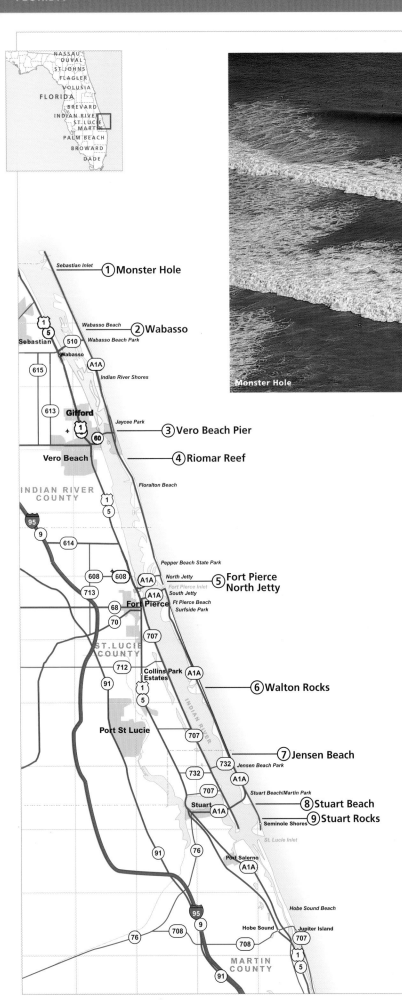

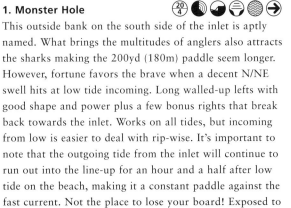

Monster Hole

DOUG WATERS

Indian River, St. Lucie and Martin Counties

1. Monster Hole

This outside bank on the south side of the inlet is aptly named. What brings the multitudes of anglers also attracts the sharks making the 200yd (180m) paddle seem longer. However, fortune favors the brave when a decent N/NE swell hits at low tide incoming. Long walled-up lefts with good shape and power plus a few bonus rights that break back towards the inlet. Works on all tides, but incoming from low is easier to deal with rip-wise. It's important to note that the outgoing tide from the inlet will continue to run out into the line-up for an hour and a half after low tide on the beach, making it a constant paddle against the fast current. Not the place to lose your board! Exposed to the wind, and the jetskiers are all over it when it's small.

Aside from the sharks, rips, and jetskis, there's also plenty of boat traffic in the inlet channel, estuary water runout, plus the added annoyance of sea-lice. Only average consistency and only sometimes crowded, but when it's firing, the length of ride, the different sections, and the strong rips all play a part in dispersing the inevitable crowd. On occasion, there are waves breaking with nobody out – because nobody wants to sit way out there on their own.

2. Wabasso

Wabasso is a heavy shorebreak when the swell is as high as the tide. When the ideal tide and swell window conditions appear, thick, boardsnapping waves break really close to the beach.

A bit of a rarity, but when it's on, it will produce some testy waves in a sometimes crowded scenario.

3. Vero Beach Pier

This pier interrupts a straight section of beach, allowing banks to form on either side. Head to the opposite side of the pier to the swell direction at mid tide for the best quality beachbreaks in the area.

A decent walk is required from the public car parks located north or south of the pier, which can sometimes help with crowd control.

4. Riomar Reef

A big-wave spot only surfed by a handful of locals for a bunch of good reasons. A very long paddle to a deep, shark-infested reef, this spot needs a strong N swell, low tide, and favorable WSW winds, which means only the locals get this one when it's on.

One of the few truly low consistency waves around. Also suffers from a complete lack of parking, unless you're one of the affluent local residents.

5. Fort Pierce North Jetty

The southern end of this picturesque beach in the Fort Pierce Inlet State Rec. Park is flanked by a long rock jetty, which can produce lengthy wedgy rights from the jetty sidewash. Consistent right and left peaks to the north help diffuse the inevitable crowd and an outer reef provides distraction on bigger swells. Due to the Bahamian islands, S groundswell is usually blocked, but a good NE or even an E swell will get the place firing on all tides. The jetty on the south side of the inlet doesn't have anything for surfers, but it's a popular windsurfing spot.

The waves, crowds, and sharks are all super consistent. State Rec. Park charges apply. "We will fight them on the beaches," applies to old locals who frequented these sands during the US Army training for the D-Day landings.

6. Walton Rocks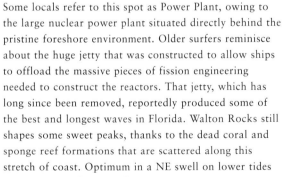

Some locals refer to this spot as Power Plant, owing to the large nuclear power plant situated directly behind the pristine foreshore environment. Older surfers reminisce about the huge jetty that was constructed to allow ships to offload the massive pieces of fission engineering needed to construct the reactors. That jetty, which has long since been removed, reportedly produced some of the best and longest waves in Florida. Walton Rocks still shapes some sweet peaks, thanks to the dead coral and sponge reef formations that are scattered along this stretch of coast. Optimum in a NE swell on lower tides up to about 12ft (3.6m) faces.

Cooling water from the nuclear reactor is discharged into the line-up, supplying a nice warm current for less hardy surfers in winter. Locals don't seem to think there's any rogue isotopes running around; they say you don't need a Geiger counter to surf here. They say.

Wabasso

7. Jensen Beach

Combination sand and rock breaks that can get good. Low incoming is best especially if it's breaking on the outside coquina reef.

Full facilities and easy parking.

8 Stuart Public Beach

Another outside reef at low tide with a decent high tide shorebreak if it's big enough.

The same conditions and facilities as Jensen Beach, but a little more consistent for waves and crowds.

9. Stuart Rocks

A series of reefs that turn a N/NE swell into good, hollow lefts and some rights. Plenty of different take-off spots disperse the large and talented local crew. Handles size. All tides are surfed, but low incoming is the best bet.

Stuart Rocks is one of those spots that people will drive a long way to surf. Consequently, there's a pecking order in the line-up and a lack of parking between the roadside shoulder (directly in front of the break) and the parking lot. Full amenities (just to the south). Jetskis are also a factor, because the St Lucie Inlet is a mere mile south.

Stuart Rocks

Martin Co. – South/Palm Beach Co. – North

1. Hobe Sound/The Refuge

Located in the Hobe Sound National Wildlife Refuge at the northern end of Jupiter Island. Low tide impedes the swell on the outside bank so mid to high is the call for the better inside shorebreak. On bigger days with N swells, longer lefts in particular will link through to the beachbreak, reforming and standing up on the inside. A half-mile out is a reef that acts as a good indicator for approaching sets. This is the southernmost point of Florida's coast that receives due E groundswells. The shadow of the Bahamas blocks long-fetch, due-E swells from reaching the breaks to the south.

This area is ostentatiously affluent and the closed community employs overzealous law enforcement officers. State-of-the-art surveillance technology means obey the low speed limits on the area's narrow streets to avoid a ticket. Beware the oyster shells in the shorebreak and the turbid water that hides abundant sea life, particularly the toothed variety. Unofficial nudist beach 1/4 mile north of here. Pay to park year round in the sometimes crowded conditions.

2. Coral Cove Park

A flat tabletop reef cultivates good lefts on small northerly swells at low to mid tides. Fast and shallow and not very suitable for beginners, who should try the beachbreaks extending south to Jupiter Inlet north jetty. The north jetty will produce some rights in a SE windchop, and the three-quarter mile walk from Coral Cove Park keeps the crowds thin.

There's a car park almost a mile north of Jupiter Inlet, or a free roadside pull-in close to the reef.

3. Jupiter Inlet South Jetty

This quality spot has a nice inside peak on all smaller swells and an outside left on bigger swells. Lower tides are best, and the jetty offers decent protection from northerly winds.

A very popular spot and one of the benchmark breaks in Palm Beach County. Crowds and hassling are de rigueur, but there are plenty more peaks to the south, especially in a N or NE swell. Full facilities to deal with the crowds, of which surfers are a small fraction.

4. Juno Pier

A brand spanking new 1,100ft (335m) pier now provides this straight section of beach with some good sandbars. Due to the pier's length, there is no trench between the outside low tide banks and the inside high tide shorebreak. From here north to the Jupiter Inlet, there are 7 miles (11km) of beachbreak with good access, including the popular break called Corners.

Surfrider Foundation's Palm Beach County chapter has brokered a deal with local authorities to allow surfing alongside the pier. Lifeguards will control the area and provide paddle-out channels next to the pier when it's big. In return, all surfers must respect the lifeguards' decisions in order to maintain this status quo. Plenty of roadside meters and a big car park make Juno an easy check, but don't expect to get it to yourself.

Map labels:
Jensen Beach Park
Stuart
707
Stuart Beach/Martin Park
Seminole Shores
St. Lucie Inlet
Port Salerno
A1A
① Hobe Sound
MARTIN COUNTY
Hobe Sound Beach
Hobe Sound
Jupiter Island
708
707
1
5
9
95
Blowing Rocks Beach
② Coral Cove Park
Jupiter Inlet Beach Colony
Jupiter
Jupiter Beach Park
③ Jupiter Inlet South Jetty
Carlin Park
811
Juno Beach Park
④ Juno Pier
Juno Beach
91
809
John D. MacArthur State Recreation Area
North Palm Beach
95
Lake Park
Howard Beach
⑤ Ocean Reef Park
9
Riviera Beach Municipal Park
Palm Beach Shores
Riviera Beach
710
⑥ Reef Road
PALM BEACH COUNTY
West Palm Beach
704
⑦ Palm Beach Jetties
Palm Beach
98 80
441
809
91
Palm Springs
Phipps Ocean Park

Jupiter Inlet

MEZ/ESM

Reef Road

DOUG WATERS

5. Ocean Reef Park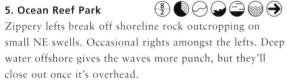

Zippery lefts break off shoreline rock outcropping on small NE swells. Occasional rights amongst the lefts. Deep water offshore gives the waves more punch, but they'll close out once it's overhead.

An oasis of green among the condos make Ocean Reef Park an aesthetically pleasing location to surf. There are a few rocks in the line-up to avoid.

6. Reef Road

Reef Road is Florida's undisputed best big-wave spot. Located off one of the most expensive oceanfront real estate strips in the world, this high-class lefthander can produce powerful, sucky rides for up to 400yds (365m). Needs an overhead N to NE swell to start breaking, then it gets better as it gets bigger. It will handle as big as Florida gets, which attracts big-wave aficionados from all over, especially in hurricane season or the depths of winter. Best at low tide incoming, when it breaks over a coquina reef outside then a shallow sandbar inside. Nearer to the south jetty of the Palm Beach Inlet, known as The Cove, there are less critical lefts and the occasional right, which offers more wind protection. Access to the north side of the inlet is also sketchy, so we won't bother describing the decent waves that break near the sand-pumping house at the base of the north jetty in the exclusive suburb of Palm Beach Shores.

No parking within a mile of Reef Road, where even unloading is not permitted. Look for a spot a mile south (no parking restrictions), or even further where the meters start, then hike in. The shoreline real estate is posted as private, but public access is allowed along the high tide line. Considering the access problems, it's quite amazing how many surfers you'll meet in the line-up, especially in

medium-size conditions. But a big swell will separate the men from the boys thanks to long paddle-outs and guaranteed drillings.

7. Palm Beach Jetties

A beach nourishment program has transformed this whole area in recent years. From Palm Beach Public Beach to Charlies Crab, 4,000 year-old gray sand has been pumped in from offshore in conjunction with building a bunch of new T-head jetties. This resulted in the loss of some consistently good lefts like Charlies Crab, while previously unsurfed areas like Flagpole began to break. An outside sandbar usually blocks the swell at low tide. Mid-high tide on a NE groundswell or SE windswell will see fast, spinning barrels that have a large local fan club.

Much of the parking requires a resident permit on weekends, so visitors have to compete for the limited meters, which primes them to compete for waves.

MEZ/ESM

Pump House

Delray

Palm Beach County – South

1. Lake Worth Pier

As with most pier breaks, south side on a northerly swell and vice versa. Good sandbars give this break more punch, which is reputedly something the locals will give you if you don't show them respect. Low tide in smaller swells, up to high in bigger swells.

Meter-feeding madness in this popular spot, where you even have to pay to walk out on the pier, which is designed like a big Lego model. It used to have a big T on the end, but the swell of '91 took the top off it. When a huge swell hits, the boardwalk planks just pop off and drift down the coast, allowing them to be retrieved and replaced. The area south of here is controlled by the rich and shameless, meaning no parking, no access, and no trespassing above the high tide line.

2. Lantana

Easy access to average beachbreak peaks without the crowds at Lake Worth. NE swell tends to close it out, so only a SE/E swell at all but low tide will serve up some rideable peaks.

Cheaper meter parking than the surrounding area and rarely crowded.

3. Boynton Inlet

The shorebreak here is under threat from a beach construction project, which will include six T-head jetties. However, about a quarter mile offshore, an outside bar produces long, hollow lefts when a big NE swell combines with a low incoming tide. There can also be some clean, uncrowded peaks on a SE windchop swell on the north side of the inlet at lower tides.

Typical example of beach replenishment/stabilization programs threatening surfers' natural habitat. The question is whether a new and improved habitat will result. Strong currents bring food to the many sharks around the inlet.

4. Boynton Beach

From here, 1.5 miles (2.5km) north to the inlet, a program to create a new 200ft (60m) wide beach is currently underway. The new sand is going to cover some existing flatbed reefs, then replacement reefs will be created, using large limestone boulders. Due to Surfrider Foundation input, these artificial reefs have been created in triangular form facing NE. High tides and a SE windchop for the beachbreaks but more likely low tide and a NE'er for the new reefs to work as they are in deeper water.

On the down side, if you are not a resident and want to park there between 8-4pm, it'll cost plenty.

5. Delray Beach

1.5 miles (2.5km) of above average beachbreak that works best at the south end (Anchor Park). Will take both NE and SE swells but tends to have better peaks on a NE'er at mid to high tides.

Delray is sometimes crowded, and it suffers from the endemic 'shark and man-o-war' syndrome.

6. 40th Street

Standard Florida beachbreak that works on all swells and tides, but best on a N/NE swell from low incoming.

Although the quality is average, 40th Street is consistent and uncrowded.

7. South Beach Pavilion

Known simply as The Pavilion, this reef and sand bottom wave needs a SE windchop to work as a NE'er will close

out. Hollow lefts and rights work up and down the beach, helping with crowding. Shallow at low, but it will break up to high.

Often a crew out when the SE wind blows. A few rocks in the line-up to avoid.

8. Boca Raton Inlet

The south side (in the county park) works on all tides in a NE swell. The peaks here hold size and are much better than on the north side, which is very inconsistent.

It's a busy inlet, so the estuary runout may not be as clean as the surrounding area. There are often as many surfers as there as there are boats using Boca Raton Inlet.

Lake Worth

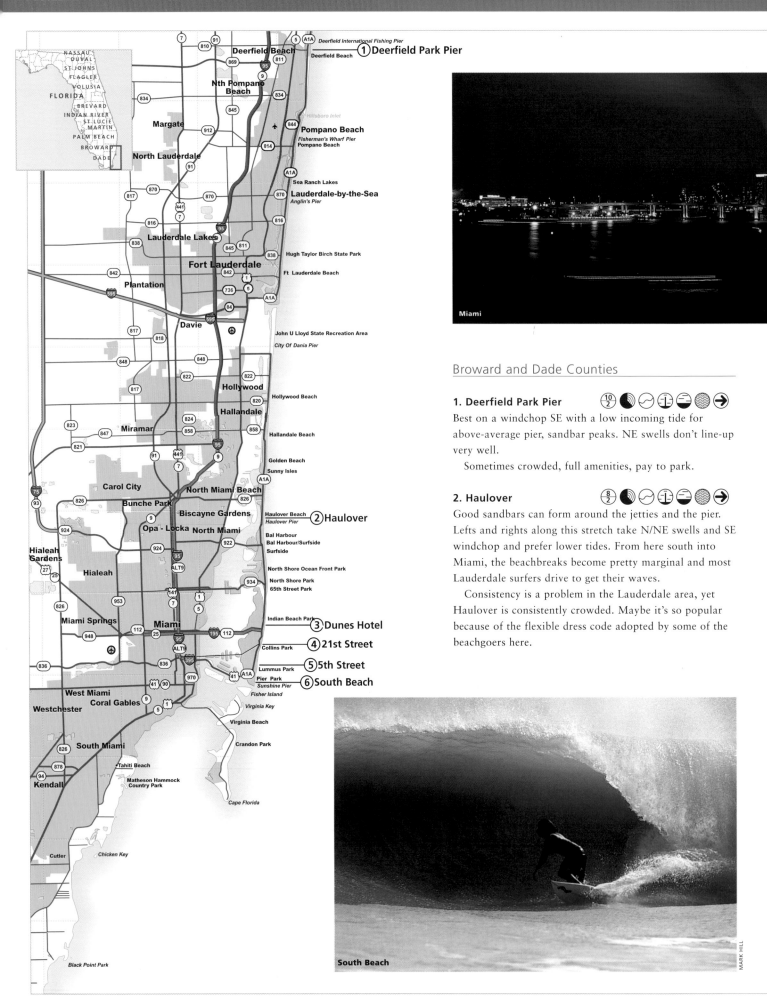

Miami

Broward and Dade Counties

1. Deerfield Park Pier

Best on a windchop SE with a low incoming tide for above-average pier, sandbar peaks. NE swells don't line-up very well.

Sometimes crowded, full amenities, pay to park.

2. Haulover

Good sandbars can form around the jetties and the pier. Lefts and rights along this stretch take N/NE swells and SE windchop and prefer lower tides. From here south into Miami, the beachbreaks become pretty marginal and most Lauderdale surfers drive to get their waves.

Consistency is a problem in the Lauderdale area, yet Haulover is consistently crowded. Maybe it's so popular because of the flexible dress code adopted by some of the beachgoers here.

South Beach

MARK HILL

PAUL KENNEDY

3. Dunes Hotel

Hard to find access on this hotel strip where average beachbreak runs left on a NE swell at lower tides. SE windchop offers some rights, and is more tidally flexible.

The beachfront is a wall of hotels, each claiming their private strip of sand and limiting public access.

4. 21st Street

A popular spot with more power than other breaks in the area, the long lefts off 21st Street peel down parallel to the beach on N-NE swells. Exposed to the wind, works best at low to mid tide.

Surfers must feed the meters to feed their addiction.

5. 5th Street

Gets good banks from being close to the jetty. Longer lefts can be had on a N-NE swell, plus occasional rights. An outside dead coral reef can break on big swells, and lower tides will yield hollow waves.

If there's any swell it'll be breaking … and crowded.

6. South Beach

Miami Beach's best wave is found on the north side of the jetty, where waves from a N-NE swell refract off the jetty and wedge up into nice peaks and A-Frames when the sand is there. Also takes a SE to S windswell, which wraps around and spins off the best rights in the area. Low incoming is best, however with size it will break through to higher tides. The jetty provides some protection from southerly winds while a westerly is dead offshore.

This is quintessential Miami and the last beach before the Florida Keys begin to stretch south and west. Attracts all species of humanity along with the countless surfers who descend on South Beach when there is any sniff of swell. An oasis of parkland amidst plenty of parking, this is an area worthy of its popularity. However, it's very close to the estuary waters of downtown Miami and there are rumors of a discharge pipe near Fisher Island, which could have an affect on water quality.

TOM DUGAN/ESM

JAMES METYKO

The Gulf of Mexico

Sometimes called the Third Coast, the Gulf Of Mexico usually plays third fiddle to the rest of the surfin' USA, and the average Gulf surfer might indeed concede they have a problem with consistency, but when it does happen, there are beachbreaks here that are as good as any on the continent. Winter storms can send sizable pulses to Texas and the Florida Panhandle, and anxiously-awaited summer hurricanes deliver their excitement in the form of solid groundswell, generally without the spectre of devastation.

The sandy barrier island configuration of the Atlantic Coast wraps around Florida and continues along the Gulf's circumference to the Mexican border. The inlets or 'passes' through these islands are usually focal points for Gulf surfers, where deeper water beckons all available swell onto sculptured inlet-jetty sandbars. Thanks to these and other man-made structures (mostly piers) that snag the shifting sands, the average Gulf surfer has plenty of options, including hundreds of miles of deserted, unnamed beachbreak peaks and channels. Factor in balmy water, warm air temperatures, endless stretches of white sand beaches, great flat day fishing, and laid-back Southern hospitality, and it all adds up: the Gulf is a valid North American surf destination.

Bob Hall Pier, Corpus Christi

MIKE BOYD

The Surf, Ocean Environment and Surf Culture

The jetties of the Gulf of Mexico attract the most preponderant waves. Fish Pass Jetties, Central Texas.

The shoreline of the Gulf of Mexico circles clockwise from Mexico to Florida and Cuba, lapping the beaches of Texas, Louisiana, Mississippi and Alabama along the way. The true definition of a gulf is "a large, deep bay," but, though the Gulf of Mexico is undoubtedly large, its coastal fringes don't exactly qualify as deep. A wide and gently sloping shelf enervates what short-lived swells the Gulf can produce within the limited fetch of its virtually landlocked environment. The problem of water depth (a

factor in swell potency) is compounded by the constant conveyance and deposition of silt by the mightiest of American rivers, the Mississippi. As a result, apart from the Padre Island beachbreaks of southern Texas and the Pensacola area of the Florida Panhandle, there are very few powerful waves for the friendly, optimistic surfers of these Southern States.

Gulf Coast states seem to suffer from about the same problems that plague East and West Coast states. Erosion, pollution, and access are common issues and Surfrider

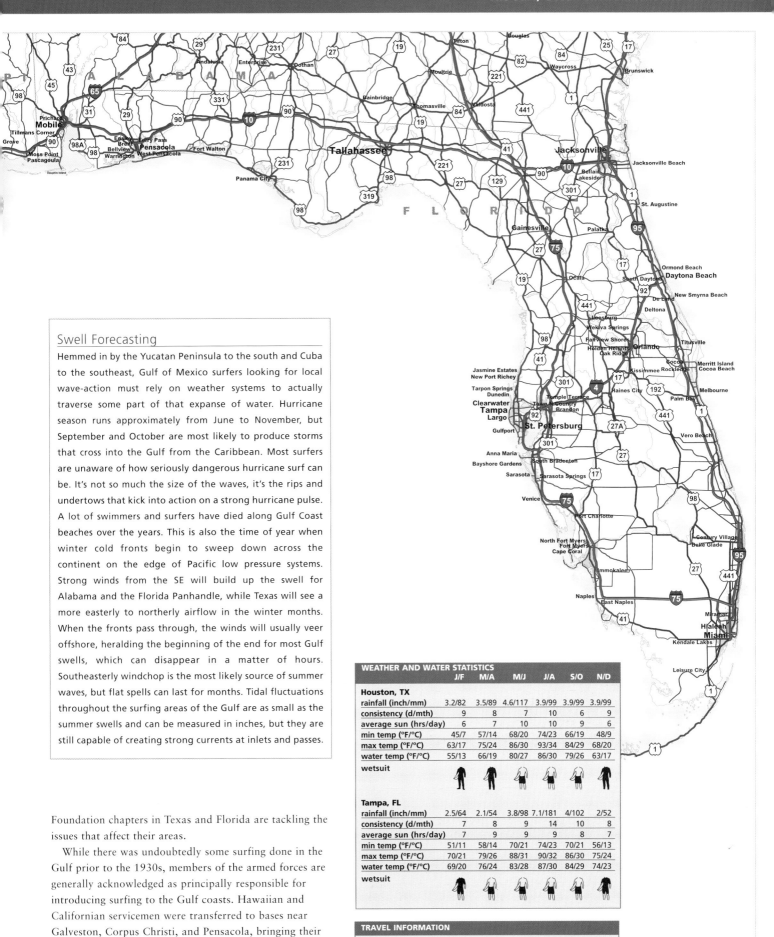

Swell Forecasting

Hemmed in by the Yucatan Peninsula to the south and Cuba to the southeast, Gulf of Mexico surfers looking for local wave-action must rely on weather systems to actually traverse some part of that expanse of water. Hurricane season runs approximately from June to November, but September and October are most likely to produce storms that cross into the Gulf from the Caribbean. Most surfers are unaware of how seriously dangerous hurricane surf can be. It's not so much the size of the waves, it's the rips and undertows that kick into action on a strong hurricane pulse. A lot of swimmers and surfers have died along Gulf Coast beaches over the years. This is also the time of year when winter cold fronts begin to sweep down across the continent on the edge of Pacific low pressure systems. Strong winds from the SE will build up the swell for Alabama and the Florida Panhandle, while Texas will see a more easterly to northerly airflow in the winter months. When the fronts pass through, the winds will usually veer offshore, heralding the beginning of the end for most Gulf swells, which can disappear in a matter of hours. Southeasterly windchop is the most likely source of summer waves, but flat spells can last for months. Tidal fluctuations throughout the surfing areas of the Gulf are as small as the summer swells and can be measured in inches, but they are still capable of creating strong currents at inlets and passes.

Foundation chapters in Texas and Florida are tackling the issues that affect their areas.

While there was undoubtedly some surfing done in the Gulf prior to the 1930s, members of the armed forces are generally acknowledged as principally responsible for introducing surfing to the Gulf coasts. Hawaiian and Californian servicemen were transferred to bases near Galveston, Corpus Christi, and Pensacola, bringing their boards and the seeds of a surf culture that has grown steadily since the early 1960s.

WEATHER AND WATER STATISTICS	J/F	M/A	M/J	J/A	S/O	N/D
Houston, TX						
rainfall (inch/mm)	3.2/82	3.5/89	4.6/117	3.9/99	3.9/99	3.9/99
consistency (d/mth)	9	8	7	10	6	9
average sun (hrs/day)	6	7	10	10	9	6
min temp (°F/°C)	45/7	57/14	68/20	74/23	66/19	48/9
max temp (°F/°C)	63/17	75/24	86/30	93/34	84/29	68/20
water temp (°F/°C)	55/13	66/19	80/27	86/30	79/26	63/17
wetsuit						
Tampa, FL						
rainfall (inch/mm)	2.5/64	2.1/54	3.8/98	7.1/181	4/102	2/52
consistency (d/mth)	7	8	9	14	10	8
average sun (hrs/day)	7	9	9	9	8	7
min temp (°F/°C)	51/11	58/14	70/21	74/23	70/21	56/13
max temp (°F/°C)	70/21	79/26	88/31	90/32	86/30	75/24
water temp (°F/°C)	69/20	76/24	83/28	87/30	84/29	74/23
wetsuit						

TRAVEL INFORMATION	
Texas	www.traveltex.com
Florida	www.flausa.com

JAMES METYKO

Texas

Like much of the Atlantic shore, the Texas coastline is
fronted by a series of barrier islands that create a 350-
mile-long (560km) Intracoastal Waterway, stretching from
the Mexican border at Port Isabel to Port Arthur and the
swampy mouth of the Sabine River. The exposed outer
beaches of this sandy barricade is entirely beachbreak,
except for the occasional rock armoring, augmented by a
series of fishing piers.

There is a definite north-south split in wave size and
consistency here. From Sabine Pass and High Island's
Meacom's Pier on the border of Louisiana, down to
Corpus Christi and North Padre Island, soft, mushy waves
are the rule, owing to the broad, gently-sloping continental
shelf. These northern areas are the closest to the
population centers of Houston and Dallas, so the
Galveston and Freeport area beaches attract daytrippers
that can put crowd pressure on the more popular spots.

The birthplace of Texas surfing, the shores of the
Galveston-Freeport area are bunkered with featureless
white sand beaches and fringed with the kind of waves
you'd expect – most always gutless junk. As with the rest
of the Texas coast, anywhere this amorphous monotony is
interrupted, things get more interesting. The game in Texas
is finding a groin, jetty or pier that will at least give a
suggestion of focus and order to approaching swells.
Galveston's series of small jetties create lots of surf spots
(like 37th and 61st Streets) but not much quality. (East
Texas guys surf at Meacom's Pier, east of Galveston.)
Outstanding (by comparison) are Galveston's Flagship Pier
(which, unfortunately, tends to overload when waves are
breaking beyond the T-head), the old Surfside Pier,
Octagon House and the Surfside Jetty.

The latter is about a half-mile long and is the premier
large-swell spot in upper Texas. When conditions are right
(a.k.a. a "jetty day"), surfers walk out the flat-topped jetty
and jump into the line-up (paddling from the beach on a
bigger day is just about impossible). The lulls between sets
are too short and the distances between sandbars are too
great, and seemingly unrelenting walls of whitewater
pummel the flagging paddler. It's brutal.

Best on a S or SW (yes, it's true) swell, which creates
sufficient wrap to smooth out the waves, the Surfside Jetty
can also handle more direct E swells if it's glassy or
offshore wind. Usually, a big E swell moves the action to
the Quintana Jetty (parallel to the Surfside Jetty on the
south side of the Freeport Channel). Quintana is usually
mushy and muddy, but when a big swell sweeps in from
the east and wraps into the lee of the jetty, it can be an
awesome sight for surf-starved locals or lucky travelers.
You can check out Quintana from the upper deck of the
Jetty Park Pavilion.

JAMES METYKO

A few times a year a huge E swell will break inside the channel – clamshell A-frames are reputed to spin off long (up to 500 yards) peeling waves. Catch this spot on a double overhead day and you'll think you're somewhere else. Most likely to 'happen' in spring or very early summer.

Away from the influence of piers and jetties, the disorganized Texas sandbars help disperse the crowds, especially when the windswell is a bit bigger and breaking further outside. Slowed by the gently sloping bottom, the weak waves are more suitable for longboarding than anything else. One exception is the isolated break called Matagorda, at the mouth of the Colorado River off the Matagorda Peninsula (about halfway between Galveston and Port Aransas). Here, the deeper waters of the inlet channel focus the swells onto shallow sandbars; the resultant barrels keep the northern shortboarders in practice. Further south, at the entrance of the Cavallo Pass to Matagorda Bay, the Port O'Connor jetties offer a definite low-key alternative. You'll need to take a boat or the ferry out to the Matagorda Island State Park to check these sometimes excellent spots.

South of Port O'Connor, the Coastal Bend area provides abundant sand beaches, interspersed with piers and rock jetties. Passes through the barrier islands (most of it the Padre Island National Seashore) are few and far between from Matagorda to Mexico, but that's where the best surf tends to concentrate.

Just north of Port Aransas, there's often good surf off San Jose Island, but it takes a ferry or boat to get there. The Horace Caldwell Pier in Port A sets up good peaks on both sides, depending on swell direction. Further down Mustang Island are the short Fish Pass Jetties (although Fish Pass isn't a pass anymore either), which create pockets of wind protection and more stable sandbars; this is a good area within Mustang Island State Park.

Down the way a bit, on Padre Island, are the JP Luby and Bob Hall piers. The former is a designated surfing pier with adjacent party beach. Bob Hall is the most consistent spot, attracting crowds of combatants for the pushier peaks on either side of the pier; it holds a larger swell. Check out Condos, a better than average section of beachbreak peaks between the two piers.

Heading south from Corpus Christi down the long expanse of Padre Island National Seashore, the general prognosis for surf improves, with empty waves breaking on even emptier beaches – a total of about 80 miles (128km) available only to 4WD vehicles. Although it's all one island from Port Aransas south, the name changes – from Mustang to Padre Island to South Padre Island. In the north, Mustang and Padre Islands were once separated by Packery Channel; its sanded-in remnants are still visible from a bridge on Highway 53 heading towards Port Aransas. There are plans afoot to reopen this pass (to provide easier Gulf access for Corpus Christi fishermen) with proposed jetties at the entrance that would add new surf spots to the area.

From time to time hurricanes have caused 'washovers' that have temporarily breached this long, narrow barrier island, but the most recent sanded-up quickly. This is not to say that the next storm won't create a new pass in the island, but for now, the low, narrow sandbar is broken in only two places – the Port Mansfield Pass about 50 miles (80km) south of the asphalt road terminus in Padre Island National Seashore, although you can access the pass from both north and south with 4WD) and the Brownsville Ship

JAMES METYKO

Below – **Southerly swells wrap in nicely on the east side of 61st Street Pier.**
Bottom – **Short period storm swells can make paddle outs laborious.**

JAMES METYKO

Channel (the Brazos Santiago Pass at the town of South Padre Island (formerly Port Isabel). Both of these passes are flanked by granite jetties, the only hard structures creating swell focus and wind protection along this 150-mile (240km) stretch. These four 'corners' hold the best Texas has to offer by way of longer, lined up waves that work on all swell directions and provide some shelter from all but dead onshore E winds. Inside both sets of jetties there can be organized sandbars creating excellent 'mysto' set-ups, particularly during hurricane swells.

South Padre Island is famed among the general population for its spring break college-student invasion; among Texas surfers it's known as the place to find the biggest surf. In fact, the popularity of this locale can likely be pinned in large part on the surf culture that flourished here in the '60s and '70s. "In those days, it was upscale beach camping," remembers Gail Hull, daughter of pioneer Don. "We had a grassy area and facilities and 'Tent City' became the cleanest, funnest, most athletic group of young partiers to ever make the news. We had a big surf contest at Easter every year; spring break was just starting to be a week holiday from school, so more people started to come. People like Pat O'Neill (he'd drive his Porsche out from California), Nancy Katin, Dru Harrison,

Top – **Ultra rare but ultra long rights between the Surfside and Quintana Jetties of the Galveston shipping channel.** Above – **Fish Pass.**

and Mike Purpus were there in the early '70s when it really started to build. So when the media came and showed how beautiful the beaches were and all the fun people were having, well...the rest is history. Now it looks more like Miami Beach."

From the Port Mansfield South Jetty, past miles of isolated 4WD beachbreak, to the jetty breaks at Port Isabel (with Brazos and Boca Chica islands beyond), the surf is regularly larger, more powerful, and in a healthier shape than the rest of the state. The waves here also tend to be more consistent, and long-period groundswells are not uncommon from fall to spring. N swells can set up a good left at Boca Chica – not as hard-breaking as the north side of the jetties, but can have excellent shape. On large swells, the classic Cove spot breaks in the channel between the

jetties, occasionally producing some very long rides.

While surfers from the West Coast or Hawaii might imagine Texas surf as small and gutless (which it typically is), it can have juice ... and size. "You hear talk of sets pushing triple overhead," writes Houston Chronicle sportswriter Joe Doggett, a surfer himself. "I'm not saying it cannot happen, but I've been following these things since 1964, and I've never seen irrefutable proof of a triple overhead wave with surfable form in Texas. But, surf in the double overhead class is for real, and the 'big days' occur more often than many inlanders and non-surfers may realize. Statistically, overhead surf hits the Texas Coast several days a month and, at least a few times each year, the ante is upped to the double overhead level."

So, there is surf in Texas, and while it may not compare with the black-diamond spots on the world tour, it can be its own flavor of delicious.

Texas has a great surfing climate with hot land and warm water temperatures for much of the year. Depth-of-winter cold fronts can bring sub-50°F (10°C) fullsuit weather for short periods, particularly in the north, but the shallow Gulf waters are prone to quick cooling, and water temps below 60°F (15°C) are common from December to March.

Surf checks along miles and miles of the extensive barrier islands require lengthy off-road drives with soft sand, high temperatures, and no services, making adequate planning and provision essential. While a small proportion of the coast has shoreline structures in place, erosion can reach 30ft-plus (9m+) a year, resulting in landowner pressure to change the Texas Open Beaches Act, which prohibits private structures on the beach and guarantees access to the state's 367 miles (587km) of coastline. In general, beach access is very good in Texas, where it is impossible to own the beach, and many counties allow on-beach driving. Water-based hazards include sharks, jellyfish, stingrays, and the irritant of a phytoplankton population explosion known as 'red tide'. Water quality is generally regarded as being acceptable despite the many petrochemical plants along the coast. Surfrider Foundation's Texas chapter (formed in 1999) implemented a beach-water testing program in Galveston and at Surfside Beach after the Texas General Land Office scrapped its own water-testing program in a cost-cutting effort by the Land Commissioner. In 2001, the EPA mandated nationwide beach-water testing, and the GLO implemented a new program. Surfrider continues to monitor the water independently of the State.

According to the now-legendary 'Doc' Dorian Paskowitz (who spent much of his youth on Texas beaches) describes the early 1930s with fondness for "the surfing joy and excitement in Galveston." According to Paskowitz, a local man had visited Hawaii in the 1920s and returned inspired to build a surfboard. The inventive fellow commissioned the Firestone tire company to make him some cylindrical innertubes – 8ft long and 6in diameter. He nestled them together and slipped them into a silk sleeve, then into a heavyweight sleeve, and finally into a heavy marine canvas

Above – **The Bob Hall Pier offers a great view of the most popular and consistent Corpus Christi surf spot.** Below – **Designated surfing and party beach, JB Luby Park Pier.**

DAVID BURHARDT

sleeve. The finished 'surfboard' was big enough to be surfed tandem. The local gremlins – including Paskowitz, the great waterman Preston Peterson, and the Columbo brothers (who ran the 'board' rental at Murdoch's Bathhouse) – caught the fever and began to surf these bulbous creations. "If you were knee-paddling and hit a wave paddling out, the board would jackknife a bit," Doc recalls, "and Columbo could use that spring to do a one-and-a-half flip and enter the water next to the board!" (In 1934, at age 13, Dorian says he talked his family into moving to California, so "lost to surfing" was he.)

In 1931, Tom Blake had received a patent on his Hawaiian Hollow Surfboard. Manufactured by the Thomas N. Rogers Company of Venice, California, the boards quickly become the ubiquitous tool of surf-

lifesavers everywhere. Galveston's Beach Patrol lifeguards (including Leroy Columbo, a deaf-mute, who went on to earn a Guinness World Record for lifesaving) were quick to adopt the 10-12ft hollow rescue paddleboards and, by extension, inspired surfing at Galveston area beaches. Like most other places in the country, however, only a few hardy souls attempted the sport.

The earliest known example of a Texan-built surfboard dates from 1946. Inspired by two traveling Californians who passed through one summer in the late '30s and let him paddle one of their boards (one red and one blue), RW Ellisor III proceeded to fashion his own out of a magnolia skeleton, skinned with shellacked muslin (marine plywood was too expensive). Still, surfing remained an obscure practice with few participants.

JAMES METYKO

MIKE BOYD

There were at least a few active surfers in the Galveston area in the 1940s and '50s, including globetrotting government undercover man, Don Hull. During the late 1950s and early '60s, as more West Coasters came to Texas, particularly in the armed forces, the surf culture gained momentum, specially on those same Galveston beaches. Mack Blaker owned and operated a watersports shop in Alameda on the road from Houston to Freeport – bait and tackle, waterski gear, SCUBA equipment, etc. – and around about 1960 a couple of Navy divers from California (Steve Bishop and Randy Woodham) turned him onto surfing. At 6'4" and 225lb, Mack couldn't find a surfboard that would float him, so he ordered a bunch of 'Malibu' boards – molded Styrofoam things with metal stringers – and that's what he started to learn on. Unfortunately they were easily damaged, so he graduated to Foss Foam popouts, and therein was a new kind of business. In 1963-4, Blaker, his son Clay, and a few other Galveston guys made a trip to California to learn how it

was done, and when they returned Blaker Surfboards became a reality.

Blaker wasn't the first surf shop in Texas, however. Depending on who you talk to. An early edition of Surfer stated that Spring Branch Surf Shop was the first in the Houston/Galveston area, and Jay's Surf Shop was first in Corpus Christi. According to Gene Bagley (who launched On The Beach, the first in Galveston was Ken Delbosco's Ken's Surf Shop, but Dickens 'Dickey' Bishop (diver Steve's brother), who partnered with Blaker and Bill Repass on the Bellaire Surf Shop in Corpus Christi, credits Henry Fry as the first shaper in Texas. Fry began making boards in 1960 and later opened the Spring Branch Surf Shop; he's still shaping under the Fry label today, some 30,000 boards later, out of the Fry Surfboards shop in Pasadena on outskirts of Houston (run by his friend, Wyman Wade).

In the early 1960s, the hot surfers were in Galveston – guys like Henry Fry, Lee Lucas, Johnny Vigianno, Skippy

Above – **Port Mansfield jetties focus swell through the shipping channel, and the dredging spoils can become groomed sandbars.**
Right – **The mid sixties foam and fibreglass boom was fed by Texan shapers Henry Fry and Mack Blaker, who competed with the flood of Californian imports.**

RON STONER/SURFER MAGAZINE

Walsh, Kirk Perry, Nathan Kapner, Leonard Guitrose, Eddie Walsh, Leonard Getrouse, Max Seukanek, and Sterling Blocker. As their skills progressed, and as surf movies music began to go more mainstream, the Texas surf boom got underway with a flurry of shop openings and booming sales. Other early Houston area shops were BJ's Surf Shop (B for Bryson Williamson, J for his father, Jack), Village Sporting Goods, Bay Surf Shop (owner Eric Rincoff also opened stores in Pasadena, Texas City, Brownsville, and Port Isabel), Locked-In Surf Shop (owner Ruth Roy showed 16mm surf movies of Surfside on weekends in the store's parking lot), Surfrider Surf Shop, Surf House (started by Lloyd & Carol Sandel it in 1967 as a combo head shop/surf shop), (Bob) Martin Surfboards, Sea and Surf (Gene Thompson and Chuck Davis), and Sunrise Surf Shop.

First shop in Port Aransas was Hawn's (owned by George Hawn), then came Pat Magee's Surf Shop (a champion surfer in the late '60s, Magee recently sold his huge shop along with the Pat Magee Surf Museum). In the Corpus Christi area, early outfitters were John's Surf Shop, Copeland's Dive Shop, and Alameda Airline; more recently Harper's (in Corpus and Port A) and Dockside (Bill Mertauve).

In South Texas, Bay Surf Shop was first in Brownsville (they later moved to Port Isabel). Paul Hammett was building boards in Brownsville by 1970, then Pop's Surf Shop and The Shop opened in Padre Island Soon there were surf shops from Beaumont to South Padre Island and as far inland as Austin and College Station. The surf biz was boomin'! Rincoff's Bay Surf Shop in Houston sold an amazing 7,500 boards one year (a record that likely remains unsurpassed); boards were manufactured in Houston and Corpus Christi.

With all these shops, the contest scene was fast and furious. Ruth Roy's Locked In Surf Shop was famous for its all-girl team, and intershop rivalries were generally intense. California surf star Mike Doyle visited Galveston in 1964 as demand for surfboards surged during the national craze. He is still warmly remembered. With thousands of spectators on the seawall to see a surf demonstration by the champ in 6-inch waves, he paddled into his first wave, jumped to his feet, and his baggies split completely open down the back.

In 1968, the annual Texas State Championships was inaugurated at Galveston Island, and on the weekend of April 6-7, 1969, a crowd of some 15,000 beachgoers (including 15-year-old Ken Bradshaw) and 750,000 television viewers watched the 2nd annual Texas State Surfing Championships, held at Galveston Island. Pat Harral and Pam Curtiss were repeat winners in decent 3-foot surf.

'Tanker surfing' became a popular if semi-underground activity in this surf-starved area during the late '60s. Large ships heading into along the 25-mile (40km) Houston Ship Channel to Galveston Bay and Houston frequently generated the largest waves of the summer.

Today, Texas embraces all the trappings of modern surf culture with plenty of contests (often national ones), shops, surf reports, even surf cams spying on the main breaks.

Louisiana and Mississippi

These two states are so marginal for waves that the few local surfers are more likely to get wet in Texas or Florida. However, there are some interesting spots around the Delta, and there are surfers in both states. "The Delta area was very complicated," Bryson Williamson summarizes. At the height of the '60s surf craze, Williamson opened a BJ's Surf Shop in Houma and sponsored a Louisiana surf team. They surfed Grand Isle, Holly Beach near Lake Charles, and the bayou La Fouce.

The islands around the Mississippi Delta do intercept some swell, and there are some pointbreaks that can be quite good by Gulf standards. They are difficult to access, however – most only by boat, and few even know of their existence. The most telling factoid for the lack of surf is a glance at pilot charts, which indicate a water depth of less than 35ft (11m) extending for miles offshore. This reflects eons of silting from the vast heartland drainage system that feeds into the Mississippi River, which has choked the muddied waters for miles around the river's delta.

Rumors of waves on offshore sandbanks out on the Mississippi Delta can't be discounted, and the Port Fourchon to Grand Isle stretch near the East Bay Peninsula may hold surf since it protrudes towards deeper water. On the whole, however, Louisiana and Mississippi are unlikely to deliver if it's surf you're lookin' for.

Freeport Pier, 1968

MICHAEL CHAPLINSKY

Alabama

Alabama's slim 50 miles (80km) of swell exposure is wedged between the worst and one of the best surfing areas on the Gulf Coast. Generally, it's more like the former. Split by Mobile Bay into two areas of possibility, Alabama needs hurricanes or SE windswell for any sort of wave action. Breaks on the skinny, sandy strip of Dauphin Island tend to be weaker and less organized, but the surf spots between Fort Morgan and the Florida state line provide the best chance of rideable waves. There is little argument among the locals that when it's good here, Florida is probably better! Still, there has been an Alabama State Championships held at State Pier in the past (won by Sammy Owen in '69), so there are definitely surfers here and surf to be had.

Right – **A brace of jetties at Destin hold some decent waves in most swells.**
Below –
Panhandle peak.

Florida

There are two distinct areas to Florida's Gulf Coast, separated by geography and also wave size. The term 'panhandle' is used to describe a narrow strip of land that projects from one state into another; this basically describes Florida's northwest territory, which extends along the Gulf shore beneath Alabama and Georgia. Directly offshore from Pensacola, the swell-sapping continental shelf is at its narrowest, providing a welcome focus for wave oscillations in the eastern Gulf. Strangely, there is enough fetch for E windswells to be produced, adding to the usual SE windchop, but SW to W swells have a lot of trouble getting over the shallow delta at the mouth of the Mississippi. But if a tropical storm enters the area from the south, the Panhandle will pump with double overhead and even larger waves, although swell duration can be extremely short. Winter is the time when the E-SE winds blow hardest before a cold front sweeps in from the NW bringing offshore winds and powerful, precipitous waves from Pensacola to Panama City.

Pensacola has miles of glaringly white, sandy beaches. Here the waves conform to the 'crumbly outside wall reforming into steeper inside shorebreak' category. However, this trend is bucked by a precious few waves at the barrier island extremities where inlet jetties provide foundations for solid, quality breaks. Furthest west are the lefts of The Point at Fort Pickens, which need a sizable swell to wrap around into the sheltered bay. Sand formation is crucial and, while hurricanes bring swell, they also destroy sandbars or rearrange them in all the wrong places, making this sand-bottomed pointbreak very fickle indeed.

Pensacola Beach has plenty of uninterrupted beachbreaks leading east along Santa Rosa Island to Navarre. Here a new pier provides constant banks from the outside to the steeper shorebreak, without the crowds of the nearby cities.

Fort Walton Beach and Destin present welcome variations from straight, open beaches; here, inlet jetties form wedging waves, which help shape consistent spots like NCOs and Jetty East. The shoreline from Destin to Sandestin offers miles of featureless peaks to choose from, and the Henderson Beach State Park is a nice respite from shoreline development. Grayton Beach State Park is a cheap camping option in otherwise expensive surroundings with proximity to some above-average sandbars.

Heading east into the popular college town/tourist destination of Panama City, look for more crowds, especially at the two piers. The concrete one is more consistent with better banks that can connect all the way from the outside through to the steeper shorebreak; the wooden pier is a less crowded, if humbler, option. Three of the best waves on the Panhandle are clustered at the southeastern end of Panama Beach. Long jetties protect the deep inlet between St Andrews State Park and Shell Island, both of which offer hard-breaking peaks with good wind protection. But the real gem is situated inside the inlet on the western side of the eastern jetty. Amazons is a long, workable lefthander that needs a decent SE or E swell to break. Handles the big stuff, but access is tricky without a boat, as paddling across the inlet is dangerous due to tidal currents, boat traffic, sharks, and zealous, ticket-writing Coastguard officials. Military bases and difficult access compound the situation, making it difficult to surf any further east.

Surfing opportunities all but disappear along the 250-mile (400km) stretch between Cape St George to Clearwater, as impenetrable marshlands exclude access, and broad, shallow offshore shoals dampen all swell activity. There aren't many waves along the heavily-populated east coast of the Florida Peninsula from Tampa south to Naples. Swells are rare, and rideable shape even rarer.

The 'Sun Coast', from Clearwater down to the entrance to Tampa Bay, is worse off than more southern areas because of shorter fetches on N swells and more extensive offshore shoals. Sandwiched between the ultra-developed, surfer-restricted stretch of Clearwater Beach and the ultra-protective, elite-residential beachbreaks of Belleair is a single inlet jetty that has recently lifted its ban on surfing. When lifeguards deem it good enough, Sand Key produces longer than average righthanders when a NW swell wraps around the jetty. Indian Rocks to Indian Shores curves enough to give options depending on swell direction, and most of the beachbreaks peak up and pitch close to shore. From Reddington Shores to St Pete, jetties are the focus for more hollow shorebreaks.

South of Tampa Bay the offshore waters deepen and the waves grow accordingly. Anna Maria Key is a pier hotspot boasting outside and inside sandbars that will produce on any swell direction, size, or tide. Holmes Beach Pier and the misnomered Twin Piers (there are 3 structures) at Bradenton Beach are regularly crowded, but nearby open beach can hold surprisingly punchy peaks. The next key down, Siesta, needs summer S or W swells as it is protected from the N swells and winds, but nearby Turtle Beach works on winter NW'ers.

Just south of Sarasota, Venice Beach is generally considered Spot X on the Gulf Coast – subject to heavy crowds in heavy swells. The North and South Inlet Jetties are swell magnets, bending in serious waves at whichever one is opposed to the swell direction. The crowds are still apparent at nearby Venice Pier but recede at the beachbreaks that extend south past Englewood. Boca Grande marks the end of the easy access spots (without a boat or surplus money to book in at one of the exclusive island resorts). The last-chance surf at Naples Pier provides sandbars on either side, and there are a couple of jetty breaks to the north, but geographically and metaphorically speaking, Naples is the last resort on the Gulf Coast.

Beyond Naples and Marco Island, the beaches of the Everglades don't offer much; for swells to reach this southern Gulf Coast, they have to come from the NW – usually courtesy of winter cold fronts. This means short fetches, onshore winds, and a fleeting lifespan. The rest of the year is even more dubious, as the best you can expect is below waist windswell junk for desperate longboarding, or the rare hurricane that takes off on the right track to send generous swells back in the opposite direction of their line of travel, bringing genuine SW swells to this tropical corner of the 48 States.

Florida's Gulf Coast waters are surprisingly clean considering the vast swathes of shoreline development. The Beach Bill brings the promise of standardized testing and the EPA has begun investigating ways to reduce the massive dead zone that extends out from the Mississippi Delta when upriver farming pollutants are deposited into the Gulf. Concentrated coastal development is a feature near the major cities of Pensacola and Tampa whose populations soar during holiday periods. This raises access issues as only 43% of sandy beaches are state owned, bringing surfers into conflict with private condo and hotel developments, where parking and beach access paths are at a premium. Oil drilling in the Gulf is one of the latest burning issues and is at odds with the main dollar earner of tourism.

The entire Gulf of Mexico is home to many species of shark, but the prevalence of attacks is lower than on the Atlantic Coast. Man o' war and moon jellyfish are constant invaders of the line-up, while the white sand reflects and doubles the intensity of the sun's burning rays.

One of the most famed Gulf surfers of all time, Yancy Spencer is a longstanding Panhandle resident. Yancy started riding in 1965 after a handful of mainly military transplants had introduced surfing to the area. The guy who ran the local hardware store, Hutson's, was hip to the trend and enlisted the help of some Navy crewmen from California to shape some boards under the Hutson logo. Spencer went on to become a successful competition surfer and surf shop-chain operator; he is generally regarded as the guru of Panhandle surfing.

Further south, Sarasota local Juan Rodriguez was repairing and reshaping old boards before gaining valuable board-building experience in California and Hawaii. This led him into a successful business, creating surf, skate, and skimboard designs. Fame has also come to the Florida West Coast surfing fraternity via the WCT top 16 pro surfing brothers from Indian Rocks Beach, Shea and Cory Lopez.

NCO's wall.

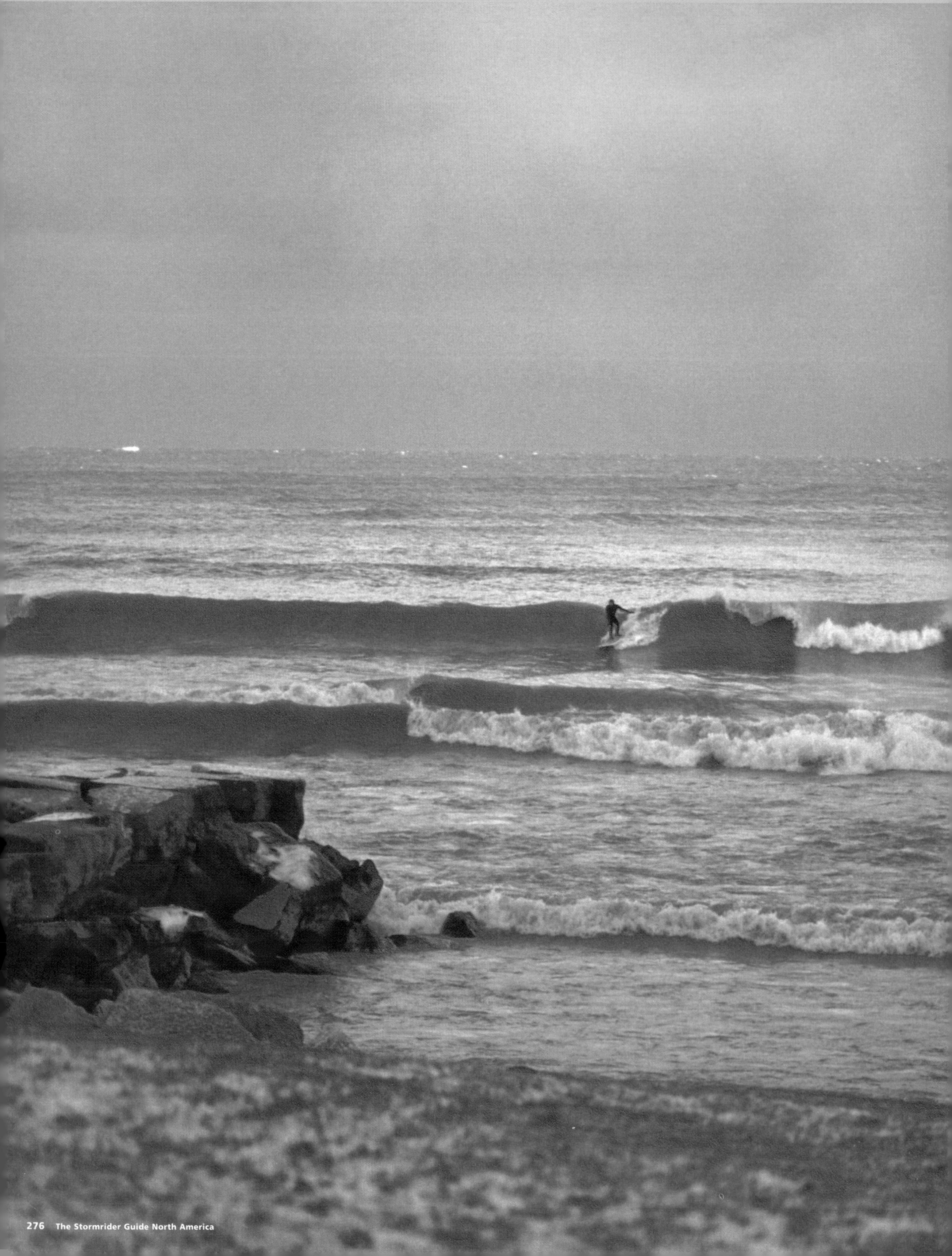

The Great Lakes

For surfers who haven't tried it, the idea of surfing on a lake might seem like a bit of a joke. But if you're one of the hardcore freshwater surfers that rely on the wind-driven waves of the Great Lakes, well, you're smiling too – because you know. Straddling the USA/Canada border, this massive system of lakes is the biggest on the planet, and when the wind blows strong enough for long enough, the waves here can also get surprisingly large. Perched at altitude, way above North America's saltwater coasts, the Great Lakes attract inland surfers to a range of beach, point, and reef waves that break on a diverse array of shorelines.

The American heartland is like a vast earth-ocean, exposed to massive seasonal weather systems. No less than on the open seas, these energies transfer readily to these expansive lake waters, transforming them from summer placidity and small-wave surfing in boardshorts to overhead surf in winter maelstroms that hurl snow at the thick-rubbered surfers dodging ice slabs in the line-up.

Wave heights are often marginal, conditions are usually onshore, but there is a growing posse just happy to paddle out and catch a few freshies. Freshwater surfing might not appeal to everyone, but the men and women who ride these waves – no matter the conditions – are undoubtedly among the most dedicated, stoked surfers on the planet.

JOHN RUEBARTSCH

The Surf, Environment and Surf Culture

Introduction

The five Great Lakes – Superior, Michigan, Huron, Erie, and Ontario – are huge bodies of H_2O, which collectively contain approximately one fifth of the world's freshwater supply (6 quadrillion gallons). The total shoreline of the lakes, including islands and channels, extends for some 10,900 miles (17,549km), almost halfway around the world. Michigan's lakeshore alone stretches for 3,288 miles (5290km), easily exceeding any other continental state's littoral expanse. It is the size and concomitant fetch of these lakes that accounts for the presence of surprisingly large, surfable waves here in the middle of the North American continent.

Many of the lakes' shores are deserted and solo surfing is always a possibility.

JOHN RUEBARTSCH

The integrated freshwater system we know as the Great Lakes began forming about 12,000 years ago when glaciers commenced their most recent retreat towards the north. More than a mile thick, these glaciers gouged mighty troughs into the earth's surface. When glacial meltwater gathered in the depressions, it created thousands of small lakes and the five great bodies of water now known as the Great Lakes. Because of the large size of the Great Lakes watershed, physical characteristics and climate vary widely at surf spots across the region. Each of the lakes is notably above sea level, ranging from a surface elevation of 600ft (147m) at Lake Superior in the west down to 240ft (74m) at Lake Ontario in the east. The mighty Niagara Falls accounts for the largest step in the 326ft descent of the Niagara River from Lake Erie down to Lake Ontario. Add to this the fact that the system spans a distance of over 700 miles (1120km) from west to east and 500 miles (800km) from north to south, and you can understand how a surf experience on the NW shore of Lake Superior can be vastly different from a session on one of Erie's southeastern beaches.

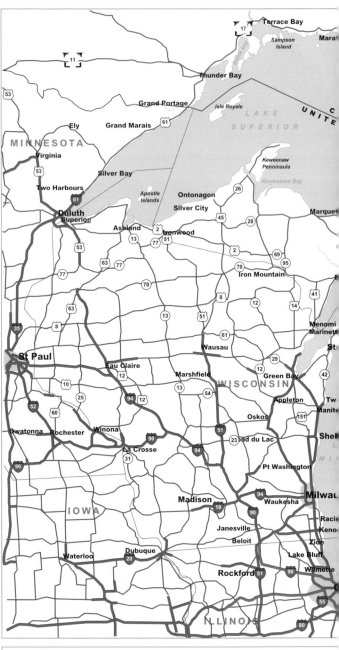

Swell Forecasting

Like anywhere, wind is the ingredient in Great Lakes wave formation, and understanding how local weather systems work is the most critical factor (outside of luck) in a successful inland surfing experience. The largest waves on the lakes easily surpass 10ft (3m) faces and waves more than 20ft (6m) are occasionally recorded by NOAA weather buoys, usually in spring and fall. Even bigger waves are possible under extreme conditions in open water, though there's a general agreement among meteorologists that 25ft (7.5m) is the upper limit.

Remember the tragic Gordon Lightfoot song, *The Ballad of the Edmund Fitzgerald*? The 729ft (219m) long vessel, the world's largest freshwater freighter, set out from Duluth Harbor for Detroit, Michigan on November 9, 1978 in mild weather. Next day, two storms swept into the area, and Lake Superior was blasted by 80mph winds plowing up 25ft (7.5m) waves. *The Fitzgerald*, making for the shelter of Whitefish Bay,

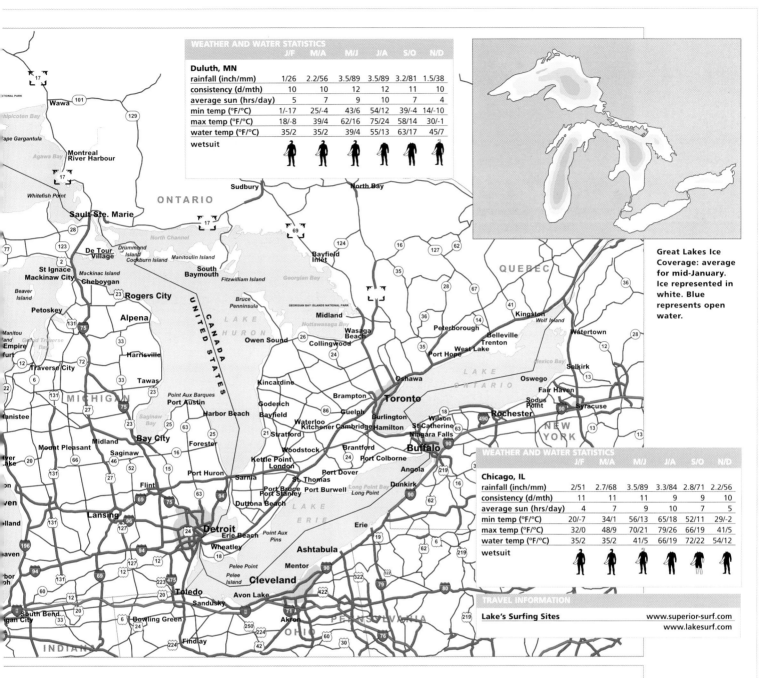

WEATHER AND WATER STATISTICS

Duluth, MN	J/F	M/A	M/J	J/A	S/O	N/D
rainfall (inch/mm)	1/26	2.2/56	3.5/89	3.5/89	3.2/81	1.5/38
consistency (d/mth)	10	10	12	12	11	10
average sun (hrs/day)	5	7	9	10	7	4
min temp (°F/°C)	1/-17	25/-4	43/6	54/12	39/-4	14/-10
max temp (°F/°C)	18/-8	39/4	62/16	75/24	58/14	30/-1
water temp (°F/°C)	35/2	35/2	39/4	55/13	63/17	45/7
wetsuit						

Great Lakes Ice Coverage: average for mid-January. Ice represented in white. Blue represents open water.

Chicago, IL	J/F	M/A	M/J	J/A	S/O	N/D
rainfall (inch/mm)	2/51	2.7/68	3.5/89	3.3/84	2.8/71	2.2/56
consistency (d/mth)	11	11	11	9	9	10
average sun (hrs/day)	4	7	9	10	7	5
min temp (°F/°C)	20/-7	34/1	56/13	65/18	52/11	29/-2
max temp (°F/°C)	32/0	48/9	70/21	79/26	66/19	41/5
water temp (°F/°C)	35/2	35/2	41/5	66/19	72/22	54/12
wetsuit						

TRAVEL INFORMATION

Lake's Surfing Sites   www.superior-surf.com
www.lakesurf.com

was holding her own until two tremendous waves slammed into her, snapping the huge vessel in two, and sinking her in less than 10 seconds.

Great Lakes' surfers have been known to exaggerate wave height, but for the most part, surfers here will usually be riding waves ranging between knee and head high.

In summer, the northern Great Lakes region generally receives cool, dry air masses from the Canadian Northwest, while the southern region is dominated by tropical air masses moving north from the Gulf of Mexico. Wind speeds are at their lowest at this time of year and are reflected in generally low wave heights, so surfable days are few and far between. This is especially unfortunate, since water temps for lakes Michigan, Huron, and especially Erie can exceed 70°F (21°C) in July and August, allowing for a comfortably stylish interlude of boardshorts weather. In fall, things start to change. The rapid movement of weather systems and the occasional clash of warm and cold air masses through the region produce frequent, strong winds. Waves are the largest they'll be all year as the dominant SW wind direction across the region shifts to include more northerly conditions. Water temps drop down to the 50°Fs or high 40°Fs (7-15°C). In winter, shelf ice, snow, and generally inhospitable conditions characterize Great Lakes surf spots. Arctic air sweeping down from the northern plains of Canada is extremely cold and dry when it hits the lakes; surfing at this time of year is pretty difficult at best. Like autumn, spring is characterized by variable and sometimes volatile weather. Alternating low and high pressure air masses move rapidly across the lakes, resulting in frequent cloud cover, thunderstorms, and high wind. SW winds resume their dominance as warmer air and increased sunshine begin to melt snow and ice, but the lakes are slow to warm. By the end of May, expect water temperatures barely into the 50°Fs (10-15°C).

JOHN RUEBARTSCH

Right – **Racine is a popular beachbreak on Lake Michigan, between Chicago and Milwaukee.** Below – **One of the stony points of Lake Superior, Minnesota**

BOB TEMA

The Surf

Lake Superior is the largest surface freshwater lake in the world. It's also the deepest and coldest of the lakes and, due to its size, has the biggest surfable waves. Minnesota's stretch of Lake Superior's north shore stretches northeast from Duluth. The beaches are very rugged, comprised of bedrock slabs and boulder bottoms with deep offshore waters making for steep and powerful surf. E, NE, and N winds are required to generate swell for this end of the lake. Known breaks are Lester River, French River, and Stony Point, all within or near Duluth's city limits. Further north and into Ontario, Canada, is a largely undiscovered coastline, which requires a less frequent SE windflow to generate waves. The rugged shoreline here is blocked in places by many small and large offshore islands.

The shores at the eastern end of Superior are mostly beachbreaks apart from the cobblestone points of Marathon. Michigan's upper peninsula touches the southern fringe of Superior and is probably the most consistent shore, picking up waves from the W around to the E with sand bottom beachbreaks in Grand Marias and long pointbreak at Au Sable Point. The southeastern corner of Superior, with its concentrated and refractory wave action and dangerous shoals is known as the Graveyard of the Lakes. Hundreds of vessels have been lost here over the past centuries. White Point Light, marking the headland west of Whitefish Bay, has been a reliable beacon for 150 years – except on the night of Nov 10, 1978, when the *Edmund Fitzgerald* went down.

Heading back west along the southern coast you'll find varying types of waves (some of them good) in and around the Marquette area. The Keweenaw Peninsula is very rugged, surrounded mostly by deep water that yields huge swells that slam mercilessly onto rock shelves, cliffs, and shoals. The western base of the Keweenaw offers some good beachbreak waves in Ontonagon, and a good pointbreak at Union Bay. The Apostle Islands have great exposure and seem likely places to find good surf, but exploration has been minimal. Certainly, waves will reach here on E, NE, or N winds.

Lake Michigan is the only one of the lakes entirely within the United States and the only lake to experience a lunar tidal influence – up to 4 inches twice a day! Heavy population pressure in the south and west from the large cities of Chicago and Milwaukee make this the most surfed of all the Great Lakes. The Chicago area is dominated by a westerly air flow, which tends to be N in the winter then S in the summer. Spring will see a definite shift around to the N/NE and brings the most promising conditions to the city's beachbreaks, which benefit from jetty and breakwall constructions. Strangely enough, all the Illinois breaks from Chicago up to Zion (about 50mi [80km] north) will work on a NW wind.

A few miles into Wisconsin is the popular break of Racine, which breaks on all E wind variations. Further north past Milwaukee and the reliable beachbreaks of Whitefish Bay is Sheboygan, where quality reefbreaks attract a crowd when the northerlies blow or when a rare SE wind springs up.

The northern extremities of Lake Michigan (upper Michigan State) hold an abundance of pointbreaks and islands well situated to accept any SE, S, or SW windswell... and few surfers to share them with. Secluded beachbreaks continue down the east side of the lake through Empire and on to Muskegon, opening up the NW wind option, which produces the best waves at piers and jetties. Grand Haven has become surf central in Michigan (it has also hosted numerous windsurfing competitions in the past), and the South Pier handles the bigger SW to NW windchop, plus there's easy access from the end of the pier. More powerful and reliable beachbreaks continue to the south through Holland and South Haven in SW to NW winds, with the action usually around the piers and breakwalls.

Indiana's short coast has some good waves around Michigan City and short, pounding beachbreak in the Ogden Dune area, but the wind must be NW to NE for anything to happen at this southernmost end of the lake. With over 300 miles (480km) of open fetch to the north, however, it can occasionally get big and powerful down here, so watch for that rare conjunction of a storm on the north end of the lake when the wind is blowing straight up from the Gulf of Mexico!

Lake Huron is the least explored of the Great Lakes due to the sparse populations around its shores, Huron has the longest coastline of the five big lakes – if you include the 30,000-plus islands that lie within its boundaries! Huron's ability to generate huge waves is reflected in its history of numerous shipwrecks, so don't be surprised at the size and power of the surf.

The western shore of Huron, from Mackinac Island in the north down to Bay City, rely on NE to SE winds, which aren't too common except either side of summer. The Port Austin beachbreaks will also break on NW winds, but the dominant wind flow is more S to W. This means that the best waves are usually found on the Ontario coastline. From Bayfield to Sauble Beach are many miles of long, sandy beaches that hold waves in SW to NW wind conditions. The jetty at Bayfield is a noted bigger wave spot where long rights will peel off the south side of the 400ft (120m) breakwall. In the southern confines of Georgian Bay, there are a few reefbreaks that break with size in the rarer NW gales, and windsurfers are attracted by the consistent sideshores. The secluded shoreline of Manitoulin Island (Ontario) is a largely unsurfed coast with plenty of potential in the SW airflow.

Lake Erie is the smallest of the lakes and the only one to completely freeze in winter. It is also the shallowest lake, which results in waves being whipped up quickly, but then not hanging around for long. Lake Erie is perfectly aligned with the very consistent wind direction of SW allowing for a decent fetch along its 241mi (388km) length. Obviously, this means that the biggest waves will be found in the eastern corner of this natural wind tunnel.

The Canadian north side starts with the perfect triangle of Pelee Point, which usually works best with some

Above – **Head high and glassy at Sheboygan, Wisconsin.**
Left – **Lester River line-up, Minnesota.**

JOHN RUEBARTSCH

Lake Ontario is at the end of the chain, as the lake's freshwater exits the east end of the lake into the St Lawrence River and so out to the Atlantic Ocean. Immensely deeper than Erie, Ontario's depth translates into a generally longer windswell duration and the chance of a cleaner wave after the wind has died down. 'Cleaner' is not a term used for Ontario's water quality, however, particularly in the vicinity of the shoreline's major cities. Industrial wastes occasionally pollute the

variation of an E wind. The SW wind fetch improves to the east, and Erie Beach will pick up these swells which also hit a decent pointbreak at Point Aux Pins. There are more sandy breaks on the north shore through the Ports of Stanley, Bruce and Burwell before the lengthy spit of Long Point protrudes into the lake. The western side of this peninsula picks up far more swell and is warmer, while the cooler east-facing beaches rely on rare SE winds for waves. The Port Colborne area receives plenty of powerful waves giving the shortboarders more of a chance, plus there's a pointbreak at Crystal Beach in large SW to W windswells.

Along Erie's south shore, the New York State coast has consistent sand-bottomed breaks from Buffalo down to Dunkirk, where there is also a pointbreak at Wright Park Beach Point. The best surf on Pennsylvania's short coast is found around the town of Erie in SW to NW conditions. Once into Ohio, the NE winds can add to the usual westerly flow. Ashtabula has a break named Surfers Point Campground, run by long-time Lake Erie surfer, Neal Luoma. Saybrook and Mentor have some powerful and reliable shorebreak. Opportunities diminish from Cleveland to Toledo due to a reliance on rare NW or NE winds.

waters at selected surf spots, sending boarders in search of cleaner waves. The US shore is less urbanized and is not as intensively farmed except for a narrow band along the southern shoreline.

Lake Ontario seems to have a slight variation on the spring and fall SW winds that energize most of these lakes. In summer, an easterly breeze is prevalent towards the western end of the lake around Toronto. While average wind speed statistics indicate a general lack of strength, when the wind does get up from the E, there are some decent breaks to choose from. Niagara Rivermouth has some offshore sandbars that can handle size, and nearby St Catherines has a few well-organized beach and pier breaks. The rocky, cobblestone shore at Grimsby leads into the established surf spots around the jetties and beaches of Hamilton. All these breaks need E or NE winds to produce.

Toronto beachbreaks are popular with surfers and windsurfers alike and can pick up the SW windchop as it starts to pump NW towards Oshawa. Further along the north shore is the rare reefbreak adjacent to the beaches of Presqu'ile Point. Sandbanks Provincial Park faces directly into the SW winds and picks up all available swell along its 5 miles (8km) of beach, reef, and pointbreaks.

The town of Kingston is near the mouth of the St Lawrence and Thousand Islands. The islands at this end of the lake receive the payoff of Ontario's wide-open 150-mile (240km) SW fetch, so the waves can get big off Richardson Beach, and Wolfe Island has some point setups to check for those who choose to bother with the ferry. The New York coastline from Stony Point and Southwick Beach State Park to Selkirk picks up anything from either side of W. South of here, the coastline bends around to the southern shore, where a northerly wind of some description is required. Best spots are Durand Beach and Ontario Beach in Rochester and the reef and pointbreaks at Hamlin Beach State Park, which work on any wind from NE to W.

Above – **Whitefish Bay, Lake Michigan, Wisconsin, as opposed to Whitefish Bay, Lake Superior, Michigan.** Below – **Zion and other Illinois breaks will work on NW winds.**

JOHN RUEBARTSCH

The Environment

Water quality across the lakes is variable. The ecosystem is vulnerable to abuse, and some of America's biggest industrial cities were built on their shores. The Great Lakes region continues to be exploited for its natural resource (i.e. Minnesota's iron) and mistreated for economic gain. Industrial practices include nutrient loading, resource extraction, deforestation and pollution associated with urbanization. The introduction of exotic aquatic species; alterations and destruction of natural habitat; and contamination of air, water and soil have all inflicted permanent damage. Heavy rain effectively transports pollutants originating in sewage systems, which are designed to overflow, into the lakes. Rivers feed huge amounts of non-specific point pollution from the system's extensive catchment areas into each lake.

The Great Lakes-St Lawrence Seaway system is one of the busiest international shipping areas in the world, and a plethora of non-indigenous species has been introduced into these waters (largely through ships' ballast) at great detriment to the region's ecosystem. Problematic exotic species now thriving in the lakes include sea lampreys, round gobies, spiny water fleas, zebra mussels, and purple loosestrife. The Aquatic Nuisance Prevention and Control Act, introduced in 1990, mandates ballast-water exchange for all saltwater vessels entering the St Lawrence. Further, the National Invasive Species Act of 1996 reauthorized and expanded 1990 federal non-indigenous species legislation for ballast water management in US waters. Even so, accidental introduction of exotics is the most serious threat to the environmental health of the Great Lakes. So, don't even think about setting your aquarium fish free in one of these lakes – a couple of cute little cichlids could wipe out an indigenous species!

While these freshwater seas may be devoid of many of the traditional surfing hazards, such as sharks and jellyfish, there are a few nasties to take their place. Cold shock and hypothermia are real dangers as the water temps drop below 40°F (4°C), necessitating a thick 5-6mm suit, hood, booties, and gloves. Wave action can break up frozen sheets of shoreline ice sending big chunks of the stuff drifting into the line-up, creating heavy obstacles that are most prevalent during the spring thaws. Traditional dangers like lightning and submerged objects are a given.

An additional area of concern for surfers is access to the coast, which is not always guaranteed in the Great Lakes region, and many restrictions exist, especially during the summer months, relating to surfcraft and designated swimming areas.

With 28 cities of 50,000 or more people lying within the Great Lakes watershed, the co-operation of business, government, and residents is critically important if there is to be any possibility of properly managing and preserving what is arguably North America's most precious natural resource. Environmental enhancement and protection groups like Surfrider Foundation (check out SF's website – www.surfrider.com – for the Lake Michigan chapter) and

the Great Lakes Information Network (www.great-lakes.net) help inform the general public about what they can do to benefit the lakes.

Top – **Lester River, Minnesota.**
Above – **Jumping off into the line-up at Sheboygan, Wisconsin.**

Surf Culture

The first reported surfer of the Great Lakes was an unknown GI who returned to Grand Haven, Michigan from Hawaii with his longboard in 1945. Twenty years later the Great Lakes Surfing Association was formed by Rick Sapinski. Then, in 1998, Lake Ontario surfer Leslie-Ann Gervais gained a spot on the Canadian National Surfing Team. It's like anyplace far from the Great Oceans – people find it hard to believe that there are rideable waves on a lake.

While the waves around the lakes vary immensely, there is one unifying factor that runs deep among the 750-odd surfers that ride them: pure stoke and an unadulterated pride in riding the unique freshwater waves that ocean surfers are all but oblivious to. When conditions are right, locals from the big cities and the countryside around the lakes get their gear together and head off in search of surf. They're a hardy bunch whose dedication and love of riding waves should be well respected. If you find yourself on the lakes and happen to meet some locals, take time to share some conversation, and hopefully you'll get the chance to experience and appreciate the unique stoke of surfing on freshwater.

FIND SURF.

Life is like a maze for most surfing people.

Some get paid to be in the right places at the best times, but the rest of us don't. We have to work, live and love our way through life, fitting in the perfect surf whenever we can get it.

And that means we have to find the time, the money and the means to make our barrels happen.

That's not always easy. But it is, as you know, a worthwhile quest.

THE WORLD, THE WAVES

While much of the world has been explored, exposed and exploited, there's still a huge blue planet out there that offers us our own moments of discovery and ecstasy. Those moments don't have to occur in exotic, far out places. They can happen at the nearest available beach on the ugliest onshore day you've ever paddled into. That's one of the joys of our quest – it's full of surprises.

And although we all share the addiction, surfers the world over vary as much as the waves we ride. That's why we don't like to be boxed, categorised and told we have to be a certain way, act or speak a certain way, or buy certain types of stuff.

We just want to ride waves – it's the mission we all share.

The Surfer's Path Magazine was established in 1997 and has become known for covering surfing in a way that you don't see in other magazines.

Our photos (big and clean as often as possible) aren't chosen for logo-visibility or by advertisers' arm bending. They're chosen because they reflect our realities and the beauty of those moments surfers witness and dream about.

And we like words, too – in-depth stories about places, people, and issues that relate to surfing, in any way. The famous names might get a look in, but so can anyone or anywhere else that entertains, informs and enlightens our journey.

And while we're happy to talk about well-known places, we won't give away any secrets. If a spot appears in the guidebooks or other magazines, we'll name it too. In some cases we'll go further in-depth than you'll usually see, because we think it's important for travelling surfers to know as much as possible about the waves, the people, the cultures and the environment that we're in. However, protection of threatened natural resources, be they crowd sensitive surf spots or endangered reefs, is important to us. So if we won't tell you exactly how to get there, we will show you what's out there.

Less hype, just a wide angled exploration of the world, the waves, the oceans and the life.

Check out our website, or look for us in your local
surf shop, bookstore or magazine stand.
We'll be there.
ALOHA

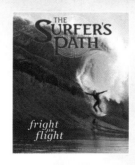 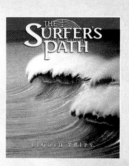 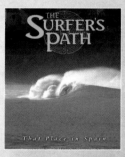

Surf Break Index

If you don't go,